THOMAS AQUINAS

Selected Commentaries on the New Testament

THOMAS AQUINAS

Selected Commentaries on the New Testament

EDITED WITH AN INTRODUCTION AND NOTES BY

JASON C. PAONE

WORD on FIRE
ACADEMIC

Published by Word on Fire Academic, an imprint of
Word on Fire, Park Ridge, IL 60068

Printed in the United States of America

Design and layout by Cassie Pease, Rozann Lee, Ikuborije Opeyemi, and Anna Manhart.

Translations of all biblical commentaries by Thomas Aquinas are from the Latin/English Edition of the Works of St. Thomas Aquinas, reproduced by permission of the Aquinas Institute, corrected and edited by Jason C. Paone.

Except in the second inaugural sermon, all biblical quotations in bold, italic font are from the Douay-Rheims translation. Except where otherwise indicated, all biblical quotations in non-bold, italic font are from the RSV-CE.

The featured translation of *The Inaugural Sermons* is by Ralph McInerny and adapted by Jason C. Paone from its original published form in *Thomas Aquinas: Selected Writings.* Reproduced by permission of Penguin Books.

All hymns and prayers of Thomas Aquinas are from *The Aquinas Prayer Book: The Prayers and Hymns of Thomas Aquinas*, reproduced by permission of Sophia Institute Press. To purchase this book, visit https://www.sophiainstitute.com.

First published August 2022
Reprinted August 2024

ISBN: 978-1-68578-014-2

Library of Congress Control Number: 2021922728

CONTENTS

Conclusion

ACKNOWLEDGMENTS

Books are always the work of a community. Certainly this one is. From the Angelic Doctor, who lectured and wrote the earliest forms of its material nearly 1000 years ago, countless hands and eyes have diligently labored over these texts—scribes and copyists, translators, editors, and scholars—far more than I could thank. But I am especially grateful to Brandon Vogt and Matthew Becklo of Word on Fire Publishing for giving me the opportunity to create this collection. I owe many thanks, also, to John Mortensen of the Aquinas Institute for providing many of the manuscripts that were used to create this collection. My teacher, Reinhard Hütter, too deserves credit both for having taught me most of what I know about Thomas Aquinas and for his help reviewing a draft of the book.

I am indebted, also, to Matthew Levering who gave me superb feedback on an early draft of the introduction and invaluable input on the project all along the way. Richard DeClue and Bobby Mixa of the Word on Fire Institute gave me crucial advice as well. James O'Neil copyedited the book and wrote the general index with his usual skill, and Dan Seseske helped me to polish up the introduction and wrote the ancient sources index. Edyta McNichol secured permissions for much of the book's previously published content. Rozann Lee and Cassie Pease of Word on Fire's design team transformed a bland Word document into a beautiful and functional book.

Lastly, I thank my beloved wife, Clara, who carried a double load on the many evenings and weekends that I spent working on this project—to say nothing of her many years of support during graduate school.

INTRODUCTION

As arguably the best-known and most-researched medieval thinker, Thomas Aquinas (1225–1274) needs little in the way of a biographical introduction here. In any case, there is a wealth of fine literature on the topic for any interested reader.[1] Many will have already encountered his well-known works of theology and philosophy, the *Summa theologiae* and *Summa contra Gentiles*. In fact, the need for a biblical commentary collection such as this is in some measure a consequence of the very prominence of these masterworks, which have tended to eclipse St. Thomas' corpus of biblical commentary, which in turn, has resulted in a somewhat skewed reception of this medieval master of the sacred page.

Ask an undergraduate what he or she knows about Thomas Aquinas, and you will likely hear about the "five ways"—his arguments for the existence of God. A student of theology might mention his systematic treatment of the Trinity, his discussion of the relation between philosophy and theology, or some other of his contributions to fundamental, systematic, or moral theology. By contrast, you will not likely hear, for instance, about his understanding of the spiritual senses of Scripture, the theme of Christ's supremacy in the *Commentary on Hebrews*, or of his comparison of contemplative and active discipleship in the *Commentary on John*. Thus, although the rediscovery of St. Thomas' biblical commentaries has been underway for some time within certain sectors of the Thomistic scholarly community, the movement has not yet become mainstream enough to register in college curricula or in the perception that students have of the kind of thinker and teacher Thomas Aquinas was.[2]

The perception that the biblical commentaries are inessential for new students and readers of Thomas Aquinas is again reflected in their exclusion from the many introductory Aquinas anthologies on offer. This collection, designed to serve readers at any level of exposure to his works, is the first and only anthology dedicated wholly to the biblical commentaries.

1. See the biographies section in the bibliography at the end of this volume.

2. For discussion of the movement of "biblical Thomism" in the twentieth century, see Christopher T. Baglow's introduction to *"Modus et Forma": A New Approach to the Exegesis of Saint Thomas Aquinas with an Application to the* Lectura super Epistolam ad Ephesios (Rome: Editrice Pontificio Istituto Biblico, 2002), 1–16. For more recent work in this research program, see the two essay collections edited by Piotr Roszak and Jörgen Vijgen: *Towards A Biblical Thomism: Thomas Aquinas and the Renewal of Biblical Theology* (Pamplona, ES: Ediciones Universidad de Navarra, 2018) and *Reading the Church Fathers with St. Thomas Aquinas: Historical and Systematical Perspectives* (Turnhout, BE: Brepols, 2021).

In a more general sense, this selective anthology of Thomas' New Testament commentaries is dedicated to raising this forgotten corpus to its proper place within the canon of works customarily held to be most representative of Thomas Aquinas. And with the great Aquinas scholar Jean-Pierre Torrell, our guiding conviction is that a well-rounded perception of Thomas Aquinas, of the theologian and his method, demands a rigorous engagement with his biblical commentaries—his premier work as a thirteenth-century theologian.[3]

The biblical commentaries—comprising roughly a third of his overall corpus—deserve a place among the works standardly included in introductory courses and anthologies on Thomas Aquinas. And they especially ought to be included in Catholic theological curricula given the special pedagogical status that St. Thomas enjoys as *Doctor Universalis* by the commendation of the Church's Magisterium.[4] If "the study of the sacred page is . . . the soul of sacred theology," as the Second Vatican Council teaches, then Thomas Aquinas is a model theologian, in the first place, as a *biblical* theologian, and it is from his biblical commentaries that we may gather the resources for a distinctively Catholic model of biblical theology—no less instructive in the twenty-first century than in the thirteenth.[5]

That Aquinas is sometimes imagined to be paradigmatic of a kind of preconciliar theological methodology that Vatican II is supposed to have put to rest, again, likely owes something to the marginalization of his biblical commentaries, in which we see a model of theology that could hardly be more opposite from the insular rationalism that postconciliar theologians railed against. The council's vision of *ressourcement*, the return to the sources of the Christian faith, is very much embodied in the commentaries, in which a typical page presents a flurry of Old and New Testament cross-references and engagements with the Fathers of the West and East, including Augustine, John Chrysostom, Origen, Jerome, Gregory the Great, Ambrose, and Athanasius, to name only a few.

To promote further reader engagement with these patristic sources, hundreds of new footnote citations have been added—by painstaking original research—to the lectures featured in this collection, connecting every one of

3. "If we wish . . . to get a slightly less one-sided idea of the whole theologian and his method, it is imperative to read and use in a much deeper fashion these biblical commentaries in parallel with the great systematic works" (*Saint Thomas Aquinas*, vol. 1, *The Person and His Work*, trans. Robert Royal [Washington, DC: The Catholic University of America Press, 1996], 55).

4. For a brief survey of the magisterial commendations that Thomas Aquinas has received, see Chrysostom Baer's introduction to his translation of the *Commentary on the Epistle to the Hebrews* (South Bend, IN: Saint Augustine's, 2006), xi–xiv.

5. Vatican Council II, *Dei Verbum* 6.24.

Thomas' patristic citations to a precise location within a source.[6] Each abbreviated source citation in the notes corresponds, in turn, to a full bibliographic reference in the "ancient works cited" section of the bibliography, where the reader can find the best and most recent translation of the respective work.

Also included in the bibliographies are recent biographies, introductions, and studies that illuminate the place and importance of Sacred Scripture in Thomas' thought and career.[7] Many of these studies link the modern neglect of his biblical commentaries with an inadequate understanding of what Thomas was by training and aspiration. It was for precisely this work of expositing Scripture that Thomas spent some fifteen years in preparation—two of which were devoted to reading the Bible from cover to cover. Only upon the completion of this lengthy, Bible-centered program of study was a theologian granted the title *magister sacrae paginae* (master of the sacred page) and authorized to give the kind of commentaries on the Bible that are collected in this volume. Scriptural commentary was the primary task for which Thomas was trained, and when he completed his training, it was his official job description. The Bible was his textbook, and for the whole period of his tenure as a master (1256–1273), he taught no other text *ex professo*.[8] Hence, although he is perhaps best-known today as a Christian exponent of Aristotelian philosophy, as Scott Hahn observes, "Thomas, in fact, never taught a class on Aristotle."[9] Nor, as John Boyle points out, did he ever teach a course on his *Summa theologiae* or *Summa contra Gentiles*.[10]

To interpret the sacred page was, for Aquinas and his contemporaries, the most important work of the theologian, and thus as Boyle suggests, Thomas Aquinas himself most likely regarded his scriptural commentaries as his most important works.[11] This is in no way meant to minimize the importance that Thomas obviously gave to the *Summa theologiae* and his other systematic *magna*

6. For the source citations in the lectures from the *Commentary on John*, I am grateful to The Catholic University of America Press's published edition, which includes source citations for nearly all of Thomas' patristic citations (many of these were borrowed, in turn, from the French edition of the *Commentary*) along with cross references to the *Summa theologiae*.

7. See especially Matthew Levering's *Paul in the* Summa Theologiae (Washington, DC: The Catholic University of America Press, 2014). By tracing Pauline themes and references in the *Summa*, Levering shows concretely how Thomas' engagement with Scripture shaped his systematic theology.

8. See Heinrich Denifle, "Quel livre servait de base à l'enseignement des maîtres en théologie dans l'Université de Paris?," *Revue Thomiste* 2 (1894): 129–161.

9. Scott Hahn, foreword to *Thomas Aquinas: Biblical Theologian*, ed. Roger Nutt and Michael Dauphinais (Steubenville, OH: Emmaus Academic, 2021), x.

10. John F. Boyle, "St. Thomas Aquinas and Sacred Scripture," *Pro Ecclesia* 4, no. 1 (1995): 92–104, at 94.

11. Boyle, 92. See also Boyle's collection of essays on Thomas' approach to Scripture in *The Order and Division of Divine Truth* (Steubenville, OH: Emmaus Academic, 2021).

opera, to which he devoted so many of his prime years and so much of his intellectual energy. The point is rather that we cannot fully appreciate these great systematic works apart from their context. They are the fruit of a biblical theologian's lifelong study of Sacred Scripture.[12] But to see the full profile of Thomas Aquinas, the biblical theologian—to appreciate the extent to which his profound engagement with Scripture shaped his thought—we must turn to his biblical commentaries and recognize their importance in his scholarly career. With the *Summa*, we must regard these commentaries as the fruit and end of Thomas' career as a medieval theologian.

In this light, it is no surprise that in the commentaries we find some of St. Thomas' richest and most sophisticated theological work. Torrell has ventured to identify the *Commentary on John* in particular as "the theological work par excellence by Saint Thomas."[13] Blending systematic and positive theological methods with the riches of medieval hermeneutics, at their best, the lectures on John achieve the quality of a rich tapestry in which strands of Scripture, New and Old, are braided together with shimmering threads of patristic commentary, and woven into a vast fabric of speculative theology—the robust warp and weft of the commentaries—that subtly glows with a contemplative and mystical radiance.

Some readers will perhaps find the florid aesthetics of this image incongruous with Thomas' own famously austere writing. It is certainly the case that the Angelic Doctor favored precision and clarity over rhetorical flourish. And yet the reader accustomed to the restrained style of the *Summa theologiae* will notice a distinctive tone and personality in many of these commentaries and a stylistic element that, though modest in comparison with Augustine or other of the fathers, is remarkable in its own right as reflecting a side of Aquinas that is seldom seen in the *Summa*.

It is quite possible, however, to overstate the literary achievement of the commentaries. As far as medieval biblical commentaries go, Thomas' are certainly not among the most pleasurable reads on offer, and at some point, the explanation of their neglect in the past few decades must gesture at their often dry and tedious scholastic form. At the opening of each lecture, for example, Thomas offers a point-by-point summary of the text under commentary, which he organizes into often lengthy hierarchies of numbered points and sub-points

12. For more on the dialectical interrelationship between Thomas' biblical exegesis and speculative theology, see Michael Dauphinais and Matthew Levering, eds., *Reading John with St. Thomas Aquinas: Theological Exegesis and Speculative Theology* (Washington, DC: The Catholic University of America Press, 2005).

13. Torrell, *Saint Thomas Aquinas*, 1:200.

(and sub-sub-points!).[14] Energetic readers may be inclined to draw diagrams in order to follow these *divisiones textus*, and in certain lectures there may be value in this approach, as often these summaries contain a key insight or something essential to the subsequent commentary.[15] In many others, however, the divisions and organization of these summaries are apparently determined as much by the exigencies of lecturing as by the inherent features of the biblical passage under analysis. Hence, it is often a valuable reading strategy to skim through them so as to discern whether further analysis is worthwhile.

Earlier editions of the translations used in this collection dedicated a separate paragraph to each point and sub-point in order to maximize the navigability of these summaries. But this approach tended to yield a rather disorienting sprawl of paragraph fragments across the initial page or two of most lectures. Given that these summaries are not always essential, in this collection, their points and subpoints are consolidated into larger paragraphs and their ordinal number terms (*first*, *second*, *third*, etc.) are highlighted with italic typeface. Likewise, and in the same interest of improving the visual presentation and readability of the lectures, the Marietti paragraph numbers, though usually featured in the body text of English translations, have been moved to the margins.

Where possible, the Douay-Rheims translation has been replaced with the RSV-CE version for biblical quotations in non-bold, italic font. For the primary biblical texts of the commentaries in this collection, the Douay-Rheims translation has been retained for most lectures as the version that most closely follows the version of the Vulgate that St. Thomas himself used and referenced in these commentaries.

Above I gestured at the significance of the fact that these commentaries were originally oral lectures. This is an important detail in understanding their form. The first textual antecedents of this collection were handwritten records produced by students or scribes who attended Thomas' lectures. These hand-recorded *reportationes*, as they were called, were sometimes published with little or no revision on the part of the lecturer. Apart from the commentaries on Romans and 1 Corinthians 1–10, all of the commentaries on the Pauline epistles (including some twenty of the lectures included in this collection) are

14. For more on Thomas' use of the *divisio textus*, see John F. Boyle, *The Order and Division of Divine Truth: St. Thomas Aquinas as Scholastic Master of the Sacred Page* (Steubenville, OH: Emmaus Academic, 2021) and Randall B. Smith, *Aquinas, Bonaventure, and the Scholastic Culture of Medieval Paris: Preaching, Prologues, and Biblical Commentary* (Cambridge: Cambridge University Press, 2021).

15. John F. Boyle goes so far as to say that "the genius of the commentaries is often in the division of the text. It is this division that sets every passage in a context, or perhaps better, in a set of nested contexts" ("St. Thomas Aquinas and Sacred Scripture," 100–101).

thought to constitute more-or-less unredacted *reportationes*.[16] The commentaries on Matthew, of which five lectures are included in this collection, are also *reportationes*. The commentaries on Romans and 1 Corinthians 1–7:9, by contrast, are classified as *ordinationes* (or *expositiones*) as composed by Thomas' own hand.

It is perhaps natural to expect a *reportatio* to be overall inferior both in quality and fidelity to a master's thought than an *ordinatio*. The inferior textual status of many biblical commentaries—compounded by the fact that there are as yet no critical editions available for any of St. Thomas' scriptural commentaries—represents yet another explanation for the reluctance of the Thomistic scholarly mainstream to give much attention to these commentaries until recently.

Nevertheless, such concerns surrounding the textual status of the biblical commentaries amount to far less than valid reasons to neglect them, as will be clear to anyone who reads them. Moreover, the *Commentary on John*—a *reportatio* transcribed by Thomas' companion, Reginald of Piperno—stands as a counterexample to the presumption that a *reportatio* as such must be of inferior quality. Of Reginald's *reportatio* of the *Commentary on John*, the medieval Church historian Thomas Prügl observes: "The quality of these notes was so remarkable that they were accepted by the University of Paris as an exemplar, that is, an official copy serving as an authentic text for further copying."[17]

The *Commentary on John*, likely produced during his second tenure at the University of Paris between 1269–1272, is an undeniable masterpiece of Thomas' theology, as Torrell has argued. I suggest, furthermore, that it represents a centerpiece of Thomas' whole theological enterprise, which revolves around the being and agency of the divine Word—the one who was sent to convey a new divine life to a world that had first received its life from him. In Thomas' view, moreover, this divine Word is the primary topic and insight of the Gospel of John. In the prologue to his commentary, Thomas explains that among the Evangelists, it is John who "sees the light of the incarnate Word more excellently," and on this account, "John's gospel contains the ultimate in revelation."[18]

16. See Torrell, 1:250–57; and James A. Weisheipl, *Friar Thomas D'Aquino: His Life, Thought, and Works* (Washington, DC: The Catholic University of America, 1983), 117.

17. Thomas Prügl, "Thomas Aquinas as Interpreter of Scripture," in *The Theology of Thomas Aquinas*, ed. Rik Van Nieuwenhove and Joseph Wawrykow (Notre Dame, IN: University of Notre Dame Press, 2005), 386–415, at 390.

18. Thomas Aquinas, *On John*, prologue 11 (pp. 18–19 below). The latter phrase in quotation marks is Torrell's quote of M.-D. Philippe's French translation of the *Commentary on John* in Torrell, *Saint Thomas Aquinas*, 1:200.

In the first of the two *Inaugural Sermons* (included below), which Thomas delivered in 1256 when he received the title *magister*, Thomas offers a *divisio textus* of the whole Bible in which he summarizes the New Testament in terms of a three-phase economy of grace. Accordingly, the Gospels give account of the *origin* of grace, the Pauline epistles its *power*, and the remaining books, especially Acts and Revelation, address the outworking of this grace in the world, especially in terms of the Church and its sacraments.[19] But to understand any phase in Thomas' economy of grace, we must first understand its origin in Christ, from whose divine fullness we have all received "grace upon grace" (John 1:16). But Christ's superlative fullness of grace, as Thomas insists, is a strict consequence of his divine nature as the Word—the consubstantial Son of God—made flesh. Thus, although John features last in the canonical order of the Gospels, Thomas gives it the place of privilege as the Gospel *par excellence*, because it peers deepest of all into the mystery of Christ's divinity. Thomas expresses this with unusual rhetorical flair in a discussion of the Gospels' four symbols:

> The other three evangelists, concerned with those things which Christ did in his flesh, are symbolized by animals which walk on the earth, namely, by a man, a bull calf, and a lion. But John flies like an eagle above the cloud of human weakness and looks upon the light of unchanging truth with the most lofty and firm eyes of the heart. And gazing on the very deity of our Lord Jesus Christ, by which he is equal to the Father, he has striven in this Gospel to confide this above all.[20]

Following Thomas' prioritization, this collection gives precedence to the *Commentary on John* both in terms of the number of lectures drawn from it—more than that of any other commentary—and in terms of the thematic organization of the collection, which generally follows the narrative flow of the Gospel of John. Hence, following the introductory *Inaugural Sermons* and Thomas' prologue to the *Commentary on John*, discussion proceeds in the order of John's Gospel and thus begins in chapter 1, not with the Nativity or genealogy of Christ, but at the absolute beginning—the Word, the consubstantial wisdom and creativity of God as elaborated in Thomas' eighteen-page commentary on the first two verses of John. Next, in his commentary on the genealogy of Matthew, Thomas sheds further light on the eternal generation of the Word by distinguishing a "twofold generation in Christ," divine and human, of which Matthew addresses the latter.

19. Thomas Aquinas, *The Division of Sacred Scripture* (p. 3 below).

20. Thomas Aquinas, *On John*, prologue 11 (pp. 18–19 below).

Chapter 2 turns to a discussion of the power of the Word by exploring his role in the creation of the heavens and earth in lectures on John 1:3–4 and Hebrews 1:10–12, and chapter 3 treats the Incarnation in Thomas' two lectures on John 1:14.

In his commentary on Hebrews 2:9–13, Thomas explains that Christ is the grace of God both in the sense that he is the source of all grace and as the gratuitous, sacrificial gift of God in his Passion and death. Following this distinction, part 2 features Thomas' lectures on Christ's gift of himself in his sacrificial Passion and death, and parts 3 and 4, his lectures on Christ's grace and the human participation in the divine life that follows from it.

Chapter 4 links the Incarnation to the cross with commentaries on John 3:16–21, Philippians 2:5–8, and Hebrews 2:9–13 that consider the Incarnation as a *kenosis,* or a self-emptying, in which the Word assumed a nature in which he was able to suffer and die for the salvation of the world. And chapters 5 and 6, introducing a welcome element of narrative, feature commentaries on the Passion, death, and Resurrection of Christ in Matthew and John. These are complemented by lectures on Hebrews, exploring the sacrificial character of Christ's death and on 1 Corinthians 15:20 and 1 Thessalonians 4:12–18 on the hopeful implications of Christ's Resurrection.

From Christ's death and Resurrection, chapters 7–9 turn to explore aspects of Christ's supernatural life in which believers participate. In chapter 7, commentaries on John 1:9–10 and Hebrews 1:1–2 explore the grace of enlightenment that Christ gives to the world as the revelation of God in human flesh. Chapter 8 features the thematic discussion of Christ's fullness of grace in John 1:16–17, followed by complementary lectures on Titus 2:11–15 and Ephesians 2:8–10. Finally, chapter 9 features commentaries that elaborate on the sacraments as the media by which Christ's soul-perfecting graces are conveyed to the world. The opening lecture on Hebrews 6:1–6 discusses the sacraments all together, and the subsequent lectures from Romans, John, 1 Corinthians, and Matthew explore the specific sacraments of Baptism and the Eucharist in a more focused way.

Part 4 considers the supernatural life in which we become participants through Christ's grace. Our union with Christ brings us into new relationships also with the Father and Spirit, and thus chapter 10 features commentaries on John 14 and Galatians 4, exploring Christ's gift of the Spirit who comes to dwell in us. From Christ, we also receive the gift of adoption wherein we come to participate in Christ's sonship, ceasing to relate to the Father as mere creatures and servants.

Chapter 11 takes up the theme of adoption in Thomas' commentaries on Romans 8 and John 15–16. Following the trajectory of our now inchoate participation in the triune life of God through Christ, chapter 12 is devoted to the beatific vision of God—the topic of the lectures on 1 Timothy 6:15–16, 1 Corinthians 13:12–13, 2 Corinthians 12:1–2, and John 17:20–23.

Having considered the glorious ultimate end to which Christ's grace orders us, we return to consider its more immediate effects now in the life of the Church and in Christian discipleship. Chapter 13 features the narrative commentaries on Peter's confession in Matthew and Jesus' threefold mandate to him ("feed my sheep") in John 21, followed by commentaries on the Pauline identification of the Church as the Mystical Body of Christ in Colossians 1 and Romans 12.

Chapter 14 explores the moral teachings of Christ and Paul in the commentaries on the Beatitudes of Matthew 5 and Galatians 5:22–23 on the fruits of the spirit. Chapter 15 studies the special theological virtues of faith, hope, and love, with commentaries on Hebrews 11:1, Romans 5:1–5, and 1 Corinthians 13:4–7, respectively. The conclusion, featuring Thomas' commentary on the epilogue of John's Gospel, qualifies the Gospel's achievement in view of the inexhaustible depth of meaning in Christ's every word and deed. "If one tried to write and tell of the nature of every one," Thomas insists, "he could not do so; indeed, the entire world could not do this. This is because even an infinite number of human words cannot equal one word of God."[21]

This remark about the depth of meaning in Christ's words brings us to a handful of final remarks that must be made about Thomas' expository approach. It bears repeating that Thomas is a medieval exegete whose approach to Scripture is bound to seem foreign in some measure to readers who are removed from his milieu, as we are, by almost a thousand years. To become acquainted with so foreign an author, it will help to observe some of the peculiar features of his work and take stock, at the same time, of our own peculiarities as readers with sensibilities no less shaped by a particular time and cultural circumstance.

One distinctive feature of Thomas' approach is his typically medieval understanding of the fourfold sense of Scripture. Accordingly, a given passage can mean several different things concurrently. Thomas distinguishes, first, between the literal and spiritual (or "mystical") senses of Scripture.[22] The literal, Thomas explains, consists in the primary meaning intended in the use of a word or sentence. Nevertheless, it would be wrong to imagine that this "primary meaning" is reached without any kind of interpretation. Thomas is conscious of the plurality of possible meanings even at the literal level and suggests that the divine author of the Scriptures may intend a given passage to have multi-

21. Thomas Aquinas, *On John*, epilogue 2660 (p. 391 below).

22. See Thomas Aquinas, *Quodlibetal Questions* 7.6.2 (available at https://Aquinas.cc).

ple literal meanings.[23] Further complicating this picture, Thomas holds that the literal meaning can sometimes be a metaphor, as where a metaphor is the meaning primarily intended. This is the case, for example, where Jesus is said to sit at the right hand of God. No nonmetaphorical literal sense could be the intended meaning of this passage, as Thomas explains, because there is no literal sense in which God the Father has a right hand.[24]

To explain the spiritual sense, in turn, Thomas distinguishes between the signification of words and of things. 'Rock' literally signifies a dense mineral object (the signification of the word), but this object in turn can itself signify Peter or Christ (the signification of the thing). Accordingly, the spiritual meaning is that conveyed by the *things* to which the words of Scripture literally refer.[25]

For Thomas, the spiritual senses are ordered to instruct the reader either regarding right action or right belief. The spiritual sense instructive of right action is called the moral (or tropological) sense. And of the two spiritual senses that instruct right belief, the allegorical sense concerns the truths of the New Testament, especially those regarding Christ and the Church. And last, the anagogical sense is eschatological, signifying especially the glorified life of the saints in heaven. Thus, the three spiritual meanings are the moral, allegorical, and anagogical meanings, one or more of which are sometimes implicated in the literal meaning of Scripture.

In the commentaries below, Thomas tends to use the term "mystical sense" indiscriminately of all three spiritual senses. We will see, moreover, that his exposition of the mystical sense is a fairly standard feature of his commentaries. Nevertheless, it should also be said that Thomas' spiritual interpretations are both rarer and more bound to the literal meaning of the text than was typical among many of his contemporary exegetes. He seems to have been more concerned with the literal meaning, but as we have seen, the literal sense, for Thomas, is often more expansive in its semantic possibility than we might

23. See Thomas Aquinas, *The Power of God* (*De potentia Dei*) 4.1 and *Summa theologiae* 1.1.10. For further discussion of Thomas' understanding of the literal sense and its possible plurality, see Mark F. Johnson, "Another Look at the Plurality of the Literal Sense," *Medieval Philosophy and Theology* 2 (1992): 115–141.

24. See Thomas Aquinas, *On Galatians* 4.7.254 and *Literal Commentary on Job* 1.6.

25. The ancient Christian practice of spiritual interpretation, largely rejected by modern scholars, has been reappraised by some scholars in light of the work of Richard Hays and others who, among other notable contributions, have drawn new attention to the pervasive metaphor, typology, and allegory inherent in both testaments and the deployment of a kind of spiritual interpretation of Old Testament on the part of New Testament authors. See Richard Hays, *The Conversion of the Imagination: Paul as Interpreter of Israel's Scripture* (Grand Rapids, MI: Eerdmans, 2005).

expect. There are passages in the Old Testament, for instance, whose literal meaning Thomas understands to refer to Christ.[26]

It goes without saying that Thomas' interest in the literal and historical was quite different from that of modern historical scholars. For Thomas, the purpose of Sacred Scripture is not to relay historical and scientific information *per se* but to manifest those truths that are essential to human salvation.[27] Consequently, in his approach to a passage, Thomas is interested in its historical and scientific import only insofar as these are in some way bound up with the salvific meaning of Scripture. Furthermore, we can see that Thomas is in no way committed to affirming the veracity of every historical or scientific detail in the Bible—even though he does insist that "nothing false can ever underlie the literal sense of scripture"—if we bear in mind that in the narratives and cosmological descriptions it presents, what Scripture is intended to *assert* need not be any historical or astronomical information.[28] And where it does seem to assert what is evidently false along these lines, Thomas takes this as a cue to look for a different meaning so as to avoid the absurdity of ascribing falsehood or factual error to an all-knowing author who by nature cannot lie.

Thomas' expository approach, again, differs rather strikingly from modern biblical commentaries in the manner of his engagement with his scriptural texts. His commentaries are less strictly exegetical and far more speculative and theological than is typical of biblical commentaries today. Many of the lectures included in this collection constitute full-blown theological treatises in their own right. Some are certainly no less systematic, no less theologically and philosophically dense than their corresponding discussions in the *Summa theologiae*. Evidently, Thomas sees the content of the passage under study as a starting point rather than a limit of his exploration of the fuller theological meaning revealed in the book to which it belongs and in the Scriptures as a whole. He explores and expands upon the meaning of both the part and whole in light of the authoritative teaching and theological tradition of the Church.

Of course, historical facts are normative of Thomas' interpretation too. In the commentary on the Passion narrative of Matthew 27, for instance, we see Thomas grappling with the problem presented by the shortage of extra-biblical

---

26. See, for instance, Thomas' literal commentary on the servant songs of Isaiah, especially chapter 53. For a helpful study of the place of Christ in Aquinas' commentary on Isaiah, see Matthew Levering, "Mystagogy and Aquinas' *Commentary on Isaiah*: Initiating God's People into Christ," in *Initiation and Mystagogy in Thomas Aquinas: Scriptural, Systematic, Sacramental and Moral, and Pastoral Perspectives*, ed. H.J.M. Schoot et al. (Leuven, BE: Peeters, 2019), 17–40.

27. See Thomas Aquinas, *Quodlibetal Questions* 7.6.1.

28. Thomas Aquinas, *Summa theologiae* 1.1.10 ad 3. Cf. Thomas Aquinas, *The Power of God* 4.1.

attestation to the eclipse described in the Gospel narrative.[29] Although Thomas worked before the advent of the historical data and research methods that are available to biblical scholars today, it would be unfair to dismiss him as simply "uncritical." At the same time, Thomas' approach to Scripture, as a dogmatic theologian of the thirteenth century, certainly differs from that of a modern historical-critical scholar in ways that are not reducible to methodology. Naturally, Thomas is innocent of many questions that we have been asking about the Bible since the Enlightenment; more significantly, though, he is innocent of our sense of the importance of certain distinctly modern kinds of questions. This is not a suggestion that Thomas was in any sense "anti-modern"; only that he was *not* modern.

Thomas' sensibilities are "naive" in the sense that, for better or worse, they are free of the hermeneutic suspicions that are encoded in our cultural DNA. Thus he evinces no doubt, for instance, about the genuine Pauline authorship of the Epistle to the Hebrews (nor that of any of the fourteen Pauline epistles). If this constitutes something of a deficiency in his approach, it should be said that Thomas' purposes—which, as we have said, are more theological than strictly expository—do not demand that he give the same level of interest to such questions as we do today.

Furthermore, the importance of the question of human authorship is relativized in some measure by the robust sense in which Thomas holds God to be "the principal author of Sacred Scripture."[30] In the first *Inaugural Sermon* featured at page 3 below, Thomas makes clear that a book's status as authoritative Scripture may in some cases have entirely nothing to do with the identity of its human author. Discussing the apocryphal books of the Old Testament, "whose teachings are not doubted but whose authors are," he explains, "they do not have force from the authority of the authors but rather from their reception by the Church."[31]

This is not to say that the question of the human authorship of a given book was insignificant for Thomas. In the *Commentary on John*, for instance, we can see how prominent John the Apostle figures as the presumed author of the Gospel. Thomas betrays a special devotion to John, whom he esteems as a model theologian, contemplative, and disciple of Christ. The unique authority that he ascribes to John's Gospel is certainly bound up with his view of its authorship by this "disciple whom Jesus loved" (John 20:2), and in some measure these

29. Thomas Aquinas, *On Matthew* 27.2 (p. 101 below).

30. Thomas Aquinas, *Quodlibetal Questions* 7.6.1 ad 5 (available at https://Aquinas.cc).

31. Thomas Aquinas, *The Division of Sacred Scripture* (p. 3 below).

points can surely be made of the Pauline epistles too, which, apart from the Gospels, Thomas cherished above all other writings.[32]

Lastly, this comment about Thomas' affection for the Scriptures brings us to a final point that, perhaps more than anything that has been said so far, is essential for any adequate appreciation of Thomas' project in the commentaries. Thomas was a devout Christian who vigorously practiced his faith. His biographer, Bernard Gui, describes his many devotions and the daily Mass that only sickness could prevent him from celebrating.[33] But by contrast to the milieu in which biblical scholars today operate, there were no academic norms in thirteenth-century Europe that demanded any pretense of secular neutrality or air of religious indifference. And thus, there is never anything calculated or cautious in the way that Thomas exhibits his faith in his writing; he has no notion that his faith is in any way incompatible with scholarly rigor or that a scientific study of the Bible could not at the same time constitute a Christian mystagogy and practice of discipleship.

To the contrary, for Thomas, a truly scientific theology is necessarily a spiritual practice of prayer and contemplation. And thus for Thomas, the apostolic model of a theologian is not his namesake, Thomas, who approached the reports of Christ's Resurrection with a cool, critical scrutiny and demanded tangible evidence; the model is John, the beloved disciple, whose noteworthy trait was not any intellectual gift or discipline but the intimate love that he shared with Jesus. It is this love, Thomas explains, that granted him the most profound theological insights of all.

Likewise, although we might be inclined to point to Aquinas' extraordinary intelligence as the explanatory factor for his towering theological and philosophical achievements, he is reported to have personally confessed to Reginald of Piperno that "prayer . . . was of greater service . . . in the search for truth than his natural intelligence and habit of study." "When perplexed by a difficulty," Bernard Gui explains, "he would kneel and pray and then, on returning to his writing or dictation, he was accustomed to find that his thought had become so clear that it seemed to show him inwardly, as in a book, the words he needed."[34]

---

32. William of Tocco, one of Thomas' contemporary biographers, makes this point in *Vita S. Thomae Aquinatis* 17, p. 88; translation in Kenelm Foster, trans. and ed., *The Life of St. Thomas Aquinas: Biographical Documents* (London: Longmans, 1959), 70.

33. Bernard Gui, *The Life of Saint Thomas Aquinas* 15, in *The Life of Saint Thomas Aquinas: Biographical Documents*, 25–81, at 37.

34. Gui, p. 37.

The practice of theology was inseparable, for St. Thomas, from the practice of prayer.[35] In this collection, we have sought to reflect this spiritual context of Thomas' biblical theology by including many of his own prayers and hymns at the beginning and end of each major section. To fully enter into Thomas' engagement with Scripture, we must also enter into his habit of prayer—his striving for intimacy with God. The end of Sacred Scripture, after all, is to lead us to this beatific intimacy or, as he says specifically of the Gospel of John, to make us "the temple of God."[36]

35. For more on this point, see Paul Murray, *Aquinas at Prayer: The Bible, Mysticism and Poetry* (London: Bloomsbury, 2013).

36. Thomas Aquinas, "The Prologue of Saint Thomas to the Gospel of John" 8 (p. 17–18 below).

Before Study

A PRAYER OF THOMAS AQUINAS

Ineffable Creator,
who, from the treasures of your wisdom,
have established three hierarchies of angels,
have arrayed them in marvelous order
above the fiery heavens,
and have marshaled the regions
of the universe with such artful skill,

You are proclaimed
the true font of light and wisdom,
and the primal origin
raised high beyond all things.

Pour forth a ray of your brightness
into the darkened places of my mind;
disperse from my soul
the twofold darkness
into which I was born:
sin and ignorance.

You make eloquent the tongues of infants;
refine my speech
and pour forth upon my lips
the goodness of your blessing.

Grant to me
keenness of mind,
capacity to remember,
skill in learning,
subtlety to interpret,
and eloquence in speech.

May you
guide the beginning of my work,
direct its progress,
and bring it to completion.

You who are true God and true man,
who live and reign, world without end.

Amen

THE INAUGURAL SERMONS

I. The Division of Sacred Scripture

This is the book of the commandments of God, and the law that is forever. All that keep it shall come to life: but they that have forsaken it, to death.

-BARUCH 4:1

According to Augustine, one skilled in speech should so speak as to teach, to delight, and to change;[1] that is, to teach the ignorant, to delight the bored, and to change the lazy. The speech of Sacred Scripture does these three things in the fullest manner. For it firmly teaches with its eternal truth: *Forever, O Lord, thy word is firmly fixed in the heavens* (Ps. 119:89). And it sweetly delights with its pleasantness: *How sweet are thy words to my taste!* (Ps. 119:103). And it efficaciously changes with its authority: *Is not my word like fire, says the Lord?* (Jer. 23:29).

Therefore in the text above Sacred Scripture is commended for three things. *First*, for the authority with which it changes: ***This is the book of the commandments of God***. *Second*, for the eternal truth with which it instructs, when it says, ***and the law that is forever***. *Third*, for the usefulness with which it entices, when it says, ***All that keep it shall come to life***. The authority of this Scripture is shown in three things. *First*, its origin, because God is its origin. Hence it says, ***the commandments of God***. Baruch 3:36: *He found the whole way to knowledge*. Hebrews 2:3: *It was declared at first by the Lord*. Such an author is infallibly to be believed, both on account of the condition of his nature, because he is truth: *I am the way, and the truth, and the life* (John 14:6). And on account of his fullness of knowledge: *O, the depth of the riches and wisdom and knowledge of God!* (Rom. 11:33). And also on account of the power of the words: *The word of God is living and active, sharper than any two-edged sword* (Heb. 4:12).

Second, it is shown to be efficacious by the necessity with which it is imposed: *He who does not believe will be condemned* (Mark 16:16). The truth of Sacred Scripture is proposed in the manner of a precept; hence the text says, ***the commandments of God***. These commandments direct the intellect through faith: *Believe in God, believe also in me* (John 14:1); inform the affections with love: *This is my commandment, that you love one another* (John 15:12); and induce to action: *Do this and you will live* (Luke 10:28).

Third, it is shown to be efficacious by the uniformity of its sayings, because all who teach the sacred doctrine teach the same thing. *Whether then it was I*

1. Augustine, *Teaching Christianity* 4.12.

or they, so we preach, and so you believed (1 Cor. 15:11). And this is necessary because they all had one teacher: *You have one teacher* (Matt. 23:8). And they had one spirit: *Did we not act in the same spirit?* (2 Cor. 12:18) and one love from above: *Now the company of those who believed were of one heart and soul* (Acts 4:32). Therefore, as a sign of the uniformity of doctrine, it says significantly, ***this is the book.***

The truth of this teaching of Scripture is immutable and eternal, hence the words, ***and the law that is forever.*** Luke 21:33: *Heaven and earth will pass away, but my words will not pass away.* This law will endure forever because of three things: *First,* because of the power of the lawgiver: *The Lord of hosts has purposed, and who will annul it?* (Isa. 14:27). *Second,* on account of his immutability: *I the Lord do not change* (Mal. 3:6); *God is not a man, that he should lie, or a son of man, that he should repent* (Num. 23:19). *Third,* because of the truth of the law: *All thy statutes are truth* (Ps. 118:86 DRB). *Truthful lips endure forever* (Prov. 12:19). *Truth remains and gathers strength eternally* (3 Ezra 4:38).[2]

The usefulness of this Scripture is the greatest: *I am the Lord thy God that teach thee profitable things* (Is. 48:17 DRB). Hence our text continues: ***All that keep it shall come to life.*** Which indeed is threefold: *First* it is the life of grace, to which Sacred Scripture disposes. *The words that I have spoken to you are spirit and life* (John 6:63). For through this life the spirit lives in God. *It is no longer I who live, but Christ who lives in me* (Gal. 2:20). *Second* is the life of justice consisting in works, to which Sacred Scripture directs. *I will never forget thy precepts; for by them thou hast given me life* (Ps. 119:93). *Third* is the life of glory which Sacred Scripture promises and to which it leads. *Lord, to whom shall we go? You have the words of eternal life* (John 6:69). *But these are written that you may believe that Jesus is the Christ, the Son of God, and that believing you may have life in his name* (John 20:31).

Sacred Scripture leads to this life in two ways, by commanding and by helping. Commanding through the mandates which it proposes, which belong to the Old Testament: *The covenant of the Most High God, the law which Moses commanded* (Sir. 24:23). Helping, through the gift of grace which the lawgiver dispenses, which pertains to the New Testament. Both of these are touched on in John 1:17: *For the Law was given through Moses; grace and truth came through Jesus Christ.*

Hence the whole of Sacred Scripture is divided into two principal parts, the Old and New Testaments, which are mentioned in Matthew 13:52: *every Scribe who has been trained for the kingdom of heaven is like a householder who brings out of his treasure what is new and old.* And Song of Solomon 7:13: *over*

2. 3 Ezra is a deuterocanonical book featured in the Septuagint and in again in the Vulgate translation that Thomas used.

our doors are all choice fruits, new as well as old, which I have laid up for you, O my beloved.

The Old Testament is divided according to the teaching of the commandments, for the commandment is of two kinds, the binding and the warning. The binding is the command of a king who can punish transgressors: *The dread wrath of a king is like the growling of a lion* (Prov. 20:2). But a warning is the precept of a father who must teach: *Do you have children? Discipline them* (Sir. 7:23). The precept of a king is of two kinds, one which establishes the laws, another which induces to observance of the law, which is customarily done through his heralds and ambassadors. Thus it is that three kinds of command are distinguished, that of the king, that of the herald, and that of the father. On this basis the Old Testament is subdivided into three parts, according to Jerome in his prologue to the book of Kings.[3]

The *first* part is contained in the law which is proposed by the king himself. *For the Lord is our judge, the Lord is our lawgiver, the Lord is our King* (Isa. 33:22 DRB).

The *second* is contained in the prophets who were, as it were, ambassadors and heralds of God, speaking to the people in the person of God, and urging them to observance of the law: *Haggai, the messenger of the Lord, spoke to the people with the Lord's message* (Hag. 1:13).

The *third* is contained in the works of hagiographers, writers who were inspired by the Holy Spirit and spoke as for themselves and not for God. Hence they are called saintly writers because they were writers of the sacred, *agios* meaning 'sacred,' and *graphia* meaning 'scripture.' Thus the precepts found in them are paternal. As is evident in Proverbs 6:20: *My son, keep your father's commandment.*

Jerome mentions a *fourth* kind of book, namely the apocryphal, so called from *apo*, that is, 'especially,' and *cryphon*, that is, 'obscure,' because there is doubt about their contents and authors.[4] The Catholic Church includes among the books of Sacred Scripture some whose teachings are not doubted but whose authors are. Not that the authors are unknown but because these men were not of known authority. Hence they do not have force from the authority of the authors but rather from their reception by the Church. Because there is the same manner of speaking in them and in the hagiographical works, they are for now counted among them.

The *first* part, which contains the law, is divided into two parts, insofar as there are two kinds of law, public and private. A private law is imposed for the observance of one person or one family. Such law is contained in Genesis, as

3. Jerome, "The Books of Samuel and Kings."

4. Jerome, "The Books of Samuel and Kings."

is evident from the first precept given to man, *but of the tree of the knowledge of good and evil you shall not eat* (2:17), and to Noah, *you shall not eat flesh with its life, that is, its blood* (9:4), and to Abraham, *As for you, you shall keep my covenant, you and your descendants after you throughout their generations* (17:9).

The public law is that which is given to the people. For the divine law was given to the Jewish people through a mediator because it was not fitting that the people should receive it immediately from God: *I was the mediator and stood between the Lord and you and at that time to show you his words* (Deut. 5:5 DRB). *Why then the law? It was added because of transgressions . . . and it was ordained by angels through an intermediary* (Gal. 3:19). Thus a twofold level is found in legislation. *First*, when the law comes from the Lord to the mediator, and this pertains to three books, Exodus, Leviticus, and Numbers. Hence we frequently read in them, *God spoke to Moses*. *Second*, when the law is given to the people by the mediator, and this pertains to Deuteronomy, as is evident from its very beginning: *These are the words that Moses spoke to all Israel* (1:1).

These three books are distinguished by the three things in which a people should be ordered. *First*, precepts bearing on equity of judgement, and this is found in Exodus. *Second*, in sacraments with respect to the establishment of worship, and this in Leviticus. And *third*, in offices, with respect to the administration of the community, and this in Numbers.

The *second* part, which is the prophets, is subdivided insofar as a herald ought to do two things. He should manifest the beneficence of the king, so that men will be inclined to obey, and he should declare the edict of the law.

There is a threefold divine beneficence that the prophets expose to the people. *First*, the effect of heredity, and this in Joshua, of which Sirach says, *Joshua the son of Nun was mighty in* war (46:1). *Second*, the destruction of armies, and this in the book of Judges, of whose destruction Psalm 83:9 says, *Do to them as to Madian, as to Sisara*. *Third*, the exultation of the people, which is twofold, namely the private exaltation of one person, and this in Ruth, and a public which is of the whole people, and this in Kings, which benefice God grants to them: *You were decked with gold and silver* (Ezek. 16:13). For these books, according to Jerome, are placed in the rank of prophets.[5]

In other books which are commonly said to be of the prophets, the prophets posed divine edicts for the observance of the law. And this is said, *first*, in general, in the major prophets who were sent to the whole people and called for the observance of the whole law; *second*, in particular, and this in the minor prophets, different ones of whom were sent for different reasons to special tribes, as Hosea to the ten tribes of Joel, Jonah to the Ninevites, and so with the rest.

5. Jerome, "The Books of Samuel and Kings."

The major prophets differ according to the different ways the prophets sought to lead the people to observance of the law, namely, cajoling by the promise of benefits, frightening with the threat of punishment, arguing by condemnation of sins. Although each of these is found in every prophet, Isaiah chiefly cajoles, as is said in Sirach 48:24: *By the spirit of might he saw the last things and comforted those who mourned in Zion*. Jeremiah chiefly warns: *He is weakening the hands of the soldiers who are left in this city by speaking such words to them* (38:4). But Ezekiel argues and scolds: *Your father was an Amorite and your mother a Hittite* (Ezek. 16:3).

They can be distinguished in another way, insofar as Isaiah chiefly foretells the mystery of the incarnation, which is why he is read during the time of Advent by the Church, and Jeremiah the mystery of the Passion, hence he is read in Passiontide, and Ezekiel the mystery of the Resurrection, hence his book finishes with the raising of the bones and the repair of the temple. Daniel, however, is included among the prophets insofar as he predicted future events in a prophetic spirit; although he did not speak to the people in the person of the Lord, he dealt with the divinity of Christ. Thus the four prophets answer to the four Evangelists, and also to the call to judgement.

The third part, which contains the hagiographic and the apocryphal books, is subdivided according to the two ways fathers instruct their sons in virtue, namely, by word and deed, since in morals examples are no less important than words. Some teach by deed alone, some by word alone, some by word and deed.

By deed, however, in two ways. One, instructing about the future by warning, and this in Joshua, whom Jerome places among the hagiographs.[6] For although one is a prophet because of the gift of prophecy, this is not his office, because he was not sent by God to prophesy to the people. Hence what is said in Wisdom 8:8 can be applied to the prophet: *She has foreknowledge of signs and wonders*. In another way, speaking of past events as examples of virtue. There are four principal virtues, namely justice, which serves the common good, an example of which is given in Chronicles, in which the condition of a whole people who were governed with justice is described. The *second* is temperance, an example of which is given in Judith, which is why Jerome says, *Take Judith as an example of the chaste widow*.[7] Judith 15:10: *thy heart has been strengthened because thou hast loved chastity*. *Third* is fortitude, which has two attributes. To attack, and an example of this is found in the book of Maccabees; and to endure, and an example of this is found in Tobit 2:12: *Now this trial the Lord therefore permitted to happen to him, that an example might be given to posterity of his patience*. The *fourth* is prudence, by which dangers are avoided, and an

6. Jerome, "The Books of Samuel and Kings."

7. Jerome, "Prologue to Judith."

example of this is given in Ezra. For in that book we are shown how Ezra and Nehemiah and other princes prudently guarded against the plots of enemies wishing to impede the building of the temple and the city. It also pertains to prudence wisely to repel the violent, and an example of this is given in Esther, where it is shown how Mordecai and Esther handled the deceptions of the most powerful Haman.

The hagiographical and apocryphal books which instruct by word, are divided insofar as words work in a twofold way to instruct, in one way, by asking for the gift of wisdom. *I prayed, and understanding was given me; I called upon God, and the spirit of wisdom came to me* (Wis. 7:7). This is how the psalter instructs, speaking to God in prayer. In another way, by teaching wisdom, and this in two ways according to the twofold work of wisdom, one of which is to expose the liar, and Job who drove out errors by way of disputation exhibits this: *I would speak to the Almighty and I desire to argue my case with God. As for you, you whitewash with lies* (Job 13:3–4). The other work is not to lie about what it knows, and thus we are instructed in a twofold way, because either wisdom is commended to us, and this in the book of Wisdom, or the precepts of wisdom are proposed, and this in the three books of Solomon, which indeed differ according to the three grades of virtue that Plotinus distinguishes since the precepts of wisdom ought to concern only the acts of virtue.[8] In the *first* grade, according to him, are political virtues, whereby a man moderately uses the things of this world and lives among men, and this in the Proverbs. In the *second* grade are the purgative virtues, whereby a man regards the world with contempt, and this in Ecclesiastes, which aims at contempt of the world, as is clear from Jerome's prologue.[9] In the *third* grade are the virtues of the purged soul, whereby a man, wholly cleansed of worldly cares, delights in the contemplation of wisdom alone, and this is found in the Song of Solomon. In the *fourth* grade are the exemplar virtues existing in God, concerning which precepts of wisdom are not given but are rather derived from them. In word and in deed Sirach instructs. Hence the precepts of wisdom in praise of fathers close his book, as is clear in chapter 44 and after.

The New Testament, which is ordered to eternal life not only through precepts but also through the gifts of grace, is divided into three parts. In the *first* the origin of grace is treated, in the Gospels. In the *second*, the power of grace, and this in the epistles of Paul, hence he begins in the power of the Gospel, in Romans 1:16 saying, *I am not ashamed of the Gospel, for it is the power of God unto salvation to everyone who believes*. In the *third*, the execution of the aforesaid virtues is treated, and this in the rest of the books of the New Testament.

8. Plotinus, *Enneads* 1.1.2.2–7.

9. Jerome, "Preface to the Commentary on Ecclesiastes."

Christ is the origin of grace. *From his fullness have we all received, grace upon grace. For the Law was given through Moses; grace and truth came through Jesus Christ* (John 1:16–17). In Christ a twofold nature is to be considered, a divine, and the Gospel of John is chiefly concerned with this, hence he begins, *In the beginning was the Word, and the Word was with God, and the Word was God.* And a human, and the other Gospels treat chiefly of this, and they are distinguished according to the threefold dignity that belongs to the man Christ. With respect to his royal honor, Matthew speaks. Hence in the beginning of his Gospel he shows that Christ descended from kings and was adored by the Magi kings. With respect to his prophetic honor, Mark speaks, hence he begins with the preaching of the Gospel. With respect to his priestly dignity, Luke speaks, and he begins with the temple and the priesthood and ends his Gospel in the temple, and frequently returns to the temple, as the *Gloss* says about Luke 2:46: *They found him sitting in the temple in the midst of the teachers.*[10]

In another way, Matthew might be said to speak of Christ chiefly with respect to the mystery of the incarnation, and thus he is depicted in the figure of a man. Luke, with respect to the mystery of the Passion, and therefore he is depicted as a bull, which is an animal to be immolated. Mark, with respect to the victory of the Resurrection, and thus he is depicted as a lion. But John, who soars to the heights of his divinity, is depicted as an eagle.

[The part dealing with the power of grace as exemplified in the epistles of Paul is missing from the text.]

The execution of the power of grace is shown in the progress of the Church, in which there are three things to consider. *First,* the beginning of the Church, and this is treated in the Acts of the Apostles, hence Jerome says, in his preface to the Pentateuch, that *the Acts of the Apostles seem to give the bare history of the birth and to clothe the infant Church.*[11] *Second,* the progress of the Church, and to this is ordered the apostolic instruction of the canonical epistles. *Third,* the end of the Church, with which the whole content of Scripture concludes in Revelation, with the spouse in the abode of Jesus Christ sharing the life of glory, to which Jesus Christ himself conducts, and may he be blessed forever and ever. Amen.

10. The *Gloss* mentioned here is a compilation of scriptural comments and well-known sayings mostly attributed to the Fathers. Early on, individual glosses were included sporadically in the margins or between the lines of Vulgate manuscripts, but over time, certain authoritative comments appeared with more regularity. By the twelfth century, more standardized gloss collections such as the *Glossa Ordinaria* were widely used. Thomas Aquinas produced his own gloss collection for the four Gospels called the *Glossa Continua super Evangelia* or the *Catena Aurea.* The two glosses most frequently cited by St. Thomas are the *Glossa Ordinaria* and Peter Lombard's *Magna Glossatura.* Versions of these glosses can be found in Latin in the Patrologia Latina series, volumes 113–114 and 192, respectively.

11. The quote is actually located in Jerome, "To Paulinus" 9.

II. Commendation of Sacred Scripture

From thy lofty abode thou waterest the mountains: the earth is satisfied with the fruit of thy work.

-PSALMS 104:13

PREFACE

The King and Lord of the heavens set down this law from all eternity that the gifts of his Providence should come to the lower through intermediaries. Hence Dionysius says, *It is the most sacred law of the divinity that things in the middle should be led to his most divine light by first things.*[1]

This is found to be a law not only in spiritual things but also in corporeal. Hence Augustine says: *As the more crass and least are ruled in a given order by more subtle bodies, so all bodies are ruled by the rational spirit of life.*[2] Therefore, in the psalm the Lord proposed this law observed in the communication of spiritual wisdom in a metaphor of bodily things: ***waterest the mountains.*** It is plain to the senses that from the highest clouds rain flows forth by which the mountains and rivers are refreshed and send themselves forth so that the satiated earth can bear fruit. Similarly, from the heights of divine wisdom the minds of the learned, represented by the mountains, are watered, by whose ministry the light of divine wisdom reached to the minds of those who listen.

There are then four things to be considered in the chosen text: the *height* of spiritual doctrine; the *dignity* of those who teach it; the *condition* of the listeners; and the *order* of communicating.

1.

Its height is expressed by the words, ***from thy lofty abode.*** The *Gloss* has, ***from thy treasure houses on high.*** The height of sacred doctrine comes from three things.

First, its origin: for this is the wisdom that is described as being from on high. *The word of God on high is the fountain of wisdom* (Sir. 1:5 DRB).

Second, because of the subtlety of its matter: *I dwelt in the high places, and my throne was in a pillar of cloud* (Sir. 24:4). There are some heights of divine wisdom to which all come, though imperfectly, because, as Damascene says: *Knowledge of the existing God is naturally inserted in all.*[3] In this respect, it is said in Job 36:25, *All men see him: everyone beholds afar off* (DRB). Other things are higher and only the wit of the wise achieves them. *What can be known about God is plain to them* (Rom. 1:19). Some are so high that they completely

1. Pseudo-Dionysius, *The Celestial Hierarchy* 5.

2. Augustine, *The Trinity* 3.1.4.

3. John of Damascus, *An Exact Exposition of the Orthodox Faith* 1.1.

transcend human reason, of which it is said in Job 28:21, *It is hid from the eyes of all living*, and Psalm 18:11: *He made darkness his covering*. But this has been made known by the Holy Spirit: *Now we have received not the spirit of this world, but the Spirit that is from God* (1 Cor. 2:12), instructing holy teachers who passed it on in the text of Sacred Scripture; and these are the highest, in which this wisdom is said to dwell.

Third, from the sublimity of the end, for it has the highest end, namely, life eternal: *These are written that you may believe that Jesus is the Christ, the Son of God, and that believing you may have life in his name* (John 20:31). *If then you have been raised with Christ, seek the things that are above, where Christ is seated at the right hand of God. Set your minds on things that are above, not on the things that are on earth* (Col. 3:1–2).

2.

Because of the height of this doctrine, there is required dignity in those who teach it, which is why they are symbolized by mountains when it is said, ***thou waterest the mountains***, and this for three reasons.

First, because of the height of mountains. For they are elevated above the earth and neighbors of the sky. Thus the holy teachers by despising earthly things cleave to heavenly things alone: *Our commonwealth is in heaven, and from it we await a Savior, the Lord Jesus Christ* (Phil. 3:20). Hence of the teacher of teachers, Christ, it is said in Isaiah: *It shall come to pass in the latter days that the mountain of the house of the Lord shall be established as the highest of the mountains . . . . and all the nations shall flow to it* (2:2).

Second, because of its splendor. For the mountains are illumined by beams. Similarly the sacred teachers of minds first receive the splendor. Like mountains the teachers are illumined by the first beams of divine wisdom. *Glorious are you, more majestic than the everlasting mountains. All the foolish of heart were troubled* (Ps. 76:4–5), that is, by the teachers who participate in eternity. *You shine as lights in the world* (Phil. 2:15).

Third, because of the protection of the mountains, for the land is defended from the enemy by mountains. So too the doctors of the Church must in defense of the faith stand against errors. The sons of Israel do not put their trust in lance or bow, but the mountains defend them. *You have not gone up into the breaches, or built a wall for the house of Israel, that it might stand to stand in battle in the day of the Lord* (Ezek. 13:5).

Therefore all the teachers of Sacred Scripture should give high thanks to their eminence of life, that they might be worthy to preach efficaciously, because as Gregory says: *The preaching of those whose life is despised will also be despised.*[4] Ecclesiastes 12:11: *The sayings of the wise are like goads, and like nails firmly fixed are the collected sayings which are given by one Shepherd.* For the heart cannot be stimulated or stirred to fear of God unless it is fixed in highness of life.

They should be enlightened, that they might fittingly teach by reading: *To me, though I am the very least of all the saints, this grace was given, to preach to the gentiles the unsearchable riches of Christ, and to make all men see what is the plan of the mystery hidden for ages in God who created all things* (Eph. 3:8–9). Armed, that they might refute errors in disputation: *I will give you a mouth and wisdom, which none of your adversaries will be able to withstand or contradict* (Luke 21:15). Of these three offices, namely, to preach, to lecture, and to dispute, it is said in Titus 1:9: *He must hold firm to the sure word as taught, so that he may be able to give instruction in sound doctrine and also to confute those who contradict it.*

3.

Third, the condition of those who hear, which are presented in the symbol of earth: ***the earth is satisfied.*** This is because the earth is lowest: *As the heavens for height, the earth for depth* (Prov. 25:3). Again, it is stable and firm: *A generation goes, and a generation comes, but the earth remains forever* (Eccles. 1:4). Again, it is fruitful: *Let the earth put forth vegetation, plants yielding seed, and fruit trees bearing fruit in which is their seed* (Gen. 1:11).

Similarly, they should be low as the earth in humility: *With the humble is wisdom* (Prov. 11:2).[5] Again, firm with the sense of rectitude *that we may be now no longer children, tossed to and fro and carried about with every wind of doctrine* (Eph. 4:14). And fruitful, as the precepts of wisdom bear fruit in them: *Hearing the word,* [they] *hold it fast in an honest and good heart and bring forth fruit with patience* (Luke 8:15).

Therefore humility is required of them with respect to the learning that comes from listening: *If you love to listen, you will gain knowledge; and if you incline your ear, you will become wise* (Sir. 6:33). Rectitude of the senses with respect to the judgement of what is heard; *Does not the ear try words?* (Job 12:11). But fruitfulness in discovery, by which from a few things heard, the good listener pronounces many things: *Give instruction to a wise man, and he will be still wiser* (Prov. 9:9).

---

4. Gregory the Great, *Forty Gospel Homilies* 12.

5. It is worth noting here that the Latin word for humble (*humilis*) is derived from the word for earth (*humus*). Hence, in Latin, 'humble' has the force of 'of the earth.'

4.

The order of its coming about is touched on here with respect to three things, namely, the order of communicating, the amount, and the quality of the gift received.

First with respect to the order of communicating, because not everything that is contained in divine wisdom can be grasped by the minds of the teachers. Hence he does not say 'from the highest mountains,' but from the upper: *Lo, these are but the outskirts of his ways* (Job 26:14). Similarly, not everything that the teachers grasp is passed on to the hearers: *He heard things that cannot be told* (2 Cor. 12:4). Hence he does not say, 'passing on to earth the fruits of the mountains,' but ***the earth is satisfied with the fruit of thy work.*** Job 26:8 says, *He binds up the waters in his thick clouds, so that they break not out and fall down together.* In explaining this, Gregory says that *the teacher should not preach to the simple as much as he knows, because he himself is unable to know how many divine mysteries there are.*[6]

Second, the order with respect to the mode of having is touched upon, because God has wisdom naturally. Hence his ***lofty abode*** is what is natural to him: *With God are wisdom and might; he has counsel and understanding* (Job 12:13). But teachers share in wisdom abundantly. Hence they are said to be watered from on high: *I will water my orchard and drench my garden plot* (Sir. 24:31). But listeners sufficiently participate in it, and the satiety of the earth signifies this: *I shall be satisfied with beholding thy form* (Ps. 17:15).

Third, with respect to the power of communicating, because God communicates wisdom by his own power. Hence by himself he is said to water the mountains. But the teachers do not communicate wisdom except as ministers. Hence the fruits of the mountains are not attributed to them but to the divine works, ***with the fruit of thy work.*** 1 Corinthians 3:4–5: *What is Paul? Servants through whom you believed.*

But *who is sufficient for these things?* (2 Cor. 2:16). For God requires innocent ministers: *He who walks in the way that is blameless shall minister to me* (Ps. 101:6); understanding: *A servant who deals wisely has the king's favor* (Prov. 14:35); fervor: *You . . . make the winds your messengers, fire and flame your ministers* (Ps. 104:4); again, obedience: *Bless the Lord, all his hosts, his ministers that do his will!* (Ps. 103:21).

But although no one by himself, of himself, is sufficient for such a ministry, he can hope to have this sufficiency from God: *Not that we are competent of ourselves to claim anything as coming from us; our competence is from God*

6. Gregory the Great, *Moralia in Job* 17.37.

(2 Cor. 3:5). He must ask it of God: *If any of you lacks wisdom, let him ask God, who gives to all men generously and without reproaching, and it will be given him* (James 1:5).

The Prologue of Saint Thomas to the Gospel of John

I saw the Lord seated on a high and lofty throne, and the whole house was full of his majesty, and the things that were under him filled the temple.

-ISAIAH 6:1

1 These are the words of a contemplative, and if we regard them as spoken by John the Evangelist, they apply quite well to showing the nature of this Gospel. For as Augustine says: *The other evangelists instruct us in their Gospels on the active life; but John in his Gospel instructs us also on the contemplative life.*[7]

The contemplation of John is described above in three ways, in keeping with the threefold manner in which he contemplated the Lord Jesus. It is described as high, full, and perfect. It is high: *I saw the Lord seated on a high and lofty throne*; it is full: *and the whole house was full of his majesty*; and it was perfect: *and the things that were under him filled the temple.*

2 As to the *first*, we must understand that the height and sublimity of contemplation consists most of all in the contemplation and knowledge of God. *Lift up your eyes on high and see who created these* (Isa. 40:26). A man lifts up his eyes on high when he sees and contemplates the Creator of all things. Now since John rose above whatever had been created—mountains, heavens, angels—and reached the Creator of all, as Augustine says, it is clear that his contemplation was most high.[8] Thus, *I saw the Lord.* And because, as John himself says below: ***Isaiah said this because he saw his glory***, namely, of Christ, ***and spoke of him*** (John 12:41), therefore the Lord seated on a high and lofty throne is Christ.

Now a fourfold height is indicated in this contemplation of John. A height of authority; hence he says, *I saw the Lord.* A height of eternity; when he says, *seated.* One of dignity, or nobility of nature; so he says, *on a high throne.* And a height of incomprehensible truth; when he says, *lofty.* It is in these four ways that the early philosophers arrived at the knowledge of God.

3 Some attained to a knowledge of God through his authority, and this is the most efficacious way. For we see the things in nature acting for an end and attaining to ends which are both useful and certain. And since they lack intelligence, they are unable to direct themselves, but must be directed and moved by one directing them, and who possesses an intellect. Thus it is that the movement of the things of nature toward a certain end indicates the existence of something higher by which the things of nature are directed to an end and governed. And so, since the whole course of nature advances to an end in an orderly way and is directed, we have to posit something higher which directs

7. Augustine, *Agreement among the Evangelists* 1.5.

8. Augustine, 1.4.

and governs them as lord; and this is God. This authority in governing is shown to be in the Word of God when he says, *Lord*. Thus a Psalm says: *You rule the raging of the sea; when its waves rise, you still them* (89:9), as though saying: 'you are the Lord and govern all things.' John shows that he knows this about the Word when he says below, ***he came unto his own*** (1:11), i.e., to the world, since the whole universe is his own.

4 Others came to a knowledge of God from his eternity. They saw that whatever was in things was changeable, and that the more noble something is in the grades of being, so much the less it has of mutability. For example, the lower bodies are mutable both as to their substance and to place, while the heavenly bodies, which are more noble, are immutable in substance and change only with respect to place. We can clearly conclude from this that the first principle of all things, which is supreme and more noble, is changeless and eternal.

The prophet suggests this eternity of the Word when he says, *seated*, i.e., presiding without any change and eternally. *Your divine throne endures forever and ever* (Ps. 45:6); *Jesus Christ is the same yesterday and today and forever* (Heb. 13:8). John points to this eternity when he says below, ***in the beginning was the Word*** (1:1).

5 Still others came to a knowledge of God from the dignity of God; and these were the Platonists. They noted that everything which is something by participation is reduced to what is the same thing by essence, as to the first and highest. Thus, all things which are fiery by participation are reduced to fire, which is such by its essence. And so since all things which exist participate in being and are beings by participation, there must necessarily be at the summit of all things something which is its existence through its own essence, i.e., whose essence is its existence. And this is God, who is the most sufficient, the most eminent, and the most perfect cause of the whole of existence, from whom all things that are participate in existence. This dignity is shown in the words, *on a high throne*, which, according to Dionysius, refer to the divine nature.[9] *The Lord is high above all nations* (Ps. 113:4). John shows us this dignity when he says below, ***the Word was God*** (1:1), with ***Word*** as subject and ***God*** as the predicate.

6 Yet others arrived at a knowledge of God from the incomprehensibility of truth. All the truth which our intellect is able to grasp is finite, since according to Augustine, *Everything that is known is bounded by the comprehension of the one knowing*;[10] and if it is bounded, it is determined and particularized. Therefore, the first and supreme truth, which surpasses every intellect, must necessarily be incomprehensible and infinite; and this is God. Hence a psalm says, *Your greatness is above the heavens* (8:1), i.e., above every created intellect, angelic

9. Pseudo-Dionysius, *The Celestial Hierarchy* 13.4.

10. Augustine, *The City of God* 12.18.

and human. The Apostle says this in the words, *He dwells in unapproachable light* (1 Tim. 6:16).

This incomprehensibility of truth is shown to us in the word *lofty*, that is, above all the knowledge of the created intellect. John implies this incomprehensibility to us when he says below, ***No one has ever seen God*** (1:18).

Thus, the contemplation of John was high as regards authority, eternity, dignity, and the incomprehensibility of the Word. And John has passed on this contemplation to us in his Gospel.

7 John's contemplation was also full. Now contemplation is full when someone is able to consider all the effects of a cause in the cause itself, that is, when he knows not only the essence of the cause, but also its power, according as it can extend out to many things. Of this flowing outward we read, *it fills men with wisdom, like the Pishon, and like the Tigris at the time of the first fruits* (Sir. 24:25); *the river of God is full with water*, since the divine wisdom has depth in relation to its knowledge of all things. *With thee is wisdom, who knows your works* (Wis. 9:9).

Since John the Evangelist was raised up to the contemplation of the nature of the divine Word and of his essence when he said, ***In the beginning was the Word, and the Word was with God*** (1:1), he immediately tells us of the power of the Word as it extends to all things, saying, ***All things were made through him*** (1:3). Thus his contemplation was full. And so after the Prophet had said, *I saw the Lord seated*, he added something about his power, *and the whole house was full of his majesty*, that is, the whole fullness of things and of the universe is from the majesty and power of God, through whom all things were made, and by whose light all the men coming into this world are enlightened. *The earth is the Lord's and the fullness thereof* (Ps. 24:1).

8 The contemplation of John was also perfect. For contemplation is perfect when the one contemplating is led and raised to the height of the thing contemplated. Should he remain at a lower level, then no matter how high the things which he might contemplate, the contemplation would not be perfect. So in order that it be perfect it is necessary that it rise and attain the end of the thing contemplated, adhering and assenting by affection and understanding to the truth contemplated. Job says, *Do you know the balancings of the clouds*, that is, the contemplation of those preaching, *the wonderous works of him who is perfect in knowledge* (37:16), inasmuch as they adhere firmly by affection and understanding to contemplating the highest truth.

Since John not only taught how Christ Jesus, the Word of God, is God, raised above all things, and how all things were made through him, but also that we are sanctified by him and adhere to him by the grace which he pours into us, he says below, ***Of his fullness we all have received—indeed, grace***

upon grace (1:16). It is therefore apparent that his contemplation is perfect. This perfection is shown in the addition, *and the things that were under him filled the temple*. For *the head of Christ is God* (1 Cor. 11:3). The things that are under Christ are the sacraments of his humanity, through which the faithful are filled with the fullness of grace. In this way, then, *the things that were under him filled the temple*, i.e., the faithful, who are the holy temple of God (1 Cor. 3:17) insofar as through the sacraments of his humanity all the faithful of Christ receive from the fullness of his grace.

9 The contemplation of John was thus full, high, and perfect. We should note, however, that these three characteristics of contemplation belong to the different sciences in different ways. The perfection of contemplation is found in moral science, which is concerned with the ultimate end. The fullness of contemplation is possessed by natural science, which considers things as proceeding from God. Among the physical sciences, the height of contemplation is found in metaphysics. But the Gospel of John contains all together what the above sciences have in a divided way, and so it is most perfect.

10 In this way then, from what has been said, we can understand the matter of this Gospel. For while the other evangelists treat principally of the mysteries of the humanity of Christ, John, especially and above all, makes known the divinity of Christ in his Gospel, as we saw above. Still, he does not ignore the mysteries of his humanity. He did this because, after the other evangelists had written their Gospels, heresies had arisen concerning the divinity of Christ, to the effect that Christ was purely and simply a man, as Ebion and Cerinthus falsely thought. And so John the Evangelist, who had drawn the truth about the divinity of the Word from the very fountainhead of the divine breast, wrote this Gospel at the request of the faithful. And in it he gives us the doctrine of the divinity of Christ and refutes all heresies.

The order of this Gospel is clear from the above. For John *first* shows us *the Lord seated on a high and lofty throne*, when he says below, ***In the beginning was the Word*** (1:1). He shows *second* how *the house was full of his majesty*, when he says, ***All things were made through him*** (John 1:3). *Third*, he shows how *the things that were under him filled the temple*, when he says, ***The Word became flesh*** (John 1:14).

The end of this Gospel is also clear, and it is that the faithful become the temple of God and become filled with the majesty of God; and so John says below, ***These things are written so that you may believe that Jesus is the Christ, the Son of God*** (John 20:31).

The matter of this Gospel, the knowledge of the divinity of the Word, is
11 clear, as well as its order and end. Then follows the condition of the author, who is described above in four ways: as to his name, his virtue, his symbol, and his

privilege. He is described as to name as John, the author of this Gospel. 'John' is interpreted as 'one in whom grace is present,' since the secrets of the divinity cannot be seen except by those who have the grace of God within themselves. *No one comprehends the thoughts of God except the Spirit of God* (1 Cor. 2:11).

As concerns his virtue, John saw the Lord seated, because he was a virgin; for it is fitting that such persons see the Lord: *Blessed are the pure in heart* (Matt. 5:8). He is described as to his symbol, for John is symbolized by an eagle. The other three evangelists, concerned with those things which Christ did in his flesh, are symbolized by animals which walk on the earth, namely, by a man, a bull calf, and a lion. But John flies like an eagle above the cloud of human weakness and looks upon the light of unchanging truth with the most lofty and firm eyes of the heart. And gazing on the very deity of our Lord Jesus Christ, by which he is equal to the Father, he has striven in this Gospel to confide this above all, to the extent that he believed was sufficient for all. Concerning this flight of John it is said: *Will the eagle*, that is, John, *fly up at your command?* (Job 39:27 DRB) And further on it says, *his eyes look far away*, because the Word of God is seen in the bosom of the Father by the eye of the mind.

John is described as to privilege since, among the other disciples of the Lord, John was more loved by Christ. Without mentioning his own name John refers to himself below as ***the disciple whom Jesus loved*** (21:20). And because secrets are revealed to friends, ***I have called you friends because everything I have heard from my father I have made known to you*** (John 15:15), Jesus confided his secrets in a special way to that disciple who was specially loved. Thus it says in Job: *From the savage*, that is, the proud, *he hides his light*, that is, Christ hides the truth of his divinity, *and shows his friend*, that is, John, *that it is his possession* (Job 36:32 DRB), since it is John who sees the light of the incarnate Word more excellently and expresses it to us, saying that he was ***the true light*** (1:9).

Now the matter, order, end, and author of this Gospel of the blessed John are clear.

PART I

FROM THE FATHER

The Being and Incarnation of the Word

The Word from Heaven Now Proceeding

A HYMN OF THOMAS AQUINAS

The Word from heaven now proceeding,
his Father's right hand never leaving,
advancing to his proper work,
approached his life's final evening.

By his disciples unto death
and to his enemies betrayed,
he first as life's true sustenance
himself to his apostles gave.

To them beneath a twofold guise
he flesh and blood distributed;
thus in corporeal substances
the entire man he justly fed.

Being born, he became our friend;
at supper, he became our food.
Dying, he was our ransom's price
and, reigning, is our eternal good.

O sacrifice for our salvation,
heavenly gates you open wide.
Our enemies press hard around us.
Give us strength; our help provide.

To the one and triune God,
be glory and eternal praise.
May he grant us life forever
and to our home our souls upraise.

Amen

Chapter 1

THE DIVINE AND HUMAN GENERATIONS OF CHRIST

John 1:1–2

The Being of the Word

On John 1.1 (23–67)

1:1 ***In the beginning was the Word, and the Word was with God, and the Word was God.***

1:2 ***He was in the beginning with God.***

23 John the Evangelist, as already indicated, makes it his principal object to show the divinity of the incarnate Word. Accordingly, his Gospel is divided into two parts. In the *first* he asserts the divinity of Christ; in the *second* he shows it by the things Christ did in the flesh, at ***and on the third day*** (2:1).

In regard to the *first,* he does two things. *First,* he shows the divinity of Christ; *second,* he sets forth the manner in which Christ's divinity is made known to us, at ***We have beheld his glory, the glory as of the only Son*** (John 1:14). Concerning the *first* he does two things. *First,* he treats of the divinity of Christ; *second* of the incarnation of the Word of God, at ***There was a man sent from God, whose name was John*** (1:6).

Because there are two items to be considered in each thing, namely, its existence and its operation or power, *first* he treats the existence of the Word as to his divine nature; *second* of his power or operation, at ***All things were made through him*** (1:3). In regard to the *first* [the existence of the Word] he does four things. *First,* he shows when the Word was: ***In the beginning was the Word***; *second,* where he was: ***The Word was with God***; *third,* what he was: ***The Word was God***; *fourth,* in what way he was: ***He was in the beginning with God.*** The first two pertain to the inquiry of whether something exists; the second two pertain to the inquiry of what something is.

24 With respect to the *first* of these four [when] we must examine the meaning of the statement ***In the beginning was the Word.*** And here three things present themselves for careful study according to the three parts of this statement. *First* it is necessary to investigate the name ***Word***; *second* the phrase ***in the beginning***; *third* the meaning of ***The Word was in the beginning.***

25 To understand the name ***Word*** we should note that, according to the Philosopher, vocal sounds are signs of the affections that exist in our soul.[1] It is customary in Scripture for the things signified to be themselves called by the names of their signs, as in the statement, *the rock was Christ* (1 Cor. 10:4). It is fitting that what is within our soul, and what is signified by our external word, be called a word. But whether the name 'word' belongs first to the exterior vocal sound or to the conception in our mind, is not our concern at present. However, it is obvious that what is signified by the vocal sound, as existing interiorly in the soul, exists prior to the vocal expression inasmuch as it is its actual cause.

Therefore if we wish to grasp the meaning of the interior word, we must first look at the meaning of that which is exteriorly expressed in words. Now there are three things in our intellect: the intellectual power itself, the species of the thing understood, which is its form, and this form being to the intellect what the species of a color is to the eye; and third, the very activity of the intellect, which is to understand. But none of these is what is signified by the exterior vocal word.

For, the name 'stone' does not signify the substance of the intellect because this is not what the one naming intends; nor does it signify the species, which is that by which the intellect understands, since this also is not the intention of the one naming; nor does it signify the act itself of understanding since to understand is not an action proceeding to the exterior from the one understanding, but an action remaining within. Therefore, that is properly called an interior word which the one understanding forms when understanding.

Now the intellect forms two things, according to its two operations. According to its operation which is called the understanding of indivisibles, it forms a definition; while according to its operation by which it unites and separates, it forms an enunciation or something of that sort. Hence, what is thus formed and expressed by the operation of the intellect, whether by defining or enunciating, is what the exterior vocal sound signifies. So the Philosopher says that the notion [*ratio*] that a name signifies is a definition.[2] Hence, what is thus expressed, i.e., formed in the soul, is called an interior word. Consequently it is compared to the intellect, not as that by which the intellect understands, but as that in which it understands, because it is in what is thus expressed and formed that it sees the nature of the thing understood. Thus we have the meaning of the name 'word.'

Second, from what has been said we are able to understand that a word is always something that proceeds from an intellect existing in act; and furthermore, that a word is always a notion and likeness of the thing understood. So

1. Aristotle, *De interpretatione* 1 (16a3–4).

2. Aristotle, 2 (16a20–16b5).

if the one understanding and the thing understood are the same, then the word is a notion and likeness of the intellect from which it proceeds. On the other hand, if the one understanding is other than the thing understood, then the word is not a likeness and notion of the one understanding but of the thing understood, as the conception which one has of a stone is a likeness of only the stone. But when the intellect understands itself, its word is a likeness and notion of the intellect. And so Augustine sees a likeness of the Trinity in the soul insofar as the mind understands itself, but not insofar as it understands other things.[3]

It is clear then that it is necessary to have a word in any intellectual nature, for it is of the very nature of understanding that the intellect in understanding should form something. Now what is formed is called a word, and so it follows that in every being which understands there must be a word.

However, intellectual natures are of three kinds: human, angelic, and divine; and so there are three kinds of words. The human word, about which it is said: *The fool said in his heart, "there is no God"* (Ps. 14:1). The angelic word, about which it is said in Zechariah, and in many places in Sacred Scripture, *The angel . . . said to me, "I will show you what they are"* (Zech. 1:9). The third is the divine word, of which it is said: *God said, "let there be light"* (Gen. 1:3).

So when the Evangelist says, ***in the beginning was the Word***, we cannot understand this as a human or angelic word, because both these words have been made since man and angel have a cause and principle of their existence and operation, and the word of a man or an angel cannot exist before they do. The word the Evangelist had in mind he shows by saying that this word was not made, since all things were made by it. Therefore, the word about which John speaks here is the Word of God.

26 We should note that this Word differs from our own word in three ways. The *first* difference, according to Augustine, is that our word is formable before being formed, for when I wish to conceive the notion of a stone, I must arrive at it by reasoning.[4] And so it is in all other things that are understood by us, with the sole possible exception of the first principles, which, since they are known in a simple manner, are known at once without any discourse of reason.

So as long as the intellect, in so reasoning, casts about this way and that, the formation is not yet complete. It is only when it has conceived the notion of the thing perfectly that for the first time it has the notion of the complete thing and a word. Thus in our mind there is both a cogitation, meaning the discourse involved in an investigation, and a word, which is formed according to a perfect contemplation of the truth. So our word is first in potency before

3. Augustine, *The Trinity* 9.5.8.

4. Augustine, 15.4.25.

it is in act. But the Word of God is always in act. In consequence, the term cogitation does not properly speaking apply to the Word of God. For Augustine says: *The Word of God is spoken of in such a way that cogitation is not included, lest anything changeable be supposed in God.*[5] Anselm was speaking improperly when he said: *For the supreme Spirit to speak is for him to look at something while cogitating.*[6]

27 The *second* difference is that our word is imperfect, but the divine Word is most perfect. For since we cannot express all our conceptions in one word, we must form many imperfect words through which we separately express all that is in our knowledge. But it is not that way with God. For since he understands both himself and everything else through his essence, by one act, the single divine Word is expressive of all that is in God, not only of the persons but also of creatures; otherwise it would be imperfect. So Augustine says: *If there were less in the Word than is contained in the knowledge of the one speaking it, the Word would be imperfect; but it is obvious that it is most perfect; therefore, it is only one.*[7] Job 33:14: *God speaks once* (DRB).

28 The *third* difference is that our word is not of the same nature as we; but the divine Word is of the same nature as God. And therefore it is something that subsists in the divine nature. For the understood notion which the intellect is seen to form about something has only an intelligible existence in our soul. Now in our soul, to understand is not the same as the nature of the soul, because our soul is not its own operation. Consequently, the word which our intellect forms is not of the essence of our soul but is an accident of it. But in God, to understand and to be are the same; and so the Word of the divine intellect is not an accident but belongs to its nature. Thus it must be subsistent, because whatever is in the nature of God is God. Thus Damascene says that God is a substantial word, and a hypostasis, but our words are concepts in our mind.[8]

29 From the above it is clear that the Word, properly speaking, is always understood as a person in the divinity, since it implies only something expressed, by the one understanding; also, that in the divinity the Word is the likeness of that from which it issues; and that it is co-eternal with that from which it issues, since it was not first formable before being formed, but was always in act; and that it is equal to the Father, since it is perfect and expressive of the whole being of the Father; and that it is co-essential and consubstantial with the Father, since it is his substance.

---

5. Augustine, 15.4.25.

6. Anselm, *Monologion* 63.

7. Augustine, *The Trinity* 15.14.23.

8. John of Damascus, *An Exact Exposition of the Orthodox Faith* 1.13.

It is also clear that since in every nature that which issues forth and has a likeness to the nature from which it issues is called a son, and since this Word issues forth in a likeness and identity to the nature from which it issues, it is suitably and appropriately called a son, and its production is called a generation.

30 So now the first point is clear, the meaning of the term ***Word***. There are four questions on this point, two of them from Chrysostom. The *first* is: why did John the Evangelist omit the Father and begin at once with the Son, saying, ***in the beginning was the Word***?[9]

There are two answers to this. One is that the Father was known to everyone in the Old Testament, although not under the aspect of Father, but as God; but the Son was not known. And so in the New Testament, which is concerned with our knowledge of the Word, he begins with the Word or Son.

The other answer is that we are brought to know the Father through the Son: ***I have manifested your name to the men whom you have given to me*** (John 17:6). And so wishing to lead the faithful to a knowledge of the Father, the Evangelist fittingly began with the Son, at once adding something about the Father when he says, ***and the Word was with God***.

31 The *second* question is also from Chrysostom: Why did he say ***Word*** and not *Son*, since, as we have said, the Word proceeds as Son?[10]

There are also two answers to this. *First*, because 'Son' means something begotten, and when we hear of the generation of the Son, someone might suppose that this generation is the kind he can comprehend, that is, a material and changeable generation. Thus he did not say 'Son,' but ***Word***, which signifies an intelligible proceeding, so that it would not be understood as a material and changeable generation. And so in showing that the Son is born of the Father in an unchangeable way, he eliminates a faulty conjecture by using the name ***Word***.

The *second* answer is this. The Evangelist was about to consider the Word as having come to manifest the Father. But since the idea of manifesting is implied better in the name ***Word*** than in the name 'Son,' he preferred to use the name ***Word***.

32 The *third* question is raised by Augustine, and it is this.[11] In Greek, where we have ***Word***, they have *Logos*; now since *Logos* signifies in Latin both notion and word, why did the translators render it as ***Word*** and not 'notion,' since a notion is something interior just as a word is? I answer that 'notion,' properly speaking, names a conception of the mind precisely as in the mind, even if through it nothing exterior comes to be; but word signifies a reference to some-

9. John Chrysostom, *Commentary on Saint John* 2.4.

10. John Chrysostom, *Commentary on Saint John* 2.4.

11. Augustine, *Eighty-Three Different Questions* 63.

thing exterior. And so because the Evangelist, when he said ***Logos***, intended to signify not only a reference to the Son's existence in the Father, but also the operative power of the Son, by which, ***all things were made through him: and without him was made nothing***, our predecessors preferred to translate it ***Word***, which implies a reference to something exterior, rather than 'notion' which implies merely a concept of the mind.

33 The *fourth* question is from Origen and is this.[12] In many passages, Scripture, when speaking of the Word of God, does not simply call him the ***Word***, but adds *of God*, saying, *the Word of God*, or *of the Lord*: *The Word of God on high is the foundation of wisdom* (Sir. 1:5 DRB); *he is called . . . the Word of God* (Rev. 19:13). Why then did the Evangelist, when speaking here of the Word of God, not say, 'in the beginning was the Word of God,' but said ***in the beginning was the Word***?

I answer that although there are many participated truths, there is just one absolute truth, which is truth by its very essence, that is, the divine act of being; and by this truth all words are words. Similarly, there is one absolute wisdom elevated above all things, that is, the divine wisdom, by participating in which all wise persons are wise. Further, there is one absolute Word, by participating in which all persons having a word are called speakers. Now this is the divine Word which of itself is the Word elevated above all words.

So in order that the Evangelist might signify this supereminence of the divine Word, he pointed out this Word to us absolutely without any addition. And because the Greeks, when they wished to signify something separate and elevated above everything else, did this by affixing the article to the name, as did the Platonists, wishing to signify the separated substances, such as the separated good or the separated man, called them the good *per se*, or man *per se*, so the Evangelist, wishing to signify the separation and elevation of that Word above all things, affixed an article to the name *Logos*, so that if it were stated in Latin we would say *Verbum* (the Word).

34 *Second*, we must consider the meaning of the phrase, ***in the beginning***. We must note that according to Origen, the word *principium* [beginning] has many meanings.[13] Since the word *principium* implies a certain order of one thing to another, one can find a *principium* in all those things which have an order.

First of all, order is found in quantified things; and so there is a principle of number and lengths, as for example, a line. *Second*, order is found in time; and so we speak of a beginning of time, or of duration.

Third, order is found in learning; and this in two ways: as to nature, and as to ourselves, and in both cases we can speak of a beginning. *By this time you*

12. Origen, *Commentary on John* 2.37–41.

13. Origen, 1.90.

ought to be teachers (Heb. 5:12). As to nature, in Christian doctrine the beginning and principle of our wisdom is Christ, inasmuch as he is the wisdom and Word of God, i.e., in his divinity. But as to ourselves, the beginning is Christ himself inasmuch as ***the Word became flesh*** (John 1:14), i.e., by his incarnation.

Fourth, order is found in the production of a thing. In this perspective there can be a *principium* on the part of the thing generated, that is, the first part of the thing generated or made; as we say that the foundation is the beginning of a house. Another is on the part of the generator, and in this perspective there are three principles: of intention, which is the purpose, which motivates the agent; of reason, which is the idea in the mind of the maker; and of execution, which is the operative faculty.

Considering these various ways of using the term, we now ask how ***begin-***
35 ***ning*** is used here when it says, ***In the beginning was the Word.*** We should note that this word can be taken in three ways. In one way so that *principium* is understood as the person of the Son, who is the principle of creatures by reason of his active power acting with wisdom, which is the conception of the things that are brought into existence. Hence, we read: *Christ the power of God and the wisdom of God* (1 Cor. 1:24). And so the Lord said about himself: *The beginning,* ***who also speak to you*** (John 8:25).

Taking ***principium*** in this way, we should understand the statement ***in the beginning was the Word*** as though he were saying 'the Word was in the Son,' so that the sense would be: the Word himself is the principle, in the sense in which life is said to be in God, when this life is not something other than God. And this is the explanation of Origen.[14]

And so the Evangelist says ***in the beginning*** here in order, as Chrysostom says, to show at the very outset the divinity of the Word by asserting that he is a principle because, as determining all, a principle is most honored.[15]

36 In a *second* way ***principium*** can be understood as the person of the Father, who is the principle not only of creatures, but of every divine process. It is taken this way in, *With you is the principality in the day of your strength* (Ps. 109:3 DRB). In this second way one reads ***in the beginning was the Word*** as though it means, 'the Son was in the Father.' This is Augustine's understanding of it, as well as Origen's.[16]

The Son, however, is said to be in the Father because both have the same essence. Since the Son is his own essence, then the Son is in whomsoever the Son's essence is. Since, therefore, the essence of the Son is in the Father by

14. Origen, 1.116–117.

15. John Chrysostom, *Commentary on Saint John* 2.3.

16. Augustine, *The Trinity* 6.2.3. Origen, *Commentary on John* 1.102.

consubstantiality, it is fitting that the Son be in the Father. Hence it is said: ***I am in the Father, and the Father in me*** (John 14:10).

37 In a *third* way, ***principium*** can be taken for the beginning of duration, so that the sense of ***in the beginning was the Word*** is that the Word was before all things, as Augustine explains it.[17] According to Basil and Hilary, this phrase shows the eternity of the Word.[18]

The phrase ***in the beginning was the Word*** shows that no matter which beginning of duration is taken, whether of temporal things, which is time, or of aeviternal things, which is the aeon, or of the whole world or any imagined span of time reaching back for many ages, at that beginning the Word already was. Hence Hilary says, *Go back season by season, skip over the centuries, take away ages. Set down whatever you want as the beginning in your opinion: the Word already was.*[19] And this is what Proverbs says: *The Lord possessed me in the beginning of his ways, before he made anything* (8:22 DRB). But what is prior to the beginning of duration is eternal.

38 And thus the *first* explanation asserts the causality of the Word; the *second* explanation affirms the consubstantiality of the Word with the Father, who utters the Word; and the *third* explanation affirms the co-eternity of the Word.

39 Now we should consider that it says that ***the Word was***, which is stated in the past imperfect tense [*erat*]. This tense is most appropriate for designating eternal things if we consider the nature of time and of the things that exist in time. For what is future is not yet in act; but what is at present is in act, and by the fact that it is in act what is present is not described as having been. Now the past perfect tense indicates that something has existed, has already come to an end, and has now ceased to be. The past imperfect tense, on the other hand, indicates that something has been, has not yet come to an end, nor has ceased to be, but still endures. Thus, whenever John mentions eternal things he expressly says ***was*** [*erat*, imperfect], but when he refers to anything temporal he says ***has been*** [*fuit*, perfect], as will be clear later.[20]

But so far as concerns the notion of the present, the best way to designate eternity is the present tense, which indicates that something is in act, and this is always the characteristic of eternal things. And so it is said: *I am who am* (Exod. 3:14 DRB). And Augustine says: *He alone truly is whose being does not know a past and a future.*[21]

17. Augustine, *The Trinity* 6.2.3.

18. Basil the Great, *Homily on the Beginning of the Gospel of John* 1. Hilary of Poitiers, *The Trinity* 2.13.

19. Hilary of Poitiers, *The Trinity* 2.13.

20. See Thomas Aquinas, *Commentary on the Gospel of John* 1.4 (not included in this collection).

21. Augustine, *The Trinity* 5.2.3.

40 We should also note that this verb ***was***, according to the *Gloss*, is not understood here as indicating temporal changes, as other verbs do, but as signifying the existence of a thing. Thus it is also called a substantive verb.

41 Someone may ask how the Word can be co-eternal with the Father since he is begotten by the Father: for a human son, born from a human father, is subsequent to his father.

I answer that there are three reasons why an originative principle is prior in duration to that which derives from that principle. *First* of all, if the originative principle of anything precedes in time the action by which it produces the thing of which it is the principle; thus a man does not begin to write as soon as he exists, and so he precedes his writing in time. *Second*, if an action is successive; consequently, even if the action should happen to begin at the same time as the agent, the termination of the action is nevertheless subsequent to the agent. Thus, as soon as fire has been generated in a lower region, it begins to ascend; but the fire exists before it has ascended, because the motion by which it tends upward requires some time. *Third*, by the fact that sometimes the beginning of a thing depends on the will of its principle, just as the beginning of a creature's coming-to-be depends on the will of God, such that God existed before any creature.

Yet none of these three is found in the generation of the divine Word. God did not first exist and then begin to generate the Word: for since the generation of the Word is nothing other than an intelligible conception, it would follow that God would be understanding in potency before understanding in act, which is impossible. Again, it is impossible that the generation of the Word involve succession: for then the divine Word would be unformed before it was formed, as happens in us who form words by cogitating, which is false, as was said. Again, we cannot say that the Father pre-established a beginning of duration for his Son by his own will, because God the Father does not generate the Son by his will, as the Arians held, but naturally: for God the Father, understanding himself, conceives the Word; and so God the Father did not exist prior to the Son.[22]

An example of this, to a limited degree, appears in fire and in the brightness issuing from it: for this brightness issues naturally and without succession from the fire. Again, if the fire were eternal, its brightness would be coeternal with it. This is why the Son is called the brightness of the Father: *the brightness of his glory* (Heb. 1:3 DRB). But this example lacks an illustration of the identity

22. The Arians were a loose group of clergy and theologians who followed the view of Arius (AD 256–336), an influential presbyter from Alexandria, Egypt, who argued that the Son, because he is begotten of the Father, can be neither co-eternal nor equal in divinity with him. Arius and his views were condemned at the Council of Nicaea in 325 AD.

of nature. And so we call him Son, although in human sonship we do not find coeternity: for we must attain our knowledge of divine things from many likenesses in material things, for one likeness is not enough. The Council of Ephesus says that the Son always coexists with the Father: for *brightness* indicates his unchangeability, *birth* points to the Word himself, but the name *Son* suggests his consubstantiality.[23]

42 And so we give the Son various names to express his perfection, which cannot be expressed by one name. We call him *Son* to show that he is of the same nature as the Father; we call him *image* to show that he is not unlike the Father in any way; we call him *brightness* to show that he is coeternal; and he is called the ***Word*** to show that he is begotten in an immaterial manner.

43 Then the Evangelist says, ***and the Word was with God***. This is the second clause which the Evangelist posits in his narration. The first thing to consider is the meaning of the two words which did not appear in the first clause, that is, ***God***, and ***with***; for what is signified by *Verbum* and *principium* has already been related. Therefore, let us diligently continue investigating that which is new in the second clause, namely ***God*** and ***with***. And to better understand the explanation of this second clause, we must say something about the meaning of each so far as it is relevant to our purpose.

44 At the outset, we should note that the name ***God*** signifies the divinity concretely and as inherent in a subject, while the name 'deity' signifies the divinity in the abstract and absolutely. Thus it cannot naturally and by its mode of signifying stand for a divine person, but only for the divine nature. But the name ***God*** can, by its natural mode of signifying, stand for any one of the divine persons, just as the name 'man' stands for any individual possessing humanity. Therefore, whenever the truth of a statement or its predicate requires that the name 'God' stand for the person, then it stands for the person, as when we say, 'God begets God.' Thus, when it says here that ***the Word was with God***, it is necessary that God stand for the person of the Father, because the preposition ***with*** signifies the distinction of the Word, which is said to be ***with God***. And although this preposition signifies a distinction in person, it does not signify a distinction in nature, since the nature of the Father and of the Son is the same. Consequently, the Evangelist wished to signify the person of the Father when he said ***God***.

45 Here we should note that the preposition 'with' signifies a certain union of the thing signified by its grammatical antecedent to the thing signified by its grammatical object, just as the preposition 'in' does. However, there is a difference, because the preposition 'in' signifies a certain intrinsic union, whereas the preposition 'with' implies in a certain way an extrinsic union.

23. The Council of Ephesus (431), "Canonical Epistle of St. Cyril, *Cum Salvator Noster*."

And we state both in divine matters, namely, that the Son is in the Father and with the Father. Here the intrinsic union pertains to consubstantiality, but the extrinsic union (if we may use such an expression, since extrinsic is improperly employed in divine matters) refers only to a personal distinction, because the Son is distinguished from the Father by origin alone. And so these two words designate both a consubstantiality in nature and distinction in person: consubstantiality inasmuch as a certain union is implied; but distinction, inasmuch as a certain otherness is signified as was said above.

The preposition 'in,' as was said, principally signifies consubstantiality, as implying an intrinsic union and, by way of consequence, a distinction of persons, inasmuch as every preposition is transitive. The preposition 'with' principally signifies a personal distinction, but also a consubstantiality inasmuch as it signifies a certain extrinsic, so to speak, union. For these reasons the Evangelist specifically used here the preposition 'with' in order to express the distinction of the person of the Son from the Father, saying, ***and the Word was with God***, that is, the Son was with the Father as one person with another.

46 We should note further that this preposition 'with' has four meanings, through which four contrary objections are eliminated. *First*, the preposition 'with' signifies the subsistence of its antecedent, because things that do not subsist of themselves are not properly said to be with another; thus we do not say that a color is with a body, and the same applies to other things that do not subsist of themselves. But things that do subsist of themselves are properly said to be with another; thus we say that a man is with a man, and a stone with a stone. *Second*, it signifies authority in its grammatical object. For we do not, properly speaking, say that a king is with a soldier, but that the soldier is with the king. *Third*, it asserts a distinction. For it is not proper to say that a person is with himself but rather that one man is with another. *Fourth*, it signifies a certain union and fellowship. For when some person is said to be with another, it suggests to us that there is some social union between them. Considering these four conditions implied in the meaning of this preposition *with*, the Evangelist quite appropriately joins to the first clause, ***in the beginning was the Word***, this second clause, ***and the Word was with God***.

For if we omit one of the three explanations of ***in the beginning was the Word***, namely, the one in which *principium* was understood as the Son, certain heretics make a twofold objection against each of the other explanations, namely, the one in which *principium* means the same as 'before all things,' and the one in which it is understood as the Father. Thus there are four objections, and we can answer these by the four conditions indicated by this preposition 'with.'

47 The *first* of these objections is this. You say that the Word was in the beginning, i.e., before all things. But before all things there was nothing. So if before

all things there was nothing, where then was the Word? This objection arises due to the imaginings of those who think that whatever exists is somewhere and in some place. But this is rejected by John when he says, ***with God***, which indicates the union mentioned in the last four conditions. So, according to Basil, the meaning is this: where was the Word? The answer is: ***with God***; not in some place, since he cannot be surrounded, but he is with the Father, who is not enclosed by any place.[24]

48 The *second* objection against the same explanation is this. You say that the Word was in the beginning, i.e., before all things. But whatever exists before all things appears to proceed from no one, since that from which something proceeds seems to be prior to that which proceeds from it. Therefore, the Word does not proceed from another. This objection is rejected when he says, ***the Word was with God***, taking ***with*** according to its second condition, as implying authority in what is causing. So the meaning, according to Hilary, is this: from whom is the Word if he exists before all things? The Evangelist answers: ***the Word was with God***, i.e., although the Word has no beginning of duration, still he does not lack a beginning or author, for he was with God as his author.[25]

49 The *third* objection, directed to the explanation in which *principium* is understood as the Father, is this. You say that ***in the beginning was the Word***, i.e., the Son was in the Father. But that which is in something does not seem to be subsistent, as a hypostasis; just as the whiteness in a body does not subsist. This objection is solved by the statement ***the Word was with God***, taking ***with*** in its first condition, as implying the subsistence of its grammatical antecedent. So according to Chrysostom, the meaning is this: ***in the beginning was the Word***, not as an accident, but he ***was with God***, as subsisting, and a divine hypostasis.[26]

50 The *fourth* objection, against the same explanation, is this. You say that the Word was in the beginning, i.e., in the Father. But whatever is in something is not distinct from it. So the Son is not distinct from the Father.

This objection is answered by the statement ***and the Word was with God***, taking ***with*** in its third condition, as indicating distinction. Thus the meaning, according to Alcuin and Bede, is this: ***the Word was with God***, and he was with the Father by a consubstantiality of nature, while still being with him through a distinction in person.

51 And so, ***and the Word was with God*** indicates: the union of the Word with the Father in nature, according to Basil; their distinction in person, accord-

24. Basil the Great, *Homily on the Beginning of the Gospel of John* 4.

25. Hilary of Poitiers, *The Trinity* 2.14.

26. John Chrysostom, *Commentary on Saint John* 4.1.

ing to Alcuin and Bede;[27] the subsistence of the Word in the divine nature, according to Chrysostom; and the authorship of the Father in relation to the Word, according to Hilary.

52 We should also note, according to Origen, that ***the Word was with God*** shows that the Son has always been with the Father.[28] For in the Old Testament it says that the Word of the Lord *came* to Jeremiah or someone else, as is plain in many passages of Sacred Scripture. But it does not say that the Word of the Lord was with Jeremiah or anyone else, because the Word comes to those who begin to have the Word after not having it. Thus the Evangelist did not say that the Word came to the Father, but ***was with*** the Father, because, given the Father, the Word was with him.

53 Then he says, ***and the Word was God.*** This is the third clause in John's account, and it follows most appropriately considering the order of teaching. For since John had said both when and where the Word was, it remained to inquire what the Word was, that is, ***the Word was God***, taking ***Word*** as the
54 subject, and ***God*** as the predicate. But since one should first inquire what a thing is before investigating where and when it is, it seems that John violated this order by discussing these latter first.

Origen answers this by saying that the Word of God is with man and with God in different ways.[29] The Word is with man as perfecting him, because it is through him that man becomes wise and good: *[He] passes into holy souls and makes them friends of God and prophets* (Wis. 7:27). But the Word is not with God as though the Father were perfected and enlightened by him. Rather, the Word is with God as receiving natural divinity from him, who utters the Word, and from whom he has it that he is the same God with him. And so, since the Word was with God by origin, it was necessary to show first that the Word was in the Father and with the Father before showing that the Word was God.

55 It is to be noted however, that this clause, ***the Word was God***, also enables us to answer two objections which arise from the foregoing.

The *first* is based on the name ***Word*** and is this. You say that ***in the beginning was the Word***, and that ***the Word was with God.*** Now it is obvious that 'word' is generally understood to signify a vocal sound and the statement of something necessary, a manifesting of thoughts. But these words pass away and do not subsist. Accordingly, someone could think that the Evangelist was speaking of a word like these.

27. Alcuin, *Commentaria in sancti Joannis Evangelium* 1. Bede, *Expositio in Evangelium Sancti Joannis* 1.

28. Origen, *Commentary on John* 2.8.

29. Origen, 2.8–10.

According to Hilary and Augustine, this question is sufficiently answered by the above account.[30] Augustine says that it is obvious that in this passage ***Word*** cannot be understood as a statement because, since a statement is in motion and passes away, it could not be said that ***in the beginning was the Word***, if this Word were something passing away and in motion.[31] The same thing is clear from ***and the Word was with God***: for to be in another is not the same as to be with another. Our word, since it does not subsist, is not with us, but in us; but the Word of God is subsistent, and therefore with God. And so the Evangelist expressly says, ***and the Word was with God***. To entirely remove the ground of the objection, he adds the nature and being of the Word, saying, ***and the Word was God***.

56 The other question comes from his saying, ***with God***. For since ***with*** indicates a distinction, it could be thought that ***the Word was with God***, i.e., the Father, as distinct from him in nature. So to exclude this he adds at once the consubstantiality of the Word with the Father, saying, ***and the Word was God***. As if to say: 'the Word is not separated from the Father by a diversity of nature, because the Word itself is God.'

57 Note also the special way of signifying, since he says, ***the Word was God***, using ***God*** absolutely to show that he is not God in the same way in which the name of the deity is given to a creature in Sacred Scripture. For a creature sometimes shares this name with some added qualification, as when it says, *I make you as God to Pharaoh* (Exod. 7:1), in order to indicate that he was not God absolutely or by nature, because he was appointed the god of someone in a qualified sense. Again, it says in a psalm: *I say, "you are gods"* (82:6) as if to say: 'in my opinion, but not in reality.' Thus the Word is called God absolutely because he is God by his own essence, and not by participation, as men and angels are.

58 We should note that Origen disgracefully misunderstood this clause, led astray by the Greek manner of speaking and this was the occasion of his error.

It is the custom among the Greeks to put the article before every name in order to indicate a distinction. In the Greek version of John's Gospel the name ***Word*** in the statement ***in the beginning was the Word***, and also the name ***God*** in the statement ***and the Word was with God***, are prefixed by the article, so as to read ***the Word*** and ***the God***, in order to indicate the eminence and distinction of the Word from other words, and the principality of the Father in the divinity. But in the statement, ***the Word was God***, the article is not prefixed to the noun ***God***, which stands for the person of the Son. Because of this Origen blasphemed that the Word, although he was Word by essence, was not God

30. Hilary of Poitiers, *The Trinity* 2.15.

31. Augustine, *Tractates on the Gospel of John* 1.8.

by essence, but is called God by participation; while the Father alone is God by essence.[32] And so he held that the Son is inferior to the Father.

59 Chrysostom proves that this is not true, because if the article used with the name ***God*** implied the superiority of the Father in respect to the Son, it would never be used with the name ***God*** when it is used as a predicate of another, but only when it is predicated of the Father.[33] Further, whenever it would be said of the Father, it would be accompanied by the article.

However, we find the opposite to be the case in two statements of the Apostle, who calls Christ *God*, using the article. For he says, *The appearing of the glory of the great God and our savior Jesus Christ* (Titus 2:13), where *God* stands for the Son, and in the Greek the article is used. Therefore, Christ is the great God. Again he says: *Christ, who is God over all things . . . blessed forever* (Rom. 9:5), and again the article is used with *God* in the Greek. Further, it is said of Jesus Christ that *he is the true God and eternal life* (1 John 5:20). Thus, Christ is not God by participation, but truly God. And so the theory of Origen is clearly false.

Chrysostom gives us the reason why the Evangelist did not use the article with the name ***God***, namely, because he had already mentioned God twice using the article, and so it was not necessary to repeat it a third time, but it was implied.[34]

Or it could be said, and this is a better reason, that ***God*** is used here as the predicate and is taken formally. And it is not the custom for the article to accompany names used as predicates, since the article indicates a distinction. But if God were used here as the subject, it could stand for any of the persons, as the Son or the Holy Spirit; then, no doubt, the article would be used in the Greek.

60 Then he says, ***he was in the beginning with God.*** This is the fourth clause and is introduced because of the preceding clause. For from the Evangelist's statement that ***the Word was God***, two false interpretations could be held by those who misunderstand. One of these is by the pagans, who acknowledge many and different gods, and say that their wills are in opposition. For example, those who put out the fable of Jupiter fighting with Saturn; or as the Manicheans, who have two contrary principles of nature.[35] The Lord said against this error: *Hear, O Israel: the Lord our God is one Lord* (Deut. 6:4).

---

32. Origen, *Commentary on John* 2.12–18.

33. John Chrysostom, *Commentary on Saint John* 4.3.

34. John Chrysostom, 4.3.

35. The Manicheans were an eclectic, Mesopotamian religious movement that emerged in the third century AD. The Manicheans held a dualistic cosmology in which good and evil were represented by two more-or-less equal deities whose rivalry constituted the fundamental dynamism of history.

Since the Evangelist had said, ***the Word was with God, and the Word was God***, they could adduce this in support of their error by understanding the God with whom the Word is to be one God, and the Word to be another, having another, or contrary, will to the former; and this is against the law of the Gospel.

And so to exclude this he says, ***he was in the beginning with God***, as if to say, according to Hilary: 'I say that the Word is God, not as if he has a distinct divinity, but he is with God, that is, in the one same nature in which he is.'[36] Further, lest his statement, ***and the Word was God***, be taken to mean that the Word has an opposed will, he added that ***the Word was in the beginning with God***, namely, the Father, not as divided from him or opposed, but having an identity of nature with him and a harmony of will. This union comes about by the sharing of the divine nature in the three persons, and by the bond of the natural love of the Father and the Son.

61 The Arians were able to draw out another error from the above. They think that the Son is less than the Father because it says: ***The Father is greater than I*** (John 14:28). And they say the Father is greater than the Son both as to eternity and as to divinity of nature. And so to exclude this the Evangelist added: ***He was in the beginning with God.***

For Arius admits the first clause, ***in the beginning was the Word***, but he will not admit that *principium* should be taken for the Father, but rather for the beginning of creatures. So he says that the Word was in the beginning of creatures, and consequently is in no sense coeternal with the Father. But this is excluded, according to Chrysostom, by this clause, ***he was in the beginning***, not of creatures, but ***in the beginning with God***, i.e., whenever God existed.[37] For the Father was never alone without the Son or Word, but ***he***, that is, the Word, was always ***with God***.

62 Again, Arius admits that the Word was God, but nevertheless inferior to the Father. This is excluded by what follows. For there are two attributes proper to the great God which Arius attributed solely to God the Father, that is, eternity and omnipotence. So in whomever these two attributes are found, he is the great God, than whom none is greater. But the Evangelist attributes these two to the Word. Therefore, the Word is the great God and not inferior. He says the Word is eternal when he states, ***He was in the beginning with God***, i.e., the Word was with God from eternity, and not only in the beginning of creatures, as Arius held; but he was with God, receiving being and divinity from him. Further, he attributes omnipotence to the Word when he adds, ***All things were made through him*** (John 1:3).

---

36. Hilary of Poitiers, *The Trinity* 2.16.

37. John Chrysostom, *Commentary on Saint John* 4.1.

63 Origen gives a rather beautiful explanation of this clause, ***He was in the beginning with God***, when he says that it is not separate from the first three but is in a certain sense their epilogue.[38] For the Evangelist, after he had indicated that truth was the Son's and was about to describe his power, in a way gathers together in a summary form, in this fourth clause, what he had said in the first three. For in saying ***he***, he understands the third clause; by adding ***was in the beginning***, he recalls the first clause; and by adding ***was with God***, he recalls the second, so that we do not think that the Word which was in the beginning is different than the Word which was God; but this Word which was God ***was in the beginning with God***.

64 If one considers these four propositions well, he will find that they clearly destroy all the errors of the heretics and of the philosophers. For some heretics, as Ebion and Cerinthus, said that Christ did not exist before the Blessed Virgin, but took from her the beginning of his being and duration; for they held that he was a mere man, who had merited divinity by his good works.[39] Photinus and Paul of Samosata, following them, said the same thing.[40] But the Evangelist excludes their errors saying, ***In the beginning was the Word***, i.e., before all things, and in the Father from eternity. Thus he did not derive his beginning from the Virgin.

Sabellius, on the other hand, although he admitted that the God who took flesh did not receive his beginning from the Virgin, but existed from eternity, still said that the person of the Father, who existed from eternity, was not distinct from the person of the Son, who took flesh from the Virgin.[41] He maintained that the Father and Son were the same person, confusing the trinity of persons in the divine. The Evangelist says against this error, ***The Word was with God***, i.e., the Son was with the Father, as one person with another.

---

38. Origen, *Commentary on John* 2.64–69.

39. Cerinthus was a first-century gnostic figure associated with the *Gospel of Cerinthus* and the view that Jesus was the natural-born son of Joseph and Mary who received the spirit of Christ during his baptism. Ebion, whom Tertullian identifies as the successor of Cerinthus, held a similar "adoptionist" view of Jesus that essentially denies the Incarnation.

40. Photinus, a bishop from the region of modern-day Serbia, was deposed in 336 for denying the Incarnation and, more generally, the divinity of Jesus Christ. Following Socrates Scholasticus, theologians have typically associated him with Paul of Samosata and Marcellus (see Sozomen, *Ecclesiastical History* 4.6).

Paul of Samosata was an especially wealthy bishop of Antioch in 260–268 who was deposed in 272 for his "adoptionist" view that Christ was initially merely human and was subsequently "adopted" and indwelt by the *Logos* (see Eusebius, *Church History* 7.27–30).

41. Sabellius, a third-century priest, advanced a position that is sometimes called "modalism," according to which the Father, Son, and Holy Spirit are not three distinct persons but three *modes* or manifestations of one divine Person.

Eunomius declared that the Son is entirely unlike the Father.[42] The Evangelist rejects this when he says, ***The Word was God.*** Finally, Arius said that the Son was less than the Father. The Evangelist excludes this by saying, ***He was in the beginning with God***, as was explained above.

65 These words also exclude the errors of the philosophers. Some of the ancient philosophers, namely, the natural philosophers, maintained that the world did not come from any intellect or through some purpose, but by chance. Consequently, they did not place at the beginning as the cause of things a reason or intellect, but only matter in flux; for example, atoms, as Democritus thought, or other material principles of this kind as different philosophers maintained. Against these the Evangelist says, ***In the beginning was the Word***, from whom, and not from chance, things derive their beginning.

Plato, however, thought that the ideas of all the things that were made were subsistent, i.e., existing separately in their own natures; and material things exist by participating in these. For example, he thought men existed through the separated idea of man, which he called man *per se*. So lest you suppose, as did Plato, that this idea through which all things were made be ideas separated from God, the Evangelist adds, ***The Word was with God.***

Other Platonists, as Chrysostom relates, maintained that God the Father was most eminent and first, but under him they placed a certain mind in which there were the likenesses and ideas of all things.[43] So lest you think that the Word was with the Father in such a way as to be under him and less than he, the Evangelist adds, ***The Word was God.***

Aristotle, however, thought that the ideas of all things are in God, and that in God, the intellect, the one understanding, and what is understood, are the same.[44] Nevertheless, he thought that the world is coeternal with him. Against this the Evangelist says, ***he***, the ***Word*** alone, ***was in the beginning with God***, in such a way that he does not exclude another person, but only another coeternal nature.

66 Note the difference in what has been said between John and the other Evangelists: how he began his Gospel on a loftier plane than they. They announced Christ the Son of God born in time, *when Jesus was born in Bethlehem* (Matt. 2:1); but John presents him existing from eternity: ***In the beginning was the Word.*** They show him suddenly appearing among men:

42. Eunomius, a fourth-century bishop of Cyzicus (in the northwestern coast of modern-day Turkey) and intellectual heir of Arius, argued that the unbegottenness and begottenness of the Father and Son respectively must constitute an essential difference between them such that they cannot even be said to be similar to one another in essence.

43. Chrysostom, *Commentary on Saint John* 2.4.

44. See Aristotle, *Physics* 8; Thomas Aquinas, *Commentary on The Metaphysics of Aristotle* 2536–2551, 2600–2663.

Lord, now let your servant depart in peace, according to your word; for my eyes have seen thy salvation which you have prepared in the presence of all peoples, a light for revelation to the gentiles, and for glory to your people Israel (Luke 2:29); but John says that he always existed with the Father: ***The Word was with God.*** The others show him as a man: *They glorified God who had given such authority to men* (Matt. 9:8); but John only says that he is God: ***The Word was God.*** The others say he lives with men: *When they abode together in Galilee, Jesus said to them* (Matt. 17:21); but John says that he has always been with the Father: ***He was in the beginning with God.***

67 Note also how the Evangelist designedly uses the word ***was*** [*erat*] to show that the Word of God transcends all times: present, past, and future. It is as though he were saying that he was beyond time: present, past, and future, as the *Gloss* says.

Matthew 1:1

The Human Nature of Christ

On Matthew 1.1 (11–22)

1:1 ***The book of the generation of Jesus Christ, the son of David, the son of Abraham:***

11 Among the Evangelists, Matthew is especially concerned with the humanity of Christ; hence according to Gregory he is signified by a man in the figure of the four animals.[45] Now, it is through his humanity that Christ entered, advanced in, and left the world. And for this reason the whole Gospel is divided into three parts. For the Evangelist treats *first* of Christ's entrance into the world through his humanity; *second*, of his advance; *third*, of his departure.

The *second* part begins at ***In those days came John the Baptist preaching in the wilderness of Judea*** (Matt. 3:1). The *third* part begins at ***when they drew near to Jerusalem and came to Bethphage, to the Mount of Olives*** (Matt. 21:1).

In the *first* part he does two things: *first*, he describes the generation of Christ; *second*, he adds a manifestation of that generation, at ***when Jesus was born in Bethlehem of Judea in the days of Herod the king*** (Matt. 2:1).

In the *first* part, he does three things: *first*, he prefaces a title as it were of the whole book, when he says, ***the book of the generation of Jesus Christ***; *second*, the series of fathers is put together, ***Abraham begot Isaac*** (Matt. 1:2); *third*, when it says ***but the generation of Christ was thus***, the generation of Christ is described in particular.

12 Now the title prefaced is this: ***the book of the generation of Jesus Christ.*** It seems to be an imperfect sentence, since a nominative is set down there without a verb, but it is not. For Matthew wrote his Gospel for the Hebrews, and so in his writing he followed the custom of the Jews. Now it is customary among the Hebrews to speak this way; for example, when it is said: *The vision of Isaiah the son of Amos* (Isa. 1:1), the phrase 'this is' is understood and does not need to be added. So here when it says, ***the book of the generation***, 'this is' is understood. And this way of speaking is also customary among us. For if we wish to give a title to some book, it is called *Priscianus the Greater* or *Lesser*, nor is it necessary to add 'this is' or 'here begins.'

13 It is also asked, why did he title his book this way, when a very small portion of this book is about the generation of Christ? And one should say that Matthew, who wrote to the Hebrews, followed the style of the Hebrews in his

45. Gregory the Great, *Homilies on the Book of the Prophet Ezekiel* 4.

writing. Now, the Hebrews customarily title books from their beginnings, as Genesis is called Genesis because it treats there of generation; hence we find, *This is the book of the generations of Adam* (Gen. 5:1). And so also the book of Exodus, which in the first part treats of the exodus of the children of Israel out of Egypt.

14 But it is asked why ***of Jesus Christ*** is added. One should say that according to the Apostle: *Just as in Adam all die, so also in Christ shall all be made alive* (1 Cor. 15:22). Now, Matthew had seen that in the first book of the Old Testament, which treats of generation, it says: *This is the book of the generations of Adam* (Gen. 5:1). In order therefore that the New Testament, which treats of regeneration and repair, might correspond to the Old Testament by contrast and to show that the same one is author of both, he says, ***the book of the generation of Jesus Christ.***

15 But here a question is asked about the fact that it says, ***the book of the generation of Jesus Christ.*** For this is contrary to Isaiah: *Who shall declare his generation?* (53:8 DRB). According to Jerome, the sense of this quotation is that there is a twofold generation in Christ.[46] There is the divine generation, of course, which cannot be recounted; even if in some way we call the Son begotten, neither man nor angel can comprehend the manner in which he is begotten. The other is the human generation, which Matthew considers, yet there are many difficulties in this generation as well. And this is why, according to Remigius, there are very few who could recount it.[47]

16 Again, a question is asked about the fact that he says ***of the generation*** when multiple generations are put together here. One should say that, although many generations are enumerated, still all are included for the sake of one, namely for the sake of the generation of Christ, concerning which it says below, ***but the generation of Christ was thus.***

17 Now, he whose generation is put together is described *first* by name, when it says ***Jesus***; *second* by office, when it says ***Christ***; *third* by origin, when it says, ***the son of David, the son of Abraham.***

18 There have been others who were also called Jesus, like Jesus the son of Nave, of whom it is said: *Valiant in war was Jesus the son of Nave, who was successor of Moses among the prophets* (Sir. 46:1 DRB); there was also another

46. Jerome, *Commentary on Matthew* 1.1.

47. Remigius of Auxerre (c. 841–908) was a Benedictine grammarist who wrote many commentaries and glosses which are mostly lost or untranslated. For the quotation alluded to here, see Thomas Aquinas, *Catena Aurea on Matthew* 1.1.

around the time of the building of the temple (Zech. 3:1).[48] But those men were Jesus in name and figure, namely insofar as they prefigured him. That Jesus led the people of Israel into the land of the promise; but this Jesus, i.e., our Savior, led us not into a fleshly land, but into a heavenly land. For we have him as *the pioneer and perfector* in his blood (Heb. 12:2).

And he is rightly called ***Jesus.*** This name befits him according to either nature, whether the divine or the human. Through the human he suffered in his flesh and completed the mystery of our redemption; but since that suffering would have had no efficacy except by the power of the divinity joined to it, it says below: ***You will call his name Jesus, for he will save his people from their sins*** (Matt. 1:21).

But it is asked why he says, ***Christ.*** Would not ***Jesus*** have been enough?
19 I respond that he said this because others were also called Jesus. Moreover he describes him by office when he says, ***Christ,*** i.e., the anointed.

Note that there were three anointings in the old law. For Aaron was anointed as a priest (Lev. 8:11–12). Saul was anointed by Samuel as a king (1 Sam. 10:1), and then David (1 Sam. 16:13). Elisha was also anointed as a prophet: *Elisha . . . you shall anoint to be prophet* (1 Kings 19:16). Since therefore Christ was a true priest, according to the Psalm: *You are a priest forever* (Ps. 110:4), and a king and a prophet, he is rightly called ***Christ,*** on account of the three offices which he exercised.

20 ***The son of David, the son of Abraham.*** Here there are two questions, namely about number and order. Regarding the *first,* the question is why he named these two. Besides the reason given in the prologue, one should say that Abraham was a prophet. The Lord said to Abimelech the king of Gerar, *Restore the man his wife, for he is a prophet* (Gen. 20:7). Similarly, he was a priest inasmuch as he exercised the function of a priest, namely by offering a victim to the Lord; *the Lord answered and said: take me a cow of three years old* (Gen. 15:9). Moreover, David was a prophet (Acts 2:30) and he was also a king (2 Sam. 2:4). Since therefore Christ was a king and a prophet and a priest, he is rightly called the son of these men. For had he named only Abraham, it would not have indicated that Christ was a king; while if David alone had been named, it would not have shown the priestly dignity in Christ. This is why he put down both.

48. The English 'Jesus' represents a third-hand transliteration of the Hebrew name *Yehosua,* which, when directly transliterated from Hebrew to English, is traditionally rendered 'Joshua.' 'Jesus' is a transliteration of the Latin *Iesus,* which in turn, is a transliteration of *Iēsous,* the Greek transliteration of the Hebrew *Yehosua.* Thus, although, in Hebrew, Jesus' name is the same as that of Joshua—as Thomas here points out—the parity is unfortunately lost in most modern English translations of the Bible (though not entirely in the DRB translation, as the quoted passage from Sirach indicates).

As regards the *second* question, according to Jerome one should say that David is put first and the order changed because he needed to put together the genealogy.[49] For if he had said first ***the son of Abraham***, and second ***the son of David***, he would have had to repeat Abraham a second time to continue the order of the genealogy. But according to Ambrose, David was named first by reason of dignity.[50] For a promise concerning the head himself was made to David, when it is said: *One of the sons of your body I will set on your throne* (Ps. 132:11). But to Abraham a promise was made concerning the members, that is, concerning the Church; hence: *By your descendants shall all the nations of the earth bless themselves* (Gen. 22:18).

21 Here it should be noted that there have been many errors about Christ. For some have erred about his divinity, as did Paul of Samosata, Photinus, and Sabellius; some have erred about his humanity; and some have erred about both. Others have erred about his person.

The *first* to err about his humanity was Mani, who said that he took up, not a true body, but the appearance of a body. Contrary to this is what the Lord says: *Handle me, and see, for a spirit has not flesh and bones as you see that I have* (Luke 24:39). *Second*, after Mani, Valentinus erred, who said that he took for himself a celestial body, and that he did not take it up from the Virgin but rather passed through her like water through a canal.[51] But contrary to this it is said: *[He] was descended from David according to the flesh* (Rom. 1:3). The *third* error was that of Apollinaris, who said that he took only a body and not a soul, but that he had the divinity in place of a soul.[52] But contrary to this is what is frequently said: *Now is my soul troubled* (John 12:27). But because of this saying, Apollinaris himself later changed his position and said that Christ had a vegetative and a sensitive soul, but nonetheless not a rational soul, but rather in its place the divinity. But in this case something unfitting would follow, namely that Christ would be no more a man than one of the brutes.

Now, the four Evangelists have divided these errors among themselves by lot, so to speak. For Mark and John have destroyed chiefly those errors which

49. Jerome, *Commentary on Matthew* 1.1.

50. Ambrose, *Commentary on Luke* 3.10.

51. Valentinus was a prominent second-century Gnostic-Christian theologian who fused elements of Christian theology into a broadly Gnostic and middle-Platonist cosmology with their typically dualist outlook. Among other heresies, Valentinus is well-known for his view that Jesus' body was of a substance different from that of ordinary human bodies. Hence Christ's apparent birth and generation from Mary constituted a kind of illusion, for Valentinus.

52. Apollinaris (the Younger) was a fourth-century bishop of Laodicea (near the West coast of modern-day Turkey) who attempted to solve the conceptual puzzle contained in the idea that Christ is a union of two different and ontologically complete things (God and man) by denying that Christ had all of the attributes of a human being. More specifically, he made conceptual space for the *Logos* by denying that Jesus had a human soul. He imagined, moreover, that the *Logos*, in some sense, was Jesus' soul. His view was condemned at the Council of Constantinople (381).

concern the divinity. Hence John says right away at the beginning of his Gospel: *In the beginning was the Word* (1:1). And Mark starts this way: *The beginning of the Gospel of Jesus Christ, the Son of God* (1:1); he does not say, 'The son of Abraham.' But Matthew and Luke at the beginning of their Gospels destroy those errors which concern his humanity.

22 So notice that when it says here, ***the son of David, the son of Abraham***, all errors which concern Christ's humanity are excluded. For one is only called someone's son through a univocal generation, which is according to a sameness in species. For however much a thing may be generated from a man, it will never be called a son unless it shares the same nature in species, as is clear from the case of lice and other such creatures. If therefore Christ is the son of David and of Abraham, he must have the same nature as they do by reason of the same species; moreover, he would not have the same nature according to species if he did not have a true and natural body, nor if he had taken it from heaven, nor if he had lacked a sensitive soul, or a rational soul. Hence the exclusion of every error is clear.

Chapter 2

CHRIST AND THE CREATION OF THE WORLD

John 1:3–4

The Word as the Creative Wisdom of the Father

On John 1.2 (68–94)

1:3 ***All things were made through him: and without him was made nothing that was made.***

1:4 ***In him was life, and the life was the light of men.***

68 After the Evangelist has told of the existence and nature of the divine Word, so far as it can be told by man, he then shows the might of his power. *First*, he shows his power with respect to all things that come into existence. *Second*, with especial respect to man, at ***and the life was the light of men***.

As to the *first*, he uses three clauses; and we will not distinguish these at present because they will be distinguished in different ways according to the
69 different explanations given by the saints. The *first* clause is ***all things were made through him***, which is used to show three things concerning the Word. *First*, according to Chrysostom, to show the equality of the Word to the Father.[1] For as stated earlier, the error of Arius was rejected by the Evangelist when he showed the coeternity of the Son with the Father by saying, ***he was in the beginning with God***.[2] Here he excludes the same error when he shows the omnipotence of the Son, saying, ***all things were made through him***. For to be the principle of all the things that are made is proper to the great omnipotent God, as it is said, *whatever the Lord pleases he does, in heaven and on earth* (Ps. 135:6). Thus the Word, through whom all things were made, is God, great and coequal to the Father.

70 *Second*, according to Hilary, this clause is used to show the coeternity of the Word with the Father.[3] For since someone might understand the earlier statement, ***in the beginning was the Word***, as referring to the beginning of creatures, i.e., that before there were any creatures there was a time in which

1. John Chrysostom, *Commentary on Saint John* 5.3.

2. See Thomas Aquinas, *Commentary on John* 1.1 above.

3. Hilary of Poitiers, *The Trinity* 2.17.

the Word did not exist, the Evangelist rejects this by saying, ***all things were made through him***. For if all things were made through the Word, then time was also. From this we can form the following argument: if all time was made through him, there was no time before him or with him, because before all these, he was. Therefore the Son and the Father are eternally coeternal.

71 *Third*, according to Augustine, this clause is used to show the consubstantiality of the Word with the Father.[4] For if all things were made through the Word, the Word himself cannot be said to have been made; because, if made, he was made through some Word, since ***all things were made through the Word***. Consequently, there would have been another Word through whom was made the Word of whom the Evangelist is speaking. This Word, through whom all things are made, we call the only begotten Son of God, because he is neither made nor is he a creature. And if he is not a creature, it is necessary to say that he is of the same substance with the Father, since every substance other than the divine essence is made. But a substance that is not a creature is God. And so the Word, through whom all things were made, is consubstantial with the Father, since he is neither made, nor is he a creature.

72 And so in saying ***all things were made through him***, you have, according to Chrysostom, the equality of the Word with the Father;[5] the coeternity of the Word with the Father, according to Hilary; and the consubstantiality of the Word with the Father, according to Augustine.[6]

73 Here we must guard against three errors. *First*, the error of Valentinus. He understood ***all things were made through him*** to mean that the Word proffered to the Creator the cause of his creating the world; so that all things were made through the Word as if the Father's creating the world came from the Word. This leads to the position of those who said that God created the world because of some exterior cause; and this is contrary to Proverbs, *The Lord has made all things for himself* (16:4 DRB). The reason this is an error is that, as Origen says, if the Word had been a cause to the Creator by offering him the material for making things, he would not have said, ***all things were made through him***, but on the contrary, that all things were made through the Creator by the Word.[7]

74 *Second*, we must avoid the error of Origen. He said that the Holy Spirit was included among all the things made through the Word; from which it follows that he is a creature.[8] And this is what Origen thought. This is heretical and blasphemous, since the Holy Spirit has the same glory and substance and

4. Augustine, *Tractates on the Gospel of John* 1.11; *The Trinity* 1.6.9.

5. John Chrysostom, *Commentary on Saint John* 5.3.

6. Augustine, *Tractates on the Gospel of John* 1.11.

7. Origen, *Commentary on John* 2.102–104.

8. Origen, 2.73.

dignity as the Father and the Son, according to what is said: *Make disciples of all nations, baptizing them in the name of the Father and of the Son and of the Holy Spirit* (Matt. 28:19). And *There are three who give testimony in heaven, the Father, the Word, and the Holy Spirit; and these three are one* (1 John 5:7 DRB). Thus when the Evangelist says, ***all things were made through him***, one should not understand ***all things*** absolutely, but in the realm of creatures and of things made. As if to say: 'all things that were made, were made through him.' Otherwise, if ***all things*** were taken absolutely, it would follow that the Father and the Holy Spirit were made through him; and this is blasphemous. Consequently, neither the Father nor anything substantial with the Father was made through the Word.

75 *Third*, we must avoid another of Origen's errors. For he said that all things were made ***through*** the Word as something is made by a greater through a lesser, as if the Son were inferior to, and an instrument of, the Father.[9] But it is clear from many places in Scripture that the preposition 'through' does not signify inferiority in the thing which is its grammatical object, i.e., in the Son or Word. For the Apostle says, speaking of the Father, *God is faithful, through whom you were called into the fellowship of his Son* (1 Cor. 1:9). If he through whom something is done has a superior, then the Father has a superior. But this is false. Therefore, the preposition ***through*** does not signify any inferiority in the Son when all things are said to have been made through him.

76 To explain this point further, we should note that when something is said to be made through someone, the preposition 'through' denotes some sort of causality in its object with respect to an operation, but not always the same kind of causality. For since an operation, according to our manner of signifying, is considered to be medial between the one acting and the thing produced, the operation itself can be regarded in two ways. In one way, as issuing from the one operating, who is the cause of the action itself; in another way, as terminated in the thing produced. Accordingly, the preposition 'through' sometimes signifies the cause of the operation insofar as it issues from the one operating: but sometimes as terminated in the thing which is produced.

It signifies the cause of the operation as issuing from the one operating when the object of the preposition is either the efficient or formal cause why the one operating is operating. For example, we have a formal cause when fire is heating through heat; for heat is the formal cause of the fire's heating. We have a movent or efficient cause in cases where secondary agents act through primary agents; as when I say that the bailiff acts through the king, because the king is the efficient cause of the bailiff's acting. This is the way Valentinus

9. Origen, 2.70–72.

understood that all things were made through the Word: as though the Word were the cause of the maker's production of all things.

The preposition 'through' [*per*] implies the causality of the operation as terminated in the thing produced when what is signified through that causality is not the cause which operates, but the cause of the operation precisely as terminated in the thing produced. So when I say that the carpenter is making a bench by means of a hatchet, the hatchet is not the cause of the carpenter's operating; but we do say that it is the cause of the bench's being made by the one acting.

And so when it says that ***all things were made through him***, if the ***through*** denotes the efficient or movent cause, causing the Father to act, then in this sense the Father does nothing by the Son, but he does all things by himself, as has been said. But if the ***through*** denotes a formal cause, as when the Father operates by his wisdom, which is his essence, he operates by his wisdom as he operates by his essence. And because the wisdom and power of the Father are attributed to the Son, as when we say, *Christ, the power of God and the wisdom of God* (1 Cor. 1:24), then by appropriation we say that the Father does all things by the Son, i.e., by his wisdom. And so Augustine says that the phrase *from whom all things*, is appropriated to the Father; *through whom all things*, is appropriated to the Son; and *in whom all things*, is appropriated to the Holy Spirit.[10] But if the ***through*** denotes causality from the standpoint of the thing produced, then the statement, *the Father does all things by the Son*, is not mere appropriation but proper to the Word, because the fact that he is a cause of creatures is had from someone else, namely the Father, from whom he has being.

However, it does not follow from this that the Word is the instrument of the Father, although whatever is moved by another for some operation, has the nature of an instrument. However, when I say that someone works through a power received from another, this can be understood in two ways. In one way, as meaning that the power both of the giver and of the receiver is numerically one and the same power; and in this way the one operating through a power received from another is not inferior but equal to the one from whom he receives it. Therefore, since it is the same power which the Father has and which he gives to the Son, and through which the Son works, when it is said that the Father works through the Son, one should not on that account say that the Son is inferior to the Father or is his instrument. This would be the case, rather, in those who receive from another not the same power, but another and created one. And so it is plain that neither the Holy Spirit nor the Son are

10. Augustine, *The Trinity* 6.10.12.

causes of the Father's working, and that neither is the minister or instrument of the Father, as Origen raved.[11]

77 If we carefully consider the words, ***all things were made through him***, we can clearly see that the Evangelist spoke with the utmost exactitude. For whoever makes something must preconceive it in his wisdom, which is the form and pattern of the thing made: as the form preconceived in the mind of an artisan is the pattern of the cabinet to be made. So, God makes nothing except through the conception of his intellect, which is an eternally conceived wisdom, that is, the Word of God, and the Son of God. Accordingly, it is impossible that he should make anything except through the Son. And so Augustine says, in *The Trinity*, that the Word is the art full of the living patterns of all things.[12] Thus it is clear that all things which the Father makes, he makes through him.

78 It should be remarked that, according to Chrysostom, all the things which Moses enumerates individually in God's production of things, saying, *God said, "let there be light"* (Gen. 1:3), and *"let there be a firmament"* (Gen. 1:6), and so forth, all these the Evangelist transcends and embraces in one phrase, saying, ***all things were made through him***.[13] The reason is that Moses wished to teach the emanation of creatures from God; hence he enumerated them one by one. But John, hastening toward loftier things, intends in this book to lead us specifically to a knowledge of the Creator himself.

79 Then he says, ***and without him was made nothing***. This is the *second* clause which some have distorted, as Augustine says in his work *The Nature of the Good*.[14] Because of John's manner of speaking here, they believed that he was using ***nothing*** in an affirmative sense as though nothing was something which was made without the Word. And so they claimed that this clause was added by the Evangelist in order to exclude something which was not made by the Word. They say that the Evangelist, having said that ***all things were made through him***, added ***and without him was made nothing***. It was as if to say: 'I say that all things were made through him in such a way that still something was made without him, that is, the ***nothing***.'

80 Three heresies came from this. *First*, that of Valentinus. He affirmed, as Origen says, a multitude of principles, and taught that from them came thirty eras.[15] The first principles he postulates are two: the Deep, which he calls God the Father, and Silence. And from these proceed ten eras. But from the Deep and from Silence, he says, there are two other principles, Mind and

11. Origen, *Commentary on John* 1.104.

12. Augustine, *The Trinity* 6.10.11.

13. John Chrysostom, *Commentary on Saint John* 5.1.

14. Augustine, *The Nature of the Good* 25.

15. Origen, *Commentary on John* 2.100–101.

Truth; and from these issued eight eras. Then from Mind and Truth, there are two other principles, Word and Life; and from these issued twelve eras; thus making a total of thirty. Finally, from the Word and Life there proceeded in time, the man Christ and the Church. In this way Valentinus affirmed many eras previous to the issuing forth of the Word. And so he said that because the Evangelist had stated that ***all things were made through him***, then, lest anyone think that those previous eras had been effected through the Word, he added, ***and without him was made nothing***, i.e., all the preceding eras and all that had existed in them. All of these John calls ***nothing***, because they transcend human reason and cannot be grasped by the intellect.

81 The *second* error to arise from this was that of Mani, who affirmed two opposing principles: one is the source of incorruptible things, and the other of corruptible things. He said that after John had stated that ***all things were made through him***, then, lest it be thought that the Word is the cause of corruptible things, he immediately added, ***and without him was made nothing***, i.e., things subject to corruption, which are called ***nothing*** because their being consists in being continually transformed into nothing.

82 The *third* error is that of those who claim that by ***nothing*** we should understand the devil, about whom is said: *Let the companions of him who is not dwell in his tabernacle* (Job 18:15 DRB). And so they say that all things except the devil were made through the Word. In this way they explain, ***without him was made nothing***, that is, the devil.

83 All these three errors, arising as they do from the same source, namely, taking ***nothing*** in a positive sense, are excluded by the fact that ***nothing*** is not used here in an affirmative, but in a merely negative sense: the sense being that all things were made through the Word in such a way that there is nothing participating in existence that was not made through him.

84 Perhaps someone will object and say that it was superfluous to add this clause, if it is to be understood negatively, on the ground that the Evangelist, in stating that ***all things were made through him***, seems to have already said adequately enough that there is not something that was not made through the Word.

The answer to this is that, according to many expositors, this clause was added in many ways for a number of reasons. One of these reasons is, according to Chrysostom, so that no one reading the Old Testament and finding only visible things listed by Moses in the creation of things, would think that these were the only things made through the Word.[16]

And so, the Evangelist, after he had said, ***all things were made through him***, namely, those that Moses listed, the Evangelist then added, ***and without***

16. John Chrysostom, *Commentary on Saint John* 5.1.

him was made nothing, as though he were saying: 'none of the things which exist, whether visible or invisible, were made without the Word.' Indeed, the Apostle also speaks in this way (Col. 1:16), saying that all things, visible and invisible, were created in Christ; and here the Apostle makes specific mention of invisible things because Moses had made no express mention of them on account of the lack of erudition of that people, who could not be raised above the things of sense.

Chrysostom also gives another reason why this clause was added.[17] For someone reading in the Gospel of the many signs and miracles worked by Christ—*the blind receive their sight, the lame walk, lepers are cleansed* (Matt. 11:5)—might believe that in saying, ***all things were made through him***, John meant that only the things mentioned in those Gospels, and nothing else, were made through him. So lest anyone suspect this, the Evangelist adds, ***and without him was made nothing***. As if to say: 'not only all the things contained in the Gospels were made through him, but none of the things that were made, was made without him.' And so, according to Chrysostom, this clause is added to bring out his total causality, and serves, as it were, to complete his previous statement.

85 According to Hilary, however, this clause is introduced to show that the Word has operative power from another.[18] For since the Evangelist had said, ***all things were made through him***, it might be supposed that the Father is excluded from all causality. For that reason he added, ***and without him was made nothing***. As if to say: 'all things were made through him, but in such a way that the Father made all things with him.' For ***without him*** is equivalent to saying, not alone, so that the meaning is: it is not he alone through whom all things were made, but he is the other one without whom nothing was made. It is as if he said: ***without him***, with another working, i.e., with the Father, ***was made nothing***, as it says, *I was with him forming all things* (Prov. 8:30 DRB).

86 In a certain homily attributed to Origen, and which begins, *the spiritual voice of the eagle*, we find another rather beautiful exposition.[19] It says there that the Greek has *choris* where the Latin has ***without***. Now *choris* is the same as 'outside' or 'outside of.' It is as if he had said: ***all things were made through him*** in such a way that outside him ***was made nothing***. And so he says this to show that all things are conserved through the Word and in the Word, *upholding the universe by the word of his power* (Heb. 1:3).

---

17. John Chrysostom, 5.1.

18. Hilary of Poitiers, *The Trinity* 2.18.

19. St. Thomas' reference here is, in fact, to a work of John Scotus Eriugena (c. 800–877); see *The Voice of the Eagle: The Heart of Celtic Christianity: John Scotus Eriugena's Homily on the Prologue to the Gospel of John*, trans. Christopher Bamford (Great Barrington, MA: Lindisfarne Books, 2000), 8, p. 83.

Now there are certain things that do not need their producer except to bring them into existence, since after they have been produced they are able to subsist without any further activity on the part of the producer. For example, a house needs a builder if it is to come into existence, but it continues to exist without any further action on the part of the builder. So lest anyone suppose that all things were made through the Word in such a way that he is merely the cause of their production and not of their continuation in existence, the Evangelist added, ***and without him was made nothing***, i.e., nothing was made outside of him, because he encompasses all things, preserving them.

87 This clause is also explained by Augustine and Origen and several others in such a way that ***nothing*** indicates sin.[20] Accordingly, because ***all things were made through him*** might be interpreted as including evil and sin, he added, ***and without him was made nothing***, i.e., sin. For just as art is not the principle or cause of the defects in its products but is through itself the cause of their perfection and form, so the Word, who is the art of the Father, full of living archetypes, is not the cause of any evil or disarrangement in things, particularly of the evil of sin, which carries the full notion of evil. The *per se* cause of this evil is the will of the creature, either a man or an angel, freely declining from the end to which it is ordained by its nature. One who can act in virtue of his art but purposely violates it, is the cause of the defects occurring in his works, not by reason of his art, but by reason of his will. So in such cases, his art is not the source or cause of the defects, but his will is. Consequently, evil is a defect of the will and not of any art. And so to the extent that it is such, it is nothing.

88 So then, this clause is added to show the universal causality of the Word, according to Chrysostom; his association with the Father, according to Hilary; the power of the Word in the preserving of things, according to Origen; and finally, the purity of his causality, because he is so the cause of good as not to be the cause of sin, according to Augustine, Origen, and a number of others.

89 Then he says, ***what was made in him was life***; and this is the *third* clause. Here we must avoid the false interpretation of Mani, who was led by this to maintain that everything that exists is alive: for example, stones, wood, men, and anything else in the world. He understood the clause this way: ***what was made in him***, comma, ***was life***. But it was not life unless alive. Therefore, whatever was made in him is alive. He also claimed that ***in him*** is the same as saying through him, since very often in Scripture *in him* and *through him* are interchangeable, as in *All things were created through him and in him* (Col. 1:16 DRB).

However, our present explanation shows that this interpretation is false.
90 There are, nevertheless, a number of ways to explain it without error. In that

20. Augustine, *Tractates on the Gospel of John* 1.13. Origen, *Commentary on John* 2.92–96.

homily, *The Spiritual Voice*, we find this explanation: ***what was made in him***, i.e., through him, ***was life***, not in each thing itself, but in its cause.[21] For in the case of all things that are caused, it is always true that effects, whether produced by nature or by will, exist in their causes, not according to their own existence, but according to the power of their appropriate cause. Thus, lower effects are in the sun as in their cause, not according to their respective existences but according to the power of the sun. Therefore, since the cause of all effects produced by God is a certain life and an art full of living archetypes, for this reason ***what was made in him***, i.e., through him, ***was life***, in its cause, i.e., in God.

91 Augustine reads this another way, as: ***what was made***, distinguished from ***in him was life***.[22] For things can be considered in two ways: as they are in themselves, and as they are in the Word. If they are considered as they are in themselves, then it is not true that all things are life or even alive, but some lack life and some are alive. For example, the earth was made, and metals were made, but none is life, none is living; animals and men were made, and these, considered in themselves, are not life, but merely living.

Yet considered as they are in the Word, they are not merely living, but also life. For the archetypes which exist spiritually in the wisdom of God, and through which things were made by the Word, are life, just as a chest made by an artisan is in itself neither alive nor life, yet the exemplar of the chest in the artisan's mind prior to the existence of the chest is in some sense living, insofar as it has an intellectual existence in the mind of the artisan. Nevertheless it is not life, because it is neither in his essence nor is it his existence through the act of understanding of the artisan. But in God, his act of understanding is his life and his essence. And so whatever is in God is not only living, but is life itself, because whatever is in God is his essence. Hence the creature in God is the creating essence. Thus, if things are considered as they are in the Word, they are life.

92 This is explained in another place. Origen, commenting on John, gives another reading, thus: ***what was made in him***; and then, ***was life***.[23] Here we should note that some things are said of the Son of God as such; for example, that he is God, omnipotent, and the like. And some things are said of him in relation to ourselves; for example, we say he is savior and redeemer. Some things are said in both ways, such as wisdom and justice. Now in all things said absolutely and of the Son as such, it is not said that he was made, for example, we do not say that the Son was made God or omnipotent. But in things said in reference to us, or in both ways, the notion of being made can be used, as in,

21. John Scotus Eriugena, *The Voice of the Eagle* 9.

22. Augustine, *Tractates on the Gospel of John* 1.17.

23. Origen, *Commentary on John* 2.114.

God made [Jesus Christ] our wisdom, our justice, our sanctification and redemption (1 Cor. 1:30). And so, although he was always wisdom and justice in himself, yet it can be said that he was newly made justice and wisdom for us.

And so Origen, explaining it along these lines, says that although in himself the Son is life, yet he was made life for us by the fact that he gave us life, as is said, *Just as in Adam all die, so also in Christ shall all be made alive* (1 Cor. 15:22).[24] And so he says ***the Word that was made*** life for us ***in himself was life***, so that after a time he could become life for us; and so he immediately adds, ***and the life was the light of men.***

93 But Hilary interprets thus: ***and without him was made nothing, which was made in him***, and later it says, ***he was life.***[25] For he says that when the Evangelist says ***without him was made nothing***, one might be perplexed and ask whether there are still other things made by him, that were not made through him, although not without him, but with respect to which he was associated with the maker; and this clause is added to correct the aforesaid error. Therefore lest this be so understood, when the Evangelist says, ***all things were made through him***, he adds, ***and without him was made nothing, which was made, in him***, that is, through him; and the reason for this is that ***he was life.***

For it is plain that all things are said to have been made through the Word inasmuch as the Word, who proceeds from the Father, is God. But let us suppose that some father has a son who does not perfectly exercise the operations of a man but reaches such a state gradually. In that case the father will do many things, not through the son, yet not without him. Since, therefore, the Son of God has from all eternity the same life that the Father has, ***as the Father has life in himself, so he has granted the Son also to have life in himself*** (John 5:26), one cannot say that God the Father, although he made nothing without the Son, nevertheless made some things not through him, because he was life. For in living things which participate life, it can happen that imperfect life precedes perfect life; but in life *per se*, which does not participate life but is simply and absolutely life, there can be no imperfection at all. Accordingly, because the Word is life *per se*, there was never imperfect life in him, but always perfect life. And so in such a way that ***without him was made nothing*** that was not also made ***in him***, i.e., through him.

94 Chrysostom has a different reading and punctuation, thus: ***without him was made nothing that was made.***[26] The reason for this is that someone might believe that the Holy Spirit was made through the Word.

24. Origen, 2.128.

25. Hilary of Poitiers, *The Trinity* 2.20.

26. John Chrysostom, *Commentary on Saint John* 5.2.

So to exclude this, the Evangelist says, ***that was made***, because the Holy Spirit is not something that is made. And afterward follows, ***in him was life***, which is introduced for two reasons. *First*, to show that after the creation of all things his causality was indefectible not only with respect to the things already produced, but also with respect to things yet to be produced. As if to say: '***in him was life***, by which he could not only produce all things, but which has an unfailing flow and a causality for producing things continually without undergoing any change, being a living fountain which is not diminished in spite of its continuous outflow; whereas collected water, that is not living water, is diminished when it flows out, and is used up.' So it is said, *With you is the fountain of life* (Ps. 36:9). The *second* reason is to show that things are governed by the Word. For since ***in him was life***, this shows that he produced things by his intellect and will, not by a necessity of his nature, and that he governs the things he made: *The Word of God is living* (Heb. 4:12).

Chrysostom is held in such esteem by the Greeks in his explanations that they admit no other where he expounded anything in Holy Scripture. For this reason, this passage in all the Greek works is found to be punctuated exactly as Chrysostom did, namely, ***without him was made nothing that was made.***

Hebrews 1:10–12

The Son, Founder of the Heavens and Earth

On Hebrews 1.5 (67–78)

1:10 ***And: "You, O Lord, founded the earth in the beginning: and the works of your hands are the heavens.***

1:11 ***They shall perish: but you shall continue: and they shall all grow old as a garment.***

1:12 ***And as a vesture shall you change them, and they shall be changed. But you are the selfsame: and your years shall not fail."***

67 Above, the Apostle mentioned four things in which Christ excelled the angels, and he proved two of them, namely, that he excels them because he is the Son and because he is the heir.[27] Now he proves the third, namely, that he excels them in his power of acting, because through him the Father made the world. But the Apostle proves this on the authority of the same prophet.

In regard to this he does two things: *first*, he shows the power of his activity inasmuch as he is Creator; *second*, inasmuch as there is a difference between Creator and creature, at ***they shall perish***. In regard to the *first* he does two things: *first*, he describes the creation of earth; *second*, of the heavens, at ***and the works of your hands***.

68 It should be noted in regard to the *first* that this can be interpreted in two ways: in one way, so that it is taken to be a word of the prophet directed to the Father. As if to say: '***you, O Lord***, namely God the Father, ***founded the earth in the beginning***, i.e., in your Son, who is the beginning: *I am the beginning, who also speak unto you* (John 8:25 DRB).' And this is the same as saying: 'you founded the earth through the Son': *in wisdom have you made them all* (Ps. 104:24). But the Son is wisdom begotten; hence, above he called him *the brightness of* [God's] *glory* (Heb. 1:3 DRB). And what he says here corresponds to what he had said above: ***by whom also he made the world***.

In another way, so that it is a word directed to the Son. As if to say: '***you, O Lord, founded the earth in the beginning***, namely of time.' This is to exclude the opinion of those who say that the world is eternal;[28] or ***in the beginning***, namely, of the production of things, to exclude the opinion of those who say

27. See Thomas Aquinas, *On Hebrews* 1.3 (not included in this collection).

28. The most prominent proponent of the view of that the world is eternal was Aristotle. See Aristotle's arguments in support of this position in books 1 and 8 of *Physics*.

that bodily things were not created with spiritual things, but after: *In the beginning God created the heavens and the earth* (Gen. 1:1); *he that lives forever created all things together* (Sir. 18:1).

69 But it should be noted that the earth can be distinguished from heaven in three ways: in *one* way, so that by the earth is understood the element earth, and by heaven the higher bodies; so that just as Moses made no mention of the air, because it exists with water, so here he understood by heaven the very heaven and the other two elements, namely, air and fire, which most resemble the nature of the heavens and which is clear from their place. And this is the way Moses took it (Gen. 1:1).

And he says, ***founded***, to show that three things pertain to the earth: *first*, the earth's rest, for all other things partake of motion, but the earth alone according to its totality remains motionless.[29] As if to say, ***founded***, i.e., firmly established: *You did set the earth on its foundations* (Ps. 104:5). *Second*, to show the perpetuity of the world, for the foundation of a building is its most enduring part: *The earth remains forever* (Eccles. 1:4). And according to this he says, ***founded the earth***, i.e., established forever. *Third*, to show the order of the earth; because just as the foundation, which is the first part of a building, is below, so earth holds the lowest place among the elements: *My hand laid the foundation of the earth* (Isa. 48:13); *his hands formed the dry land* (Ps. 95:5).

He does not say, 'you made the heavens,' but ***the works of your hands are the heavens***, because that which a person makes with his hands, he seems to make with greater care. Consequently, he speaks this way to signify their nobility and beauty: *My right hand spread out the heavens* (Isa. 48:13).

70 In another way, so that by earth he understands every bodily nature; ***founded the earth***, because matter is the place and foundation of forms; but by heavens, he understands spiritual substances: *praise him, you highest heavens* (Ps. 148:4). And these are the works of his hands, because he made them to his own image and likeness.

Or, by earth, he means those who are imperfect in the Church and are the foundation of the others (for if there were no active life in the Church, the

29. Here St. Thomas reveals his geocentric view of the earth's position in relation to the rest of the universe. This was, and would remain for centuries, the standard cosmological view. In general, however, it would be a mistake to interpret and evaluate the discussion of this lecture in the terms of modern physics. St. Thomas' interest and claims here, in fact, are primarily ontological and metaphysical (even if they are in many ways inevitably bound up with a distinctly medieval physics and cosmology). More simply put, St. Thomas is less concerned with the physical interrelationships among created things than with the relationship of the universe as a whole to God (and especially to the Son), its Creator. It should be observed, however, that St. Thomas expresses some doubt about the adequacy of the prevailing Ptolemaic, geocentric model. In *De caelo* 2.17.451, after explaining Ptolemy's model, with its hypothesis of epicyclic orbits, he remarks, "although these suppositions save appearances, we are nevertheless not obliged to say that [they] are true, because perhaps there is some other way men have not yet grasped by which things which appear as to the stars are saved."

contemplative life could not exist), and by heavens, he means the contemplatives. And these were made in the Church in the beginning, i.e., by the Son: *I have placed my words in your mouth . . . that you might found the earth*, i.e., the imperfect, *and plant the heavens* (Isa. 51:16 DRB).

But in regard to the heavens, he says, ***the works of your hands are the heavens***. He says, ***the works of your hands***, and not simply, *you made the heavens*, for four reasons: *first*, to exclude the error of those who say that God is the soul of the world and, consequently, that the whole earth and its parts should be worshipped as God, as idolaters did. But he excludes this when he says, ***the works of your hands are the heavens***. As if to say: 'they are not proportioned to you as the body is to the soul, but they are subject and proportioned to your power and will': *Beware lest you lift up your eyes to heaven, and when you see the sun and the moon and the stars, all the host of heaven, you be drawn away and worship them* (Deut. 4:19).

Second, to designate the dignity and beauty of the heavens because we say that we make that with our hands which we make carefully. Therefore, to show that the heavens were made by divine wisdom in a more excellent way than the other bodily creatures, he says, ***the works of your hands are the heavens***, and this is clear; because the diversity in those lower things can be reduced to the disposition of the matter, but the diversity of heavenly bodies can be reduced only to divine wisdom. That is why, whenever mention is made of the creation of the heavens, prudence and understanding or something of that sort are also mentioned: *By understanding he established the heavens* (Prov. 3:19); *who, by understanding, made the heavens* (Ps. 136:5).

Third, to show that in the heavens the divine power of the Creator is more striking; for there is nothing in creatures in whose condition so much of God's power appears; and this is because of their magnitude and order: *By the greatness of the beauty and of created things comes a corresponding perception of their Creator* (Wis. 13:5).

Fourth, to show that of all bodies the heavenly body receives God's influence more directly: *Do you know the ordinances of the heavens? Can you establish their rule on the earth?* (Job 38:33). As if to say: 'if you consider carefully the disposition of the heavens, you cannot attribute the cause of its order to any earthly thing, but to God.'

It can be explained in another way, so that by earth is meant all bodily matter, and by heavens, spiritual substances. Then the sense is this: ***in the beginning*** of time, ***the earth***, i.e., corporeal matter, ***you founded***, i.e., you have established it as the foundation of forms. This is the way to understand the statement: *Praise the Lord from the earth* (Ps. 148:7). But the heavens, i.e., spiritual substances: *Praise him, you highest heavens* (Ps. 148:4) are the works of your hands, because you made them to your image and likeness.

It can be explained a *third* way, so that by earth is understood the lowly ones in the Church, and by the heavens is understood the great ones, and thus the sense is that ***in the beginning***, that is, through the Son, you ***founded the earth***, that is, the active and lowly ones in the Church; and they are said to be founded because they are, as it were, the foundation of the others: for unless there were actives in the Church, the contemplatives would have no subsistence; but ***the heavens***, the contemplatives and more perfect, are ***the works of your hands***, i.e., endowed with a more outstanding excellence: *the heavens are telling the glory of God* (Ps. 19:1); *hear, O heavens*, i.e., the great ones, *and give ear, O earth*, i.e., the lowly ones (Isa. 1:2).

71 Then when he says ***they shall perish***, he shows the difference between
Creator and creature, and this in regard to two things which are proper to the
Creator; the *first* is eternity; the *second* is immutability, at ***and they shall all
grow old***. In regard to the *first*, he does two things: *first*, he puts a limitation on
72 the creature; *second*, no limitation on God, at ***but you will continue***. He says,
therefore: ***they***, i.e., the heavens, ***shall perish***. But Ecclesiastes says: *the earth
stands forever* (1:4). Therefore, it seems that it will last longer than the heavens.

I answer that, according to Augustine and the Philosopher, in every change there is a coming into existence and a ceasing to exist.[30] Therefore, when he says that the heavens ***shall perish***, this is not to be understood of their substance, concerning which Job says, *The heavens . . . are most strong, as if they were of molten brass* (37:18 DRB), but of their state, which they now have: *I saw a new heaven and a new earth* (Rev. 21:1); *the fashion of this world passes away* (1 Cor. 7:31 DRB).

But how will they change their state? In various ways, because the higher
heavens are moving in regard to place, but are not altered, whereas the lower
heavens, namely, fire and air, are moved and altered and subject to corruption.
Therefore, the state of all the heavens is changeable; but then, movement will
cease in the higher heavens and corruption in the lower heavens, because the
air will be purged by fire: *By the same word the heavens and earth that now exist
have been stored up for fire, being kept until the day of judgment* (2 Pet. 3:7). All
will perish from the state in which they are now, and thus in a certain way
they will perish, *but you, O Lord, are enthroned forever; your name endures to
73 all generations* (Ps. 102:12). Here he shows the permanence of the Creator. As
if to say: *With [him] there is no variation or shadow due to change* (James 1:17);
but you, O Lord, shall remain forever, your throne from generation to generation

30. See Augustine, *The Trinity* 5.1.3; Aristotle, *Physics* 8.

(Lam. 5:19 DRB). This can be understood of Christ as man: ***Jesus Christ is the same yesterday and today and forever*** (Heb. 13:8).

74 Then when he says ***and they shall all***, he shows the difference between God and creature so far as immutability is concerned. In regard to this, he does two things: *first*, he mentions the mutability of the creature; *second*, the immutability of God, at ***but you are the selfsame***. In regard to the *first*, he does two things: *first*, he describes the nature of the creature's mutability; *second*, he mentions that mutability, at ***and as a vesture***.

75 In regard to the *first* it should be noted that old and new follow upon time. Hence, only that can grow old which is somehow measured by time. The motion of the heavens is measured by time; but the mobile thing is measured by the 'now' of time; therefore, newness and oldness can be found in the heavens. But the heavens do not grow old as though their substance shrank or were changed into something else, but only in regard to the length of time by which they will no longer be measured. Therefore, he says, ***as a vesture will you change them***, not as though the cause of their change will be the loss of their power; for if the motion of the heavens ceased from a lack of power, that cessation would have a natural cause and could be isolated by natural reason, the contrary of which is stated in Matthew: *Of that day and hour no one knows, not even the angels of heaven . . . but the Father only* (24:36). Therefore, it will be due to some end that this motion will cease, because all bodily creatures are ordained to spiritual creatures, and all changes which serve generation and ceasing-to-be are ordained to the generation of man. Therefore, when the generation of men ceases, i.e., when the number of the elect and predestined is filled, that motion will cease.

Thus, it is called a garment, which is put on to be used and cast off when it can be used no more, as a man removes a warm garment in summer and a cool one with the coming of winter. Thus, therefore, the state of the world, which is now adjusted to that end, will no longer be adjusted, when the number of the elect is filled. Then it will be cast aside as a garment: *Heaven and earth will pass away* (Luke 21:33).

76 Then he posits that mutability when he says, ***and as a vesture will you change them***, i.e., the heavens. Well does he say, ***will you change***, because it will not be by their own power, nor of themselves, but by God's power that they will be changed from motion, as a garment which is put on to be used and after it is used is put off, as the seasons require.

He says, ***a vesture***, because man's glory is both disclosed and hidden by a garment. So, too, God is both revealed and hidden by creatures: *Ever since the creation of the world his invisible nature . . . has been clearly perceived in the things* *that have been made* (Rom. 1:20); *for by the greatness of the beauty of created things comes a corresponding perception of their Creator* (Wis. 13:5).

He says, ***they shall be changed***, because they will remain changed forever. The same is true of the spiritual heavens, which will perish from the present life through the death of the body: *We must all die, we are like water spilt on the ground, which cannot be gathered again* (2 Sam. 14:14); *the righteous man perishes, and no one lays it to heart* (Isa. 57:1).

Likewise, ***they shall all grow old***, because as it says below: ***That which decays and grows old is near its end*** (Heb. 8:13). And you shall ***change***, namely, their bodies, when this bodily thing puts on incorruption (1 Cor. 15:53); and they shall be changed, namely, as to their mind, when they pass from seeing in a dark manner to seeing face to face: *All the days of my service I would wait, till my release should come* (Job 14:14).

77 Then he mentions God's immutability when he says, ***but you are the selfsame***. Here he does two things: *first*, he states his intention; *second*, he shows this by a sign; ***and your years shall not fail***.

He says, therefore, ***they shall perish: but you***, namely, the Son of God, ***are the selfsame***, i.e., you continue the same and are never changed, and this is against the Arians: *I the Lord do not change* (Mal. 3:6); *with whom there is no variation or shadow due to change* (James 1:17).

He gives the sign of this immutability when he says, ***your years shall not fail***. Here it should be noted that God's years are his duration, just as a man's years are. But a man's duration fails in two ways: *first*, in its parts, because, since he is temporal, one part succeeds another, and when one succeeds, the predecessor fails; *second*, as a whole, because it ceases altogether. But neither of these failures is found in God's duration, because he continues forever, and the parts of his duration are eternal, and all exist together without succession: *The number of his years is unsearchable* (Job 36:26).

78 But if his duration is one and unchangeable, why say ***years*** in the plural and not *year* in the singular? The reason is that our intellect takes its knowledge of the intelligible through the sensible, for all our knowledge is drawn from the senses; hence even God, who is absolutely simple, is described under a likeness of bodily things: *I saw the Lord sitting upon a throne, high and lifted up* (Isa. 6:1). So, too, his duration is described by us in terms of what is familiar, even though it is uniform and simple. Hence, it is sometimes called a year, and sometimes a day or a month, because it includes all of time's differences.

Chapter 3

CHRIST: THE INCARNATION OF THE WORD

John 1:14a

The Word's Assumption of Human Nature

On John 1.7 (165–178)

1:14a And the Word was made flesh and dwelt among us.

165 Having explained the necessity for the Word's coming in the flesh as well as the benefits this conferred, the Evangelist now shows the way he came, at ***The Word was made flesh.*** He thus resumes the thread with his earlier statement, ***He came unto his own*** (John 1:11). As if to say: the Word of God ***came unto his own.*** But lest anyone suppose that he came by changing his location, he shows the manner in which he came, that is, by an incarnation. For he came in the manner in which he was sent by the Father, by whom he was sent, i.e., he was made flesh. *God sent his Son, born of woman* (Gal. 4:4). And Augustine says about this that *he was sent in the manner in which he was made.*[1]

According to Chrysostom, however, he is here continuing the earlier statement, ***He gave them power to be made the sons of God*** (John 1:12).[2] As if to say: 'if you wonder how he was able to give this power to men, i.e., that they become sons of God, the Evangelist answers': because ***the Word was made flesh,*** he made it possible for us to be made sons of God. *God sent his Son . . . so that we might receive our adoption as sons* (Gal. 4:4–5).

But according to Augustine, he is continuing the earlier statement, ***who are born . . . of God*** (John 1:13).[3] For since it seemed a hard saying that men be born from God, then, as though arguing in support of this and to produce belief in the existence of the Word, the Evangelist adds something which seems less seemly, namely, that ***the Word was made flesh.*** As if to say: 'do not wonder if men are born from God, because ***the Word was made flesh,*** i.e., God became man.'

166 It should be noted that this statement, ***the Word was made flesh,*** has been misinterpreted by some and made the occasion of error. For certain ones have presumed that the Word became flesh in the sense that he or something of him

1. Augustine, *The Trinity* 5.19.26.

2. John Chrysostom, *Commentary on Saint John* 11.1.

3. Augustine, *Tractates on the Gospel of John* 2.15.

was turned into flesh, as when flour is made into bread, and air becomes fire. One of these was Eutyches, who postulated a mixture of natures in Christ, saying that in him the nature of God and of man was the same.[4]

We can clearly see that this is false because, as was said above, ***The Word was God*** (John 1:1). Now God is immutable, as is said, *I the Lord do not change* (Mal. 3:6). Hence in no way can it be said that he was turned into another nature. Therefore, one must say in opposition to Eutyches, ***The Word was made flesh***, i.e., the Word assumed flesh, but not in the sense that the Word himself is that flesh. It is as if we were to say: the man became white, not that he is that whiteness, but that he assumed whiteness.

167 There were others who, although they believed that the Word was not changed into flesh but assumed it, nevertheless said that he assumed flesh without a soul; for if he had assumed flesh with a soul, the Evangelist would have said, ***The Word was made flesh*** with a soul. This was the error of Arius, who said that there was no soul in Christ, but that the Word of God was there in place of a soul.

The falsity of this opinion is obvious, both because it is in conflict with Sacred Scripture, which often mentions the soul of Christ, as: *My soul is sorrowful, even to death* (Matt. 26:38), and because certain affections of the soul are observed in Christ which cannot possibly exist in the Word of God or in flesh alone: *He began to be sorrowful and troubled* (Matt. 26:37). Also, God cannot be the form of a body. Nor can an angel be united to a body as its form, since an angel, according to its very nature, is separated from body, whereas a soul is united to a body as its form. Consequently, the Word of God cannot be the form of a body.

Furthermore, it is plain that flesh does not acquire the specific nature of flesh except through its soul. This is shown by the fact that when the soul has withdrawn from the body of a man or a cow, the flesh of the man or the cow is called flesh only in an equivocal sense. So if the Word did not assume flesh with a soul, it is obvious that he did not assume flesh. But ***the Word was made flesh***; therefore, he assumed flesh with a soul.

168 And there were others who, influenced by this, said that the Word did indeed assume flesh with a soul, but this soul was only a sensitive soul, not an intellectual one; the Word took the place of the intellectual soul in Christ's

4. Eutyches (c. 380–456) first rose to prominence for his opposition to Nestorius (c. 386–450), who denied the appropriateness of Mary's epithet "Mother of God" (Gk. *theotokos*) on the ground that she could only have been the mother of Christ's human nature. Nestorius' view was condemned at the Council of Ephesus (431) as implying that Christ comprised two distinct persons or hypostases. At the opposite extreme, Eutyches defended the *theotokos* by denying any duality of natures in Jesus, in whom, he argued, humanity and divinity were fused into a single nature (*monē-physis*). At the Council of Chalcedon (451), this *monophysite* view of Jesus as possessed of a single hybrid nature was condemned as a heresy.

body. This was the error of Apollinaris. He followed Arius for a time, but later in the face of the authorities cited above, was forced to admit a soul in Christ which could be the subject of these emotions. But he said this soul lacked reason and intellect, and that in the man Christ their place was taken by the Word.

This too is obviously false, because it conflicts with the authority of Sacred Scripture in which certain things are said of Christ that cannot be found in his divinity, nor in a sensitive soul, nor in flesh alone; for example, that Christ marveled, as in Matthew (8:10). For to marvel or wonder is a state which arises in a rational and intellectual soul when a desire arises to know the hidden cause of an observed effect. Therefore, just as sadness compels one to place a sensitive element in the soul of Christ, against Arius, so marveling or amazement forces one to admit, against Apollinaris, an intellectual element in Christ.

The same conclusion can be reached by reason. For as there is no flesh without a soul, so there is no human flesh without a human soul, which is an intellectual soul. So if the Word assumed flesh which was animated with a merely sensitive soul to the exclusion of a rational soul, he did not assume human flesh; consequently, one could not say: 'God became man.'

Besides, the Word assumed human nature in order to repair it. Therefore, he repaired what he assumed. But if he did not assume a rational soul, he would not have repaired it. Consequently, no fruit would have accrued to us from the incarnation of the Word; and this is false. Therefore, ***the Word was made flesh***, i.e., assumed flesh which was animated by a rational soul.

169 But you may say: 'if the Word did assume flesh with such a soul, why did the Evangelist not mention rational soul, instead of only flesh, saying, ***the Word was made flesh***?' I answer that the Evangelist had four reasons for doing this. *First*, to show the truth of the incarnation against the Manicheans, who said that the Word did not assume true flesh, but only imaginary flesh, since it would not have been becoming for the Word of the good God to assume flesh, which they regarded as a creature of the devil. And so to exclude this the Evangelist made special mention of the flesh, just as Christ showed the truth of the resurrection to the disciples when they took him for a spirit, saying: *A spirit has not flesh and bones, as you see that I have* (Luke 24:39).

Second, to show the greatness of God's kindness to us. For it is evident that the rational soul has a greater conformity to God than does flesh, and that it would have been a great sign of compassion if the Word had assumed a human soul, as being conformed to himself. But to assume flesh too, which is something far removed from the simplicity of his nature, was a sign of a much greater, indeed, of an incomprehensible compassion. As the Apostle says: *obviously great is the mystery of godliness which was manifested in the flesh* (1 Tim. 3:16 DRB). And so to indicate this, the Evangelist mentioned only flesh.

Third, to demonstrate the truth and uniqueness of the union in Christ. For God is indeed united to other holy men, but only with respect to their soul; so it is said: *She passes into holy souls and makes them friends of God, and prophets* (Wis. 7:27). But that the Word of God is united to flesh is unique to Christ, according to the Psalmist: *I am alone until I pass* (Ps. 140:10 DRB), and *gold . . . cannot equal it* (Job 28:17). So the Evangelist, wishing to show the uniqueness of the union in Christ, mentioned only the flesh, saying, ***the Word was made flesh.***

Fourth, to suggest its relevance to man's restoration. For man was weak because of the flesh. And thus the Evangelist, wishing to suggest that the coming of the Word was suited to the task of our restoration, made special mention of the flesh in order to show that the weak flesh was repaired by the flesh of the Word. And this is what the Apostle says: *God has done what the law, weakened by the flesh, could not do: sending his own Son in the likeness of sinful flesh and for sin, he condemned sin in the flesh* (Rom. 8:3).

170 A question arises as to why the Evangelist did not say that the Word assumed flesh, but rather that ***the Word was made flesh.*** I answer that he did this to exclude the error of Nestorius. He said that in Christ there were two persons and two sons, the other being the son of the Virgin. Thus he did not admit that the Blessed Virgin was the mother of God. But if this were so, it would mean that God did not become man, for one particular *suppositum* cannot be predicated of another.[5] Accordingly, if the person or *suppositum* of the Word is different than the person or *suppositum* of the man, in Christ, then what the Evangelist says is not true, namely, ***the Word was made flesh.*** For a thing is made or becomes something in order to be it; if, then, the Word is not man, it could not be said that the Word became man. And so the Evangelist expressly said ***was made***, and not assumed, to show that the union of the Word to flesh is not such as was the lifting up of the prophets, who were not taken up into a unity of person, but for the prophetic act. This union is such as would truly make God man and man God, i.e., that God would be man.

171 There were some, too, who, misunderstanding the manner of the incarnation, did indeed admit that the aforesaid assumption was terminated at a oneness of person, acknowledging in God one person of God and man. But they said that in him there were two hypostases, i.e., two *supposita*; one of a human nature, created and non-eternal, and the other of the divine nature, non-created and eternal. This is the first opinion presented in the *Sentences*.[6]

5. '*Suppositum*' (pl. *supposita*) is most simply defined in terms of the distinction between properties and their bearers. A *suppositum*, accordingly, is an individual bearer of properties that is not itself a property. Cf. under "suppōno," in Roy J. Deferrari, *A Lexicon of Saint Thomas Aquinas*. Fitzwilliam, NH: Loreto, 2004.

6. Peter Lombard, *Sentences* 3.6.

According to this opinion the proposition, that God was made man and man was made God, is not true. Consequently, this opinion was condemned as heretical by the Fifth Council, where it is said: *If anyone shall assert one person and two hypostases in the Lord Jesus Christ, let him be anathema.*[7] And so the Evangelist, to exclude any assumption not terminated at a oneness of person, says, ***was made.***

172 If you ask how the Word is man, it must be said that he is man in the way that anyone is man, namely, as having human nature. Not that the Word is human nature itself, but he is a divine *suppositum* united to a human nature.

The statement, ***the Word was made flesh***, does not indicate any change in the Word, but only in the nature newly assumed into the oneness of a divine person. ***And the Word was made flesh*** through a union to flesh. Now a union is a relation. And relations newly said of God with respect to creatures do not imply a change on the side of God, but on the side of the creature relating in a new way to God.

173 Now follows, ***and dwelt among us.*** This is distinguished in two ways from what went before.

The *first* consists in stating that above the Evangelist dealt with the incarnation of the Word when he said, ***the Word was made flesh***; but now he touches on the manner of the incarnation, saying, ***and dwelt among us.*** For according to Chrysostom and Hilary, by the Evangelist saying ***the Word was made flesh***, someone might think that he was converted into flesh and that there are not two distinct natures in Christ, but only one nature compounded from the human and divine natures.[8] And so the Evangelist, excluding this, added ***and dwelt among us***, i.e., in our nature. Furthermore, something which is not distinct from another does not dwell in it, because to dwell implies a distinction between the dweller and that in which it dwells. But the Word dwelt in our nature; therefore, he is distinct in nature from it. And so, inasmuch as human nature was distinct from the nature of the Word in Christ, the former is called the dwelling place and temple of the divinity: ***He spoke of the temple of his body*** (John 2:21).

174 Now although what is said here by these holy men is orthodox, care must be taken to avoid the reproach which some receive for this. For the early doctors and saints were so intent upon refuting the emerging errors concerning the faith that they seemed meanwhile to fall into the opposite ones. For example, Augustine, speaking against the Manicheans, who destroyed the freedom of

7. The Second Council of Constantinople (553), canon 3.

8. John Chrysostom, *Commentary on Saint John* 11.2. Hilary of Poitiers, *The Trinity* 10.22.

the will, disputed in such terms that he seemed to have fallen into the heresy of Pelagius.[9]

In this way, lest through saying ***the Word was made flesh*** it might be thought that there was a confusion or change of natures in Christ, John the Evangelist added ***and dwelt among us.*** Nestorius misunderstood this phrase and said that the Son of God was united to man in such a way that there was not one person of God and of man. For he held that the Word was united to human nature only by an indwelling through grace. From this, however, it follows that the Son of God is not man.

175 To clarify this we should know that we can consider two things in Christ: his nature and person. In Christ there is a distinction in nature, but not in person, which is one and the same in the two natures, since the human nature in Christ was assumed into a oneness of person. Therefore, the indwelling which the saints speak of must be referred to the nature, so as to say, he ***dwelt among us***, i.e., the nature of the Word inhabited our nature; not according to the hypostasis or person, which is the same for both natures in Christ.

176 The blasphemy of Nestorius is further refuted by the authority of Sacred Scripture. For the Apostle calls the union of God and man an emptying, saying of the Son of God: *Though he was in the form of God . . . [he] emptied himself, taking the form of a servant* (Phil. 2:6). Clearly, God is not said to empty himself insofar as he dwells in the rational creature by grace, because then the Father and the Holy Spirit would be emptying themselves, since they too are said to dwell in man through grace: for Christ, speaking of himself and of the Father says, ***We will come to him, and will make our abode with him*** (John 14:23); and of the Holy Spirit the Apostle says: *God's Spirit dwells in you* (1 Cor. 3:16).

Furthermore, if Christ was not God as to his person, he would have been most presumptuous to say: ***I and the Father are one*** (John 10:30), and ***before Abraham was, I am*** (John 8:58). Now ***I*** refers to the person of the speaker. And the one who was speaking was a man, who, as one with the Father, existed before Abraham.

177 However, another connection with what went before is possible, by saying that above he dealt with the incarnation of the Word, but that now he is treating the manner of life of the incarnate Word, saying, he ***dwelt among us***, i.e., he lived on familiar terms with us apostles. Peter alludes to this when he says,

9. Cf. Thomas Aquinas, *Liber contra errores Graecorum* 1 where he elaborates this point. The point is not that Augustine had actually held to a form of Pelagianism in his polemics against the Manicheans but that prior to the Pelagian controversy there had been no need for him to qualify his affirmations of the freedom of the will. The broader point is that the teaching of earlier fathers, because it is often underqualified in relation to later controversies, needs to be interpreted carefully and reverently in light of the teaching of the Church.

during all the time that the Lord Jesus went in and out among us (Acts 1:21). *He was seen upon earth* (Bar. 3:38 DRB).

178 The Evangelist added this for two reasons. *First*, to show the marvelous likeness of the Word to men, among whom he lived in such a way as to seem one of them. For he not only willed to be like men in nature, but also in living with them on close terms without sin, in order to draw to himself men won over by the charm of his way of life.

Second, to show the truthfulness of the Evangelist's statements. For the Evangelist had already said many great things about the Word and was yet to mention more wonderful things about him; and so that his testimony would be more credible he took as a proof of his truthfulness the fact that he had lived with Christ, saying, he ***dwelt among us***. As if to say: 'I can well bear witness to him, because I lived on close terms with him.' *That . . . which we have heard, which we have seen with our eyes . . . [we] proclaim to you* (1 John 1:1); *God raised him on the third day and made him manifest; not to all the people but to us who were chosen by God as witnesses, who ate and drank with him* (Acts 10:40).

John 1:14b

Christ's Glory, Grace, and Truth

On John 1.8 (179–190)

1:14b ***We saw his glory, the glory as it were of the only begotten of the Father, full of grace and truth.***

179 Having set forth the incarnation of the Word, the Evangelist then begins to give the evidence for the incarnate Word. He does two things about this. *First*, he shows the ways in which the incarnate Word was made known. *Second*, he clarifies each way, at ***Of his fullness we have all received*** (John 1:16).

Now the incarnate Word was made known to the apostles in two ways: *first* of all, they obtained knowledge of him by what they saw; *second*, by what they heard of the testimony of John the Baptist. So *first*, he states what they saw about the Word; *second*, what they heard from John, at ***John bears witness to him*** (John 1:15).

He states three things about the Word. *First*, the manifestation of his glory; hence he says, ***We saw his glory.*** *Second*, the uniqueness of his glory, when he adds, ***as it were of the only begotten.*** *Third*, the precise nature of this glory,
180 because ***full of grace and truth. We saw his glory*** can be connected in three ways with what went before.

First, it can be taken as an argument for his having said, ***The Word was made flesh.*** As if to say: 'I hold and know that the Word of God was incarnate because I and the other apostles have seen his glory.' ***We speak what we know, and we testify what we have seen*** (John 3:11). *That . . . which we have heard, which we have seen with our eyes . . . [we] proclaim to you* (1 John 1:1).

181 *Second*, according to Chrysostom, the connection is made by taking this statement as expressing many benefits.[10] As if to say: 'the incarnation of the Word not only conferred on us the benefit of becoming sons of God, but also the good of seeing his glory.' For dull and feeble eyes cannot see the light of the sun; but they can see it when it shines in a cloud or on some opaque body. Now before the incarnation of the Word, human minds were incapable of seeing the divine light in itself, the light which enlightens every rational nature. And so, in order that it might be more easily seen and contemplated by us, he covered it with the cloud of our flesh: *They looked towards the wilderness, and behold, the glory of the Lord appeared in a cloud* (Exod. 16:10), i.e., the Word of God in the flesh.

10. John Chrysostom, *Commentary on Saint John* 12.1.

182 According to Augustine, however, the connection refers to the gift of grace.[11] For the failure of the spiritual eyes of men to contemplate the divine light is due not only to their natural limitations but also to the defects incurred by sin: *fire*, that is, of concupiscence, *has fallen on them, and they shall not see the sun* (Ps. 57:9 DRB). Hence in order that the divine light might be seen by us, he healed our eyes, making an eye salve of his flesh, so that with the salve of his flesh the Word might heal our eyes, weakened by the concupiscence of the flesh. And this is why just after saying, ***the Word was made flesh***, he says, ***we saw his glory***. To indicate this the Lord made clay from his saliva and spread the clay upon the eyes of the man born blind (John 9:6). For clay is from the earth, but saliva comes from the head. Similarly, in the person of Christ, his human nature was assumed from the earth; but the incarnate Word is from the head, i.e., from God the Father. So, when this clay was spread on the eyes of men, ***we saw his glory***.

183 This is the glory of the Word Moses longed to see, saying, *Show me your glory* (Exod. 33:18). But he did not deserve to see it; indeed, he was answered by the Lord: *You shall see my back* (Exod. 33:23), i.e., shadows and figures. But the apostles saw his brightness: *We all, with unveiled face, beholding the glory of the Lord, are being changed into his likeness from one degree of glory to another* (2 Cor. 3:18).

For Moses and the other prophets saw obscurely and in figures the glory of the Word that was to be manifested to the world at the end of their times, as the Apostle says (1 Cor. 13:12). Thus, it is also said: ***Isaiah said this because he saw his glory and spoke of him*** (John 12:41). But the apostles saw the very brilliance of the Word through his bodily presence: *We all, with unveiled face, beholding the glory of the lord*, and so forth (2 Cor. 3:18); *blessed are the eyes which see what you see! For . . . many kings and prophets desired to see what you see and did not see it* (Luke 10:23).

184 Then when he says, ***the glory as it were of the only begotten***, he shows the uniqueness of his glory. For since it is written of certain men that they were in glory, as of Moses it says that *the skin of his face shone* (Exod. 34:29), or was *horned*, according to another text, someone might say that from the fact that they saw him in glory, it should not be said that the Word of God was made flesh. But the Evangelist excludes this when he says, ***the glory as it were of the only begotten of the Father***. As if to say: 'his glory is not like the glory of an angel, or of Moses, or Elijah, or Elisha, or anything like that but ***the glory as it were of the only begotten***'; for as it is said, *Jesus has been counted worthy of as much more glory than Moses as the builder of a house has more honor than the house* (Heb. 3:3); *who among the sons of God is like God?* (Ps. 89:6).

11. Augustine, *Tractates on the Gospel of John* 2.16.

185 The word ***as***, according to Gregory, is used to express the fact.[12] But according to Chrysostom, it expresses the manner of the fact: as if someone were to see a king approaching in great glory and being asked by another to describe the king he saw, he could, if he wanted to be brief, express the grandeur of his glory in one word, and say that he approached as a king, i.e., as became a king.[13] So too, here, the Evangelist, as though asked by someone to describe the glory of the Word which he had seen, and being unable to fully express it, said that it was ***as it were of the only begotten of the Father***, i.e., such as became the only begotten of God.

186 It should be noted that the uniqueness of the glory of the Word is brought out in four ways. *First*, in the testimony which the Father gave of the Son. For John was one of the three who had seen Christ transfigured on the mountain and heard the voice of the Father saying: *This is my beloved Son, with whom I am well pleased* (Matt. 17:5). Of this glory it is said, *He received honor and glory from God the Father and the voice was borne to him by the Majestic Glory, "This is my beloved Son"* (2 Pet. 1:17).

Second, it is brought out by the service of the angels. For prior to the incarnation of Christ, men were subject to the angels. But after it, angels ministered, as subjects, to Christ. *Angels came and ministered to him* (Matt. 4:11).

Third, it is brought out by the submission of nature. For all nature obeyed Christ and heeded his slightest command, as something established by him, because ***all things were made through him*** (John 1:3). This is something granted neither to angels nor to any creature, but to the incarnate Word alone. And this is what we read, *What sort of man is this that even winds and sea obey him?* (Matt. 8:27).

Fourth, we see it in the way he taught and acted. For Moses and the other prophets gave commands to men and taught them not on their own authority, but on the authority of God. So they said: *the Lord says this*; and *the Lord spoke to Moses* (Num. 3:14). But Christ speaks as the Lord, and as one having power, i.e., by reason of his own power. Hence he says, *I say to you* (Matt. 5:22). This is the reason why, at the end of the Sermon on the Mount, it is said that *he taught as one who had authority* (Matt. 7:29). Furthermore, other holy men worked miracles, but not by their own power. But Christ worked them by his own power, hence it is said, *What is this? A new teaching! With authority he commands even the unclean spirits, and they obey him.* (Mark 1:27). In these ways, then, the glory of the Word is unique.

187 Note that sometimes in Scripture we call Christ the only begotten, as here and elsewhere: ***The only Son, who is in the bosom of the Father, he has made***

12. Gregory the Great, *Moralia in Job* 18.6.

13. John Chrysostom, *Commentary on Saint John* 12.1.

him known (John 1:18). At other times we call him the firstborn: *When he brings the firstborn into the world, he says, "Let all God's angels worship him"* (Heb. 1:6). The reason for this is that just as it belongs to the whole Blessed Trinity to be God, so it belongs to the Word of God to be God Begotten. Sometimes, too, he is called God according to what he is in himself; and in this way he alone is uniquely God by his own essence. It is in this way that we say there is but one God*: Hear, O Israel: the Lord our God is one* (Deut. 6:4). At times, we even apply the name of deity to others, insofar as a certain likeness of the divinity is given to men; in this sense we speak of many gods: *There are many "gods" and many "lords"* (1 Cor. 8:5).

Along these lines, if we consider what is proper to the Son as begotten and consider the way in which this sonship is attributed to him, that is, through nature, we say that he is the only begotten of God: because, since he alone is naturally begotten by the Father, the begotten of the Father is one only. But if we consider the Son, insofar as sonship is conferred on others through a likeness to him, then there are many sons of God through participation. And because they are called sons of God by a likeness to him, he is called the firstborn of all. *Those whom he foreknew he also predestined to become conformed to the image of his Son, so that he might be the firstborn of many brothers* (Rom. 8:29).

So, Christ is called the only begotten of God by nature; but he is called the firstborn insofar as from his natural sonship, by means of a certain likeness and participation, a sonship is granted to many.

188 Then when he says, ***full of grace and truth***, he determines the glory of the Word. As if to say: 'his glory is such that he is full of grace and divinity.' Now these words can be applied to Christ in three ways.

First, from the point of view of union. For grace is given to someone so that he might be united to God through it. So he who is most perfectly united to God is full of grace. Now some are joined to God by participating in a natural likeness: *Let us make man in our image, after our likeness* (Gen. 1:26). Some are joined by faith: *that Christ may dwell in your hearts through faith* (Eph. 3:17). And others are united by charity, because *he who abides in love abides in God* (1 John 4:16). But all these ways are partial: because one is not perfectly united to God through the participation of a natural likeness; nor is God seen as he is by faith; nor is he loved to the extent that he is lovable by charity—for since he is the infinite Good, his lovableness is infinite, and the love of no creature is able to love this infinitely. And so these unions are not able to be full.

But in Christ, in whom human nature is united to the divinity in the unity of a *suppositum*, we find a full and perfect union with God. The reason for this is that this union was such that all the acts not only of his divine but also of his human nature were acts of the person. So he was ***full of grace*** insofar as he did not receive any special gratuitous gift from God, but that he should be God himself. God . . . *bestowed on him* (i.e., God the Father gave to the Son) *the name which is above every name* (Phil. 2:9). He was *designated Son of God in power* (Rom. 1:4). He was also ***full of truth***, because the human nature in Christ attained to the divine truth itself, that is, that this man should be the divine truth itself. In other men we find many participated truths, insofar as the first truth gleams back into their minds through many likenesses; but Christ is truth itself. Thus it is said: *In [him] are hid all the treasures of wisdom and knowledge* (Col. 2:3).

189 *Second*, these words can be applied in relation to the perfection of his soul. Then he is said to be ***full of grace and truth*** inasmuch as in his soul there was the fullness of all graces without measure, ***for God does not give the Spirit by measure*** (John 3:34). Yet it was given in fractions to all rational creatures, both angels and men. For according to Augustine, just as there is one sense common to all the parts of the body, namely, the sense of touch, while all the senses are found in the head, so in Christ, who is the head of every rational creature, and in a special way of the saints who are united to him by faith and charity, all virtues and graces and gifts are found superabundantly;[14] but in others, i.e., the saints, we find participations of the graces and gifts, although there is a gift common to all the saints, and that is charity. We read about this fullness of Christ's grace: *There shall come forth a shoot from the stump of Jesse, and a branch shall grow out of his roots. And the Spirit of the Lord shall rest upon him, the spirit of wisdom and understanding, the spirit of counsel and might, the spirit of knowledge and the fear of the Lord* (Isa. 11:1).

Further, Christ was also ***full of truth*** because his precious and blessed soul knew every truth, human and divine, from the instant of his conception. And so Peter said to him, ***You know all things*** (John 21:17). And it is also said: *my truth*, i.e., the knowledge of every truth, *and my mercy*, i.e., the fullness of all graces, *shall be with him* (Ps. 88:25 DRB).

190 In a *third* way these words can be explained in relation to his dignity as head, i.e., inasmuch as Christ is the head of the Church. In this way it is his prerogative to communicate grace to others, both by producing virtue in the minds of men through the inpouring of grace and by meriting, through his teaching and works and the sufferings of his death, superabundant grace for an infinite number of worlds, if there were such. Therefore, he is ***full of grace*** insofar as he conferred perfect justice upon us. We could not acquire this perfect justice through the law, which was infirm and could make no one just or bring anyone to perfection. As we read: *God has done what the law, weakened*

14. Augustine, *The Presence of God* 13.40.

by the flesh, could not do: sending his own Son in the likeness of sinful flesh and for sin, he condemned sin in the flesh (Rom. 8:3).

Again, he was ***full of truth*** insofar as he fulfilled the figures of the old law and the promises made to the fathers. *Christ became a servant to the circumcised . . . to confirm the promises given to the patriarchs* (Rom. 15:8); *all the promises of God find their Yes in him* (2 Cor. 1:20).

Further, he is said to be ***full of grace*** because his teaching and manner of life were most gracious. *Grace is poured upon your lips* (Ps. 45:2). And so it is said that *all the people came early in the morning to him*, i.e., in the morning they were eager to come (Luke 21:38). He was ***full of truth***, because he did not teach in enigmas and figures, nor gloss over the vices of men, but preached the truth to all, openly and without deception. As it says below: ***Now you are speaking plainly*** (John 16:29).

PART II

BY HIM

The Redemptive Passion and Death of Christ

At the Elevation of the Body of Christ

A PRAYER OF THOMAS AQUINAS

O Sacrifice for our salvation,
heavenly gates you open wide.
Our enemies press hard around us.
Give us strength; our help provide.

You are Christ, the king of glory.
  You are the Son, coeternal with the Father.

To liberate mankind,
  you did not disdain to enter a virgin's womb.

Having conquered the sting of death,
  you opened heavenly realms to the faithful.

You sit at the right hand of God
  in the glory of the Father.

We believe
  you are the judge who is to come.

Therefore we ask you
  to come to the aid of your servants
    redeemed by your precious blood.

Include us among your saints in eternal glory.

Bring salvation to your people, Lord,
  and bless them as your heirs.

Govern them and lead them into eternity.

Day after day we bless you.
  We praise your name now and forever.

Lord, preserve us this day from sin.
  Have mercy upon us, Lord, have mercy.

Grant us your mercy, Lord,
  even as we have placed our hope in you.

In you, Lord, have I trusted;
  let me not be confounded in eternity.

Amen

Chapter 4

THE SACRIFICIAL END OF THE INCARNATION

John 3:16–21

The Gift of the Only Begotten Son

On John 3.3 (476–496)

3:16 ***For God so loved the world that he gave his only begotten Son; so that whoever believes in him should not perish but have eternal life.***

3:17 ***For God did not send his Son into the world to judge the world, but that the world might be saved through him.***

3:18 ***He who believes in him is not judged; but whoever does not believe is already judged, because he does not believe in the name of the only begotten Son of God.***

3:19 ***And this is the judgment: that the light has come into the world, and men loved darkness more than the light: for their works were evil.***

3:20 ***For everyone who does evil hates the light and does not come to the light, so that his works may not be reproved.***

3:21 ***But he who practices truth comes to the light, so that his works may be made manifest, because they are done in God.***

476 Above, the Lord assigned as the cause of spiritual regeneration the coming down of the Son and the lifting up of the Son of man; and he set forth its fruit, which is eternal life.[1] But this fruit seemed unbelievable to men laboring under the necessity of dying. And so now the Lord explains this. *First*, he proves the greatness of the fruit from the greatness of God's love. *Second*, he rejects a certain reply, at ***God did not send his Son into the world to judge the world.***

477 Here we should note that the cause of all our good is the Lord and divine love. For to love is, properly speaking, to will good to someone. Therefore, since the will of God is the cause of things, good comes to us because God loves

1. See John 3:13–15 and Thomas Aquinas, *On John* 3.2.

us. And God's love is the cause of the good of nature: *You love all things that exist* (Wis. 11:24). It is also the cause of the good which is grace: *I have loved you with an everlasting love, therefore have I drawn you*, i.e., through grace (Jer. 31:3 DRB). But it is because of his great love that he gives us the good of glory.

So he shows us here, from four standpoints, that this love of God is the greatest. *First*, from the person of the one loving, because it is God who loves, and immeasurably. So he says, ***God so loved***; *he loved his people; all those consecrated to him were in his hand* (Deut. 33:3). *Second*, from the condition of the one who is loved, because it is man, a bodily creature of the world, i.e., existing in sin: *God shows his love for us in that while were yet sinners Christ died for us. . . . we were reconciled to God by the death of his Son* (Rom. 5:8). Thus he says, ***the world***. *Third*, from the greatness of his gifts, for love is shown by a gift; as Gregory says: *The proof of love is given by action*.[2] But God has given us the greatest of gifts, his only begotten Son, and so he says, that he gave his only begotten Son. *He . . . did not spare his own Son but gave him up for us all* (Rom. 8:32).

He says ***his Son***, i.e., his natural Son, consubstantial, not an adopted son, i.e., not those sons of which the Psalmist says: *"You are gods"* (Ps. 82:6). This shows that the opinion of Arius is false: for if the Son of God were a creature, as he said, the immensity of God's love through the taking on of infinite goodness, which no creature can receive, could not have been revealed in him. He further says ***only begotten***, to show that God does not have a love divided among many sons, but all of it is for that Son whom he gave to prove the immensity of his love: ***The Father loves the Son and shows him all things that he himself is doing*** (John 5:20). *Fourth*, from the greatness of its fruit, because through him we have eternal life. Hence he says, ***so that whoever believes in him should not perish but have eternal life***, which he obtained for us through the death of the cross.

478 But did God give his Son with the intention that he should die on the cross? He did indeed give him for the death of the cross inasmuch as he gave him the will to suffer on it. And he did this in two ways. *First*, because as the Son of God he willed from eternity to assume flesh and to suffer for us; and this will he had from the Father. *Second*, because the will to suffer was infused into the soul of Christ by God.

479 Note that above, when the Lord was speaking about the coming down which belongs to Christ according to his divinity, he called him the Son of God; and this because of the one *suppositum* of the two natures, as was explained above. And so divine things can be said about the *suppositum* of the human nature, and human things can be said about the *suppositum* of the divine

2. Gregory the Great, *Forty Gospel Homilies* 30.1.

nature, but not with reference to the same nature. Rather, divine things are said with reference to the divine nature, and human things with reference to the human nature. Now the specific reason why he here calls him the Son of God is that he set forth that gift as a sign of the divine love, through which the fruit of eternal life comes to us. And so, he should have been called by that name which indicates the power that produces eternal life; and this power is not in Christ as Son of man but as Son of God: *This is the true God and eternal life* (1 John 5:20); ***in him was life*** (John 1:4).

480 Note also that he says, ***should not perish***. Someone is said to be perishing when he is hindered from arriving at the end to which he is ordained. But the end to which man is ordained is eternal life, and as long as he sins, he turns himself from that end. And although while he is living he cannot entirely perish in the sense that he cannot be restored, yet when he dies in sin, then he entirely perishes: *The way of the wicked will perish* (Ps. 1:6).

He indicates the immensity of God's love in saying, ***have eternal life***: for by giving eternal life, he gives himself. For eternal life is nothing else than enjoying God. But to give oneself is a sign of great love: *God, who is rich in mercy . . . made us alive together with Christ* (Eph. 2:5), i.e., he gave us eternal
481 life. Here the Lord excludes an objection that might be made. For in the old law it was promised that the Lord would come to judge: *The Lord will enter into judgment* (Isa. 3:14 DRB). So someone might say that the Son of God had not come to give eternal life but in order to judge the world. The Lord rejects this.

First, he shows that he has not come to judge. *Second*, he proves it, at ***He***
482 ***who believes in him is not judged***. So he says: the Son of God has not come to judge, because ***God did not send his Son***, referring to his first coming, ***into the world to judge the world, but that the world might be saved through him***. The same thing is said later: ***I did not come to judge the world, but to save the world*** (John 12:47).

Now man's salvation is to attain to God: *In God is my salvation* (Ps. 61:8 DRB). And to attain to God is to obtain eternal life; hence to be saved is the same as to have eternal life. However, because the Lord says, ***I did not come to judge the world*** (John 12:47), men should not be lazy or abuse God's mercy, or give themselves over to sin, because although in his first coming he did not come to judge but to forgive, yet in his second coming, as Chrysostom says, he will come to judge but not to forgive.[3] *At the time set which I appoint I will judge with equity* (Ps. 75:2).

483 However, this seems to conflict with what is said: ***For judgment I came into this world*** (John 9:39). I answer that there are two kinds of judgment. One is the judgment of distinction, and the Son has come for this in his first

3. John Chrysostom, *Commentary on Saint John* 28.1.

coming; because with his coming men are distinguished, some by blindness and some by the light of grace. The other is the judgment of condemnation; and he did not come for this as such.

484 Now he proves what he had said, as though by a process of elimination, in the following way: whoever will be judged will be either a believer or an unbeliever. But I have not come to judge unbelievers, because they are already judged. Therefore, from the outset, ***God did not send his Son into the world to judge the world.***

So *first* he shows that believers are not judged. *Second*, that unbelievers are
485 not judged, at ***Whoever does not believe is already judged.*** He says therefore: ***I did not come to judge the world*** (John 12:47): because he did not come to judge believers, for ***he who believes in him is not judged***, with the judgment of condemnation, with which no one who believes in him with faith informed by love is judged: ***He does not come into judgment but has passed from death to life*** (John 5:24). But he is judged with the judgment of reward and approval, of which the Apostle says: *It is the Lord who judges me* (1 Cor. 4:4).

486 But will there be many believing sinners who will not be damned? I reply that some heretics have said that no believer, however great a sinner he may be, will be damned, but he will be saved by reason of his foundation of salvation, namely, his faith, although he may be allowed to suffer some punishment. They take as the basis of their error the statement of the Apostle: No other foundation can anyone lay than that which is laid, which is Jesus Christ (1 Cor. 3:11); and further on: *If any man's work is burned up . . . he himself will be saved, but only as through fire* (1 Cor. 3:15). But this view is clearly contrary to what the Apostle says: *The works of the flesh are plain: fornication, impurity . . . . those who do such things shall not inherit the kingdom of God* (Gal. 5:19–21).

Therefore we must say that the foundation of salvation is not faith unformed, but formed, which operates through charity. Significantly therefore the Lord did not say: 'he who believes in him,' but ***whoever believes in him***, that is, whoever by believing tends toward him through love, ***is not judged***, because he does not sin mortally, through which the foundation is removed. Or one could say, following Chrysostom, that everyone who acts sinfully does not believe:[4] *They profess to know God, but they deny him by their deeds* (Titus 1:16); but he who acts worthily *by [his] works will show you [his] faith* (James 2:18); such a one who is not judged and not condemned for unbelief.

487 Here he shows that unbelievers are not judged. *First* he makes the state-
488 ment; *second*, he explains it at: ***and this is the judgment.*** Concerning the *first* we should note, according to Augustine, that Christ does not say that he that

4. John Chrysostom, 28.1.

does not believe is judged, but rather ***is not judged.***[5] This can be explained in three ways. For, according to Augustine, whoever does not believe is not judged because he is already judged, not in fact, but in God's foreknowledge, that is, it is already known to God that he will be condemned: *The Lord knows who are his* (2 Tim. 2:19).

In another way: according to Chrysostom, ***whoever does not believe is already judged,*** indicates that the very fact of unbelief is a condemnation for the unbeliever.[6] For not to believe is not to adhere to the light—which is to live in darkness, and this is a momentous condemnation: *With one chain of darkness they were all bound* (Wis. 17:17). *What kind of joy can I have, I who sit in darkness and do not see the light of heaven?* (Tob. 5:12 DRB).

In a *third* way: also according to Chrysostom, ***whoever does not believe,*** being already condemned, displays the obvious reason for his condemnation.[7] This is like saying that a person who is proven guilty of death is already dead, even before the sentence of death has been passed on him, because he is as good as dead. Hence Gregory says that in passing judgments there is a twofold order.[8] Some will be sentenced by a trial; such are the ones who have something not deserving of condemnation, namely, the good of faith, that is, sinners who believe. But unbelievers, whose reason for condemnation is manifest, are sentenced without trial; and of these it is said, ***whoever does not believe is already judged.*** *The wicked will not stand in the judgment* (Ps. 1:5), that is, stand in trial.

489 It should be noted that to be judged is the same as to be condemned; and to be condemned is to be shut out from salvation, to which only one road leads, that is, the name of the Son of God: *There is no other name under heaven given among men by which we are saved* (Acts 4:12); *save me, O God, by your name* (Ps. 54:1). Therefore, those who do not believe in the Son of God are cut off from salvation, and the cause of their damnation is evident.

490 Here the Lord explains his statement that unbelievers have an evident cause for their condemnation. *First,* he sets forth the sign which shows this. *Second,* the fittingness of this sign, ***for everyone who does evil hates the light.***

491 In the sign he sets forth he does three things. *First,* he mentions the gift of God. *Second,* the perversity of mind in unbelievers. *Third,* the cause of this perversity. So he says: it is abundantly clear that ***whoever does not believe is already judged,*** which is apparent from the kindness of God, because ***the light has come into the world.*** For men were in the darkness of ignorance, and God destroyed this darkness, sending a light into the world in order that men might

5. Augustine, *Tractates on the Gospel of John* 12.12.

6. John Chrysostom, *Commentary on Saint John* 28.2.

7. John Chrysostom, 28.2.

8. Gregory the Great, *Moralia in Job* 26.27.

know the truth: ***I am the light of the world: he who follows me will not walk in darkness but will have the light of life*** (John 8:12); *to give light to those who sit in darkness and in the shadow of death* (Luke 1:78). Now the light came into the world because men could not come to it, for *he dwells in unapproachable light, whom no man has seen or can see* (1 Tim. 6:16).

It is also clear from the perversity of mind in unbelievers who ***loved darkness more than the light***, i.e., they preferred to remain in the darkness of ignorance rather than be instructed by Christ: *They are those who rebel against the light* (Job 24:13); *woe to you . . . .who put darkness for light and light for darkness* (Isa. 5:20).

And the cause of this perversity is that ***their works were evil***: and such works do not conform to the light but seek the darkness: *Let us then cast off the works of darkness* (Rom. 13:12), i.e., sins, which seek the darkness; *those who sleep, sleep at night* (1 Thess. 5:7); *the eye of the adulterer also waits for the twilight* (Job 24:15). Now it is by withdrawing from the light, which is unpleasant to him, that one does not believe the light.

492 But do all unbelievers produce evil works? It seems not: for many gentiles have acted with virtue; for example, Cato, and many others. I answer, with Chrysostom, that is it one thing to work by reason of virtue, and another by reason of a natural aptitude or disposition.[9] For some act well because of their natural disposition because their temperament is not inclined in a contrary way. And even unbelievers can act well in this way. For example, one may live chastely because he is not assailed by concupiscence; and the same for the other virtues. But those who act well by reason of virtue do not depart from virtue, in spite of inclinations to the contrary vice, because of the rightness of their reason and the goodness of their will; and this is proper to believers. Or, one might answer that although unbelievers may have done good things, they do not do them for love of virtue but out of vainglory. Further, they did not do all things well; for they failed to render to God the worship due him.

493 Then when he says, ***for everyone who does evil hates the light***, he shows the appropriateness of the sign he used. *First*, with respect to those who are evil. *Second*, with respect to the good, at ***but he who practices truth comes to the light***.

494 So he says: they did not love the light because ***their works were evil***. And this is plain because ***for everyone who does evil hates the light***. He does not say: 'did,' but rather ***does***: because if someone has acted in an evil way, but has repented and is sorry, seeing that he has done wrong, such a person does not hate the light but comes to the light. But ***everyone who does evil***, i.e., persists

9. John Chrysostom, *Commentary on Saint John* 28.2.

in evil, is not sorry, nor does he come to the light, but he hates it; not because it reveals truth, but because it reveals a person's sins.

For an evil person still wants to know the light and the truth; but he hates to be unmasked by it. *If the morning suddenly appear, it is to them the shadow of death* (Job 24:17 DRB). And so ***he does not come to the light***; and this ***so that his works may not be reproved.*** For no one who is unwilling to desert evil wants to be rebuked; this is fled from and hated. *They hate the one who reproves in the gate* (Amos 5:10); *a corrupt man does not love the one who reproves him* (Prov. 15:12 DRB).

495 Now he shows the same things with respect to the good, who practice the truth, i.e., perform good works. For truth is found not only in thought and words, but also in deeds. Every one of these ***comes to the light.*** But did anyone practice the truth before Christ? It seems not, for to practice the truth is not to sin; and before Christ *all have sinned* (Rom. 3:23).

I answer, according to Augustine, that he practices the truth in himself who is displeased at the evil he has done;[10] and after leaving the darkness, keeps himself from sin, and repenting of the past, ***comes to the light***, with the special intention ***so that his works may be made manifest.***

496 But this conflicts with the teaching that no one should make public the good he has done; and this was a reason why the Lord rebuked the Pharisees. I answer that it is lawful to want one's works to be seen by God so that they may be approved: *It is not the man who commends himself that is accepted, but the man whom the Lord commends* (2 Cor. 10:18); *my witness is in heaven* (Job 16:19). It is also lawful to want them to be seen by one's own conscience, so that one may rejoice: *Our boast is this, the testimony of our conscience* (2 Cor. 1:12). But it is reprehensible to want them to be seen by men in order to be praised or for one's own glory. Yet, holy persons desire that their good works be known to men for the sake of God's glory and for the good of the faith: *Let your light so shine before men that they may see your good works and give glory to your Father who is in heaven* (Matt. 5:16). Such a person ***comes to the light, so that his works may be made manifest, because they are done in God,*** that is, according to God's commandment or through the grace of God. For whatever good we do, whether it be avoiding sin, repenting of what has been done, or doing good works, it is all from God: *You have wrought for us all our works* (Isa. 26:12).

10. Augustine, *Tractates on the Gospel of John* 12.13.

Philippians 2:5–8

Christ's Obedient Self-Emptying

On Philippians 2.2 (51–66)

2:5 ***For let this mind be in you, which was also in Christ Jesus:***

2:6 ***Who being in the form of God, thought it not robbery to be equal with God:***

2:7 ***But emptied himself, taking the form of a servant, being made in the likeness of men, and in habit found as a man.***

2:8 ***He humbled himself, becoming obedient unto death, even to the death of the cross.***

51 After giving his exhortation, the Apostle urges them to the virtue of humility
according to Christ's example.[11] *First,* he exhorts them to follow the example
52 of Christ; *second,* he gives the example, at ***who being in the form of God.*** He
says, therefore: be humble, as I have said; hence ***let this mind be in you,*** i.e.,
acquire by experience the mind ***which was also in Christ Jesus.***

It should be noted that we should have this mind in five ways according to the five senses: *first,* to see his glory, so that being enlightened, we may be conformed to him: *Your eyes will see the king in his beauty* (Isa. 33:17); *and we all, with unveiled face, beholding the glory of the Lord, are being changed into his likeness from one degree of glory to another* (2 Cor. 3:18); *second,* to hear his wisdom, in order to become happy: *Happy are these your servants, who continually stand before you and hear your wisdom* (1 Kings 10:8); *as soon as they heard of me, they obeyed me* (Ps. 18:44). *Third,* to smell the grace of his meekness, that we may run to him: *Your anointing oils are fragrant. . . . Draw me after you* (Song of Sol. 1:3–4); *fourth,* to taste the sweetness of his mercy, that we may always be in God: *Taste and see that the Lord is good* (Ps. 34:8); *fifth,* to touch his power, that we may be saved: *If I only touch his garment, I shall be made well* (Matt. 9:21).

53 Then when he says, ***who being in the form of God,*** he proposes the example of Christ. *First,* he mentions Christ's majesty; *second,* his humility, at ***he humbled himself;*** *third,* his exaltation, at ***for which cause*** (Phil. 2:9). He mentions Christ's majesty first in order that his humility might be more easily recom-

11. See Phil. 2:2–4 and Thomas Aquinas, *On Philippians* 2.1 (not included in this collection).

mended. In regard to his majesty he proposes two things, namely, the truth of his divine nature, and second, his equality, at ***thought it not robbery.***

54 He says, therefore: ***who***, namely, Christ, ***being in the form of God.*** For it is through its form that a thing is said to be in a specific or generic nature; hence the form is called the nature of a thing. Consequently, to be in the form of God is to be in the nature of God. By this is understood that he is true God: *Jesus Christ . . . the true God and eternal life* (1 John 5:20). However, it should not be supposed that the form of God is one thing and God himself another, because in simple and immaterial things, and especially in God, the form is the same as that whose form it is.

But why does he say, ***in the form***, rather than *in the nature*? Because this belongs to the proper names of the Son in three ways: for he is called the Son, the Word, and the Image. Now the Son is the one begotten, and the end of begetting is the form. Therefore, to show the perfect Son of God he says, ***in the form***, as though having the form of the Father perfectly. Similarly, a word is not perfect unless it leads to a knowledge of a thing's nature; and so the Word of God is said to be in the form of God, because he has the entire nature of the Father. Finally, an image is not perfect, unless it has the form of that of which it is the image: *He reflects the glory of God and bears the very stamp of his nature* (Heb. 1:3).

55 But does he have it perfectly? Yes, because he ***thought it not robbery to be equal with God.*** This can be taken two ways. In one way, of his humanity. But this is not the way Paul understood it, because it would be heretical; for it would be a robbery if it referred to his humanity.

Therefore, it must be explained in another way, namely, of his divinity, according to which equality with God is said of Christ. It is contrary to reason to say otherwise: because the nature of God cannot be received in matter; but the fact that someone existing in a certain nature participates in that nature to a greater or lesser degree is due to the matter; which is not the case here. Therefore, we must say that he ***thought it not robbery to be equal with God***, because he is ***in the form of God*** and knows his own nature well. And because he knows this, it is stated in John: *He . . . called God his Father, making himself equal with God* (John 5:18). But this was not a robbery, as it was when the devil and man wished to be equal to him: *I will make myself like the Most High* (Isa. 14:14); *you will be like God* (Gen. 3:5), for which Christ came to make satisfaction: *What I did not steal must I now restore?* (Ps. 69:4).

56 Then when he says, ***but emptied himself***, he commends Christ's humility. *First*, as to the mystery of the incarnation; *second*, as to the mystery of the passion, at ***he humbled himself.***

In regard to the *first*: *first*, he mentions his humility; *second*, its manner
57 and form. He says, therefore, ***he emptied himself.*** But since he was filled with the divinity, did he empty himself of that? No, because he remained what he was; and what he was not, he assumed. But this must be understood in regard to the assumption of what he had not, and not according to the assumption of what he had. For just as he descended from heaven, not that he ceased to exist in heaven, but because he began to exist in a new way on earth, so he also emptied himself, not by putting off his divine nature, but by assuming a human nature.

How beautiful to say that ***he emptied himself***, for the empty is opposed to the full! For the divine nature is sufficiently full, because every perfection of goodness is there. *I will show you all good* (Exod. 33:19 DRB). But human nature and the soul are not full, but capable of fullness, because it was made as a slate not written upon. Therefore, human nature is empty. Hence he says, ***he emptied himself***, because he assumed a human nature.

58 *First*, he touches on the assumption of human nature when he says, ***taking the form of a servant.*** For by reason of his creation man is a servant, and human nature is the form of a servant: *Know that the Lord is God! It is he that made us, and we are his* (Ps. 100:3); *behold my servant, whom I uphold* (Isa. 42:1); *you, O, Lord, are a shield about me* (Ps. 3:3).

But why is it more fitting to say ***the form of a servant***, rather than *servant*? Because servant is the name of a hypostasis, which was not assumed, but the nature was; for that which is assumed is distinct from the one assuming it. Therefore, the Son of God did not assume a man, because that would mean that he was other than the Son of God; nevertheless, the Son of God became man. Therefore, he took the nature to his own person, so that the Son of God and the Son of man would be the same in person.

59 *Second*, he touches on the conformity of his nature to ours when he says, ***being made in the likeness of men***, namely, according to species: *He had to be made like his brethren in every respect* (Heb. 2:17). If you say that it is not fitting to speak of a species in the Lord Jesus Christ: it is true in the sense that a new species does not arise from his divinity and humanity, as though his divinity and humanity agreed in having one common species of nature, for it would follow that his divine nature, so to say, would have changed.

60 *Third*, he mentions the conditions of his human nature when he says, ***and in habit found as a man.*** For he assumed all the defects and properties associated with the human species, except sin; therefore, he says, ***and in habit found as a man***, namely, in his external life, because he became hungry as a man and tired, and so on, as *one who in every respect has been tempted as we are, yet without sin* (Heb. 4:15); *he was seen upon earth and conversed with men* (Bar. 3:38 DRB). Thus, we can refer ***habit*** to outward activities.

61 Or ***in habit***, because he put humanity on as a habit. For there are four kinds of habit or ways in which something is 'had': one changes a person without itself being changed, as a fool by wisdom; another is changed and also changes the possessor, as food; a third neither changes the possessor nor is changed, as a ring worn on the finger; another is changed and does not change the possessor, as a dress. And by this likeness the human nature in Christ is called a habit or 'something had'; because it comes to the divine person without changing it, but the nature itself was changed for the better, because it was filled with grace and truth: *We have beheld his glory, glory as of the only Son from the Father, full of grace and truth* (John 1:14).

He says, therefore, ***being made in the likeness of men***, but in such a way
62 that he is not changed, because ***in habit found as a man***. It should be noted that some have fallen into error on account of this phrase, ***in habit found as a man***. Hence he touches on several opinions:

The *first* is that Christ's humanity accrues to him as an accident. This is false, because the person existing in the divine nature became a person existing in the human nature; therefore, it is present not as an accident, but substantially: not that the humanity is united to the Word in his nature, but in his person. By this is excluded the error of Photinus, who said that Christ was true man but not of the Virgin:[12] however, Paul says, ***being in the form of God***; therefore, he was in the form of God before receiving the form of a servant, as a result of which he is less than the Father, because he ***thought it not robbery to be equal with God***. He is limited, therefore, who merited through the form of a servant.

The error of Arius is also excluded, for he said Christ was less than the Father; but Paul says, he ***thought it not robbery to be equal with God***. Likewise is excluded the error of Nestorius, who said that the union should be taken as an indwelling, so that God dwells in the man as in a temple, and that the son of man is a person distinct from the Son of God. And Rabanus says that the Apostle calls the incarnation an emptying.[13] Now it is evident that the Father and the Holy Spirit are involved in every indwelling; therefore, they too are emptied. But this is false. Furthermore, Paul says, he ***emptied himself***; therefore

12. This is a somewhat puzzling description of Photinus' position (cf. *On John* 1.5, below, where Thomas ascribes to Photinus the view that Christ *was* born of the virgin). Considering that, in this commentary, Photinus is presented as a foil of St. Paul whose view of the Incarnation implies the preexistence of Christ as the Son, it may be that by "Christ" here Thomas means specifically *the Son*. In Photinus' view, the Son cannot be properly said to have been "born" of Mary (nor for him, as for Nestorius, is Mary rightly to be called the "Mother of God"), since in his view, Jesus was not the Son by birth but became the Son during his life and in virtue of his meritorious way of living.

13. Rabanus, *Expostio in Epistolam ad Philippenses* 2.

the person emptied and the one emptying are the same. But this is the Son of God, because he ***emptied himself.*** Therefore, the union is in the person.

Also the error of Eutyches, who said that one nature results from the two. Therefore, he did not receive the form of a servant, but a different one, which is contrary to what the Apostle says. Also the error of Valentinus, who said that he took his body from heaven. Also the error of Apollinaris, who said that he had no soul. If this were so, he would not have been ***made in the likeness of men.***

63 Then when he says, ***he humbled himself,*** he commends Christ's humility as indicated in his passion. *First,* he shows Christ's humility; *second,* its manner, at
64 ***becoming obedient unto death.*** Therefore he was man, but very great, because the same one is God and man; yet ***he humbled himself***: *The greater you are, the more you must humble yourself* (Sir. 3:18); *learn from me, for I am gentle and lowly in heart* (Matt. 11:29).

65 The manner and the sign of his humility is obedience, whereas it is characteristic of the proud to follow their own will for a proud person seeks greatness. But it pertains to a great thing that it not be ruled by something else, but that it rule other things; therefore, obedience is contrary to pride. Hence, in order to show the greatness of Christ's humility and passion, he says that he became ***obedient***; because if he had not suffered out of obedience, his passion would not be so commendable, for obedience gives merit to our sufferings.

But how was he made ***obedient***? Not by his divine will, because it is a rule; but by his human will, which is ruled in all things according to the Father's will: *Not as I will but as you will* (Matt. 26:39).

66 And it is fitting that he bring obedience into his passion, because the first sin was accomplished by disobedience: *As by one man's disobedience many were made sinners, so by one man's obedience many will be made righteous* (Rom. 5:19); *an obedient man shall speak of victory* (Prov. 21:28 DRB).

That this obedience is great and commendable is evident from the fact that obedience is great when it follows the will of another against one's own. Now the movement of the human will tends toward two things, namely, to life and to honor. But Christ did not refuse death: *Christ also died for sins once for all, the righteous for the unrighteous* (1 Pet. 3:18). Furthermore, he did not flee ignominy; hence he says, ***even to the death of the cross,*** which is the most shameful: *Let us condemn him to a shameful death* (Wis. 2:20). Thus, he neither refused death nor an ignominious form of death.

Hebrews 2:9–13

Christ Condescended to Suffer for All

On Hebrews 2.3 (121–135)

2:9 ***But we see Jesus, who was made a little lower than the angels, for the suffering of death, crowned with glory and honor: that, through the grace of God he might taste death for all.***

2:10 ***For it became him, for whom are all things and by whom are all things, who had brought many children into glory, to perfect the author of their salvation, by his passion.***

2:11 ***For both he that sanctifies and they who are sanctified are all of one. For which cause he is not ashamed to call them brethren,***

2:12 ***saying, "I will declare your name to my brethren: in the midst of the church will I praise you."***

2:13 ***And again, "I will put my trust in him." And again, "behold I and my children, whom God has given me."***

121 Above, the Apostle, desiring to prove Christ's eminence over the angels, relied on the authority of a prophet who said something pertaining to Christ's dignity, such as, ***you have subjected all things under his feet***, and something pertaining to his passion, namely, ***you have made him a little lower than the angels.***[14] But this seems to militate against his chief intention, which is to prefer Christ over the angels. Consequently, he explains this more fully in this section, where he does two things: *first*, he shows in what sense that lessening is to be understood; *second*, he describes the suitability of the passion, at ***for it became him.***

In regard to the *first*, he does two things: *first*, he explains a statement he made; *second*, he describes the passion, at ***that through the grace of God.***

122 He said therefore: ***What is man, that you are mindful of him? . . . You have crowned him with glory and honor . . . you have subjected all things under his feet; you have made him a little lower than the angels.*** These are the things the prophet predicted of Christ, and already we see many of them fulfilled. Hence, it is certain that the rest will be fulfilled, namely, that all things will be subjected under his feet. *The accomplishments of the past give assurance for the future.*[15]

14. See Thomas Aquinas, *Commentary on Hebrews* 2.2 (not included in this collection).

15. Gregory the Great, *Forty Gospel Homilies* 3.

Then he continues, ***We see Jesus, who was made a little lower than the angels***, and not only this, but ***for the suffering of death, crowned with glory and honor***, which was the cause of his exaltation: *Therefore God has highly exalted him* (Phil. 2:9). He says, ***of death***, because he did not endure just any death, but the bitterest and most shameful: *Let us condemn him to a most shameful death* (Wis. 2:20 DRB).

Or, another way: ***we see Jesus***, and when asked who he is, he answers: he ***who was made a little lower than the angels, for the suffering of death, crowned with glory and honor***. As if to say that this lessening was due only to his suffering of death. Nor is this strange, because in this respect he is not only lower than the angels, but lower than men, *despised and the most abject of men* (Isa. 53:3 DRB). A gloss of Augustine says that Christ was made a little lower than the angels, not because of a condition of his nature, but because of the passion.[16] For as to the nature of the human mind, which Christ assumed without sin, nothing is greater but the Trinity alone.

In body he is less than the angels because he suffered in his body. But this seems to be contrary to Dionysius, who says that angels are greater than men by reason of their natural participation in light.[17] The answer is that we can speak in two ways about the nature of the human mind and the angelic mind: in one way, according to what is natural, and then the nature of angels is more excellent and more noble than the nature of the human mind, because an angel receives knowledge of divine truth in a more excellent and fuller intellectual light, but man from creatures. In another way, we can consider the nature of each without sin in relation to happiness; they are then equal: *They . . . are like angels in heaven* (Matt. 22:30). Yet by reason of his excellent grace, Christ in his human nature is greater than the angels. Consequently, his lessening is not in relation to the nature of his divinity nor absolutely according to his human nature, but in the sense that he suffered according to it.

But we can say that Christ was crowned with a triple glory, namely, with the glory of holiness, which he had in the first instant of his conception; *second*, with the glory of the beatific vision, because from the first instant of his conception he possessed it; *third*, with the glory of incorruptibility, which he merited after the passion.

123 Then when he says ***that, through the grace of God***, he describes Christ's passion from three viewpoints. *First*, from its cause, when he says ***that, through the grace of God***; *second*, from its utility, when he says ***for all***; *third*, from the manner, when he says ***he might taste***.

16. Augustine, *Answer to Maximinus the Arian* 2.28.6.

17. Pseudo-Dionysius, *The Celestial Hierarchy* 4–5.

124 Only God's grace was the cause. Hence, he continues, ***we see Jesus***, who was lower, and this, ***through the grace of God***, for that alone led him to give his only begotten Son: *God so loved the world as to give his only begotten Son* (John 3:16); *God shows his love for us in that while we were yet sinners Christ died for us* (Rom. 5:8).

Or, according to a gloss of Augustine, ***that, through the grace of God***, i.e., Christ himself, who is the grace of God, ***he might taste death for all.***[18] Here ***grace*** is in the nominative case. But Christ is called grace because he is the author of grace: *Grace and truth came through Jesus Christ* (John 1:17). Or, because he is given freely: *To us a son is given* (Isa. 9:6). Then the sense is this: he was made a little lower in order that he who is the grace of God might taste death for all. Either position follows the *Gloss.*

125 ***For all***: behold the usefulness. But ***for all*** can be understood in two ways: *first*, as applying to all the predestined, since it is only in the predestined that it is efficacious. *Second*, as applying absolutely to all so far as sufficiency is concerned; for of itself it is sufficient for all: *The living God . . . is the savior of all men, especially of those who believe* (1 Tim. 4:10). Chrysostom says, *He died for all in general, because the price was sufficient for all. And if all do not believe, he nevertheless fulfilled his part.*[19]

126 ***Might taste***: behold the manner. For a person who has not eaten or drunk much is said to have tasted. Therefore, because Christ did not continue in death but rose at once, he tasted death: *He shall drink of the brook by the way* (Ps. 110:7). One who is on the way hurries.

Furthermore, taste is a discerner of flavor; hence, one who tastes discerns more than one who drinks. Therefore, to indicate that he tasted death and pain, and that his death was not imaginary, as Mani and Apollinaris claim, he says that ***he might taste death.***

But the manner is mentioned when he says, ***taste.*** Matthew says the same thing: *If it be possible, let this cup pass from me* (26:39). He says this for three reasons: *first*, to express the bitterness of death, which is experienced by taste: *All you who pass by the way, look and see if there is any sorrow like my sorrow* (Lam. 1:12); *the drink shall be bitter to those who drink it* (Isa. 24:9); *second*, because just as tasting or not tasting lie in the power of the taster, so also the passion of Christ was voluntary: *No one takes [my life] from me but I lay it down of my own accord* (John 10:18). *Third*, because to taste is to take little; Christ, however, persisted little in death: *You do not give me up to Sheol* (Ps. 16:10).

18. This quote is likely misattributed to Augustine. Lee Gatiss argues that the quote (or some form of it) belongs, in fact, to Peter Lombard. See Lee Gatiss, "Grace Tasted Death for All: Thomas Aquinas on Hebrews 2:9," *The Tyndale Bulletin* 63, no. 2 (2012): 217–236.

19. John Chrysostom, *On 1 Corinthians* 36.

127 Then when he says ***for it became him***, he shows the suitability from its usefulness. For God the Father is the cause of Christ's death, since he is the one ***by whom are all things*** as by an efficient cause, and ***for whom are all things***, as for a final cause. All things are for him, because they are for communicating his goodness: and this was the cause inducing him to produce things, and thus all things are finally for God: *The Lord has made all things for himself* (Prov. 16:4 DRB). But effectively, all things are by him, *who made heaven and the sea and all that is in them* (Ps. 146:6); *I am the Alpha and the Omega, the beginning and the end* (Rev. 1:8 DRB); *from him and through him and to him are all things* (Rom. 11:36). Therefore, it became him as the author of all things to provide for all: *He takes thought for all alike* (Wis. 6:8).

Second, it was fitting on the part of the cause, which, as has been stated, was the grace of God. But grace is ordained to glory: *The grace of God [is] life everlasting* (Rom. 6:23 DRB). But God from all eternity predestined those whom he would lead to glory, i.e., all those who are adopted sons of God, because *if sons, heirs also* (Rom. 8:17 DRB). Therefore, he says, ***who has brought many children into glory***. As if to say: 'he has one perfect Son naturally': *a beloved son* (Mark 12:6); who is naturally ***the brightness of his glory*** (Heb. 1:3 DRB). But the others are adopted and, therefore, must be brought into glory. Hence, he says: ***who has brought***, i.e., foreordained them to be brought.

128 And what was fitting for him? This, namely, that he should make ***perfect the author of their salvation***. This salvation consists in two things, namely, that they become sons and be brought into their inheritance. That they are sons they owe to the natural Son: *Those whom he foreknew he also predestined to be conformed to the image of his Son* (Rom. 8:29). But they obtain glory and the inheritance only through him whose inheritance it is by right and who is the splendor of glory. Therefore, because we obtain those two things through the Son, he is fittingly called the author of salvation, *for he will save his people from their sins* (Matt. 1:21); ***looking to Jesus, the pioneer and perfecter of our faith*** (Heb. 12:2). Therefore it was fitting that the Father send the author of salvation, namely, his Son, ***who had brought many children into glory***.

To perfect . . . by his passion, i.e., by faith. For he, as the natural Son, is altogether perfect, but because he was lessened in the passion, he had to be made perfect by the merit of the passion. From this consummation, therefore, the fittingness of the manner is clear, concerning which he said that Christ tasted. For he only tasted death, for he did not receive it, except that it might be ended through the merit of the passion. For this very consummation is his glorification: *Was it not necessary that Christ should suffer these things and enter into his glory?* (Luke 24:26). He also tasted that he might lead the sons to glory, just as a doctor tastes a medicine lest the sick man shrink back from it, but rather that he drink it confidently, thus he tastes death, so that because without entering the necessity of death, no one is saved, let no one flee death.

129 Then when he says ***for both he that sanctifies***, he proves what he had said. Here he does two things: *first*, he proves his conclusion on the part of the Father sanctifying; *second*, on the part of Christ sanctified, at ***the children share in flesh and blood*** (Heb. 2:14).

In regard to the *first*, he does two things: *first*, he states his conclusion;
130 *second*, he proves it by an authority, at ***for which cause***. He says, therefore: ***Both he that sanctifies and they who are sanctified are all of one***. But it should be noted that the Apostle had said three things above: *first*, that Christ is the cause of salvation, in which he shows that we depend on him as on a Savior; *second*, he shows that the Father is the finisher of Christ by the merit of the passion, so that in this, Christ depends on the Father; *third*, that the Father brings us into glory, which also shows that we depend on God. Accordingly, the Apostle does three things here.

First, he shows that we depend on Christ, for the one sanctified depends on the sanctifier: ***Jesus also, that he might sanctify the people by his own blood, suffered without the gate*** (Heb. 13:12). Therefore, it has been well said that because he is the author and sanctifier, we depend on him; but he depends on the Father, from whom he has power to sanctify; which is the *second* thing the Apostle shows. But ***all***, namely, ***he that sanctifies and we who are sanctified***, have one origin, namely, of the Father; this is the *third* thing: *heirs of God and fellow heirs with Christ* (Rom. 8:17).

131 Then he proves three points by three authorities: *first*, that Christ, as the mediator and author of salvation, brings God's gifts to us. Hence, he says, ***for which cause***, namely, because he and we depend on the Father, ***he is not ashamed to call them brethren***, because all are of the same Father: *Have we not all one Father?* (Mal. 2:10); *that he might be the firstborn among many brethren* (Rom. 8:29). Therefore, it is said: *I will tell your name to my brethren* (Ps. 22:22); *go to my brethren* (John 20:17).

But note that he says, ***He is not ashamed to call them brethren***, because some born of an ignoble race are ashamed to recognize their brethren, if they are promoted: *The brethren of the poor man hate him* (Prov. 19:7 DRB). But not Christ, for he says, ***I will declare your name to my brethren***: *I have manifested your name to the men whom you gave me* (John 17:6); *the only Son, who is in the bosom of the Father, he has made him known* (John 1:18).

132 Then he shows the fruit of this manifestation when he says, ***In the midst of the Church will I praise you***. As if to say: 'this forms a great Church in the midst of which I will praise you.' He says, ***in the midst***, because just as a pillar in the midst of a house supports it, and a lamp in the midst of a house gives

light, and the heart in the midst of the body gives life, so Christ is in the midst of the Church.

Furthermore, ***in the midst***, because he was not sent to one people, as Moses was: *In Judea God is known; his name is great in Israel* (Ps. 76:1), but he was sent for the salvation of all: *He has wrought salvation in the midst of the earth* (Ps. 74:12). Therefore, it is stated in Luke that *Jesus stood in the midst of* his disciples (24:36).

On this point it should be noted that before the law it was the custom that all the firstborn were priests, and this pertained to the right of primogeniture. But Christ is a brother and firstborn; therefore, he is a priest. But a priest who sanctifies the people is a mediator between God and the people: *I was the mediator and stood between the Lord and you at that time* (Deut. 5:5). Therefore, it pertains to him to announce the things of God to the people and to bring the things of the people to God. He does the *first* by preaching; hence, he says, ***I will declare your name to my brethren***, i.e., I will bring them to know you, and this to *sanctify them in the truth* (John 17:17). The *second* he accomplishes by doing, when he makes men burst forth in praise of God. Hence, he says, ***in the midst of the church will I praise you.***

133 Then when he says, ***and again***, he shows that Christ himself depends on the Father by the fact that he says, ***I will put my trust in him.*** This, following Jerome, is considered in Isaiah, where we have: *I will wait for the Lord, who is hiding his face from the house of Jacob* (8:17).[20] But Isaiah says expressly: *I will trust and will not be afraid* (12:2).

I will put my trust in him for the glory of the head and members, which is why above he spoke of perfection: *In you, O Lord, have I hoped* (Ps. 30:1 DRB). But he shows the kind of hope he has, namely, firm hope, which is called trust: for hope, even though it is not concerned with the impossible, sometimes has fear joined to it, and then it is properly called hope. But sometimes hope is firm and without fear; then it is called trust. This is the hope Christ had.

134 He says, therefore, ***I will put my trust in him***, i.e., I will have confidence in his help, namely, the Father, for the glory of the body that he will raise, both of the members and the soul: *In you, O Lord, have I hoped* (Ps. 30:1 DRB); *blessed is the man who trusts in the Lord* (Jer. 17:7).

But the saints say that in Christ there is neither faith nor hope, but only charity. I answer that hope is one thing and trust another: for hope is the expectation of future happiness; and this was not in Christ, because he was happy from the instant of his conception. But trust is the expectation of help, and in regard to this there was hope in Christ, inasmuch as he awaited help from the Father during his passion. Therefore, whenever we read that Christ

20. Jerome, *Commentary on Isaiah* 3.27.

had hope, this is not to be understood as referring to its principal object, which is happiness, but as referring to the glory of the resurrection and of the glory conferred on his body.

135 Then when he repeats ***and again***, he shows that we depend on the Father: ***behold I and my children, whom God has given me***: *Yours they were and you gave them to me* (John 17:6); *children, have you any fish?* (John 21:5). They are called children on account of their purity, *if the young men be clean, especially from women* (1 Sam. 21:4); and a bit later he continues: *the vessels of the young men are holy* (21:5). They are called children because of their purity: *I and the children whom the Lord has given me are signs and portents in Israel from the Lord of hosts* (Isa. 8:18). Also on account of their simplicity: *Brethren, do not become children in your thinking; be babes in evil* (1 Cor. 14:20); also because of their humility: *Unless you turn and become like children . . .* (Matt. 18:3).

Again, they are called children on account of their facility to the good: *Let the children come to me* (Matt. 19:14). He shows that not only is he from God, but also the children; hence he continues, ***whom God has given me***. This shows that both he that sanctifies and they that are sanctified have all one origin, because it says in John: *No one can come to me, unless the Father who sent me draws him* (6:44).

Chapter 5

THE SACRIFICIAL DEATH OF CHRIST

Matthew 27:27–66

The Passion of Christ

On Matthew 27.2 (2345–2416)

27:27 *Then the soldiers of the governor, taking Jesus into the praetorium, gathered together to him the whole cohort;*

27:28 *and stripping him, they put a scarlet cloak about him.*

27:29 *And plaiting a crown of thorns, they put it on his head, and a reed in his right hand. And bowing the knee before him, they mocked him, saying:, "Hail, king of the Jews."*

27:30 *And spitting upon him, they took the reed, and struck his head.*

27:31 *And after they had mocked him, they took the cloak off of him, and put on him his own garments, and led him away to crucify him.*

27:32 *And going out, they found a man of Cyrene, named Simon: him they forced to take up his cross.*

27:33 *And they came to the place which is called Golgotha, which is the place of Calvary.*

27:34 *And they gave him wine to drink mixed with gall. And when he had tasted, he would not drink.*

27:35 *And after they had crucified him, they divided his garments, casting lots; that it might be fulfilled what was spoken by the Prophet, saying, "They divided my garments among them; and upon my vesture they cast lots."*

27:36 *And they sat and watched him.*

27:37 *And they put over his head, his cause written, "THIS IS JESUS THE KING OF THE JEWS."*

27:38 *Then there were crucified with him two thieves, one on the right hand, and one on the left.*

27:39 *And those who passed by, blasphemed him, wagging their heads,*

27:40 *and saying, "Vah, you who destroy the temple of God, and in three days rebuild it, save your own self: if you are the Son of God, come down from the cross."*

27:41 *In like manner also the chief priests, with the scribes and elders mocking, said,*

27:42 *"He saved others; himself he cannot save. If he is the king of Israel, let him now come down from the cross, and we will believe him.*

27:43 *He trusted in God; let him now deliver him if he will have him; for he said: I am the Son of God."*

27:44 *And with the same thing the thieves, who were crucified with him, also reproached him.*

27:45 *Now from the sixth hour there was darkness over the whole earth, until the ninth hour.*

27:46 *And about the ninth hour Jesus cried with a loud voice, saying, "Eli, Eli, lamma sabacthani?" That is: my God, my God, why have you forsaken me?*

27:47 *And some who stood there and heard, said: "this man calls Elijah."*

27:48 *And immediately one of them, running, took a sponge, and filled it with vinegar; and put it on a reed, and gave him to drink.*

27:49 *And the others said, "Wait, let us see whether Elijah will come to deliver him."*

27:50 *And Jesus again crying with a loud voice, yielded up the spirit.*

27:51 *And behold the veil of the temple was rent in two from the top even to the bottom, and the earth quaked, and the rocks were rent.*

27:52 *And the graves were opened, and many bodies of the saints who had slept arose,*

27:53 *and coming out of the tombs after his resurrection, came into the holy city, and appeared to many.*

27:54 *Now the centurion, and those who were with him watching Jesus, having seen the earthquake, and the things that were done, were much afraid, saying, "Indeed this was the Son of God."*

27:55 *And there were there many women afar off, who had followed Jesus from Galilee, ministering to him;*

27:56 *among whom was Mary Magdalene, and Mary the mother of James and Joseph, and the mother of the sons of Zebedee.*

27:57 *And when it was evening, there came a certain rich man of Arimathea, named Joseph, who himself was also a disciple of Jesus.*

27:58 *He went to Pilate and asked for the body of Jesus. Then Pilate commanded that the body should be delivered.*

27:59 *And Joseph, taking the body, wrapped it up in a clean linen cloth,*

27:60 *and laid it in his own new monument, which he had hewed out in a rock. And he rolled a great stone to the door of the monument and went his way.*

27:61 *And there was there Mary Magdalene, and the other Mary sitting over against the sepulcher.*

27:62 *And the next day, which followed the Day of Preparation, the chief priests and the Pharisees came together to Pilate,*

27:63 *saying, "Lord, we have remembered, that that seducer said, while he was yet alive: after three days I will rise again.*

27:64 *Command therefore that the sepulcher be guarded until the third day, lest perhaps his disciples come and steal him away, and say to the people, 'He is risen from the dead'; and the last error will be worse than the first."*

27:65 *Pilate said to them, "You have a guard; go, guard it as you know."*

27:66 *And departing, they made the sepulcher sure, sealing the stone, and setting guards.*

2345 After having dealt with the condemnation, here he treats of the passion and death; *second*, of the burial, at ***and when it was evening.***

Concerning the *first*, he does two things. For *first*, he recounts what he undeservedly suffered; *second*, what he magnificently did, at ***From the sixth hour there was darkness.***

The *first* part is in three parts. In the *first*, he treats of the soldiers' mockery; *second*, of the crucifixion; *third*, of the Jews' mockery of the crucified one. The *second* is at ***after they had mocked him***; the *third*, at ***and those who passed by.***

Concerning the *first*: *first*, the mockers are described; *second*, the mock-
2346 ery. It says, ***Then the soldiers . . . gathered together to him the whole cohort.*** A cohort means a company of soldiers, and anyone who had judicial power had a cohort of soldiers to carry out his judgment. The praetorium is said to be the place where judgments were carried out. Hence both gentiles and Jews were gathered together to him, that no one might be exempt, because he had to redeem all. For this reason, what is said is fitting: *God has consigned all men to disobedience, that he may have mercy on all* (Rom. 11:32). And, *They surrounded me like bees* (Ps. 118:12).

2347 ***And stripping him, they put a scarlet cloak about him.*** Here the mockery is described. And *first*, as regards clothing; *second*, as regards honor; *third*, as regards reproach.

The *second* is at ***Bowing the knee before him, they mocked him***; the *third*, at ***and going out, they found a man of Cyrene, named Simon.***

2348 One should note that although they had accused him of many things, yet he suffered for nothing else than that he called himself a king, as is found, *If you release this man, you are not Caesar's friend* (John 19:12). Hence Pilate was afraid more for this reason. So when they wished to mock him, they put on him the signs of a king. For it is the custom that kings are clothed in purple; and in place of this, they clothed him with a scarlet garment. Likewise, they usually have a crown; and in place of this they made a crown of thorns. Likewise,
2349 they usually have a scepter; and in place of this, they gave him a reed. It says therefore, ***They put a scarlet cloak about him***, i.e., a red one.

But why does Mark say that they clothed him in purple (15:17)? Augustine resolves it: he said this owing to the likeness of the colors.[1] Or it can be said that although it was scarlet, yet it had something of purple.

By the fact that he was stripped of his own clothes and clothed with another man's, those heretics are caught up who said that he was not a true man. The cloak can signify Christ's body, stained with his blood, for *he was wounded for our iniquities, he was bruised for our sins* (Isa. 53:5). Or, it signifies

1. Augustine, *Agreement Among the Evangelists* 3.9.

the blood of the martyrs, who washed their robes in the blood of the Lamb (Rev. 7:14). Or, the sin of the gentiles.

2350 ***Plaiting a crown of thorns, they put it on his head.*** Hence instead of a crown of glory, they imposed on him a crown of indignity; *he will crown you with a crown of tribulation* (Isa. 22:18 DRB). These thorns signify the prickles of sinners, which prick their consciences: and Christ received these for us, for he died for our sins (1 Cor. 15:3). Or it can be referred to Adam's curse, where it was said: *Thorns and thistles [the ground] shall bring forth to you* (Gen. 3:18). Hence it signified that this curse was undone.

2351 And in place of a scepter, ***a reed in his right hand.*** And it signifies the power of the demons, according to Origen, which Christ tore from their hands;[2] *you are relying now on Egypt, that broken reed* (2 Kings 18:21). For it can signify the uselessness of the gentiles, whom Christ still took to himself; *ask of me, and I will give you the gentiles for your inheritance* (Ps. 2:8 DRB). And they are well compared to a reed, because as a reed is bent by every wind, so the gentiles by every error.

Also, a reed is used for writing. Also, for killing with poison. Thus Christ also drew and reckoned the faithful to himself, but the persecutors unto death.

2352 Then he treats of the mockery by honor, and they showed this by deed; hence it says, ***Bowing the knee before him, they mocked him.*** And although they did this by way of mockery, yet it signified that every knee should bend before him: *At the name of Jesus every knee should bow* (Phil. 2:10). Then they mocked him by word, saying to him, ***Hail, king of the Jews.*** And they signify those who *profess to know God, but . . . deny him by their deeds* (Titus 1:16).

2353 Likewise, they inflicted various indignities, for they spat on his face; *I hid not my face from shame and spitting* (Isa. 50:6). Likewise, they struck his head as though he were a fool. And who are those who strike Christ's head? *The head of Christ is God,* as is said (1 Cor. 11:3). Therefore, those strike Christ's head who blaspheme Christ's divinity. The reed signified the Sacred Scriptures. Such men support their error with Sacred Scripture.

2354 ***And going out, they found a man of Cyrene, named Simon.*** After the mockery, he treats of the crucifixion, and concerning this he does two things. *First,* he describes the place of the crucifixion; *second,* the condition, and the things which were done in that place. *first,* he recounts how Christ was led to the place; *second,* how the cross was carried; *third,* how they arrived at the passion.

2355 ***And after they had mocked him, they took off,*** namely the cloak with which they had clothed him. Note that he is mocked in another's clothing but led away in his own; which signifies that to be mocked was not his own, but to be killed:

2. Origen, *Commentary on Matthew,* series 125.

for, as is said, *He humbled himself and became obedient unto death* (Phil. 2:8). For his strength was made apparent there: *The right hand of the Lord has wrought strength* (Ps. 118:16 DRB); *he shall be led as a sheep to the slaughter* (Isa. 53:7 DRB).

2356 ***And going out, they found a man of Cyrene.*** Here he treats of the carrying of the cross. And this signified that he did not wish to suffer in the city, but outside. And the reason is given where it says, *Jesus also suffered outside the gate in order to sanctify the people through his own blood* (Heb. 13:12). It also agrees with a figure, for, as it is said that the goat which had to be offered for sin was cast outside the camp (Lev. 16:19), so also Christ, for he was the people's sacrifice.

Likewise for our edification, that we might understand that we must go out to him outside our way of life; *let us go forth to him outside the camp and bear the abuse he endured* (Heb. 13:13). Also, he suffered outside the gate so that the strength of his passion would not be shut up in one nation; *he died that all nations might be gathered into one* (John 11:52).

2357 ***Him they forced to take up his cross.*** Here there seems to be a disharmony because John says that *he went out, bearing his own cross* (19:17). There is one solution here according to Jerome, that he carried it at first, but after they left they met Simon, and forced him.[3] Origen says that it happened the other way around, that Simon carried it at first, and Christ later.[4] And there is a mystical reason why he carried the cross. For above, ***If any man would come after me, let him deny himself and take up his cross, and follow me*** (Matt. 16:24).

And one should notice that this Simon was a foreigner, and he signified the gentile people, who bore the Lord's cross; *for the word of the cross, to those indeed who perish, is foolishness; but to those who are saved, that is, to us, it is the power of God* (1 Cor. 1:18). ***Simon*** means 'obedient,' and the gentile people obeyed: *People whom I had not known served me. As soon as they heard of me they obeyed* (Ps. 18:43–44). And he came from a village. What is called a village in Latin [*villa*] is called a 'pagos' in Greek. Hence he who comes from a village is one who came from paganism.

And it is also fitting that it says, ***of Cyrene***, which means 'inheritance of a reward'; *ask of me, and I will give you the gentiles for your inheritance* (Ps. 2:8 DRB). And when it says that they forced him, it signifies those who bear the cross exteriorly; but interiorly they bear it as one who is forced, for they do it not for God's sake, but for the world's. *Those who belong to Christ Jesus have crucified the flesh with its passions and vices* (Gal. 5:24).

2358 Next, the place is set down: ***They came to the place that is called Golgotha, which is the place of the skull.*** Among men, a skull is something said to be stripped bare, as is clear in cemeteries. Hence in Greek it is called 'kranios.'

---

3. Jerome, *Commentary on Matthew* 27.32.

4. Origen, *Commentary on Matthew*, series 126.

And some say that Adam was buried in that place. Jerome disproves this, since he was buried in Hebron (Josh. 14).[5] And why did he suffer there? One should note that in any city there is a certain place where the condemned are usually tormented: hence it was the place of the condemned.

2359 Then what was done at his crucifixion is recounted. And *first*, his drink; *second*, his crucifixion; *third*, other things which were done. And concerning the *first*: *first*, what was offered is set down; *second*, how he dealt with the thing offered.

2360 It says therefore, ***They gave him wine to drink mixed with gall.*** They wanted all his senses to suffer: his vision suffered by spittle and wakefulness, his hearing by blasphemies and mocking words, his touch because he was scourged; so they desired that his taste should also suffer. And what is said in the Psalm was fulfilled: *They gave me gall for my food, and in my thirst they gave me vinegar to drink* (Ps. 69:21 DRB); and, *How then are you turned unto me into that which is good for nothing, O strange vineyard?* (Jer. 2:21 DRB).

But there is a question, for it says that they gave him wine mixed with myrrh (Mark 15:23). One should say that myrrh is most bitter, and wine mixed with gall is bitter. But usually everything bitter is named under the species of gall. So in fact it was wine mixed with myrrh, but it is named by a likeness to gall. And this signified that he bore the bitterness of our sins.

2361 After this, how he dealt with it is set down: ***When he had tasted, he would not drink.*** But why does Mark say that he did not take it, while here it says that he tasted it? One can say that he only took it to taste it. And this signifies that he tasted death: for he quickly arose, and hardly seemed dead, because he was *free among the dead* (Ps. 88:5).

2362 ***And after they had crucified him.*** But one can ask why he wished to die by this death rather than another. One reason is on the side of those who crucified him, that they wanted him to be defamed by this, in accord with *Let us condemn him to a shameful death* (Wis. 2:20), and this is the death of the cross. Also, on the part of God's decree, for Christ willed to be our teacher, that he might give us an example of suffering death. For he suffered death that he might free us through death, as is said (Heb. 2:14). But there are many who are quite willing to suffer death but flee from a base death; so the Lord gave an example, lest they should flee from any kind of death.

Likewise, it fits with the redemption, because he died as satisfaction for the sin of the first man: but the first man sinned on a tree; for this reason, the Lord willed to suffer on a tree. *Blessed is the wood, by which righteousness comes* (Wis. 14:7). Also, Christ was to be exalted through his suffering, so he willed to be lifted up by suffering on the cross. Again, he willed to draw our hearts to

5. Jerome, *Commentary on Matthew* 27.33.

himself; *I, when I am lifted up from the earth, will draw all men to myself* (John 12:32). Again, that our hearts might be raised up.

2363 ***They divided his garments.*** Here are set down the things which were done as an insult to the crucified one. And *first*, the division of his garments is set down; *second*, the placing of a title over him; *third*, the association.

2364 Concerning the *first*: *first*, he sets down the deed; *second*, a prophecy. He says therefore, ***they divided.*** Chrysostom says that this was done as a great disparagement.[6] For usually a condemned man was only stripped if he was a most vile man: so, to inflict a great insult on him, they stripped him, that we might learn that we should strip ourselves of every effect of carnal acts.

Matthew passes over when this was done, but John recounts that each soldier took his own part of the other garment; but they cast lots over the seamless tunic (19:23).

2365 Then a prophecy is set down: ***that it might be fulfilled what was spoken by the prophet.*** The ***that*** is not set down causatively, but consecutively, for when Christ suffered it happened that what had been said was fulfilled. ***And they sat and watched him***, namely so that he would not be buried; *they stare and gloat over me* (Ps. 22:17).

2366 Then there follows the title: ***They put over his head, his cause written.*** And one should note carefully that what they did in order to shame him fell to his honor. Hence ***they put . . . his cause***, i.e., the cause for which he suffered; it is found written, *King of kings and Lord of lords* (Rev. 19:16). Therefore, when it says, ***KING OF THE JEWS***, this pertains to his honor, because he was going to be king over all nations; *but I am appointed king by him over Zion his holy mountain* (Ps. 2:6 DRB).

2367 Then his company is set down: ***Then there were crucified with him two thieves.*** These were his company, because he was in the middle of two thieves as though an evildoer; hence, *[he] was numbered with the transgressors* (Isa. 53:12). But one was at his right, the other at his left. He took up the cross as a judge: for just as in a judgment one is at the right and the other at the left, so it is here. Hence this signifies the judge of the living and the dead; *God has highly exalted him and bestowed on him the name which is above every name, that at the name of Jesus every knee should bow, in heaven and on earth and under the earth* (Phil. 2:9); *you are full of judgment on the wicked; judgment and justice seize you* (Job 36:17). Likewise, the fact that one was at the right and the other at the left signifies that Christ suffered for all; yet some believe, and some do not. *But we preach Christ crucified, unto the Jews indeed a stumbling block, and unto the gentiles foolishness* (1 Cor. 1:23). Or, it can be said that some suffer the

6. John Chrysostom, *Homilies on the Gospel of Saint Matthew* 87.

cross for God's sake, and these are at the right; while others suffer the cross not for God's sake, but for the world's sake, and these are at the left.

2368 Then he treats of the mockery of the crucified one: ***Those that passed by, blasphemed him, wagging their heads***; and *first*, he treats of what the people did; *second*, of what the rulers did; *third*, of what the thieves did.

Concerning the *first*: *first*, he describes the blasphemers; *second*, the blasphemies.

2369 *First* therefore he describes them, at ***those who passed by***, i.e., those going along the road. About such men it says, *Turn aside from the path, let us hear no more of the Holy One of Israel* (Isa. 30:11). Likewise, they are described at ***wagging their heads***: and they did this for mockery. The head signifies reason, and the feet signify the affections; hence first they moved their affections, then they moved their heads, because they are made foolish in sins.

2370 They laugh at him for three things. *First*, for words; *second*, for the works he did; *third*, for the dignity which he claimed for himself.

About the *first*, it says, ***vah, you who destroy the temple of God. Vah*** is an interjection of derision. For he was already well known, and they did not want to believe; hence Jeremiah says about them, *They hold fast to deceit; they refuse to return* (8:5). As though to say: 'if you wish to rebuild the temple, rebuild yourself'; but he could not have rebuilt unless he had first been destroyed; so he first willed that he be destroyed, because he had said this about the temple of his own body.

Then over the work: ***save your own self***, as though to say: 'you save others, save yourself. But you did not truly save others, nor can you save yourself.'

Likewise, over the dignity: ***If you are the Son of God, come down from the cross.*** This conditional statement is not a good one, but rather on the contrary, if he is the Son of God, he should be obedient to the Father. For he was *obedient unto death* (Phil. 2:8). Likewise, they should rather say that: if you are the Son of God, ascend, and not ***come down***; *no one has ascended into heaven but he who descended from heaven, the Son of man* (John 3:13). They use the same words which the devil used when tempting him: ***If you are the Son of God, throw yourself down*** (Matt. 4:6). For it does not belong to the Son of God to come down: hence the devil was speaking by way of persuasion, desiring to obstruct his passion.

2371 Then there follows the chief priests' mockery: ***in like manner also the chief priests . . . mocking.*** Hence not only the people, but even the chief priests were mocking him. Some are not disturbed if they are condemned by the least of men, but they cannot endure the scorn of the great. For man naturally desires to be honored, and honor comes in testimony to virtue; hence ridicule comes due to disgrace. And these men are described by authority, ***the chief priests.***

Likewise by teaching, ***the scribes.*** Likewise, by life, since they were Pharisees, who were pre-eminent in life; *"I will go to the great and will speak to them, for they know the way of the Lord, the law of their God." But they alike had broken the yoke, they had burst the bonds* (Jer. 5:5).

And they say three things: *first,* they scoff at the miracles he did; *second,* his kingly dignity; *third,* that he made himself the Son of God.

2372 As regards the *first,* they say: ***He saved others; himself he cannot save.*** They wished to say: if he saved others, he would have been able to save himself; but he cannot save himself, therefore neither did he save others. But we should argue the other way around: he saved others, therefore he can save himself; but he was able to save himself by rising again, therefore he was also able to save us. *He became, to all who obey him, the cause of eternal salvation* (Heb. 5:9). For these men meant nothing but temporal salvation, while Christ wished to show that eternal salvation should be put first; hence they say, ***If he is the king of Israel, let him now come down from the cross.***

2373 Here they scoff at his kingly dignity, and they make a false promise, and draw a false consequence. For if he is the king of Israel, he should not come down, because he should ascend through the cross; *the Lord has reigned from the wood* (Ps. 96:10), and *the government,* i.e., the cross, *will be upon his shoulder* (Isa. 9:6). Likewise, he did something greater, for he rose from the grave, and yet they did not believe; hence they were lying. *Do not listen to the words of the prophets who prophesy to you, filling you with vain hopes,* and there follows, *they speak visions of their own minds* (Jer. 23:16).

2374 Likewise, they scoff at the fact that he called himself the Son of God: ***He trusted in God; let him now deliver him if he will have him.*** *He committed his cause to the Lord, let him deliver him; let him rescue him, for he delights in him* (Ps. 22:8). He could have freed him, if he wished; but he did not want to, for he wanted to abandon him to death for a time, that he might gain salvation for us, and honor for himself. Hence what is said, was fulfilled: *All of them curse me* (Jer. 15:10).

2375 ***And with the same thing the thieves who were crucified with him also reproached him.*** But why does it say here that both scoffed at him, while in Luke it says that only one did? (Luke 23:39). Augustine resolves it, saying that sometimes it is the custom in the Scriptures that the plural is set down instead of the singular, as, *the prophets . . . stopped the mouths of lions* (Heb. 11:33), i.e., he *stopped the mouths,* namely Daniel.[7] And this is a common way of speaking, as it is said that "these peasants have harassed me," even if only one is thus harassing him. This is how Matthew speaks. Or in another way, according to Jerome, that both scoffed at him at first, but one, seeing the miracles he

7. Augustine, *Agreement among the Evangelists* 3.16.

was working, repented.[8] And this, as Chrysostom says, was done by divine arrangement.[9] Hence it signifies those who turn back to Christ after many sins.

2376 ***Now from the sixth hour there was darkness over the whole earth.*** Above, the Evangelist recounted how the Lord suffered on the cross; here, how he worked great things. And *first,* he sets down the things he worked before death; *second,* the things he worked after death, at ***Jesus again crying with a loud voice, yielded up the spirit.***

Concerning the *first,* he does two things: *first,* he recounts darkness falling; *second,* the cry, at ***and about the ninth hour Jesus cried.***

2377 It says therefore, ***From the sixth hour there was darkness over the whole earth.*** As Origen recounts, gentiles hearing the Evangelist recount this as a miracle laughed at him and said that this had happened naturally;[10] for this reason they thought that he spoke as one ignorant, since the sun suffered naturally. But this was not a natural eclipse, but a miraculous one. But if you wish to see, hear what Dionysius says, who was twenty-five years old, and studying the heavenly bodies in the city of Heliopolis.[11] And when they saw it, they marveled, he and Apollonius; and it seemed to them that it was not natural, and they carefully examined four miracles.

First, on the part of the time, for when it was the day on which the Pasch was supposed to take place, it was the fifteenth moon, where the moon stands opposite to the sun; but a natural eclipse comes from a conjoining of the moon to the sun. The *second* miracle was that when the sun is in the west, the moon should be in the east; but here the course of the moon was changed. Likewise a *third* sign is that darkening always begins from the western side, because all the planets have a double motion, their own proper motion and a common one. The moon is faster as regards its own proper motion, and when it approaches the body of the sun, it comes from the west; but it was not so here, for it came from the east. The *fourth* miracle was that a darkening of the sun begins, and the illumination returns from the same part; but this did not happen then, for the part it occupied first was the part it left last, for the moon came from the east up to the sun's body, and then went backwards, hence that part was the first to be illuminated again. And this is why, considering these things, when Paul came, he converted himself and later converted his companion. The *fifth* miracle, which as he says is greater, is that when there is a natural eclipse, it lasts only a little while: for the sun does not suffer, but rather a darkening is caused by the interposition of the moon; but the moon's body is not bigger

8. Jerome, *Commentary on Matthew* 27.44.

9. John Chrysostom, *Homilies on the Gospel of Saint Matthew* 87.

10. Origen, *Commentary on Matthew,* series 134.

11. Pseudo-Dionysius, "Letter Seven: to Polycarp" 2.

than the sun's, so it has no delay. But this one went on for three hours, and so it was a great miracle.

2378 But Origen asks: *If this was such a great miracle, why does not any astronomer describe it?* He responded, and said that this darkening was not universal, but around the land of Judea.[12] Or, it says, ***over the whole earth***, namely Judea. A similar way of speaking is when it says, *There is no nation or kingdom, where my lord has not sent to seek you* (1 Kings 18:10), for it should be understood as about this nation; so it is here. But Chrysostom says that it is understood as ***over the whole earth***, i.e., over the whole world, because he died for the whole world;[13] so he willed to make it known to all through a sign of the passion. But Dionysius says that he was in Egypt, and he himself saw it, and so he could know that it reached all the way to Asia; hence one should believe him more.[14]

A certain astronomer does tell of a certain eclipse which happened at the time of Tiberius, but he does not say when, or how long it lasted, or the manner of it; yet one can say that, since it was not then the time for an eclipse, he did not consider carefully the manner. Hence some have said that many clouds were positioned between us and the sun; but others have said the sun withdrew its rays, hence, *I will make the sun go down at noon* (Amos 8:9).

2379 But there is a question, because it says here that he was crucified in the sixth hour, while Mark says it was the third hour (15:25). One should say that Matthew recounts the history, because he was crucified in the sixth hour, and died in the ninth hour. And this pertains to a mystery, for at noon the sun is in the middle of the sky; and so it befits the Son of God, who is the true sun. *For you who fear my name the sun of righteousness shall rise* (Mal. 4:2). Likewise it fits with the first man's transgression, for Adam sinned after noon (Gen. 3:8); so Christ willed to make satisfaction in that hour.

2380 Why then does Mark say that it was in the third hour? One should say that he was crucified in the third hour by the tongue of the Jews, but in the sixth hour by the hands of the soldiers. Likewise, there was darkness for three hours, and it was prefigured by what is written, that *Moses stretched out his hands to the sky for three hours, and a darkness was cast over the whole land of Egypt for three days* (Exod. 10:22). Thus Christ spread out his hands on the cross, and a darkness was cast for three hours, to signify that they were deprived of the light of the Trinity.

2381 ***And about the ninth hour Jesus cried with a loud voice.*** Here he sets down Christ's cry. And *first*, the cry is set down; *second*, the effect, at ***and some who stood there.***

12. Origen *Commentary on Matthew*, series 134.

13. John Chrysostom, *Homilies on the Gospel of Saint Matthew* 88.

14. Pseudo-Dionysius, "Letter Seven: to Polycarp" 2.

2382 It says therefore, ***About the ninth hour Jesus cried with a loud voice.*** According to Origen, Christ cries out in a loud voice, and signifies a multitude of mysteries.[15] *One cried to another and said: holy, holy, holy, is the Lord of hosts* (Isa. 6:3). Hence the one who wants to take it that he cried out from a weariness of death has not understood the mystery. So one should not understand it this way, but since he willed it to be understood that he is equal to the Father, he said in the Hebrew language, ***Eli, Eli, lamma sabacthani?*** Also, because he willed to signify that he was foretold by the prophets, and so he spoke the words of the Psalm: *My God, my God, why have you forsaken me?* (Ps. 22:1). Hence Jerome says that they are impious who wish to explain this Psalm otherwise than about Christ's passion.[16]

2383 Note that some have understood this badly. Hence you should know that there have been two heresies. There was one which did not hold that the Word was united in Christ, but that the Word stood in place of a soul; and Arius held this. But there was another, that the Word was not united naturally, but through grace, as in any just man, as in the prophets; and this is what Nestorius said. Whence they explained ***My God, my God, why have you forsaken me?*** They say that the Word of God said this, and he calls him God, because he is his creature, and he laments because the Word united this creature to himself, and then abandoned him. But this is an impious explanation, because he is always with him; hence the divinity left neither the body nor the soul. Hence, *He who sent me, is with me* (John 8:29).

What then? One should say that it is clear from the very manner of speaking that it should be understood as about Christ, for John says of him: *I ascend to my Father and to your Father, to my God and your God* (20:17). He calls him Father, because he is God; he calls him God, because he is man. And so when he says, ***my God, my God***, it is clear that he speaks according as he is a man; this is why he repeats it, to indicate the magnitude of human feeling. And when he says, ***why have you forsaken me***, he speaks by way of similitude, because what we have, we have from God; hence just as when someone is exposed to an evil, he is called abandoned, in the same way when the Lord has left a man to fall into the evil of punishment, or of guilt, he is called abandoned. So Christ is called ***forsaken*** not as regards the union, nor as regards grace, but as regards the passion; *for a brief moment I forsook you* (Isa. 54:7). And he says, ***why?*** not as though out of weariness, but it can indicate his compassion for the Jews. Hence he only said it after there was darkness; so he wishes to say: why have you willed that I should be handed over to suffering, and that these men should be darkened? Likewise, it indicates astonishment, for the charity

15. Origen, *Commentary on Matthew*, series 135.

16. Jerome, *Commentary on Matthew* 27.46.

of God is astonishing. *God shows his love for us in that while we were yet sinners Christ died for us* (Rom. 5:8).

2384 Then there follows the effect: ***and some who stood there.*** And *first,* he sets down the effect common on all; *second,* the effect on one of them, at ***and immediately one of them, running.***

2385 It says then, ***Some who stood there and heard, said, "This man calls Elijah."*** Who were these men? Jerome believes that these were the soldiers, who did not know the Hebrew language, and owing to this thought that he called Elijah, because Elijah was very famous, since he was caught up into heaven (2 Kings 2:11).[17] Or, one can say that these men were Jews, and wished to show by this that Christ is a man, and not God, because he begs for the help of another.

2386 Then the effect on one man is described: and *first,* it says what he himself did; *second,* what the others did. It says therefore, ***Immediately one of them, running, took a sponge, and filled it with vinegar.*** It does not say here why he did this, but in John it says that Christ, seeing that everything was finished, said: *I thirst* (19:28). So this man, wishing to satisfy him, gave him the drink of the condemned. Hence what is said in the Psalm was fulfilled: *They gave me gall for my food, and in my thirst they gave me vinegar to drink* (Ps. 69:21 DRB).

2387 One should note that it was wine mixed with myrrh, but it is called gall, or vinegar, because it is bitter. Mystically, the wine mixed with myrrh signifies those who have nothing of the faith. Or vinegar, which comes from the corruption of wine, signifies the corruption of human nature. And Christ drank this bitterness. Or, the vinegar signifies the Jews' malice. And it is put in a sponge, which is porous, and signifies the carefulness and cunning of the Jews. But he put it on a reed. The reed signifies the Sacred Scriptures; hence they wish to support their malice with Scripture.

And it can be that this man was moved by compassion; hence this man wished to give him help, while the others did not wish to, and so they said: ***Wait, let us see whether Elijah will come to deliver him.***

2388 ***And Jesus again crying with a loud voice, yielded up the spirit.*** Here he treats of those things which were done after his death. And *first,* Christ's death is set down; *second,* the things which were done; *third,* the effect. The *second* is at ***Behold the veil of the temple was rent in two***; the *third,* at ***now the centurion.***

Concerning the *first,* he touches on the death, and the manner of the death.

2389 Three reasons are given for the death. One reason was to show how much he loved us. Augustine: *There is no greater reason for love than to be preceded in loving.*[18] *God shows his love for us in that while we were yet sinners Christ died for us* (Rom. 5:8). Likewise, to teach us to despise death. Through death he

17. Jerome, *Commentary on Matthew* 27.47.

18. Augustine, *Instructing Beginners in Faith* 4.

destroyed all sins. Likewise, to bear the penalty of Adam's sin, namely that he might free us from Adam's sin. For it was said to him, *In the day that you eat of it you shall die* (Gen. 2:17); he freed us from this death. Likewise since the devil, who is the wielder of death, attacked him who had not deserved it, he lost his power over others; this is why he handed his soul over to death, that he might free us.

2390 Likewise, the condition of the death is indicated: ***Jesus again crying with a loud voice, yielded up the spirit.*** Some have said that the divinity had died; but this is false, because life cannot die, and God is not only living, but also life. Some have said that the soul died with the body: but this cannot be, because then it could not lay hold of immortality.

Also, one should note that all men die by necessity, but Christ by his own will. Hence it does not say 'he died,' but rather he ***yielded up***, because it was by will, and this indicates power, as is said in another place, *I have power to lay it down, and I have power to take it again* (John 10:18).

And he willed to die ***with a loud voice*** to indicate that he died by his power, and not out of necessity: for he laid down his soul when he willed, and he took it up when he willed. So it was easier for Christ to lay down his soul and to take it up than for someone else to sleep and wake up. But why was it blamed on them? Because they did what was in them.

2391 ***And behold the veil of the temple was rent in two.*** In this part, he treats of the effect: *first*, he treats of the things done concerning the temple; *second*, of the things done in the elements; *third*, of the things done in men.

2392 And it seems that Matthew tells things in an order different from what Luke says (Luke 23:44). Augustine says that Matthew recounts the order of history; and this is clear, because he says, ***Behold the veil of the temple was rent in two.***[19] But in Luke no such thing is found.[20]

And one should note that there were two veils in the temple, as in the tabernacle, for there was a veil inside the holy of holies, and there was another veil which was not in the holies. And these two signified a double veiling, for the interior veiling signified the veiling of the heavenly mysteries, which will be revealed to us: for then we will be like him, when he appears in his glory. The other, which was exterior, signified the veiling of the mysteries which pertain to the Church. Hence this exterior one was split in two, not the other, to signify that those mysteries which pertain to the Church were manifested through Christ's death; but the other was not divided, because the heavenly secrets still

---

19. Augustine, *Agreement among the Evangelists* 19.56.

20. Here St. Thomas is *not* saying that there is no reference to the rending of the temple veil in Luke. Rather, although it is somewhat unclear here, when he says, "in Luke no such thing is found," he is speaking of the Matthean phrase ***and behold***, which Augustine sees as an indication of Matthew's intent to preserve a chronological ordering in his presentation of the Passion events.

remain veiled. Hence the Apostle: *When a man turns to the Lord, the veil is removed* (2 Cor. 3:16). Hence through the passion all the mysteries which were written in the law and the prophets were opened, as is said, *Beginning with Moses and all the prophets, he interpreted to them in all the Scriptures the things concerning himself* (Luke 24:27).

Or, it signified the dispersion of the Jewish people. And since their glory was in the veil that was torn in two during the Lord's passion, it signified that the whole glory was cut off from them.

2393 ***And the earth quaked, and the rocks were rent.*** Above was set down the miracle which was worked concerning the sacred temple; here he sets down the miracle which was worked concerning the elements. And these things are found to be fitting: *first*, as regards the power of the passion; *second*, as regards the effect of salvation; *third*, as regards the judicial power which Christ merited by suffering.

It is fitting that ***the earth quaked*** because it cannot endure the presence of such great majesty without trembling; hence, he *looks on the earth, and it trembles* (Ps. 104:32). ***And the rocks were rent***, which signified that no power can resist him; *and behold the Lord passed by, and a great strong wind rent the mountains and broke in pieces the rocks* (1 Kings 19:11). ***And the graves were opened.*** Graves are enclosures for dead bodies. Hence it signifies that he burst the bonds of death; *O death, I will be your death; O hell, I will be your bite* (Hos. 13:14 DRB). Likewise, *death is swallowed up in victory* (1 Cor. 15:54).

Likewise, it is fitting as regards the effect. The earth quakes when any part of the earth is thrown down. *You have moved the earth and have troubled it: heal you the breaches thereof, for it has been moved* (Ps. 60:2). Similarly, rocks are broken when hardness of heart is moved to compassion; *is not my word*, namely about the passion, *like fire . . . and like a hammer which breaks the rock in pieces?* (Jer. 23:29). Similarly, that graves were opened signifies that those who are dead in sin should rise again; *Awake, O sleeper, and arise from the dead* (Eph. 5:14).

Likewise it fits with his coming for judgment, for when he comes the earth will be shaken; *in a little while, and I will shake the heavens and the earth* (Hag. 2:7). Again, the rocks are broken, because the loftiness of men is humbled. Also, the graves are opened, because the dead will rise for the judgment; *the hour is coming, when all who are in the tombs will hear his voice* (John 5:28).

2394 Next he treats of the miracle in men. And *first*, he touches on the resur-
2395 rection; *second*, the manifestation. It says therefore, ***Many bodies of the saints who had slept arose.***

There is usually a question about these people, whether they rose again and died again, or did not die. It is agreed that some have arisen and later died, like Lazarus. But one can say about these people that they rose and did not die again, because they rose for the manifestation of Christ's resurrection, and it is certain that *Christ, being raised from the dead, will never die again* (Rom. 6:9). Also, if they had risen only to die again, it would not have been a kindness shown them but rather an injury; therefore they rose to enter into heaven with Christ.

2396 ***And coming out of the tombs after his resurrection, came into the holy city.*** And one should note that although this was said in the description of Christ's death, yet one should understand that it was said by way of anticipation, because it was done after the resurrection; for Christ is *the firstborn of the dead* (Rev. 1:5).

And they came ***into the holy city,*** not because it was holy now, but because it had been before: *How the faithful city has become a harlot, she that was full of justice!* (Isa. 1:21). Or, it is called holy because holy things were done there. Or, following Jerome, ***into the holy city,*** namely the heavenly city, because they went with Christ into glory.[21] ***And appeared to many.*** For just as Christ has the power of manifesting himself to whom he wishes, so it should be understood with glorified bodies.

2397 ***Now the centurion.*** Here he treats of the effect of the miracles. And *first*, on the gentiles; *second*, on the women, at ***There were there many women afar off.***

2398 Concerning the *first*, he does three things. *First*, their diligent consideration is set down; *second*, their fear; *third*, their true confession of the faith, which came from fear.

It says therefore, ***Now the centurion and they who were with him watching Jesus, having seen the earthquake, and the things that were done, were much afraid.*** In Luke, it says that this man was terrified by the fact that Christ expired while crying out (Luke 23:42); but here it says that it was after ***having seen the earthquake.*** And Augustine says that this would not be easy to resolve if it did not say, ***and the things that were done.***[22] Now, this man signified the gentile people, who confessed the Lord with a healthy fear; hence, *I will say to that which is not my people, "you are my people," and they will say, "you are my God"* (Hos. 2:24 DRB). *We have conceived by your face, O Lord, and we have born a spirit of salvation* (Isa. 26:18).[23]

Then the true confession is set down, at ***Indeed this was the Son of God.*** By this Arius is confounded, who does not confess that he is truly the Son of

---

21. Jerome, *Commentary on Matthew* 27.52–53.

22. Augustine, *Agreement among the Evangelists* 3.20.

23. This quotation of Isaiah 26:18 differs significantly from both the DRB and RSV-CE, the latter of which says "We were with child, we writhed, we have as it were brought forth wind. We have no deliverance in the earth, and the inhabitants of the world have not fallen."

God while he is in heaven, whom the centurion confessed while he was dead; *this is the true God and life eternal* (1 John 5:20).

2399 There follows the women's devotion: ***There were there many women.*** And *first,* they are described with respect to the past, and with respect to the present. In which one should consider that when the people drew back, the women clung to him, so that what is said in Isaiah was fulfilled: *I came, and there was not a man* (50:2 DRB).

2400 But one should consider that it says here that they stood ***afar off.*** Now, John says that they were *standing by the cross of Jesus* (19:25). Augustine says that one can say that there were some women there who were near, and some who were at a distance;[24] except it says it of both, because Mary Magdalene was one of them.[25]

So one should say otherwise, that just as many and few are said relatively, so are near and far: and just as the same thing can be called many and few with respect to different things, so it can be called near and far with respect to different things. Thus one should consider that the centurion and the gentiles were next to the cross; but the women were after them, and the crowds indeed further off. Hence they were near and far, according to different comparisons: far off in comparison to the centurion and the gentiles, but near in comparison to the crowds. Or one can say that at first they stood near, but when he sent forth the spirit, they stood at a distance.

2401 Also, notice that it says that they ***had followed Jesus from Galilee, ministering to him.*** For he to whom angels were ministering permitted that the women minister to him. By this he gave an example to the apostles who were following that they should accept temporal things from those to whom they were ministering spiritual things. And this was an ancient custom, that teachers received the necessary things from the good people whom they taught. But Paul, since he preached to the gentiles, among whom there was not this custom, did not wish to accept anything, lest it seem that he preached for money.

2402 ***Among whom was Mary Magdalene, and Mary the mother of James and Joseph.*** Helvidius took an occasion for error from these words, who said that Jesus was born from the seed of Joseph.[26] Jerome says to this that there were

---

24. Augustine, *Agreement among the Evangelists* 3.21.

25. Matthew and Mark name Mary Magdalene as one of the women standing at a distance from the cross, but John locates her near the cross. Following Augustine, St. Thomas explains the discrepancy by suggesting that she was "far off" in comparison to some (i.e., the centurion) but "near" in comparison to others.

26. Helvidius (not to be confused with the Stoic philosopher Helvidius Priscus) was a leading opponent of monastic celibacy in Rome during the late fourth century. In a now-lost treatise, Helvidius rejected the perpetual virginity of Mary, arguing that Mary engaged in sexual relations with Joseph after the birth of Jesus from which were born children who are referred to in the Gospels as the "brothers" of the Lord.

two Jameses: the Greater, who is called the brother of John, and the Lesser, who was the son of Alpheus, whose mother was also the mother of Joseph.[27] Hence the woman who was the mother of James the Greater was not the mother of James the Lesser, for it immediately adds ***and the mother of the sons of Zebedee.***

2403 But why does it say, *Mary of Cleophas*, and *Mary of Alpheus*?[28] Jerome resolves it, suggesting that it could have been that this Mary had a husband who had two names: hence he was called Cleophas and Alpheus.[29] Or, one can say that first she married Cleophas, and when he died she married Alpheus. Or, one can say that Cleophas was the father, and the mother was called Salome, because Mark says, *and Salome* (15:40); hence Salome is the name of a woman.

Hence the error of the Master in the gloss on the second chapter of Galatians is clear, that it was the name of a man.[30] And also the error of the teacher in the *History*, because in Greek it has *Salomei*, which is a feminine ending, which is never found in the masculine.

2404 ***And when it was evening.*** In this part, *first*, he treats of the burial; *second*, of the veneration; *third*, of the watch. The *second* is at ***Joseph taking the body, wrapped it up in a clean linen cloth***; the *third*, at ***and the next day.***

Concerning the *first*: *first*, he sets down the condition of the one who buried
2405 him; *second*, his request. Four conditions are set down; hence ***when it was evening***, for it was necessary that the body be removed, so it would not remain on the Sabbath, ***There came a certain rich man of Arimathea.*** And he is described by resources, ***rich***; *blessed is the rich man who is found without blemish, and who does not go after gold, nor put his trust in money nor in treasures* (Sir. 31:8).

But why does he call him rich? One should say that he does not say this for the sake of his praise or boasting, but in this connection, that he was able to obtain the body from Pilate, which one poor man could not have done.

Likewise, he is described by homeland, ***of Arimathea***, which is the same as Rama, which was Samuel's city of residence. And it means 'exalted,' and this man was exalted. Likewise by name, ***Joseph***, which means 'increasing.'

27. Jerome, *On the Perpetual Virginity of the Blessed Mary* 12.

28. To clarify, a "Mary of Cleophas" is referenced as present at the cross only in John (19:25) whereas "Mary of Alpheus" appears only in the synoptics (Matt. 3:18; Luke 6:15) but not in the crucifixion scene.

29. See, Jerome, *On the Perpetual Virginity of the Blessed Mary* 13. Jerome in fact does not go so far as to suggest that Mary's husband had two names (although this is surely possible). His point is rather that Mary seems to go by two names. He suggests, moreover, that "Mary of Cleophas" is so surnamed by John "after her father or some relationship of her family or for some other reason" (Jerome, 13).

30. "The Master" is St. Thomas' standard epithet for Peter Lombard. The passage to which St. Thomas refers appears to be from his commentary on the first chapter of Galatians, the Latin text of which is published in Patrologia Latina 192:101d.

Likewise, by religion, ***who himself was also a disciple of Jesus***, for he had not fallen away from the faith; *if you continue in my word, you are truly my disciples* (John 8:31).

2406 Then he treats of the obtaining; and *first* the request is set down, *second* the obtaining. ***He went to Pilate and asked for the body of Jesus.*** And he is commended, for ***he went.*** There follows the obtaining: ***Then Pilate commanded***
2407 ***that the body should be delivered.*** There follows the description of the burial: ***Joseph, taking the body, wrapped it up in a clean linen cloth.*** And he treats of the veneration, and the burial.

Of the veneration: it was simple veneration, for it was a simple linen cloth. And for this reason, according to Jerome, veneration with excessively big sepulchers is censured.[31]

According to a mystery, this linen cloth signifies three things. *First,* it signifies the clean flesh of Christ: for it comes from flax, which is whitened by great pressure; thus the flesh of Christ through great pressure arrived at the radiance of the resurrection; *thus it is written that the Christ should suffer and on the third day rise from the dead* (Luke 24:46).

Or, it signifies the Church, which has neither spot nor wrinkle (Eph 5:27): and this is signified by the linen, which is woven together out of various fibers. Likewise, it signifies a clean conscience, where Christ rests.

2408 ***And laid it in his own new monument.*** And he says four things about this tomb. *First,* that it was his own. And it was fitting enough that the one who had died for the sins of others should be buried in the tomb of others. Also, he says, ***new,*** for if another body had been placed there, it would not be known who had risen. Also, he says that it was ***in a rock,*** not in a tomb built out of different stones, that every false accusation might be removed.

But why not under the ground? The reason was lest it should be thought that the disciples had dragged him out through caves in the ground. Also, he says that ***he rolled a great stone.*** And since it was big, it took more than a few men to roll it away, especially since there were guards.

2409 Then there follows the women's devotion. For the women, who were more ardent, followed him all the way to the tomb: hence it says, ***There was there Mary Magdalene, and the other Mary.*** And he does not mention Mary of Zebedee, who was not there, because she did not love as ardently.

2410 ***And the next day***; here he treats of the watch over the tomb: and he does three things: *first,* the request is set down; *second,* the consent; *third,* the execution of the request. Concerning the *first,* the time is set down; and the reason; and the request; and the threatening danger.

31. Jerome, *Commentary on Matthew* 27.59.

2411 The time: ***the next day, which followed the Day of Preparation***. 'Parasceves' means 'preparation.' For the Jews, who did nothing on the Sabbath, prepared on the day before, and for this reason it was called the Day of Preparation. For even though they might have some solemnity, still a greater observance belonged to the Sabbath, hence they prepared nothing on the Sabbath, due to the commandment, where the Lord commanded that Friday they should collect enough of the manna for two days (Exod. 16:22).

Then ***the chief priests and the Pharisees came together to Pilate***, for they intended to persecute [Jesus] greatly, for it was not enough to persecute him until death, but they intended to persecute him even after death; hence they desired to prevent the resurrection.

2412 But why did they come together? The reason follows: ***Lord, we have remembered, that that seducer said . . .*** They call him a ***seducer***; hence John says that some of them were saying that he is good, but others that he is not, but rather he seduces the crowds (7:12). ***After three days I will rise again***. They knew this from what he had said before, that ***as Jonah was three days and three nights in the belly of the whale, so will the Son of man be three days and three nights in the heart of the earth*** (Matt. 12:40). And the part is put down for the whole, as was explained above.

2413 Likewise, the request is set down: ***Command therefore that the sepulcher be guarded***. The very zeal of the Jews is profitable for us, for certitude: hence the more they meant to do harm, the more they were profitable for the salvation of those who believe. *Who catches the wise in their craftiness* (Job 5:13), because the Lord turns what they intend into something else.

2414 Then the intention behind the request is set down: ***lest perhaps his disciples come and steal him away and say to the people, "He is risen from the dead."*** And in this they prophesied, and so they sinned the more, for they had seen marvelous things, and yet did not believe that he could rise again.

2415 The consent follows: ***Pilate said to them: you have a guard***, i.e., you should
2416 have guard, as though to say, 'it is on you to guard him.' There follows the execution: ***Departing, they made the sepulcher sure, sealing the stone, and setting guards***. Hence it was not enough that they should place guards around, but they also sealed it. Nor was it enough for them that the soldiers should do this, but they even sealed it themselves; *a company of evildoers encircle me* (Ps. 22:16).

Hebrews 2:14–18

Christ's Triumph in Death

On Hebrews 2.4 (136–154)

2:14 ***Therefore because the children are partakers of flesh and blood, he also himself in like manner has been partaker of the same: that, through death, he might destroy him who had the empire of death, that is to say, the devil:***

2:15 ***And might deliver them, who through the fear of death were all their lifetime subject to servitude.***

2:16 ***For nowhere does he take hold of the angels: but of the seed of Abraham he takes hold.***

2:17 ***Wherefore, it behooved him in all things to be made like unto his brethren, that he might become a merciful and faithful high priest before God, that he might be a propitiation for the sins of the people.***

2:18 ***For in that wherein he himself has suffered and been tempted he is able to succor them also that are tempted.***

136 Having shown the suitability of Christ's death from the standpoint of the Father causing it, the Apostle now shows the same thing from the standpoint of Christ enduring it.[32] Therefore, he intends to show how he was made the author of salvation by his passion.

And concerning this, he does three things. *First,* he shows the condition of the nature through which he could suffer and die; *second,* the benefits he obtained by dying, at ***that, through death***; *third,* he proves what he had proposed, at ***for nowhere does he take hold.***

137 He says, therefore, I have said that he and the children have all one origin and that he called them brethren. Consequently, it was fitting that he be like them, not only because he confers on them a participation in the divine nature, which is from grace, but also because he assumed their nature. Hence, he says, ***Because the children are partakers of flesh and blood, he also himself in like manner has been partaker of the same.***

138 Here it should be noted that by the name flesh and blood is sometimes understood the nature of flesh and blood: *This is now bone of my bones and flesh*

32. See Thomas Aquinas, *On Hebrews* 2.3 (not included in this collection).

of my flesh (Gen. 2:23); then by flesh is understood the body: *You did clothe me with skin and flesh* (Job 10:11) and by blood, the soul: not as though the soul were blood, but because it is not preserved in the body without blood. Sometimes by flesh and blood are understood the vices of flesh and blood: *Flesh and blood has not revealed this to you* (Matt. 16:17).

But sometimes they signify the corruptibility of flesh and blood: *Flesh and blood cannot inherit the kingdom of God, nor does the perishable inherit the imperishable* (1 Cor. 15:50). But here it does not refer to vices, for Christ assumed a nature without sin, but with the possibility of suffering, because he assumed a flesh similar to the sinner: *in the likeness of sinful flesh* (Rom. 8:3). Therefore, like the children, he is partaker of flesh and blood, and all in the same way: for it was not imaginary flesh, as the Manicheans say, nor was it assumed as an accident, as Nestorius said. But true flesh and blood, such as children have, were assumed into the unity of the person.

139 That Christ is a partaker of flesh and blood is not to be understood as referring to the vices of flesh and blood, because he did not take on sin or commit any, but as referring to the very substance of animated flesh, because he assumed flesh and soul. It also included the possibility of suffering because he assumed our nature capable of suffering. Therefore, the sense is: ***because the children***, i.e., the faithful, have a nature capable of suffering, Christ ***himself in like manner has been partaker of the same***; or ***the children***, namely, in the nature of flesh and blood; or ***the same***, i.e., of flesh and blood, not indeed, in appearance, as Mani said deliriously, nor in an accidental way, as Nestorius imagined, but ***in like manner***, namely, as us, that is, in the same way that we partake, that is, according to the truth of the thing, namely, in a personal and substantial way. For we partake of flesh and blood through our person; and Christ in like manner assumed them to his person: *The Word became flesh* (John 1:14). By flesh and blood can also be understood the flesh and blood of Christ according to the statement *he who eats my flesh and drinks my blood* (John 6:55), of which ***the children***, i.e., the apostles, partook at the last supper and of which Christ partook, as Chrysostom expressly says about Matthew 26: *He drank his own blood.*[33] Hence, *I have earnestly desired to eat this passover with you, before I suffer* (Luke 22:15).

140 Then, he shows the benefits his death brought when he says ***that through death he might destroy***. In regard to this he does two things. *First*, he shows its usefulness on the part of the devil, who had the power; *second*, on our part who
141 were held, at ***and might deliver them***. He says, therefore: he ***has been partaker*** of flesh and blood, i.e., he assumed a nature in which he could suffer and die,

33. John Chrysostom, *Homilies on the Gospel of Saint Matthew* 82.

which he could not do in the divine nature, ***that, through death, he might destroy him who had the empire of death, that is to say, the devil.***

But how does the devil have the power of death? For this is God's prerogative: *The Lord kills and brings to life* (1 Sam. 2:6); *I kill, and I make alive* (Deut. 32:39).

I answer that a judge has the power of death in one way, because he inflicts death, when he punishes with death; but a thief has it another way in the sense of deserving death because of demerit. God has the power of death in the *first* way: *In the day that you eat of it you shall die* (Gen. 2:17). But the devil in the *second* way, because by persuading man to sin, he yielded him over to death: *Through the devil's envy death entered the world* (Wis. 2:24).

But he says, that ***he might destroy him***, not as to his substance, which is indestructible, nor as to his malice, so that the devil would become good at some time (as Origen says), but as to his power.[34] *Now is the judgment of this world; now shall the prince of this world be cast out* (John 12:31). *He disarmed the principalities and powers* (Col. 2:15).

142 This was accomplished by the death of Christ in three ways: *first*, on the part of Christ, for the true nature of justice is that the victor subject the vanquished to himself: *Whatever overcomes a man, to that he is enslaved* (2 Pet. 2:19). But Christ overcame the devil: *The Lion of the tribe of Judah . . . has conquered* (Rev. 5:5). Therefore, it is just that the devil be subject to him: *When a strong man, fully armed, guards his own palace, his goods are in peace* (Luke 11:21).

Second, on the part of the devil: for justice requires that a person who unjustly uses power granted him should lose it. But the devil has been given power over the sinners he seduced, but not over the good. Therefore, because he presumed to extend this power even to Christ, who did not sin: *The ruler of this world is coming. He has no power over me* (John 14:30), he deserved to lose it.

The *third* reason is on our part: for it is just that the vanquished be the servants of the victor. But man by sin was the servant of the devil: *Everyone who commits sin is a slave to sin* (John 8:34); consequently, he was subject to the devil and liable to sin. But Christ paid the price for our sin: *What I did not steal must I now restore* (Ps. 69:4). Therefore, when the cause of servitude was taken away, man was set free by Christ.

143 But it should be noted that no other satisfaction was suitable. For man was in debt; but one man can satisfy for another out of charity, although no one can satisfy for the entire human race, because he does not have power over it, nor could the entire human race satisfy sufficiently, because it was entirely subject to sin; nor could an angel, because this satisfaction was unto glory, which exceeds the power of an angel. Therefore, it was necessary that the one

34. Origen, *On First Principles* 3.6.5.

who satisfied be man and God, who alone has power over the whole human race. By the death of God and man, therefore, he destroyed him who had the empire of death.

144 Then when he says ***and might deliver them***, another advantage on our part is mentioned. In regard to this it should be noted that a man is a servant of sin to the extent that he is induced to sin. But the most effective inducements to sin are the love of transitory goods and the fear of present punishments: *burned with fire* speaks to the first, and, *cut down*, to the second (Ps. 80:16).

But these two amount to the same thing, because the more a person loves something, the more he fears its evil contrary. These are the things by which man is bound and retained in sin; but he is moved more by fear than by love. Hence, we see that savage beasts are kept from the greatest pleasures through fear of punishment; and thus fear most of all binds men. Among all fears, however, the fear of death is the greatest. For it is the end of terrible things. Hence, if a man overcomes this fear, he overcomes all; and when fear is overcome, all disordered love of the world is overcome.

Thus Christ by his death broke this fear because he removed the fear of death, and consequently the love of the present life. For when a person considers that the Son of God, the Lord of death, willed to die, he no longer fears death. That is why before the death of Christ, it was said: *O death, how bitter is the remembrance of you* (Sir. 41:1); but after Christ's death the Apostle expresses *a desire to depart and be with Christ* (Phil. 1:23): Hence, we are told: *Do not fear those who kill the body* (Matt. 10:28).

He says, therefore, ***and might deliver them, who through the fear of death were all their lifetime***, as they were desiring too much, ***subject to servitude***,
145 namely, the servitude of sin. Or in another way: for man was subject to a double servitude, namely, that of the law and that of sin, since the law is called *a yoke . . . which neither our fathers nor we have been able to bear* (Acts 15:10); *and Moses' hands were heavy* (Exod. 17:12); *God sent forth his son . . . to redeem those who were under the law* (Gal. 4:5). For they were subject to the servitude to sin. Christ delivered us from that double servitude. Now the difference between the Old and the New Testament is fear and love. In the New, there is love: *If you love me, you will keep my commandments* (John 14:15). But the Old was the law of fear: *You did not receive the spirit of slavery to fall back into fear* (Rom. 8:15). Therefore, he says, ***and might deliver them, who through the fear of death***, bodily death, which the law inflicted, ***were all their lifetime subject to servitude.***

146 But why did he not free us at once from death but only from the fear of death? I answer that he freed us immediately from the cause of death, but not from death itself, although he freed us from the fear of death. The reason for this was that if he had freed us from bodily death, men would serve Christ

only for their bodily good, and then the merit of faith and hope would be destroyed. Furthermore, bodily evils enable us to merit eternal life: *Through many tribulations we must enter the kingdom of God* (Acts 14:21).

It should be noted that he freed us from the fear of death, *first* of all, by showing the immortality that awaited us. As a result, man could scorn temporal death: *Christ is risen from the dead, the firstfruits of those who sleep* (1 Cor. 15:20); *second*, by giving us a foretaste of death he made us more ready to undergo death for Christ: *Christ also suffered for you, leaving you an example* (1 Pet. 2:21). *Third*, by opening the gate to glory, which was closed before his death; as a result, we not only do not fear death, but we desire it: *My desire is to depart and be with Christ, for that is far better* (Phil. 1:23).

147 Then when he says ***for nowhere does he take hold***, the Apostle proves the benefits which Christ's death obtained. In regard to this he does three things: *first*, he shows that by his death Christ freed us by reason of the condition of the nature he assumed; *second*, he concludes a likeness, at ***wherefore, it behooved him***; *third*, he shows the benefit of the likeness, at ***that he might become***.

148 He says, therefore: so I have stated that Christ by his death freed us from sin and death. Nor is there any doubt that in regard to the condition of its nature an angel is greater than man; but because the angels were not subject to servitude or deserving of death, he did not assume an angel. But if he had, this would have been on account of the dignity of its nature. But we have never read that he assumed an angel, but only ***of the seed of Abraham***, i.e., a human nature, not in the abstract but in an individual, and from the seed of Abraham: *Jesus Christ . . . the son of Abraham* (Matt. 1:1). He adds this in order that the Jews, who glory in being of the seed of Abraham, might venerate Christ more.

But he says significantly ***take hold of***, because that is properly said to be taken hold of, which flees. But not only the human nature fled from God, but also the children of Abraham *refused to hearken and turned a stubborn shoulder* (Zech. 7:11). This taking hold of human nature unto the unity of the person of the Son of God exalts our nature beyond measure. Hence, Chrysostom says: *It is a great and marvelous thing for our flesh to be seated above and to be adored by angels and archangels. As I turn this over in my mind, I experience excessive joy, imagining great things about the human race.*[35]

149 But it would have seemed better to assume an angelic nature than a human nature. For likeness is the reason making the incarnation of a divine person fitting. But a more express likeness of God is found in the angelic nature than in the human, because the former is *the seal of resemblance* (Ezek. 28:12). Therefore, it would seem more fitting to take hold of an angel than of the seed of Abraham.

35. John Chrysostom, *Homilies on Hebrews* 5.

Furthermore, sin is found in the angelic nature as in the human nature: *In his angels he found wickedness* (Job 4:18 DRB). Therefore, if he took hold of human nature to free it from sin, it seems there was more reason to take hold of the angelic.

I answer that a nature is assumable by the Son of God depending on its fitness to be united to the person of the Word. But this fitness depends on the dignity, so that the nature is assumable which is likely to attain to the Word himself by knowing and loving him; and also depending on the need, in the sense that it is subject to a reparable sin. The first and second are found in human nature, which is capable of knowing and loving God, and which has a reparable sin; consequently, it is assumable. But although the first is found in an angelic nature, it lacks the second: for a sin is irreparable not by reason of its gravity, but by reason of the condition of the nature. But what death was to men, the fall was to the angels. But it is clear that all the sins of man, whether they be small or great, are reparable before death; after death they are irreparable and remain forever. Therefore, the angelic nature is not assumable. By this the solution to the objections is clear, for while there is a fitness of dignity in the angelic nature, nevertheless a fitness of necessity is lacking.

150 Then when he says ***wherefore, it behooved him in all things to be made like unto his brethren***, he concludes to a likeness. As if to say: 'therefore, because he did not assume an angel but the seed of Abraham, it behooved him in all things to become like unto his brethren. In all things, I say, in which they are brethren, not in guilt but in punishment. Therefore, it behooved him to have a nature that could suffer'; hence ***one tempted in all things as we are, without sin*** (Heb. 4:15). Likewise, they are brethren as to grace: *See what love the Father has given us, that we should be called children of God; and so we are* (1 John 3:1); *those whom he foreknew he also predestined to be conformed to the image of his Son* (Rom. 8:29).

151 Then he shows the usefulness of that resemblance when he says, ***that he might become a merciful and faithful high priest.*** Here he does two things: *First*, he mentions the likeness; *second*, he explains it, at ***for in that wherein.***

152 Christ as mediator has two functions: one sets him over the whole human race as judge: *The Father . . . has given him authority to execute judgment, because he is the Son of man* (John 5:26–27); the other is in relation to God, before whom he intercedes for us as our advocate because he attends before his face for us: ***always living to make intercession for us*** (Heb. 7:25); *we have an advocate with the Father, Jesus Christ the righteous* (1 John 2:1).

In a judge, mercy is desired particularly by the guilty; but in an advocate, fidelity. But the Apostle insinuates that these two qualities are in Christ during his passion. For mankind desired mercy in Christ, inasmuch as he is a judge, and fidelity in Christ, inasmuch as he is an advocate. And both of these qualities were exhibited by Christ during his passion. Hence, in regard to the first, he says that by his passion he was ***made like unto his brethren, that he might become a merciful and faithful high priest.***

153 But was he not merciful from all eternity? It seems so, because *his tender mercies are above all his works* (Ps. 145:9 DRB). Again, he had mercy from the beginning: *From my infancy mercy grew up with me* (Job 31:18 DRB).

I answer that mercy consists in having a heart grieved at another's misfortune: in one way, by merely recognizing the misfortune, which is the way God recognized our wretchedness without suffering, as it is said in the Psalm: *He knows our frame* (Ps. 103:14); in another way, by experiencing our misfortune, which is how Christ experienced our misery, especially during the passion.

And thus it is said that he who was merciful through apprehension of our misery was merciful by experience: *I shall cry out and say, here I am, because I the Lord your God am merciful* (Isa. 58:9). And thus it is, because he was merciful, as is clear concerning the woman caught in adultery. He taught mercy, *Blessed are the merciful* (Matt. 5:7). He commanded mercy: *I will have mercy, and not sacrifice* (Matt. 12:7 DRB). In addition, he is a faithful advocate.

Hence, he is called a ***faithful high priest***: ***Christ, taking the position of high priest of the good things to come*** (Heb. 9:11). And it is required that he be faithful: *It is required among the dispensers that a man be found faithful* (1 Cor. 4:2 DRB): and all this that he might be a propitiation for the sins of the people, for whom he willed to die.

154 Then when he says, ***for in that wherein***, he shows its utility. As if to say: 'I do not speak of Christ as God, but as man. Therefore, in that, i.e., in that nature which he assumed, in order to experience in himself that our cause is his own.' Hence he says, he ***has suffered and been tempted***; therefore, ***he is able to succor them also that are tempted.***

Or, another way: he became merciful and faithful because in suffering and being tempted he has a kinship to mercy. He says, ***tempted***, not by the flesh but by the enemy: *Jesus was led up by the spirit into the wilderness to be tempted by the devil* (Matt. 4:1). For in Christ there was no rebellion of the lower powers against the higher, but he suffered for us in the flesh: *Christ also suffered for you, leaving you an example that you should follow* (1 Pet. 2:21); *Christ suffered in the flesh, arm yourselves with the same thought* (1 Pet. 4:1).

Hebrews 9:23–28

Christ the High Priest and Sacrifice

On Hebrews 9.5 (461–478)

9:23 ***It is necessary therefore that the patterns of heavenly things should be cleansed with these: but the heavenly things themselves with better sacrifices than these.***

9:24 ***For Jesus is not entered into the holies made with hands, the patterns of the true: but into heaven itself, that he may appear now in the presence of God for us.***

9:25 ***Nor yet that he should offer himself often, as the high priest enters into the holies every year with the blood of others:***

9:26 ***For then he ought to have suffered often from the beginning of the world. But now once, at the end of ages, he has appeared for the destruction of sin by the sacrifice of himself.***

9:27 ***And as it is appointed unto men once to die, and after this the judgment:***

9:28 ***So also Christ was offered once to exhaust the sins of many. The second time he shall appear without sin to those who expect him unto salvation.***

461 Having shown what is common to the Old and New Testaments,[36] the Apostle now shows the difference between the two. In regard to this he does two things. *First*, he shows that there is a better cleansing in the New; *second*, that it is more complete, at ***nor yet that he should.***

In regard to the *first* he does two things. *First*, he shows that both as to what is cleansed and as to that by which the cleansing is effected, there is a better cleansing in the New; *second*, he clarifies what he has said, at ***for Jesus is not entered.***

462 He says, therefore, ***it is necessary therefore that the patterns of heavenly things***, namely, the tabernacle itself, which, so far as we are concerned, is a pattern, although, absolutely speaking, it is the thing exemplified and its figure, and, therefore, of less value, because the thing exemplified is superior to the figure, as the body is superior to its shadow: ***should be cleansed with these,***

36. See Thomas Aquinas, *On Hebrews* 9.4 (not included in this collection).

i.e., with the sacrifices. ***But the heavenly things themselves***, namely, the New Testament, ***with better sacrifices than these***: ***better***, because the others were cleansings with the blood of animals, but in the New Testament the cleansing is accomplished with the blood of Christ. Now better things are always cleansed with better things. But they were heavenly things, that is, the figures of heavenly things. If therefore they were cleansed with blood, these heavenly things ought to be cleansed with better blood.

463 But on the other hand, there is no uncleanness in heaven. I answer that according to a gloss, by heavenly things are understood things which pertain to the state of the present Church, which are called heavenly. Furthermore, believing men bear the image of heavenly things, inasmuch as they mentally dwell in heaven.

Or, in another way and better: by heavenly things is understood the heavenly home. And the Apostle is speaking here in the way that the tabernacle was said to be cleansed in the Old Testament; not that it had any uncleanness in itself, but because certain irregularities were washed away, by which they were hindered from coming to the sanctuary. And heavenly things are said to be cleansed inasmuch as a sacrament of the new law cleanses sins, which hinder one from entering heaven.

464 But he says, ***sacrifices***, in the plural. Yet there is but one sacrifice of Christ: ***By a single offering oblation he has perfected for all time those who are sanctified*** (Heb. 10:14). I answer that although it is one in itself, it was prefigured by several sacrifices of the old law.

This text also shows that the sacrifices of the old law were good, for something is called better in relation to something good.

465 Then when he says ***for Jesus is not entered into the holies***, he shows that heavenly things are cleansed by better sacrifices. For the high priest expiated the sanctuary, which was made with hands, but Christ has entered into the holies not ***made with hands***, for they were not, so far as they were concerned, ***the patterns of the true***: ***but into heaven itself***, which he expiated not in itself but in regard to us, as has been said. But he did not expiate it with fleshly sacrifices because Christ did not come to offer such things: *Sacrifice and offering you do not desire* (Ps. 40:6); *were I to give a burnt offering, you would not be pleased* (Ps. 51:16); ***for it is evident that our Lord sprung out of Judah: in which tribe Moses spoke nothing concerning priests*** (Heb. 7:14). But he entered ***into heaven itself***: *The Lord Jesus . . . was taken up to heaven* (Mark 16:19); *this Jesus who was taken up from you into heaven, will come in the same way as you saw him go* (Acts 1:11).

466 But why? ***That he may appear now in the presence of God for us***. Here the Apostle alludes to a rite of the old law according to which the high priest, who

entered the holy of holies, stood before the mercy seat to pray for the people. Similarly, Christ entered into heaven to stand before God for our salvation.

But not in the same way, because the high priest could not see the holy of holies or any face on account of the smoke ascending from the censer; but Christ appears before the face of God: not that a bodily face is there, or a cloud,
467 but clear vision. But when Christ was on earth, could he not appear before the face of God, since God sees all things?

I answer that, as Augustine speaking of God says: *you were with me, but I was not with you*, namely, because God is in all things by his essence, power, and presence; but the wicked are not with God through grace.[37] Thus, Christ is said to have entered to appear before the face of God, for although he always saw him clearly as one perfectly happy, yet the state of pilgrims, as such, does not confer this, but only the heavenly state. Therefore, when he ascended perfectly happy in body and soul he entered, to appear ***in the presence of God***, i.e., he entered the place where God is seen clearly.

And this ***for us***. For he entered heaven to prepare the way for us: *I go and prepare a place for you. But I will come again and will take you to myself* (John 14:3); *he shall go up that shall open the way before them* (Mic. 2:13 DRB). For the body should follow the head: *Wherever the body is, there the eagles will be gathered together* (Matt. 24:28).

468 Then when he says ***nor yet that he should offer***, he shows that the cleansing effected by the New Testament is more complete than that of the Old. But he shows this in two ways: *first*, by the fact that the former were repeated every day, but this only once. Likewise, as to its effects, because the former could not remove sin, but this one can.

In regard to this he does two things. *First*, he describes the first; *second*, the second, at ***the law has but a shadow of the good things to come*** (Heb. 10:1).

But it should be noted that above, the Apostle had said three things about Christ: *first*, that he is a high priest; *second*, what is the dignity of the place he entered; *third*, how he entered, namely, with blood. But since he has already explained these three things, he now explains how he entered because, as the high priest entered once a year, so Christ entered only once.

In regard to this he does three things. *First*, he shows what was accomplished in the Old Testament; *second*, that it would not be fitting for the same to be accomplished in the New Testament, at ***for then he ought***; *third*, he shows what is accomplished in the New Testament, at ***but now once, at the end of ages***.

469 For in the Old Testament, although the high priest could not enter lawfully but once a year, yet according to the law he had to enter it every year with the blood of others, as it says in Leviticus (16). But Christ has not entered into the

37. Augustine, *The Confessions* 10.27.

place ***made with hands . . . nor yet that he should offer himself often, as the high priest enters into the holies every year with the blood of others.***

470 Then when he says, ***for then he ought to have suffered,*** he proves that it would have been unbecoming to do the same thing in the New Testament because the greatest impropriety would follow, because since Christ entered with his blood, it would follow that he would have ***to have suffered often from the beginning of the world.*** For this is not the case in the sacrifices of the Old Testament because they were offered for the sins of the children of Israel. But that people began when the law was given; therefore, it was not fitting that it be offered from the beginning of the world. But Christ offered himself for the sins of the whole world, because he was made the propitiation for our sins and for those of the whole world (1 John 2:2). Therefore, if he were offered frequently, it would have been necessary for him to have been born and to suffer from the beginning of the world; but this would have been most unbecoming.

But against this view is Revelation, which states, *the Lamb which was slain from the beginning of the world* (13:8 DRB). I answer that it is true that the Lamb was slain, that is, the slaying was prefigured from the beginning of the world, as in the slaying of Abel.

471 Then when he says ***but now once,*** he shows what is done in the New. In regard to this he does two things. *First,* he gives two reasons why the sacrifice is not repeated in the New Testament; *second,* he explains them, at ***and as it***
472 ***is appointed.*** He says, therefore: ***but now once, at the end of the ages, he has appeared***: *These things . . . were written down for our instruction, upon whom the end of the ages has come* (1 Cor. 10:11).

And he says this on account of the number of years, because already more than a thousand years had passed since he said this. For the ages of the world are taken according to the ages of men, which are chiefly distinguished according to the state of progress and not according to the number of years. The first age was before the deluge, in which there was no written law or punishment, as in infancy. Another was from Noah to Abraham; and so on for the ages, so that the final age is the present one, after which there is no other state of salvation, just as there is no other age after old age. But just as in the other ages of men there is a definite number of years, but not in old age, which begins at sixty, and some live for a hundred and twenty years, so it has not been determined how long this state of the world will continue. Yet it is the end of the ages, because no other age remains for salvation.

But Christ appeared once during that age, and he gives two reasons why he was offered only once: the *first* is because in the Old Testament sins were not taken away, but this was accomplished by the offering of Christ. The *second* is because the high priest of the law did not offer his own blood as Christ did.

Hence, he says, ***He has appeared for the destruction of sin by the sacrifice of himself.*** Therefore, the former are repeated, but not this one: *Christ also died for sins once for all* (1 Pet. 3:18).

473 Then when he says ***and as it is appointed***, he explains the two reasons. *First*, the second one; *second*, the first one, at ***the law has but a shadow of the good things to come*** (Heb. 10:1).

He explains the *second* by reason of a likeness to other men; hence, he does two things. *First*, he shows what has happened to other men; *second*, what happened to Christ, at ***so also Christ was offered.***

474 In every man we find two things, namely, the need to die; *second*, that he should rise, not to be cleansed but to be judged according to his deeds. He touches on the first when he says, ***and as it is appointed unto men once to die.***

475 But on the other hand, it seems that this is not appointed, but that man brought this about by sinning, for it says in Wisdom: *God did not make death, and he does not delight in the death of the living* (1:13); and shortly after, *Ungodly men by their words and deeds summoned death* (Wis. 1:16).

I answer that there are three things to consider in death: *first* of all, the material cause, and in this respect it has been appointed for man once to die by reason of the condition of his nature; *second*, the gift which was bestowed, and in this respect there was given to man the gift of original justice, by which the soul contained the body, so that it would not die; *third*, the deservedness of dying, and accordingly, by sinning man deserved to lose that gift and became subject to death. Hence, he says that the wicked called death to themselves by touching the forbidden fruit. Therefore, man is the cause of death by default, but God as the judge: *The wages of sin is death* (Rom. 6:23).

He says ***once*** because this is certainly true of common experience, though it was permitted for some to be raised, as Lazarus and the widow's son, who afterwards died.

476 However, as regards the *second*, he says, ***and after this the judgment***, because after they shall rise, they will not die again, but the judgment will immediately follow. *For we must all appear before the judgment seat of Christ, so that each one may receive good or evil, according to what he has done in the body* (2 Cor. 5:10).

477 Then when he says ***so also Christ***, he shows how three things fit Christ. In regard to the *first*, he says, ***so also Christ was offered once***, in which he agrees with the others. But he differed in two respects: *first*, since Christ had not descended from Adam by way of human seed, but merely as to bodily substance, he did not contract original sin; consequently, he was not obliged by that statute: *In the day that you eat of it you shall die* (Gen. 2:17), but he underwent death by his own will: *No one takes [my life] from me but I lay it*

down of my own accord (John 10:18). Therefore, he says that he ***was offered***: *He was offered because it was his own will* (Isa. 53:7 DRB); *Christ also died for sins once for all* (1 Pet. 3:18).

He differs, *second*, because our death is the effect of sin: *The wages of sin is death* (Rom. 6:23). But Christ's death destroys sin; therefore, he says, ***to exhaust the sins of many***, i.e., to remove them. He does not say 'of all' because Christ's death, even though it was enough for all, has no efficacy except in regard to those who are to be saved: for not all are subject to him by faith and good works.

478 In regard to the *second*, he says, ***The second time he shall appear without sin***. He says two things about the second coming: *first*, how it differs from the first, because the second will be without sin. For even though he had no sin in the first coming, he came *in the likeness of sinful flesh* (Rom. 8:3). In the first coming he was also made a victim for sin: *For our sake he was made to be sin who knew no sin* (2 Cor. 5:21). But those things are not to be found in the second coming; hence, he says that ***he shall appear without sin***.

Second, he states what will be peculiar to the second coming, because he will appear not to be judged, but to judge and to reward according to merits; hence, he says that ***he shall appear***. And although he will appear to all in the flesh, even to those who wounded him, he will appear according to his divinity to the elect that eagerly ***expect him*** by faith ***unto*** their ***salvation***: *Blessed are all those who wait for him* (Isa. 30:18); *we await a Savior, the Lord Jesus Christ, who will change our lowly body to be like his glorious body* (Phil. 3:20–21).

John 13:31–32

The Cross: Christ's Glory

On John 13.6 (1825–1830)

13:31 When he therefore had gone out, Jesus said, "Now is the Son of man glorified, and God is glorified in him.

13:32 If God is glorified in him, God also will glorify him in himself; and immediately he will glorify him."

1825 After Judas left to bring about our Lord's death, Jesus mentions that he himself will be leaving for glory. *First,* to console them, he mentions the glory to which he is going; *second,* he foretells his leaving: ***Little children, yet a little while I am with you*** (John 13:33).

1826 The glory to which he is going is the glorification and exaltation of Christ insofar as he is the Son of man. ***When he,*** that is Judas, ***therefore had gone out Jesus said,*** to his disciples, ***Now is the Son of man glorified, and God is glorified in him.***

The word used was actually 'clarified' and not 'glorified.' But both words mean the same thing. To be clarified is the same as to be glorified, for glory is a kind of splendor. According to Ambrose, someone has glory when he is known with clarity and praised.[38] Whence the commentators use 'clarified' in Greek, translating 'glorified,' and the converse. The same is said here, ***now is the Son of man clarified,*** that is ***glorified.***

We can understand this statement in four ways, by referring it to the four kinds of glory which Christ had: the glory of the cross; the glory of his judicial power; the glory of his resurrection; and the glory of being known by the faith of the people.

1827 Scripture attributes this fourfold glory to Christ. *First,* then, Christ was glorified by being lifted up on the cross. Even Paul said that his own glory was in the cross: *Far be it from me to glory except in the cross of our Lord Jesus Christ* (Gal. 6:14). This is the glory Chrysostom has in mind in his explanation of the text.[39] In this explanation our Lord mentions four things about the glory of the cross: the glory itself; the fruit of this glory; the author of the glory; and the time of the glory.

38. This definition of glory, misattributed here to Ambrose, belongs in fact to Augustine, *Answer to Maximinus the Arian* 2.13.2.

39. John Chrysostom, *Commentary on Saint John* 72.2.

As to the *first* he says, ***now is the Son of man glorified.*** Note that when something is beginning, it seems in a way to already exist. Now when Judas went out to bring back the soldiers, this seems to be the beginning of Christ's passion, the passion by which he was to be glorified. This is why he says, ***now is the Son of man glorified***, that is, the passion by which he will be glorified is now beginning. Indeed, Christ was glorified by the passion of the cross because by it he conquered the enemies of death and the devil: *that through death he might destroy him who has the power of death* (Heb. 2:14). Again, he acquired glory because by his cross he joined heaven and earth: *to reconcile to himself all things, whether on earth or in heaven, making peace by the blood of his cross* (Col. 1:20). Further, he was glorified by his cross because by it he acquired all kingship; *say among the nations, "the Lord reigns"* from his cross (Ps. 96:10). Again, Christ was glorified by the cross because he accomplished many miracles on it: the curtain of the temple was split, an earthquake occurred, rocks were split and the sun was darkened, and many saints arose (Matt. 27:51). So with his passion drawing near, these are the reasons why our Lord said, ***now is the Son of man glorified.*** It is like saying: 'now my passion is beginning, the passion which is my glory.'

The fruit of this glory is that God is glorified by it. So he says, ***and in him God is glorified***, that is, in the glorified Son of man. For the glory of the passion leads to the glory of God. If God was glorified by the death of Peter, he was much more glorified by the death of Christ: ***This he said to show by what death he was to glorify God*** (John 21:19).

The author of this glory is not an angel or a human being, but God himself. He says, ***if God is glorified in him***, that is, if his glory is so great that God is glorified by it, he does not need to be glorified by another. But ***God will also glorify him in himself***, that is, through himself: ***Now glorify me, O Father, with yourself, with the glory which I had, before the world was, with you*** (John 17:5).

The time for this glory is fast approaching, because ***immediately***—that is, straightaway—***God will glorify him***, that is, he will give him the glory of the cross. For the cross, although it is foolish to the gentiles and to those who are lost, yet to us who believe, it is the very great wisdom of God and the power of God (1 Cor. 1:18–24).

1828 The *second* glory of Christ is the glory of his judicial power: *They will see the Son of man coming in clouds with great power and glory* (Mark 13:26). This is the glory about which Augustine speaks, as the *Gloss* says.[40] In reference to this, he does four things here: *first*, he mentions the glory of the judicial power of Christ; *second*, he shows the merit from which he acquired it; *third*, he expounds on this; *fourth*, he shows the source of Christ's glory.

40. Augustine, *Tractates on the Gospel of John* 63.2.

As to the *first*, he says, ***now is the Son of man glorified***. We should note that in Sacred Scripture, one thing is not explicitly said to signify another, and the word for the signifying thing is also used for the thing signified. For example, we do not read that the rock signified Christ; rather, it says, *and the rock was Christ* (1 Cor. 10:4). In the departure of Judas away from the apostles we have a kind of image of the future judgment, when the wicked will be separated from the good, and Christ will put the sheep on his right and the goats on his left (Matt. 25:33). Since this departure of Judas signified the future judgment, right after this our Lord began to speak of the glory of his judicial power, saying, ***now is the Son of man glorified***; that is, this departure or separation represents the glory which the Son of man will have in the judgment, where none of the good will perish and none of the evil will be with them. He does not say: 'now is the glorification of the Son of man signified,' but rather, ***now is the Son of man glorified***, in keeping with the above-mentioned custom of Scripture.

Now the merit of this glorification is that God would be glorified in him. For God is glorified by those who seek to do his will, and not their own. Christ was like this: ***I have come down from heaven, not to do my own will, but the will of him who sent me*** (John 6:38). And this is why ***in him God is glorified***.

He amplifies this when he says, ***if God is glorified in him***, that is, if, by doing the will of God, he glorifies God, then rightly ***God will also glorify him in himself***, so that the human nature assumed by the eternal Word will be given an eternal glory. Thus, ***in himself***, that is, in his own glory: *Therefore God has highly exalted him and bestowed on him the name which is above every name* (Phil. 2:9). Therefore the glorification by which God is glorified in Christ is the merit in virtue of which Christ as man is glorified ***in himself***, that is, in the glory of God. This will occur when his human nature, its weakness having been laid down by the death of the cross, receives the glory of immortality at the resurrection. So the resurrection itself was the source from which this glory began. Accordingly he says, ***Immediately he will glorify him***, at the resurrection, which will quickly come: *I will arise in the morning early* (Ps. 108:3 DRB): and also, *You will not give your Holy One to see corruption* (Ps. 15:10 DRB).

1829 The *third* glory of Christ is the glory of his resurrection, about which we read, *We were buried therefore with him by baptism into death, so that as Christ was raised from the dead by the glory of the Father, we too might walk in newness of life* (Rom. 6:4). It is in terms of this glory that Hilary explains this passage, and Augustine also in part.[41]

From this aspect, Christ *first* foretells this glory of his, saying, ***Now is the Son of man glorified***. Here he is speaking of the future as if it has already happened, because what we think will quickly happen we regard as good as

41. Hilary of Poitiers, *The Trinity* 11.42; Augustine, *Tractates on the Gospel of John* 63.3.

done. Now the glory of the resurrection was very near, and so he says, ***now is the Son of man glorified***, as if his body, by its union with the divine nature, had in a way acquired the glory of the divinity.

Second, he mentions the cause of this glory quite subtly. As he said, in the resurrection the humanity of Christ was glorified because of its union with the divine nature; and there was one person, that of the Word. For we read: *You will not leave my soul in Sheol; you will not let your Holy One*, who is the holiest of all, *see corruption* (Ps. 15:10 DRB). Such glory is also due to this human being, Christ, insofar as he is God. We too will have the glory of the resurrection to the extent that we share in the divinity: *He who raised Christ Jesus from the dead will give life to your mortal bodies also through his Spirit who dwells in you* (Rom. 8:11). So he says that ***the Son of man***, that is, Christ considered in his human nature, ***is glorified***, by his resurrection. And who will glorify him? He says, ***God will also glorify him in himself***, so that this human being, Christ, who reigns in the glory which is from the glory of God, may himself pass into the glory of God, that is, might entirely abide in God, as though deified by the way his human nature is possessed. It is like saying: 'a lamp is bright because a fire is burning brightly within it.' That which sends the rays of brightness into the human nature of Christ is God; and thus the human nature of Christ is glorified by the glory of his divinity, and the human nature of Christ is brought into the glory of his divinity, not by having its nature changed, but by a sharing of glory in so far as this human being, Christ, is adored as God: *Therefore God has highly exalted him and bestowed on him the name which is above every name, that at the name of Jesus every knee should bow* (Phil. 2:9). So he says, ***if God is glorified in him***, that is, if it is true that the glory of his divinity overflows to the glory of his humanity, subsequently ***God will also glorify him in himself***, give him a share of his own glory by assuming him into that glory: *Every tongue [should] confess that Jesus Christ is Lord to the glory of the Father* (Phil. 2:11).

Thus, Christ has a twofold glory. One is in his human nature but is derived from his divinity. The other is the glory of his divinity, into which his human nature is in a way taken up. But each glory is different. The first-mentioned glory had a beginning in time. For this reason he speaks of it as past, saying, ***and God is***, or has been, ***glorified in him***, on the day of the resurrection. The other glory is eternal, because from eternity the Word of God is God. And the human nature of Christ, assumed into this glory, will be glorified forever. And so he speaks of this as in the future: ***and will glorify him at once***, that is, he will always establish him in that glory forever.

1830 The *fourth* glory of Christ is the glory of being known by the faith of the people. Origen has this kind of glory in mind in his exposition.[42] According to

42. Origen, *Commentary on John* 32.26–28.

him, glory means one thing in ordinary speech, and another thing in Scripture. In ordinary speech, glory is the praise given by a number of people, or the clear knowledge of someone accompanied by praise, as Ambrose says.[43] While in Scripture, glory indicates that a divine sign or mark is upon one; *the glory of the Lord appeared over the tabernacle* (Exod. 40:34), that is, a divine sign rested over it. The same happened to the face of Moses, when it was glorified. Just as glory, in the physical sense, indicates that a divine sign rests upon one, so, in the spiritual sense, that intellect is said to be glorified when it is so deified and so transcends all material things that it is raised to a knowledge of God. It is by this that we are made sharers of glory: *We all, with unveiled face, beholding the glory of the Lord, are being changed into his likeness from one degree of glory to another* (2 Cor. 3:18). Therefore, if anyone who knows God is glorified and made a sharer of glory, it is clear that Christ, who knows God most perfectly, since he is the brightness of the entire divine glory (Heb. 1:3), and able to receive the splendor of the entire divine glory, if, I say, this is so, then Christ is most perfectly glorified. And all who know God owe this to Christ.

But men did not yet realize that Christ was so glorified by this most perfect knowledge and participation in the divinity. And so, although he was glorified in himself, he was not yet glorified in the knowledge of men. He began to have his glory at his passion and resurrection, when men began to recognize his power and divinity. Our Lord, speaking here of this glory, says, ***now is the Son of man glorified***, that is, now, in his human nature, he is receiving glory in the knowledge of men because of his approaching passion. ***And God***, the Father, ***is glorified in him***. For the Son not only reveals himself, but the Father as well: ***I have manifested your name*** (John 17:6). Consequently, not only is the Son glorified, but the Father also: *No one knows the Father except the Son and anyone to whom the Son chooses to reveal him* (Matt. 11:27). He says, ***in him***, because one who sees the Son also sees the Father (John 14:9). It is characteristic of one who is greater to return what is greater. And thus he adds, ***if God is glorified in him***, that is, if the glory of God the Father somehow increases because of the glory of the Son of man, because the Father becomes better known, ***God will also glorify him in himself***, that is, make it known that Christ Jesus is in his glory. This will not be delayed for he ***will glorify him at once***.

43. This definition of glory, misattributed here to Ambrose, belongs in fact to Augustine, *Answer to Maximinus the Arian* 2.13.2.

Chapter 6

CHRIST'S VICTORY OVER DEATH

John 20:1–9

Racing to the Tomb

Models of Devotion to Christ

On John 20.1 (2470–2489)

20:1 ***And on the first day of the week, Mary Magdalene came early, when it was still dark, to the sepulcher; and she saw the stone had been taken away from the sepulcher.***

20:2 ***She ran, therefore, and came to Simon Peter, and to the other disciple whom Jesus loved, and said to them, "They have taken the Lord out of the sepulcher, and we do not know where they have laid him."***

20:3 ***Peter therefore went out, and that other disciple, and they came to the sepulcher.***

20:4 ***And they both ran together, and the other disciple outran Peter, and came to the sepulcher first.***

20:5 ***And when he stooped down, he saw the linen cloths lying there; but he did not go in.***

20:6 ***Then Simon Peter came, following him, and went into the sepulcher, and saw the linen cloths lying there,***

20:7 ***and the napkin that had been on his head, not lying with the linen cloths, but apart, wrapped up in one place.***

20:8 ***Then the other disciple also went in, who had come to the sepulcher first, and he saw, and believed.***

20:9 ***For as yet they did not know the Scripture, that he must rise again from the dead.***

2470 Having related the mysteries of the passion of Christ, the Evangelist now speaks of the resurrection.[1] *First*, he says the resurrection was made known to certain women; *second*, to the disciples: ***now when it was late on that same day*** (John 20:19).

The revelation of Christ's resurrection to the women went in stages: *first*, there is the open tomb; *second*, the appearance of the angel: ***The disciples therefore went back to their homes*** (John 20:10); *third*, the sight of Christ: ***When she had said this, she turned around, and saw Jesus standing*** (John 20:14).

In regard to the *first*, he *first* mentions the sight of the open tomb; *second*, this news is reported to the disciples: ***She ran, therefore, and came to Simon Peter***; and *third*, they see for themselves: ***Peter therefore went out.***

2471 Four things can be noted about the *first*. *First*, the time; it was one day of the Sabbath, that is, ***the first day of the week***. The Jews considered the Sabbath as a very sacred day, and all the other days were described in reference to the Sabbath. Thus they spoke of the first day of the Sabbath, the second day of the Sabbath, and so on. Matthew says, *after the Sabbath* (28:1). But John speaks of ***the first day of the week*** because he is referring to a mystery, for this day of the resurrection was the beginning of a new creation: *When you send forth your Spirit, they are created; and you renew the face of the ground* (Ps. 104:30); *neither circumcision counts for anything, nor uncircumcision, but a new creation* (Gal. 6:15). In Genesis, when Moses is speaking of the first day of creation, he does not say 'the first day,' but he says *one day* (1:5). And so the Evangelist uses these words of Moses because he wants to express a newness.

And also because this day begins the day of eternity, which is one day, no night interrupting it, because the sun which makes this day will never set. *The city has no need of sun or moon to shine upon it, for the glory of God is its light, and its lamp is the Lamb* (Rev. 21:23); *there shall be continuous day . . . not day and not night, for at evening time there shall be light* (Zech. 14:7).

2472 *Second*, the person who saw the tomb is given, ***Mary Magdalene came early, when it was still dark, to the sepulcher***. A question arises here because Mark makes mention of *Mary Magdalene, and Mary the mother of James, and Salome* (16:1); and Matthew also mentions *the other Mary* (28:1).

According to Augustine the resolution is that Mary Magdalene was more ardent and more devoted to Christ than the other women.[2] Thus we read that *her sins, which are many, are forgiven, for she loved much* (Luke 7:47). And for this reason the Evangelist mentions her by name. This is also the reason why the Lord appeared to her first: *He appeared first to Mary Magdalene* (Mark 16:9); *she hastens to make herself known to those who desire her* (Wis. 6:14).

1. See John 18–19.

2. Augustine, *Agreement among the Evangelists* 3.24.

2473 *Third*, the time is given, ***early, when it was still dark.*** Luke tells us that the women who had come with Christ from Galilee saw his tomb and how his body was laid, and they prepared spices and ointments for it (23:55). They rested on the Sabbath according to the commandment. As soon as the Sabbath was over, on the first day of the week, before daylight, she came to the tomb, incited by her exceedingly great love, *its flashes*, the flashes of love, *are flashes of fire* (Song of Sol. 8:6).

2474 The question arises why Mark says *very early . . . when the sun had risen* (16:2), while the Evangelist says, ***when it was still dark.*** The answer is that what Mark says should be understood as referring to the breaking of the day, so that the sun had risen, not that it had appeared above the earth, but that it approached our region.

2475 *Fourth*, we are told what Mary saw, she ***saw the stone had been taken away from the sepulcher.*** This was a sign that either someone had taken Christ away, or that he had arisen. When Matthew says that *an angel of the Lord descended from heaven and came and rolled back the stone*, we should not think the stone was rolled away before Christ arose, but only after (28:2). For since Christ came forth from the closed womb of the Virgin even though his body was not glorified, it is not surprising if he passed through the tomb with his glorified body. The stone was taken away so that people could see that Christ was not there, and more easily believe in his resurrection.

2476 Next the Evangelist mentions that ***she ran, therefore, and came to Simon Peter***, and the events of this vision were announced. Because of Mary's exceeding love she could not delay telling what she had seen to the disciples, ***She ran, therefore, and came to Simon Peter and to the other disciple whom Jesus loved***: *This day is a day of good news; if we are silent and wait until the morning light, punishment will overtake us* (2 Kings 7:9). And so one who hears the words of God should tell it to others without delay: *Let him who hears say, "come"* (Rev. 22:17). Mary came to those who were more important and who loved Christ more ardently, so that they might either look for Jesus with her or share her sorrow.

She said to them, ***they have taken the Lord out of the sepulcher.*** Mary saw the empty tomb, and not yet having it in her heart that Christ had risen, she said, ***and we do not know where they have laid him.*** We can see from this that Mary had not been alone at the tomb, and that she still had doubts about the resurrection. So it was not without reason that the Evangelist wrote that ***it was still dark***, for this indicated the condition of their minds, in which there was the darkness of doubt: *They have neither knowledge nor understanding, they walk about in darkness* (Ps. 82:5).

Note that in the Greek manuscripts it reads, ***my Lord***, which shows the impetus of her love and her affectionate devotion: *Whom have I in heaven but you? And there is nothing upon earth that I desire besides you. . . . God is the strength of my heart and my portion forever* (Ps. 73:25–26).

2477 The Evangelist next shows how this was investigated: ***Peter, therefore, went out, and that other disciple.*** *First*, he indicates the eagerness with which Peter and John acted, for they left the place where they were and ***Peter, therefore, went out, and that other disciple.*** Those who want to look into the mysteries of Christ have in a sense to come out from themselves and from their carnal way of living: *Go forth, O daughters of Zion, and behold King Solomon* (Song of Sol. 3:11).

2478 *Second*, we see the details of their search. *First*, it is said that they ran. ***They both ran***, they who loved Christ more than the others: *I will run in the way of your commandments* (Ps. 119:32); *so run that you may obtain it*, the prize (1 Cor. 9:25).

2479 *Second*, we see how the disciples arrived, ***The other disciple outran Peter.*** John arrived first, and Peter followed: ***Then Simon Peter came, following him.***

2480 It is not without reason that the Evangelist is careful to tell us the smallest details. For these two disciples signify two peoples, the Jews and the gentiles. Although the Jews were the first to have knowledge of the one true God, the gentiles were an older people, because even the Jews originated from the gentiles: *Go from your country and your kindred* (Gen. 12:1). These two people were both running over the course of this world: the Jews using the written law, the gentiles using the law of nature. Or, they were both running by their natural desire for happiness and for a knowledge of the truth, which all men desire to know by their very nature. ***The other disciple***, that is, the younger one, ***outran Peter***, because the gentiles came to a knowledge of the truth more slowly than the Jews, since formerly God was known only in Judea. So the Psalm says, *He has not dealt thus with any other nation* (Ps. 147:20). ***And came to the sepulcher first***, because he first considered the mysteries of Christ, as it was first to the Jews that the promise of Christ was made, *and to them belong the sonship, the glory, the covenants and the giving of the law, the worship, and the promises; to them belong the patriarchs, and of their race, according to the flesh, is the Christ, who is God over all* (Rom. 9:4–5).

And when he stooped down, he saw the linen cloths lying there; but he did not go in. He stooped, under the yoke of the law: *All that the Lord has spoken we will do* (Exod. 24:7). ***He saw the linen cloths lying there***, that is, the figures or foreshadowings of all the mysteries: *Their minds were hardened; for to this day, when they read the Old Covenant, that same veil remains unlifted* (2 Cor. 3:14). ***But he did not go in***, for as long as he was unwilling to believe in the one who was dead he had not yet come to the knowledge of the truth. Another who did not go in was the brother of the prodigal son, for when he heard the celebrations, the music and the dancing, he *refused to go in* (Luke 15:28). Nevertheless, David promised that they would enter: *I will go to the altar of God* (Ps. 43:4).

2481 Now the Evangelist recounts the arrival of Peter. As for the literal meaning, the fact that they ran together was a sign of their passionate devotion. John arrived first because he was a younger man than Peter.

But considering the mystical sense, Peter follows John because the gentiles who were converted to Christ were not joined to another church different from the church of the Jews but were grafted on to the already existing olive tree and Church. The Apostle praises them saying, *You, brethren, became imitators of the churches of God in Christ Jesus which are in Judea* (1 Thess. 2:14).

2482 *Third*, we see the order in which they entered: ***and went into the sepulcher***, Peter first, and then John: ***Then the other disciple also went in.***

2483 The Evangelist says that Peter entered the tomb. According to the literal meaning, although John arrived first, he did not enter because of his respect for Peter. But considering the mystical interpretation, this signifies that the Jewish people, who were the first to hear of the mysteries of the incarnation, would be converted to the faith after the gentiles: *That gentiles, who did not pursue righteousness have attained it . . . but that Israel who pursued the righteousness which is based in law did not succeed in fulfilling that law* (Rom. 9:30).

John saw only the linen cloths. Peter also ***saw the linen cloths lying there*** because we do not reject the Old Testament, for as Luke says, *He opened their minds to understand the Scriptures* (24:45).

But in addition Peter saw ***the napkin which had been on his head***: *The head of Christ is God* (1 Cor. 11:3). Thus to see the napkin which had been on the head of Jesus is to have faith in the divinity of Christ, which the Jews refused to accept. This napkin is described as ***not lying with the linen cloths, but apart, wrapped up in one place***, because the divinity of Christ is covered over, and it is apart from every creature because of its excellence: *God who is over all, be blessed forever* (Rom. 9:5); *truly, you are a God who hides yourself* (Isa. 45:15). He saw the napkin ***wrapped up***, to form a circle. And when linen is rolled this way one cannot see its beginning or end, for the eminence of the divinity neither begins nor ends: *Jesus Christ is the same yesterday and today and forever* (Heb. 13:8); *you are the same, and your years have no end* (Ps. 102:27). The napkin was in one place, ***apart***, because God does not dwell where minds are divided; those who merit his grace are those who are one in charity: *His place is in peace* (Ps. 76:2 DRB); *for God is not a God of confusion but of peace* (1 Cor. 14:33).

2484 Or, in another interpretation, the napkin, which workers use to wipe the sweat off their faces, can be understood to indicate the labor of God. For while

God always remains tranquil, he presents himself as laboring and burdened when he endures the stubborn depravity of mankind: *They have become a burden to me, I am weary of bearing them* (Isa. 1:14). Christ took on this burden in a special way when he took on a human nature: *Let him give his cheek to the smiter and be filled with insults* (Lam. 3:30).

This napkin is found separate and apart from the other cloths because the sufferings of our Redeemer are far apart and separate from our sufferings. The other linen cloths, which are related to the members of the body as the napkin is to the head, indicate the sufferings of the saints, which are separate from the napkin, that is, the sufferings of Christ, for Christ suffered without fault what we suffer because of our faults: *for Christ also died . . . the righteous for the unrighteous* (1 Pet. 3:18). He went to his death willingly: ***No one takes [my life] from me but I lay it down of my own accord*** (John 10:18); *Christ loved us and gave himself up for us* (Eph. 5:2), while the saints go to their death reluctantly, ***Another will gird you and carry you where you do not wish to go*** (John 21:18).

2485 Why was the Evangelist so careful to mention all these details? Chrysostom says this was done to counter the false rumor spread by the Jews that the body of Christ had been secretly taken away (Matt. 28:13).[3] For if Christ's body had been stolen away as they said, the disciples would surely not have removed the wrappings, especially since they had to work fast because the guards were near. Nor would they be so careful to lift off the napkin and roll it up and place it in a separate place. They would simply have taken the body as they found it. This was why he allowed himself to be buried with myrrh and aloes, because they glue the cloths to the body so that they cannot be quickly removed.

2486 When the Evangelist says, ***then the other disciple also went in, he who had come to the sepulcher first***, he tells of John's entrance. John did not remain outside but entered after Peter, because when the world is ending, the Jews will also be gathered into the faith: *A hardening has come upon part of Israel, until the full number of the gentiles come in, and so all Israel will be saved* (Rom. 11:25); *the remnant shall be converted* (Isa. 10:21 DRB).

2487 Or, another interpretation, in the mystical sense. These two disciples stand for two kinds of people; John represents those who are devoted to the contemplation of truth, and Peter stands for those whose main interest is to carry out the commandments. In fact, Simon means obedient.

Now it very often happens that contemplatives, because they are docile, are the first to become acquainted with a knowledge of the mysteries of Christ, but they do not enter, for sometimes there is knowledge, but little or no love follows. While those in the active life, because of their continuing fervor and earnestness, even though they are slower to understand: *Through your precepts*

3. John Chrysostom, *Commentary on Saint John* 85.4.

I get understanding (Ps. 119:104), enter into them more quickly, so that those who are later to arrive, are the first to penetrate the divine mysteries: *The last will be first, and the first last* (Matt. 20:16).

2488 Next when he says, ***he saw, and believed***, we see the effect of the investigation. At first glance it seems to mean that ***he saw*** the situation ***and believed*** that Christ had arisen. But according to Augustine this is not correct, because the next thing the Evangelist says is, ***for as yet they did not know the Scripture, that he must rise again from the dead.***[4] Therefore, one must say that ***he saw*** the empty tomb ***and believed*** what the woman had said, which is that someone had taken the Lord. Then we read, ***for as yet they did not know the Scripture***, because the meaning of the Scripture was not yet opened to them so they could understand it (Luke 24:45).

But certainly Christ had foretold his passion and resurrection? *I will rise on the third day* (Matt. 20:19). I answer that we should say that in keeping with the way they heard his parables, they failed here also to understand many things which he had said plainly, thinking that he meant something else.

2489 Or, according to Chrysostom's understanding, ***he saw*** the linen cloths so folded and arranged which would not have been the case if the body had been furtively snatched away;[5] ***and believed***, with a true faith, that Christ had risen from the dead. What follows, ***for as yet they did not know the Scripture***, refers to the statement, ***he saw and believed.*** It was like saying: 'before he saw these things he did not understand the Scripture ***that he must rise again from the dead***; but when he saw he believed that he had risen from the dead.'

4. Augustine, *Tractates on the Gospel of John* 120.9.

5. John Chrysostom, *Commentary on Saint John* 85.4.

John 20:10–13

Magdalene's Tears

Hope Born of Inconsolable Love

On John 20.2 (2490–2503)

20:10 ***The disciples therefore went back to their homes.***

20:11 ***But Mary stood outside the sepulcher, weeping. Now as she was weeping, she stooped down, and looked into the sepulcher,***

20:12 ***and she saw two angels in white, sitting, one at the head, and one at the feet, where the body of Jesus had been laid.***

20:13 ***They said to her, "Woman, why do you weep?" She said to them, "Because they have taken away my Lord; and I do not know where they have laid him."***

2490 Having told how Mary Magdalene came to the opened tomb, the Evangelist now tells how she came to see the angels: *first*, we see her devotion; *second*, she sees the angels: ***and she saw two angels in white***; *third*, we have her conversation with them: ***They said to her, "Woman, why do you weep?"***

Her devotion, which made her fit to see the angels, is praised for three
2491 things. *First*, it was constant, and it deserves praise, especially considering that the disciples left, ***the disciples therefore went back***, not yet understanding ***the Scripture that he must rise from the dead*** (John 20:9), ***back to their homes***, where they were staying and from where they had run to the tomb. Their fear was so great that they did not stay together: *Strike the shepherd that the sheep may be scattered* (Zech. 13:7); *the holy stones lie scattered at the head of every street* (Lam. 4:1).

Further, she stood there, lingering near the tomb: ***Mary stood outside the sepulcher weeping.*** The disciples had left, but a stronger and more burning affection fixed the weaker sex to the spot.

2492 A question arises here, because Mark says that the women *went out and fled from the tomb* (16:8). Therefore, they must have been within it. Why then does John say that ***Mary stood outside***?

I answer that the tomb of Christ was hewn out of rock and surrounded by a garden, as was stated before. Sometimes, therefore, the Evangelists call only the place where the body of Christ had been laid the tomb, and at other times the entire enclosure is called the tomb. Thus when the women are said to enter into the tomb (Mark 16:5), this should be understood to mean the entire enclosure. But when it says here that ***Mary stood outside***, the Evangelist is referring to the tomb hewn out of rock. But this rock-hewn tomb was within the enclosure they had already entered. Mary was standing here because of the unwavering love which had inflamed her heart: *Be steadfast, immovable, always abounding in the work of the Lord* (1 Cor. 15:58); *our feet have been standing within your gates* (Ps. 122:2).

2493 *Second*, Mary's devotion is admired because it overflowed in tears, for she stood there ***weeping***: *She weeps bitterly in the night* (Lam. 1:2). There are two kinds of tears: tears of compunction, to wash away sins, *Every night I flood my bed with tears* (Ps. 6:6), and tears of devotion, from a desire for heavenly things: *He . . . goes forth*, hastening towards heavenly things, *weeping, bearing the seed for sowing* (Ps. 126:6). Mary Magdalene had copious tears of compunction at the time of her conversion, when she had been the village sinner. Then, in her love for the truth, she washed the stains of her sins with her tears: *Her sins, which are many, are forgiven, for she loved much* (Luke 7:47). She also shed abundant tears of devotion over the passion and resurrection of Christ, as we see here.

2494 *Third*, her devotion is admired because of her earnest search for Christ, and ***as she was weeping she stooped down and looked into the sepulcher***. This weeping of Mary came from the desire of love. For it is the nature of love to want its beloved present; and if the beloved cannot be really present, it at least wants to think of the beloved, for *where your treasure is, there will your heart be also* (Matt. 6:21). Mary shed these bitter tears because the eyes which had sought her Lord and did not find him were now freed for tears, and she grieved the more because he had been taken from the tomb. The life of such a teacher had been destroyed, but his memory remained. Since Mary could not have him present, she wanted at least to look at the place where he had been buried, so ***she stooped*** to look into the tomb. We learn from this that we should look at the death of Christ with a humble heart: *You have hidden these things from the wise and understanding and revealed them to babes* (Matt. 11:25). She stooped ***and looked***, giving us the example to look continually on the death of Christ with the eyes of our mind, for one look is not enough for one who loves, for the force of love increases the desire to explore, *looking to Jesus the pioneer and perfecter of our faith, who for the joy that was set before him endured the cross, despising the shame* (Heb. 12:2).

She stooped down and looked, pressed down by the love of Christ: *The charity of Christ presses us* (2 Cor. 5:14 DRB). Or again, according to Augustine, by a divine impulse in her soul she was made to look about, and saw something greater, the angels;[6] *For all who are led by the Spirit of God are sons of God* (Rom. 8:14).

2495 Next the Evangelist describes the sight of the angels: ***She saw two angels in***
2496 ***white, sitting.*** He mentions four things. *First,* what Mary saw, which was that ***she saw two angels,*** which goes to show that all orders of angels, both those assisting and those ministering, were in service to Christ: *Let all God's angels worship him* (Heb. 1:6).

A question arises here because Matthew and Mark say that Mary and the other women saw one angel on the right side of the tomb (Matt. 28:2; Mark 16:5), while here we have two angels, and they are inside.

Each one is correct, for Matthew and Mark tell what occurred first, when the women first came, and believing that Christ was taken, returned to the disciples. But John recounts what happened after Mary returned with the disciples and remained after they had left.

2497 *Second,* he mentions their raiment, ***in white.*** This shows the splendor of the resurrection and the glory of the risen Christ: *They shall walk with me in white* (Rev. 3:4). Indeed, we read that the armies of heaven followed him and were clothed in white, that is, raised to heavenly glory (Rev. 19:14).

2498 *Third,* we see that they were ***sitting.*** This indicates the calmness and power of Christ, who being now at rest from all afflictions, reigns in immortal flesh and sitting at the right hand of the Father: *Sit at my right hand* (Ps. 110:1); he will sit *upon the throne of David, and over his kingdom* (Isa. 9:7).

2499 *Fourth,* we see how they were positioned, ***one at the head, and one at the feet.*** We can refer this to three things. *First,* to the two Testaments. The word 'angel' in Greek [*aggelos*] means messenger, and both Testaments brought messages about Christ: *The crowds that went before him and that followed him shouted, "Hosanna to the Son of David!"* (Matt. 21:9). So the angel sitting at the head signifies the Old Testament, and the angel at the feet the New Testament.

Second, we can relate this to those who preach Christ. There are two natures in Christ, the divine and the human; the head of Christ is God (1 Cor. 11:3), and the feet of Christ are his human nature: *Let us worship at his footstool* (Ps. 132:7). So, those who preach the divinity of Christ, as in ***In the beginning was the Word*** (John 1:1), are sitting at the head; those who preach his humanity, as in ***The Word became flesh*** (John 1:14), are sitting at the feet.

Third, this can refer to the time when the mysteries of Christ are announced. Then one angel sits at the head and the other at the feet because they signified that the mysteries of Christ would be announced from the head or beginning of the world to its end: *You proclaim the Lord's death until he comes* (1 Cor. 11:26).

---

6. Augustine, *Tractates on the Gospel of John* 121.1.

2500 Next, the Evangelist gives the greeting of the angels: ***They said to her: woman, why do you weep?*** *First* their question; and then Mary's answer.
2501 Concerning the *first*, the angels knew that Mary was uncertain about the resurrection and so as if beginning anew they asked her the reason for her tears: ***they***, the angels, ***said to her, woman, why do you weep?*** This was like saying: 'do not cry for there is no need for it, because *weeping may tarry for the night* of the passion, *but joy comes with the morning* of the resurrection' (Ps. 30:5); *keep your voice from weeping and your eyes from tears, for your work shall be rewarded* (Jer. 31:16).

In this regard we can recall to mind that Gregory said that the very same sacred words which excite our tears of love console those same tears when they promise us hope in our Redeemer: *When the cares of my heart are many, your consolations cheer my soul* (Ps. 94:19).[7]

2502 Mary thought that they were questioning her because of their ignorance and regarded them not as angels but as men; so she gave the reason for her tears: ***They have taken away my Lord***, that is, the body of my Lord. Here she was referring to a part by mentioning the whole, just like we profess that the Lord Jesus Christ the Son of God was buried, although only his flesh was buried, because his divinity did not desert his flesh.[8] ***And I do not know where they have laid him***. This was the reason for her desolation; she did not know where to go to find him to soothe her sorrow.

2503 Is it a consolation for one who loves to have something that belonged to the beloved? According to Augustine, in his *Confessions*, this would be more a cause of sorrow.[9] For this reason he said that he fled from all the places where he had formerly spent time with his friend. Still, Chrysostom says that this would be a cause of consolation.[10]

Each of these is true. In all cases where there is a mixture of joy and sadness, the hope for the thing desired brings pleasure: *Rejoice in your hope, be patient in tribulation* (Rom. 12:12), and also brings sorrow: *Hope deferred makes the heart sick* (Prov. 13:12). But hope does not cause these from the same point of view. Hope causes joy because it regards the thing loved as able

7. Gregory the Great, *Forty Gospel Homilies* 25.4.

8. The Divine Word, although inseparably united even to the dead body of Christ, cannot properly be said to have been *buried* because the Word is not properly a body—or a physical being—such as can be buried. Moreover, St. Thomas understands the death of Jesus in terms of a separation of Christ's body and soul such that, although both remained united to the Word in death, his soul was separated from his body (sojourning in hell, in fact) until his Resurrection. If to be buried is to be located in a tomb or grave, then we can see in what sense the Word cannot be said to have been buried simpliciter, since, although he was with his body in the tomb, he was also with his soul, which was not in the tomb. See also Thomas Aquinas *Summa theologiae* 3.50.2–3.

9. Augustine, *The Confessions* 4.7.12.

10. John Chrysostom, *Commentary on Saint John* 86.1.

to be obtained; but insofar as this thing is actually absent it produces sorrow. It is like that here; something belonging to a friend, because it stands for the friend, is pleasant to the lover; while inasmuch as it recalls the absence of the one loved it produces sadness.

John 20:14–18

"Whom Do You Seek?"

Recognizing the Glorified Lord

On John 20.3 (2504–2522)

20:14 ***When she had said this, she turned around, and saw Jesus standing; and she did not know that it was Jesus.***

20:15 ***Jesus said to her, "Woman, why do you weep? Whom do you seek?" She, thinking it was the gardener, said to him, "Lord, if you have taken him from here, tell me where you have laid him, and I will take him away."***

20:16 ***Jesus said to her, "Mary." She, turning, said to him, "Rabbi," which is to say, Master.***

20:17 ***Jesus said to her, "Do not touch me, for I have not yet ascended to my Father. But go to my brethren and say to them: I ascend to my Father and to your Father, to my God and your God."***

20:18 ***Mary Magdalene went and said to the disciples, "I have seen the Lord, and he said these things to me."***

2504 Now the Evangelist shows how Mary came to see Christ: *first*, he tells how she
saw Christ; *second*, how he was recognized by her: ***Jesus said to her, "Do not
touch me."*** Concerning the *first*, we see her seeing Christ; and then what Christ
2505 said to her: ***Jesus said to her, "Woman, why do you weep?"*** *First*, then, ***when she
had said this***, that is, when Mary said this to the angels, ***she turned around.***

Chrysostom wonders why Mary, who was speaking to the angels, whom she considered to be at least men deserving of respect, turned around [away from them] before they had answered her.[11]

The answer is that while Mary was responding to the angels' question, Christ arrived, and the angels stood out of reverence. When Mary saw this, she was puzzled and turned around to see what had made them stand up. Thus in Luke mention is made that the two angels were seen standing (24:4). ***She turned around and saw Jesus standing; and she did not know that it was Jesus***; she was seeing him not in the splendor of his glory, whom the blessed angels honor in glory.

11. John Chrysostom, *Commentary on Saint John* 86.1.

We see from this that if anyone desires to see Christ, they must turn round to him: *Return to me, says the Lord of hosts, and I will return to you* (Zech. 1:3). Those come to the point of seeing him who entirely turn themselves to him by love: *She hastens to make herself known to those who desire her* (Wis. 6:14).

Mystically, this signifies that at one time Mary had turned her back to Christ by her disbelief, but when she turned her soul to knowing him, she turned round to him.

2506 Why did Mary not recognize Christ, since he was the same person as before? We should say that it was either because she did not believe that the one she had seen dead had risen, or else her eyes were held so that she would not recognize him, like the two disciples on their way to Emmaus (Luke 24:16).

2507 The words of Christ are now given: ***Woman, why do you weep?*** *First,* we see Christ's question, then Mary's answer.

2508 Concerning the *first,* note that Mary was advancing step by step; for the angels asked her why she was weeping, but Christ asked her whom she was looking for, for her weeping was caused by the desire which led her to look. Christ asked her whom she was looking for in order to increase this desire, for when she spoke of the one she was seeking, her love burned more intensely, and so she would continue to seek him. *Seek his presence continually* (Ps. 105:4); *the path of the righteous is like the light of dawn, which shines brighter and brighter until full day* (Prov. 4:18).

2509 When the Evangelist says, ***she, thinking it was the gardener, said to him,*** we see Mary's answer: *first,* whom she thought was questioning her; then her response.

2510 Mary thought the ***gardener*** was speaking to her, because she knew that the guards had already fled, frightened by the earthquake and the sight of the angels, and that the only one who would be there would be the one taking care of the place, the gardener. As Gregory says: *This woman, in erring did not err, when she thought that Christ was a gardener, for he planted the seeds of virtue in her heart by the strength of his love.*[12] It is written: *I will water my orchard and drench my garden plot* (Sir. 24:31).

2511 Mary said to Jesus, ***Lord, if you have taken him from here, tell me.*** She calls him ***lord*** in order to gain his good will. But since this gardener had just arrived, and Mary had not told him whom she was looking for, why does she say, ***if you have taken him from here***? Who was ***him***?

We should say that the force of love causes the lover to think that no one would be ignorant of the one who is always in his thoughts. For, we read in Luke that our Lord asked, *What is this conversation which you are holding with each other as you walk?* And one of the disciples answered, *Are you the only*

12. Gregory the Great, *Forty Gospel Homilies* 25.4.

visitor to Jerusalem who does not know the things that have happened there in these days? (24:17–18).

2512 When Mary says, ***tell me where you have laid him, and I will take him away***, she shows a wonderful courage which would not be driven off by the sight of a dead person, and that she would have tried to carry the body away even though it was beyond her strength. But this is what is spoken of: *Love hopes all things* (1 Cor. 13:7). She wanted to take him so the Jews would not violate the dead body and to carry it to another secret grave.

2513 Next the Evangelist shows Mary recognizing Christ; ***Jesus said to her, "Mary."*** The Evangelist uses the name ***Mary***, while before he had used the general word ***woman*** (John 13:15). He calls her by her own name, ***Mary***, to show that she was well known to the saints. *He determines the number of the stars, he gives to them their names* (Ps. 147:4); *I know you by name* (Exod. 33:12); and to indicate that although all things are moved by God with a general motion, yet a special grace is needed for a person's justification.

The effect of her being called by Christ was that ***she, turning, said to him***,
2514 in Hebrew, ***"Rabbi," which is to say, Master***. Was not Mary always looking at Christ when he was speaking to her?

According to Augustine, this present turning refers to her interior state of mind; before, although she was facing Christ, she thought he was someone else, the gardener; but now her heart was turned, and she recognized him for who he was.[13]

Or, one could say that, as was said, she thought he was someone else, and so while she was talking to him she did not look at him but was concerned with the Christ she carried in her heart and was looking about for some trace of him. And, therefore, Christ recalling her, called out her proper name, saying, ***Mary***, as if he says: whom do you look back at? Recognize him, by whom you are recognized. And, at once, when she is called by name, she recognized the speaker, saying, ***Rabbi, which is to say, Master***, for so she was accustomed to call him.

We can understand from this that the cause of our justification and of our profession of faith is to have been called by Christ.

2515 Next, at ***Jesus said to her, "Do not touch me,"*** the Evangelist shows Mary receiving instructions from Christ; one of them is negative, the other positive:
2516 ***Go to my brethren***. He does two things about the *first*: he states the prohibition, and then gives the reason for it.

Christ warns Mary not to touch him, saying, ***Do not touch me***. Even though we do not read here that Mary wanted to touch Christ, Gregory says we can see from this that Mary fell at the feet of Christ and wanted to grasp

13. Augustine, *Tractates on the Gospel of John* 121.2.

the one she had recognized.[14] He adds the reason, ***for I have not yet ascended to my Father***. It seems from this that after his resurrection, Christ did not want to be touched before he ascended. But the opposite is found in Luke: *Handle me and see, for a spirit has not flesh and bones as you see that I have* (24:39).

It is no answer to say that Christ wanted to be touched by his disciples, but not by the women, for we see in Matthew, that Mary Magdalene and other women came to him and did grasp him by his feet (28:9).

Therefore, we should understand, according to the letter of the text, that Mary saw angels at two times: the first time was with the other women, when she saw one angel sitting on the stone (Matt. 28:2; Mark 16:5); the second time was when she returned and saw two angels inside the tomb (John 20:12). Similarly, she also saw Christ two times; *first* in the garden, when she thought he was the gardener, as we just saw; *second*, she saw him when she was running with the other women to tell the disciples what they had seen, in order to strengthen them in their faith in the resurrection. It was this second time that they approached and held Christ's feet (Matt. 28:9; Mark 16:9).

2517 There are two mystical reasons why Christ did not want to be touched. *First*, because this particular woman signified the church of the gentiles, which was not to touch Christ by faith until he had ascended to the Father: *A congregation of people will surround you; for their sakes return on high* (Ps. 7:7 DRB).

The other reason is given by Augustine in his work *The Trinity*. It is that touch is the last stage of knowledge: when we see something, we know it to a certain extent, but when we touch it our knowledge is complete.[15] Now this particular woman had some faith in Christ, which was that he was a holy man; and this was why she called him ***Master***. But she had not yet reached the point of believing that he was equal to the Father and one with God. Thus Christ says, ***do not touch me***, that is, do not allow what you now believe of me to be the limit of your faith, ***for I have not yet ascended to my Father***, that is, in your heart, because you do not believe that I am one with him; yet she did believe this later. In a way, Christ did ascend to the Father within her when she had advanced in the faith to the point of believing that he was equal to the Father.

2518 Or, we could say, with Chrysostom, that after this woman saw that Christ had arisen, she thought he was in the same state as he was before, having a life subject to death.[16] She wanted to be with him as she was before his passion, and in her joy thought there was nothing extraordinary about him, although Christ's flesh had become much better by arising. To correct this impression Christ said, ***do not touch me***. It was like saying: 'do not think that I have a

14. Gregory the Great, *Forty Gospel Homilies* 25.5.

15. Augustine, *The Trinity* 1.9.18.

16. John Chrysostom, *Commentary on Saint John* 86.2.

mortal life and can associate with you as before': *Even though we once regarded Christ from a human point of view, we regard him thus no longer* (2 Cor. 5:16). This is what he adds when he says, ***for I have not yet ascended to my Father.*** Accordingly, this statement does not give the reason for his prohibition, but an answer to an implicit question. It was like saying: 'although you see me remaining here, it is not because my flesh is not glorified but because ***I have not yet ascended to my Father.***' For before he ascended he wanted to strengthen in the hearts of the apostles their faith in his resurrection and in his divinity.

2519 After this he gives his positive directions, ***go to my brethren***, that is the apostles, because they are his brethren by his having the same nature: *He had to be made like his brethren in every respect* (Heb. 2:17); and they are his brethren by being adopted through grace, because they are the adopted children of his Father, of whom he is the natural Son.

Note the three privileges given to Mary Magdalene. *First*, she had the privilege of being a prophet because she was worthy enough to see the angels, for a prophet is an intermediary between angels and the people. *Second*, she had the dignity or rank of an angel insofar as she looked upon Christ, on whom the angels desire to look. *Third*, she had the office of an apostle; indeed, she was an apostle to the apostles insofar as it was her task to announce our Lord's resurrection to the disciples. Thus, just as it was a woman who was the first to announce the words of death, so it was a woman who would be the first to announce the words of life.

2520 ***And say to them, "I ascend to my Father and to your Father."*** As above: ***I am going to him who sent me*** (John 16:5);[17] *he who descended is he who also ascended far above all the heavens* (Eph. 4:10).

Arius based his error on these words, ***my Father and to your Father.*** He took it to mean that God is the Father of the Son in the same way that he is our Father, and that he is the God of the Son in the same way that he is our God. The answer to this is that the meaning of these words must be gathered from the circumstances in which they were spoken. Christ said before, ***go to my brethren.*** But Christ had these brethren insofar as he had a human nature, and in his human nature he is subject to the Father as a creature to the creator, for the body of Christ is something created.

2521 Or, according to Augustine, Christ is speaking of himself and referring to each of his natures.[18] ***I ascend to my Father and to your Father*** refers to his divine nature, and from this point of view he has as Father God, to whom he is equal and like in nature. Thus, the meaning is my Father by nature, and your Father by grace. It is saying in effect: 'the fact that you are adopted children by

17. See Thomas Aquinas, *On John* 16.1 (not included in this collection).

18. Augustine, *Tractates on the Gospel of John* 121.3.

grace is due to me': *God sent forth his Son . . . so that we might receive adoption as sons* (Gal. 4:4); *for those whom he foreknew he also predestined to be conformed to the image of his Son, in order that he might be the firstborn among many brethren* (Rom. 8:29). When he adds, ***to my God and your God***, he is referring to his human nature. From this point of view God rules him; thus he says, ***my God***, under whom I am a man. ***And your God***, and between him and you, I am the mediator: for God is our God because through Christ we are pleasing to him: *Since we are justified by faith, we have peace with God through our Lord Jesus Christ. Through him we have obtained access to this grace in which we stand, and we rejoice in our hope of sharing the glory of God* (Rom. 5:1–2); *in Christ God was reconciling the world to himself* (2 Cor. 5:19).

2522 Mary was quick to obey, as we see from ***Mary Magdalene went, and said to the disciples, "I have seen the Lord, and he said these things to me."*** She came from the place in the garden in front of the stone of the sepulcher, announcing to the disciples. *For I received from the Lord what I also delivered to you* (1 Cor. 11:23); *what I have heard from the Lord of hosts, the God of Israel, I announce to you* (Isa. 21:10).

1 Corinthians 15:20–28

Christ as Firstfruits of the Resurrection

On 1 Corinthians 15.3 (926–950)

15:20 ***But now Christ is risen from the dead, the firstfruits of those who sleep:***

15:21 ***For by a man came death: and by a man the resurrection of the dead.***

15:22 ***And as in Adam all die, so also in Christ all shall be made alive.***

15:23 ***But everyone in his own order: the firstfruits, Christ: then they who are of Christ, who have believed in his coming.***

15:24 ***Afterwards the end: when he shall have delivered up the kingdom to God and the Father: when he shall have brought to naught all principality and power and virtue.***

15:25 ***For he must reign, until he has put all his enemies under his feet.***

15:26 ***And the enemy, death, shall be destroyed last:***

15:27 ***For he has put all things under his feet. And whereas he says, "All things are put under him"; undoubtedly, he is excepted, who put all things under him.***

15:28 ***And when all things shall be subdued unto him, then the Son also himself shall be subject unto him that put all things under him, that God may be all in all.***

926 Here he proves that the conditional statement above set forth is true, namely, if Christ arose, the dead will rise.[19] In regard to this he does three things: *first,* he shows how Christ's resurrection is related to that of others; *second,* he shows the order of the resurrection, at ***but everyone in his own order***; *third,* he shows the end of the resurrection, at ***afterwards the end.***

19. Thomas seems to be referring here to 1 Cor. 15:13, which says *if the dead are not raised, then Christ has not been raised,* (see *On 1 Corinthians* 15.2 [not included in this collection]). Here he presents what is actually the logically equivalent contrapositive (as having applied *modus tollens*) of the former conditional. Accordingly, if it is false that Christ has not risen, then it is false that there is no resurrection of the dead.

In regard to the *first* he does two things: *first*, he shows the relationship of Christ's resurrection to that of others; *second*, he proves this relationship, at ***for***
927 ***by a man***. He says, therefore: ***now***, i.e., inasmuch as the aforesaid incongruities follow, if Christ has not risen, then to avoid them, let us say: ***Christ is risen***. This is true according to what is stated in the last chapter of Matthew and in other texts of the Gospels.

But Christ's resurrection is related to that of others as the firstfruits to those that follow, for the former excel in relation to the latter both in time and superiority or dignity; therefore, he says, ***He is risen***, not as the others, but as ***the firstfruits***, i.e., first in time and dignity: *the firstborn of the dead* (Rev. 1:5). ***The firstfruits***, I say, ***of those who sleep***, i.e., of the dead who rest in hope of the resurrection. From this can be inferred the conditional statement, because, as we say and is true, if Christ, who is ***the firstfruits of those that sleep***, arose, then so also will the others who sleep.

928 But something seems contrary to this, namely, that Christ did not resurrect as the firstfruits of those who sleep, because Lazarus was raised by Christ before his passion, and certain prophets raised others from the dead, as it says in the Old Testament. The answer is that resurrection is twofold: one is to mortal life, to which Lazarus and the others had been raised. The other is to immortal life, and it is about this that the Apostle speaks.

929 But on the other hand it is said in Matthew: *Many bodies of the saints who had fallen asleep were raised* (27:52). Therefore, since this happened before the resurrection of Christ and it is obvious that they did not rise to an immortal life, it seems that the first question still remains. I answer that what Matthew says about the resurrection of those souls, he says by anticipation, because although it is written in the tract on the passion, they did not rise then, but after Christ arose.

930 ***For by a man came death: and by a man the resurrection of the dead***. Here he proves the relationship posited, namely, that Christ is the firstfruits of them that sleep. *First*, he proves this in general terms; *second*, in particular terms, at ***and as in Adam all die***.

931 He proves it in a general way with the following reason: God willed to reintegrate human nature, which had been corrupted by man, because death entered through a man. Therefore, it pertained to the dignity of human nature that it be reintegrated by a man, but this is so that it be brought back to life. Therefore, it was fitting that just as death entered through a man, namely, Adam, so ***the resurrection of the dead*** be accomplished ***by a man***, namely, Christ: *If, because of one man's trespass, death reigned through that one man, much more will those who receive the abundance of grace and the free gift and of righteousness reign in life through the one man Jesus Christ* (Rom. 5:17).

932 ***And as in Adam.*** Here he proves the same in specific terms, saying that as in Adam we all die a bodily death, so too we are all made alive in Christ: *As sin came into the world through one man and death through sin . . .* (Rom. 5:12). He does not say 'through Eve,' which seems contrary to Sirach: *From a woman sin had its beginning* (25:24). This *from a woman* is said of Eve as the one who suggested [the original sin], but through Adam as cause. For if Eve alone had sinned, original sin would not have been passed on to their descendants.

All shall be made alive, I say, ***in Christ***, namely, the good and the bad with the life of nature, but the good only with the life of grace. Yet the Apostle speaks here of a resurrection to a life of nature, to which all shall be made alive. *As the Father has life in himself, so he has granted the Son also to have life in himself* (John 5:26), i.e., the power to grant life: *All who are in the tombs will hear his voice* (John 5:28).

933 ***But everyone in his own order.*** Here he shows the order of the resurrec-
tion. *First*, he gives the order itself; *second*, he exhibits what he had said, at ***the***
934 ***firstfruits, Christ.*** Therefore I say that it is true that in Christ shall all be made alive but in different ways, because there will be a difference between head and members and a difference as to the good and the evil. And therefore he says that ***everyone*** will rise ***in his own order***, namely in dignity: *Those that exist have been instituted by God* (Rom. 13:1).

935 Then he clarifies this order, because ***the firstfruits, Christ***, for he is prior in time and dignity, and of greater glory: *We have beheld his glory, glory as of the only Son from the Father* (John 1:14). ***Then they who are of Christ*** will also rise, those who are posterior in time and dignity. They are those who crucified their flesh with its vices: *When the time had fully come, God sent forth his Son* (Gal. 4:4); *I charge you to keep the commandment unstained and free from reproach until the appearing of our Lord Jesus Christ* (1 Tim. 6:14). He explains who are Christ's when he says: ***who have believed*** by faith working through love: *Whoever would draw near to God must believe that he exists* (Heb. 11:6), ***and in his coming*** both the first and the second.

But it should be noted that among the other saints there will be no order in time, as all will rise in the twinkling of an eye, but there will be an order in dignity, because a martyr will rise as a martyr, and an apostle as an apostle, and so on.

936 ***Afterwards the end.*** Here he shows the end of the resurrection, and it is twofold: one as to attaining the good; the other as to removal of the wicked, at ***for he must reign.*** In regard to the *first* he does two things: *first*, he shows that the attainment of the good itself consists in cleaving to God; *second*, he shows that it consists in a direct cleaving, at ***when he shall have brought to naught.***

937 He says, therefore: that ***afterwards***, i.e., after this, will be ***the end*** of the resurrection. And an end of this kind will not be such as to live a life of the body and for its pleasures, as the Jews and Saracens pretend, but that they will cleave to God by immediate vision and blessed enjoyment: and this is to hand over the kingdom to God and the Father.

Therefore, he says: ***when he shall have delivered up***, i.e., brings ***the kingdom***, i.e., his believers, whom he acquired by his own blood: *You were slain and by your blood did ransom men for God* (Rev. 5:9), ***to God and the Father***, i.e., before the sight of God, i.e., of his Creator, inasmuch as he is man, and of the Father, inasmuch as he is God. And this is what Philip sought: *Lord, show us the Father and we shall be satisfied* (John 14:8). But he will deliver it up in such a way that he does not take it from himself; indeed, he, the one God with the Father and the Holy Spirit will reign.

Or ***when he shall have delivered up the kingdom to God and the Father***, i.e., when he will show God the Father reigning. For in Scripture something is said to be done, when it first becomes known, and such knowledge is made by Christ: *No one knows the Father except the Son and anyone to whom the Son chooses to reveal him* (Matt. 11:27).

938 ***When he shall have brought to naught all principality and power and virtue.***[20] Here he shows the immediacy of the aforementioned adherence. For as it is said: *As long as the heir is a child, he . . . is under tutors* (Gal. 4:1 DRB). But when he is a great and mature man, then at home he is free of his teacher and tutor as the immediate subordinate of his father.

But the condition of this present life is akin to childhood; therefore, in this life we are under angels as under tutors inasmuch as they are over us and direct us. But when the kingdom is delivered over to God the Father, then we will be directly under God, and all other powers will cease. And this is what he says: ***when he shall have brought to naught all principality and power and virtue***, i.e., when all dominion both human and angelic shall have ceased, then we shall be immediately under God: *The Lord alone will be exalted on that day* (Isa. 2:11); *and no longer shall each man teach his neighbor . . . for they shall all know me . . . says the Lord* (Jer. 31:34).

939 But will not the orders of angels remain distinct? It seems so, as to the eminence of glory, by which one excels another, but not as to the efficacy of their activity toward us. Therefore, he says that those will be done away with whose names pertain to outward activity, namely, principalities, powers, and

20. This term 'virtue,' from the DRB translation of the Vulgate, is misleadingly antiquated in relation to contemporary usage. As used here, 'virtue' does not reference any moral quality, but an order of angelic or demonic beings. This use of 'virtue' derives from the Latin *virtus* which, although it can signal a moral quality, primarily means *manliness* and connotes *strength*, *vigor*, *power*, etc.

virtues. He does not name those who belong to the higher hierarchy, because they are not outwardly active; not angels, because it is their common name. He does not say that dominations will be done away with, because although they are among the outwardly active, they do not perform outward activity, but they direct and command. For it belongs to lords to direct and command, not to act outwardly. Archangels are included with the principalities, for *archos* is the same as prince.

According to Gregory these three orders are presented in descending order, because according to him principalities are above powers, and powers above virtues;[21] but according to Dionysius in ascending order, because he wants the virtues over the powers, and the powers over the principalities.[22]

Or in another way: ***when he shall have brought to naught***, i.e., then it will be known that principalities and powers and dominations had no power of themselves but from God, from whom are all things.

940 ***For he must reign***. Here the Apostle shows the end of the resurrection as to the removal of the wicked. This he shows by the destruction of all enemies of Christ: *first*, he mentions their destruction; *second*, the perfection of subjection, at ***and the enemy, death***; *third*, the end of the destruction, at ***and when all things shall be subdued***.

941 *First*, therefore, he says: I have said that the end will be when he has delivered the kingdom to God the Father. But will Christ have a kingdom in which he should reign: *All authority in heaven and on earth has been given to me* (Matt. 28:18); *and he will reign over the house of Jacob forever* (Luke 1:32)? ***He must reign***, I say, ***until he has put all his enemies under his feet***.

But aren't they under his feet now, i.e., under Christ's power? The answer is that the enemies of Christ are now under his power, but in two ways: either because they are converted by him, as Paul, whom he caused to fall on the ground (Acts 9:3); or inasmuch as Christ does his own will, even in regard to those who act here against Christ's will. So he puts his enemies under his feet by punishing them; but in the future he will put them under his feet, i.e., under Christ's humanity. For just as by the head is understood Christ's godhead, because ***the head of Christ is God*** (1 Cor. 11:3), so by the feet, his humanity. *Let us worship at his footstool* (Ps. 132:7). Thus, therefore, the enemies will not only be under the godhead, but also under the humanity of Christ: *At the name of Jesus every knee should bow* (Phil. 2:10).

942 But why does he say, ***until he has put all his enemies under his feet?*** Will he not reign until he does that? The answer is that this can be taken in two ways: for ***until*** sometimes determines a time and stands for what comes to an

21. Gregory the Great, *Forty Gospel Homilies* 34.

22. Pseudo-Dionysius, *The Celestial Hierarchy* 6.

end, as if I should say: I will not see God, until I die; because until then I will not see, but after that I shall see. But sometimes it stands for what does not come to an end, as when it is said in Matthew: *[Joseph] knew her not until she born a son* (1:25). Not that he wanted to say that he did not know her only up to the birth of her son, but neither did he afterwards ever know her, as Jerome says.[23] This manner is observed when one intends to exclude only those things about which there is doubt. Hence, the Gospel excluded only that which seems to be in doubt, namely, that Joseph knew the Blessed Virgin *before* she gave birth. But the fact that he did not know her after giving birth is doubted by no one, since he saw so many mysteries concerning the child, and he was so often warned by angels, and Jesus had been adored by the Magi; hence he could already have known that she was the Mother of God and, therefore, he did not wish to preclude this. This is the way the Apostle speaks here.

For the fact that anyone should reign with his enemies not yet subdued, seems to be doubtful, but that he should reign after his enemies have been subjugated, no one doubts. Therefore, he excludes the first, saying: ***until he has put all his enemies***. As if to say: 'it is true that Christ has a kingdom and although there are some enemies, while they do not do his will, nevertheless he rules' and ***put all his enemies under his feet***.

943 The phrase, ***until he has put all his enemies*** can be understood in another way, so that ***until*** determines a time and stands for what is to come. As if to say: ***he must reign***. But when? ***Until he has put all his enemies under his feet***. As if to say: 'until then he will reign, until he puts his enemies under his feet, but after that he will not reign.'

But according to this explanation 'to reign' does not imply having a kingdom, but in making progress in reigning and increasing the kingdom, and this as to a perfect manifestation of a kingdom of Christ. As if to say: 'Christ's kingdom grows gradually, namely, inasmuch as it is manifested and becomes known, ***until he has put all his enemies under his feet***, i.e., until all enemies admit that he rules: for the good will admit this with the joy of beatitude but the evil with confusion. And afterward he does not reign, i.e., his kingdom does not grow and it is not further manifested, because it will already be fully manifest.'

944 So, therefore, the subjection of all adversaries is clear, which subjection will, indeed, be most complete, because even that which is extremely hostile will be subjected to him. This, however, is death, which is contrary to life most of all; and therefore, he says: ***the last enemy***, where he does three things. *First*, he mentions death's subjection; *second*, he proves this by an authority, at ***for***

23. Jerome, *On the Perpetual Virginity of the Blessed Mary* 6.

he has put all things under his feet; *third*, he argues from this authority: ***and whereas he says.***

945 He says, therefore: I have said that he has subjected all enemies under his feet. But how? Most completely, I say, because ***the enemy, death, shall be destroyed last***, namely, at the end, because it could not exist with life, when all shall be alive through the resurrection: *I will be your death, O death* (Hos. 13:14 DRB); *he will swallow up death forever* (Isa. 25:8).

946 It should be noted that from this word Origen took the occasion of his error.[24] For he wanted the punishments of the damned to be a cleansing and not eternal, and he wanted that all in hell will be converted to Christ at some time and be saved, including the devil; and he confirms this with the words, ***until I have put all my enemies under my feet.*** And he understands by ***enemies under my feet*** the subjection which occurs when sinners are converted to God, not of the subjection by which those are subject to Christ who are never converted to Christ, inasmuch as he punishes them in hell. Therefore, he says: ***He must reign, until he has put all his enemies under his feet***, because at that time all the damned and those in hell will be saved, inasmuch as they will be converted to him and will serve him, and not only those condemned men; but ***the enemy, death***, i.e., the devil, ***shall be destroyed***, not that he will not exist at all, but that he will not be death, because even in the end the devil himself will be saved. But this is heretical and condemned by a Council.[25]

947 Again it should be noted that the Apostle clearly stated that ***The enemy, death, shall be destroyed last***, in order to remove two questions which can arise concerning things predicted about the resurrection, namely, whether Christ could give life to the dead. And this is solved, because he has put all his enemies under his feet, and even death itself.

And why has he not raised all at once? The answer to this is that he must first subject the enemies under his feet, and finally when death itself is destroyed, then all will rise to life. Therefore, he delays, not because he is unable, but that he might preserve order, because things that are from God are in order.

948 That death itself will be subjected to Christ he proves with an authority: *You have put all things under his feet* (Ps. 8:6), i.e., under his humanity, namely, Christ's. *And every tongue [should] confess that Jesus Christ is Lord* (Phil. 2:11); *to me every knee shall bow, every tongue shall swear* (Isa. 45:23).

949 From this authority he argues, saying: ***and whereas he says.*** The reasoning is this: the prophet says, ***all things are put under him***; by saying ***all things***,

24. See Origen, *On First Principles* 1.6.1–2. and 3.6.5.

25. St. Thomas seems to be speaking here of the *Canons against Origen* (see especially canon 9), promulgated originally at the Synod of Constantinople (543) and subsequently ratified at the Second Council of Constantinople (553).

nothing is excluded, except the one who subjects. Therefore, all things including death are subjected to Christ. He says, therefore: ***when it says, all things are put under him***, namely, Christ as man, ***he is excepted***, namely, the Father, ***who put all things under him*** and put *everything in subjection to him* (Heb. 2:8); *all authority in heaven and on earth has been given to me* (Matt. 28:18).

But on the other hand. If the Father subjected all things to the Son, the Son is less than the Father. The answer is that the Father subjected all to the Son as man, as has been stated, and so the Father is greater than the Son. For he is less according to his humanity, but equal according to his divinity. Or it might be said that even the Son himself as God subjected all things to himself, because as God he can do all that the Father does: *We await a Savior who will change our lowly body to be like his glorious body, by the power which enables him even to subject all things to himself* (Phil. 3:20).

Then when he says: ***and when all things shall be subdued unto him***, he shows that the end of this resurrection is not in the humanity of Christ, but the rational creature will be further led to contemplating the divinity, and in it is our happiness.

950 Therefore, he says, ***when all things shall be subdued*** as if to say: 'God has not yet subjected all things to Christ, but when all things shall have been subjected to him, namely, to Christ, then the Son himself according to his humanity will be subjected to him, namely, to the Father': *The Father is greater than I* (John 14:28), and even now Christ as man is subjected to the Father, but this will be more manifest then.

The reason for this subjection is ***that God may be all in all***, i.e., that the soul of men may rest entirely in God, and God alone be beatitude. For now there is life and virtue in one and glory in another; but then God will be the life and salvation and virtue and glory and all things.

Or in another way: ***that God may be all in all***, because then it will be clear that whatever good we have is from God.

1 Thessalonians 4:12–18

Christ's Resurrection Raises the World

On 1 Thessalonians 4.2 (92–105)

4:12 ***And that you walk honestly towards those who are without: and that you want nothing of any man's.***

4:13 ***And we will not have you ignorant, brethren, concerning those who are asleep, that you be not sorrowful, even as others who have no hope.***

4:14 ***For if we believe that Jesus died and rose again: even so will God bring with him those who have slept through Jesus.***

4:15 ***For this we say unto you in the word of the Lord, that we who are alive, who remain unto the coming of the Lord, shall not prevent those who have slept.***

4:16 ***For the Lord himself shall come down from heaven with commandment and with the voice of an archangel and with the trumpet of God: and the dead who are in Christ shall rise first.***

4:17 ***Then we who are alive, who are left, shall be taken up together with them in the clouds to meet Christ, into the air: and so shall we be always with the Lord.***

4:18 ***Therefore, comfort one another with these words.***

92 In what went before Paul aimed at bringing them to the practice of continence in place of their concupiscence, and at curtailing their idleness.[26] Now he urges them to lessen their inordinate sorrow. *First,* he provides a warning; *second*, he assigns a reason for the warning, at ***for if we believe.***

93 Therefore, he forbids them to indulge in inordinate sorrow when he tells them, ***even as others.*** It seems, though, that the Apostle views sorrow for the dead benignly. Nevertheless, he cautions them not to grieve overmuch, ***even as others.***

Someone who grieves for the dead does possess compassion. A person grieves *first* because of the dissolution of the frail body; for we ought to take care of the body for the sake of the soul. *O death, how bitter is the reminder of*

26. See 1 Thessalonians 4:1–11 and Thomas Aquinas, *On 1 Thessalonians* 4.1 (not included in this collection).

you to one who lives at peace among his possessions (Sir. 41:1). *Second,* a person grieves because of the separation and departure which is so painful to friends. *Surely the bitterness of death is past* (1 Sam. 15:32). *Third,* we mourn because death reminds us of our own sin. *The wages of sin is death* (Rom. 6:23). *Fourth,* because death reminds us of our own death. *For this is the end of all men, and the living will lay it to heart* (Eccles. 7:2).

So moderate sorrow is permitted. *Weep less bitterly for the dead, for he has attained rest* (Sir. 22:11). Therefore, he says, ***even as others who have no hope,*** that is, because these people believe that these negative aspects of death are eternal; but we do not believe so. *Our commonwealth is in heaven, and from it we await a Savior, the Lord Jesus Christ, who will change our lowly body to be like his glorious body* (Phil. 3:20–21). So he says clearly, ***concerning those who are asleep.*** *Our friend Lazarus has fallen asleep* (John 11:11).

A person who decides to go to sleep does three things. *First,* he lies down with the hope of eventually getting up: *Shall he that sleeps arise again no more?* (Ps. 41:8 DRB). A person who passes away abiding in the faith feels the same way. *Second,* the soul in a sleeping person remains vigilant. *I slept, but my heart was awake* (Song of Sol. 5:2). *Third,* after sleep a man gets up much more refreshed and restored. In this same manner the saints will rise incorruptibly (1 Cor. 15:52).

94 Then when Paul says, ***for if we believe,*** he provides a reason for the warning he had given. *First,* he establishes the resurrection; *second,* he rules out the faint suspicion of a delay, at ***for this we say***; *third,* he outlines the order of resurrection, at ***for the Lord himself.***

95 It should be realized that the Apostle constructs the case for our resurrection on the basis of the resurrection of Christ (1 Cor. 15:12), for Christ's resurrection is the cause of our resurrection. So Paul makes his point here by a causal analysis. Christ's resurrection is not only the cause but also the pattern of our resurrection. The Word made flesh revives our bodies, while the Word as such revives our souls. Christ is the pattern of our resurrection in that Christ assumed flesh and also rose embodied in flesh. Nor is Christ only the pattern; he is also the efficient cause of our resurrection, for the things done by Christ's humanity were done not only by the power of his human nature, but also by virtue of his divinity united in him. Just as his touch cured the leper as an instrument of his divinity, so also Christ's resurrection is the cause of our resurrection, not merely because it was a body that arose, but a body united to the Word of life.

So the Apostle, firmly presupposing this, declares, ***for if we believe*** firmly ***that Jesus died and rose again: even so will God bring with him those who have slept through Jesus.*** Those have ***slept through Jesus*** who were conformed to his death through baptism; or he says ***through Jesus***, because God will bring them with him, that is, with Christ himself. *The Lord your God will come, and all the holy ones with him* (Zech. 14:5). *The Lord enters into judgment with the elders and princes of his people* (Isa. 3:14).

96 Then when he says, ***for this we say***, he rules out a delay in regard to the resurrection, as if saying: we know that they shall rise and shall come with Christ; therefore, we ought not to grieve so much. For those who shall be found alive will not achieve the glory of resurrection before those who are dead. And for this reason he says: ***for this we say unto you***, not as the conjecture of a man, but ***in the word of the Lord***, whose words do not fail. ***That we who are alive***, that is, those who are living, shall not receive the consolation accompanying the coming of Christ before the dead. As a result Paul says, ***We who are alive, who remain unto the coming of the Lord, shall not prevent those who have slept.***

It would seem to those who do not fully understand what the Apostle is saying here that all this shall come about while the Apostle is still alive; it seemed this way to the Thessalonians. Because of this misunderstanding he wrote them a second letter in which he says: *Now concerning the coming of our Lord Jesus Christ . . . we beg you, brethren, not to be quickly shaken in mind or excited, either by spirit or by word, or by letter purporting to be from us, to the effect that the day of the Lord has come* (2 Thess. 2:2). But he is not talking at present about himself and his contemporaries, but about those who shall be found alive at the time of Christ's coming. ***We . . . who remain***, that is, those who shall be left after the persecution of the Antichrist, ***shall not prevent those***, that is, those who are living shall not receive their consolation first. *In a moment, in the twinkling of an eye, at the last trumpet* (1 Cor. 15:52).

97 Then when he says, ***for the Lord himself shall come down from heaven***, he shows the order and manner of the resurrection. *First*, he discusses the cause of the resurrection; *second*, he presents its order and manner, at ***and the dead***; *third*, he ends with a consideration of their mutual consolation, at ***therefore, comfort one another.***

98 He proves his *first* point by saying, ***the Lord himself.*** It should be noted here, as was already mentioned before, that the cause of the general resurrection is Christ's resurrection. But if you should say: since it has already occurred (that is the resurrection of Christ), why does not its effect follow?

I would reply to this by saying that it is the cause of our resurrection according to the activity of the divine power. God, however, acts according to the order of his wisdom. Therefore, our resurrection will occur when the order of divine wisdom shall determine it.

In order to prove that Christ is the cause of the resurrection, he shows that all the dead shall rise in the presence of Christ. Three causes cooperate in the accomplishment of the general resurrection: the *principal* cause is the divine power; the *second* cause is instrumental, that is, the power of the humanity of Christ. The *third* cause might be termed a ministering cause in that the power of the angels will have some effect in the resurrection.

For Augustine shows that the things that occur now by virtue of corporeal creatures actually occur through God, by their mediation.[27] In the resurrection, some things shall be done through the angels, such as the collection of the dust. But the restoration of the bodies and the soul's reunion with the body will be accomplished immediately through Christ.

99 Paul then presents these three causes. *First*, he sets forth the glorious humanity of Christ when he says, ***the Lord himself.*** *Jesus . . . will come in the same way as you saw him go into heaven* (Acts 1:11). ***With commandment.*** In the first coming, he came as obedient: *He became obedient unto death* (Phil. 2:8). And that happened because it was the coming of humility; but this one will be the coming of glory, *and then they will see the Son of man coming . . . with power and great glory* (Luke 21:27).

Second, he presents the power of the angels when he says, ***with the voice of an archangel***, not that anything is done by his voice, but rather by his ministry. He says, ***of an archangel*** for all angels minister to the Church under one archangel. This is Michael, the prince of the Church (Rev. 12:7). Or perhaps, ***with the voice of an archangel***, that is, Christ's, who is prince of the angels, *wonderful counselor* (Isa. 9:6). And the resurrection shall be through Christ's voice, corporeal or spiritual. *All who are in the tombs will hear his voice* (John 5:28); in other words, the dead shall rise and come to judgment, and they shall obey the bodily voice.

Third, he considers the divine power when he says, ***with the trumpet of God.*** This is the divine power which is referred to as the voice of the Archangel insofar as it will act through the ministry of the Archangel. It is called the trumpet of God since the resurrection does come about by divine power. It is called a trumpet because of its resonance, which is derived from God who raises the dead. In addition, the trumpet, which had many uses in the Old Testament, brings people together for war, *and creation will join with him to fight* (Wis. 5:20). The trumpet was also used for celebrations, as it will be employed in the heavenly Jerusalem. In addition, the trumpet was used for deploying the armies; in this way holy men assisted in the movement of troops. And so if it is a sound that you can hear, it is called a trumpet; but if it is not a sound, then it is the divine power of Christ present and manifest to the whole world.

100 Then when Paul says, ***and the dead***, he mentions the order that the resurrection will follow. In doing so he makes three points. *First*, he treats the

27. Augustine, *The Trinity* 3.1.1.

resurrection of the dead; *second*, he considers the meeting of the living with Christ, at ***then we who are alive***; finally, he refers to the happiness of the saints with Christ, at ***and so shall we be always.***

101 Because of these words some people believed that the last people alive would never die, as Jerome mentions in his letter.[28] For Paul has said, ***then we who are alive, who are left, shall be taken up together with them***. It might seem that there would be no other reason for distinguishing the living from the dead.

But on the contrary: *We shall all indeed rise* (1 Cor. 15:51 DRB). *Just as in Adam all die, so also in Christ shall all be made alive* (1 Cor. 15:22). *So death spread to all men* (Rom. 5:12).

And so I say that some shall be alive at the time when Christ shall come for judgment, but in that moment they shall die and immediately afterwards they will rise. Because of the minimal time involved they are regarded as living.

102 But then another problem presents itself because it is said: ***and the dead in Christ shall rise first*** and ***then we who are alive.*** So it seems that the dead will rise before the living will meet Christ, and that the living will die when they meet him. So it appears that some will rise ahead of these others, and that there will not be a resurrection of everyone at the same time. This is contrary, however, to what is found in 1 Corinthians: *in a moment, in the twinkling of an eye, at the last trumpet* (15:52).

I wish to point out that there are two opinions on this matter. For some say that the resurrection will not take place at the same time for everybody, but that first the dead will come with Christ, and during the time that Christ is coming the living will be taken up into the clouds and they will die and rise while they are being taken up. So that what is said to happen in a moment may be understood as occurring in a brief amount of time. And if you insist that it will happen in an instant, then it should not be applied to the total resurrection of all, but rather to the resurrection of individuals, for every individual will rise in an instant.

But there are others, who maintain that everyone will rise at the same time and in an instant. They feel that where Paul says ***shall rise first***, he denotes the
103 order of dignity, not the order of time. This does seem difficult to maintain, for many still alive will suffer in the persecution of the Antichrist and be more distinguished than those who had died before.

And so it seems necessary to answer the question in a different way, saying that all will die and all will rise at the same time. For the Apostle does not say that the dead will rise first and then the living, but that the dead will rise before the living will meet Christ. Therefore he is not speaking about the resurrection in terms of the order in which they shall rise, but of the order in

28. Jerome, *Epistle* 119.7.

which they will be taken up to meet Christ. For when the Lord does come, first those who are found alive will die and then, immediately together with those who had died before, they will rise up and be taken up into the clouds to meet Christ, as Paul clearly says.

But there is a difference between the good and the evil people, because the evil people will remain on the earth that they loved, while the good people will be taken up to the Christ whom they had sought. *Wherever the body is, there the eagles will be gathered together* (Matt. 24:28). In the time of the resurrection the saints will be conformed to Christ, not only with regard to the glory of the body (Phil. 3:21), but also with respect to place, for Christ will be in a cloud. *A cloud took him out of their sight* (Acts 1:9), and *Jesus will come in the same way as you saw him go into heaven* (Acts 1:11). And so the saints too will be taken up into the clouds.

The reason for this is to show their likeness to God. For in the Old Testament the glory of the Lord appeared in the form of a cloud. *The Lord said that he would dwell in a cloud* (1 Kings 8:12 DRB). These clouds will be prepared by divine power in order to show the glory of the saints. Or, the resplendent bodies of the glorified will appear as clouds to the evil people who will remain on earth. *Behold, the bridegroom! Come out to meet him* (Matt. 25:6).

104 Then when Paul says, ***And so we shall be always with the Lord***, he shows the beatitude of the saints, for they shall always be with the Lord and derive constant enjoyment from him. *I will come again and will take you to myself, that where I am you may be also* (John 14:3). The saints desire this: *My desire is to depart and be with Christ* (Phil. 1:23).

105 Then when he says, ***Comfort one another with these words***, Paul concludes that they should comfort one another about the dead. He feels that since the saints will rise without suffering any loss, the Thessalonians should comfort one another about the dead. *Comfort, comfort my people, says your God* (Isa. 40:1).

PART III

IN HIM

Participation in Christ's Life

Praise, O Zion, Your Redeemer

A HYMN OF THOMAS AQUINAS

Praise, O Zion, your redeemer.
Praise your prince and shepherd
with canticle and hymn.

Dare to praise him as you can,
for he is greater than all praise.
Our brightest praises are but dim.

A theme of special praising now
—life-giving bread, the Bread of Life—
is proclaimed this day.

This bread at holy supper
to brethren twelve was portioned out.
Let none this beauty betray.

Let praise be full, let praise resound,
let joyful and harmonious be
our souls' deep jubilation.

For now we observe a solemn day;
we now recall this founding,
our feast's first celebration.

At this supper of our new king,
the Paschal feast's new covenant
has put the old to flight.

The old will flee from what is new
as shadows flee from truth
and day casts out the night.

What Christ enacted at that meal
we evermore should re-enact,
his memory to perpetuate.

By this sacred action taught,
the bread and wine for our salvation
as victim now we consecrate.

This truth to Christians is proclaimed:
that to flesh, bread is transformed,
and transformed to blood is wine.

What you can neither grasp nor see,
a lively faith will yet affirm
beyond this world's design.

Under different guises there
—which act as signs, not things—
wonderous matters are enshrined.

Flesh is food and blood is drink.
Christ, however, still remains
fully in each kind.

Left entire for each partaker,
neither broken nor divided,
he is received into the soul.

If one or multitudes consume,
however many, he still is one.
Consumed, he yet stays whole.

Whether good or evil men receive,
they have unequal destinies:
eternal life or else perdition,

death for the bad, life for the good.
See how similar acts can end
in opposite condition.
When the host at last is broken
from all doubting be restrained:
as much remains in a single part
as the primal whole contained.

No actual thing is cut apart,
breaking but a sign is gained.
State and stature undiminished,
the signified is yet retained.

Behold the bread of angels,
as pilgrims' food inherited!
It is the bread of all true heirs
not to lowly dogs outspread.

In prototypes it was foreshadowed:
when Isaac to sacrifice was led,
when Passover lambs were set aside
and manna to our fathers fed.

Good Shepherd, Bread of Truth,
Lord Jesus, show your clemency.
May you feed us, may you guard us,
may you let us see good things
in our homeland eternally.

You who know and do all things
feed us though still captive here.
Make us fellow citizens,
co-heirs, and friends of all the saints
in that City bright and clear.

Amen

Chapter 7
CHRIST'S REVELATION OF THE FATHER

John 1:9–10
The World's Ignorance of the Word
On John 1.5 (124–141)

1:9 ***He was the true light, which enlightens every man coming into this world.***

1:10 ***He was in the world, and through him the world was made, and the world did not know him.***

124 Above, the Evangelist considered the precursor and his witness to the incarnate Word; in the present section he considers the incarnate Word himself. As to this he does three things. *First*, he shows why it was necessary for the Word to come. *Second*, the benefit we received from the coming of the Word, at ***He came unto his own*** (John 1:11). And *third*, the way he came, at ***The Word was made flesh*** (John 1:14).

The necessity for the Word's coming is seen to be the lack of divine knowledge in the world. He points out this need for his coming when he says, ***For this I was born, and for this I came into the world, that I should give testimony to the truth*** (John 18:37). To indicate this lack of divine knowledge, the Evangelist does two things. *First*, he shows that this lack does not pertain to God or the Word. *Second*, that it does pertain to men, at ***and the world did not know him.*** He shows in three ways that there was no defect in God or in the Word that prevented men from knowing God and from being enlightened by the Word. *First*, from the efficacy of the divine light itself, because ***He was the true light, which enlightens every man coming into this world.*** *Second*, from the presence of the divine light, because ***he was in the world.*** *Third*, from the obviousness of the light, because ***through him the world was made.***

So the lack of divine knowledge in the world was not due to the Word, because he is efficacious. *First*, he shows the nature of this efficiency, that is, ***he was the true light.*** *Second*, its very efficiency, ***which enlightens every man.***

125 The divine Word is efficacious in enlightening because ***he was the true light.*** How the Word is light, and how he is the light of men need not be

discussed again, because it was sufficiently explained above.[1] What we must discuss at present is how he is the ***true light***.

To explain this, we should note that in Scripture the *true* is contrasted with three things. Sometimes it is contrasted with the false, as in *Putting away falsehood, let everyone speak the truth* (Eph. 4:25). Sometimes it is contrasted with what is figurative, as in ***The law was given through Moses; grace and truth came through Jesus Christ*** (John 1:17), because the truth of the figures contained in the law was fulfilled by Christ. Sometimes it is contrasted with what is something by participation, as in *we are in him who is true, in his Son, Jesus Christ* (1 John 5:20), who is not his Son by participation.

Before the Word came there was in the world a certain light which the philosophers prided themselves on having; but this was a false light, because as is said, *They became futile in their thinking, and their senseless minds were darkened. Claiming to be wise, they became fools* (Rom. 1:21–22); *every man is become a fool for knowledge* (Jer. 10:14 DRB). There was another light from the teaching of the law which the Jews boasted of having; but this was a symbolic light: *The law has but a shadow of the good things to come instead of the true form of these realities* (Heb. 10:1). There was also a certain light in the angels and in holy men in so far as they knew God in a more special way by grace; but this was a participated light, *Upon whom does his light not arise?* (Job 25:3), which is like saying: 'whoever shines, shines to the extent that he participates in his light, i.e., God's light. But the Word of God was not a false light, nor a symbolic light, nor a participated light, but the true light, i.e., light by his essence.' Therefore he says, ***he was the true light***.

126 This excludes two errors. *First*, that of Photinus, who believed that Christ derived his beginning from the Virgin. So, lest anyone suppose this, the Evangelist, speaking of the incarnation of the Word, says, ***he was the true light***, i.e., eternally, not only before the Virgin, but before every creature.

This also excludes the error of Arius and Origen; they said that Christ was not true God, but God by participation.[2] If this were so, he could not be the true light, as the Evangelist says here, *God is light* (1 John 1:5), i.e., not by participation, but ***the true light***. So if the Word was the true light, it is plain that he is true God.

Now it is clear how the divine Word is effective in causing divine knowl-
127 edge. The effectiveness or efficiency of the Word lies in the fact that he ***enlightens every man coming into this world***. For everything that is what it is by participation is derived from that which is such by its essence; just as everything afire is so by participation in fire, which is fire by its very essence.

1. See Thomas Aquinas, *On John* 1.3 (not included in this collection).

2. Origen, *Commentary on John* 2.17–18.

Then since the Word is the true light by his very essence, then everything that shines must do so through him, insofar as it participates in him. And so he ***enlightens every man coming into this world.***

128 To understand this, we should know that *world* is taken in three ways in Scripture. Sometimes, from the point of view of its creation, as when the Evangelist says here, ***through him the world was made.*** Sometimes, from the point of view of its perfection, which it reaches through Christ, for *in Christ God was reconciling the world to himself* (2 Cor. 5:19). And sometimes it is taken from the point of view of its perversity, as in *The whole world is in the power of the evil one* (1 John 5:19).

On the other hand, *enlightenment* or *being enlightened* by the Word is taken in two ways. *First*, in relation to the light of natural knowledge, as in *The light of your countenance, O Lord, is signed upon us* (Ps. 4:6 DRB). *Second*, as the light

129 of grace: *Be enlightened, O Jerusalem* (Isa. 60:1 DRB). With these two sets of distinctions in mind, it is easy to solve a difficulty which arises here. For when the Evangelist says, ***enlightens every man***, this seems to be false, because there are still many in darkness in the world.

However, if we bear in mind these distinctions and take ***world*** from the standpoint of its creation, and ***enlightens*** as referring to the light of natural reason, the statement of the Evangelist is beyond reproach. For all men coming into this visible world are enlightened by the light of natural knowledge through participating in this true light, which is the source of all the light of natural knowledge participated in by men. When the Evangelist speaks of ***man coming into this world***, he does not mean that men had lived for a certain time outside the world and then came into the world, since this is contrary to the teaching of the Apostle: *They were not yet born and had done nothing either good or bad* (Rom. 9:11). Therefore, since they had done nothing before they were born, it is plain that the soul does not exist prior to its union with the body.

He refers to ***every man coming into this world***, to show that men are enlightened by God with respect to that according to which they came into the world, i.e., with respect to the intellect, which is something external. For man is constituted of a twofold nature, bodily and intellectual. According to his bodily or sensible nature, man is enlightened by a bodily and sensible light; but according to his soul and intellectual nature, he is enlightened by an intellectual and spiritual light. Now man does not come into this world according to his bodily nature, but under this aspect, he is from the world. His intellectual nature is derived from a source external to the world, as has been said, i.e., from God through creation; as in *The dust returns to the earth as it was, and the spirit returns to God who gave it* (Eccles. 12:7). For these reasons, when the Evangelist speaks of ***coming into this world***, he is showing that this enlightenment refers to what is from without, that is, the intellect.

130 If we understand *enlightenment* with respect to the light of grace, then ***he enlightens every man*** may be explained in three ways. The *first* way is by Origen in his homily *The Great Eagle* and is this.[3] ***World*** is understood from the point of view of its perfection, which man attains by his reconciliation through Christ. And so we have, ***he enlightens every man coming***, by faith, ***into this world***, i.e., this spiritual world, that is, the Church, which has been enlightened by the light of grace.

Chrysostom explains it another way.[4] He takes ***world*** under the aspect of creation. Then the sense is: ***he enlightens***, i.e., the Word does, in so far as it depends on him, because he fails no one, but rather *desires all men to be saved and to come to the knowledge of the truth* (1 Tim. 2:4); ***every man coming***, i.e., who is born into this sensible world. If anyone is not enlightened, it is due to himself, because he turns from the light that enlightens.

Augustine explains it a *third* way.[5] For him, 'every' has a restricted application, so that the sense is: ***he enlightens every man coming into this world***, not ***every man*** universally, but every man who is enlightened, since no one is enlightened except by the Word. According to Augustine, the Evangelist says, ***coming into this world***, in order to give the reason why man needs to be enlightened, and he is taking ***world*** from the point of view of its perversity and defect.[6] It is as though he were saying: 'man needs to be enlightened because he is coming into this world which is darkened by perversity and defects and is full of ignorance.' This followed the spiritual world of the first man: *To give light to those who sit in darkness and in the shadow of death* (Luke 1:79).

131 The above statement refutes the error of the Manicheans, who think that men were created in the world from an opposing principle, i.e., the devil. For if man were a creature of the devil when coming into this world, he would not be enlightened by God or by the Word, for *the Son of God appeared . . . to destroy the works of the devil* (1 John 3:8).

132 So it is clear, from the efficacy of the divine Word, that the lack of knowledge in men is not due to the Word, because he is effective in enlightening all, being ***the true light, which enlightens every man coming into this world***. But

3. The author of the homily referenced here is actually John Scotus Eriugena (c. 800–877). For an English translation of the homily, see *The Voice of the Eagle: The Heart of Celtic Christianity: John Scotus Eriugena's Homily on the Prologue to the Gospel of John*, trans. Christopher Bamford (Great Barrington, MA: Lindisfarne Books, 2000).

4. John Chrysostom, *Commentary on Saint John* 8.1.

5. Augustine, *The Enchiridion* 27.103.

6. Augustine, *Tractates on the Gospel of John* 2.7.

so you do not suppose this lack arose from the withdrawal or absence of the true light, the Evangelist rules this out adding, ***he was in the world***.

A comparable statement is found in Acts: *He is not far from any one of us*, that is, God, *for in him we live, and move, and are* (17:28). It is as though the Evangelist were saying: 'The divine Word is effective and is at hand in order to enlighten us.'

133 We should remark that something is said to be in the world in three ways. In one way, by being contained, as a thing in place exists in a place: ***They are in the world*** (John 17:11). In another way, as a part in a whole; for a part of the world is said to be in the world even though it is not in a place. For example, supernatural substances, although not in the world as in a place, are nevertheless in it as parts: *God, who made heaven and earth, the sea, and all things that are in them* (Ps. 146:6).

But the true light was not in the world in either of these ways, because that light is neither localized nor is it a part of the universe. Indeed (if we can speak this way), the entire universe is in a certain sense a part since it participates in a partial way in his goodness. Accordingly, the true light was in the world in a *third* way, i.e., as an efficient and preserving cause: *Do I not fill heaven and earth?* (Jer. 23:24).

However, there is a difference between the way the Word acts and causes all things and the way in which other agents act. For other agents act as existing externally: since they do not act except by moving and altering a thing qualitatively in some way with respect to its exterior, they work from without. But God acts in all things from within, because he acts by creating. Now to create is to give being to the thing created. So, since existence is innermost in each thing, God, who by acting gives existence, acts in things from within. Hence God was in the world as one giving existence to the world.

134 It is customary to say that God is in all things by his essence, presence, and power. To understand what this means, we should know that someone is said to be by his power in all the things that are subject to his power; as a king is said to be in the entire kingdom subject to him, by his power. He is not there, however, by presence or essence. Someone is said to be by presence in all the things that are within his range of vision as a king is said to be in his house by presence. And someone is said to be by essence in those things in which his substance is, as a king is in one determinate place.

Now we say that God is everywhere by his power, since all things are subject to his power: *If I ascend into heaven, you are there . . . if I take the wings of the morning and dwell in the uttermost parts of the sea, even there your hand shall lead me, and your right hand shall hold me* (Ps. 139:8–10). He is also everywhere by his presence, and *all are open and laid bare to the eyes of him* (Heb. 4:13). He is present everywhere by his essence, because his essence is innermost in all things. For every agent, as acting, has to be immediately joined to its effect, because mover and moved must be together. Now God is the maker and preserver of all things with respect to the existence of each. Hence, since the existence of a thing is innermost in that thing, it is plain that God, by his essence, through which he creates all things, is in all things.

135 It should be noted that the Evangelist significantly uses the word ***was*** [*erat*] when he says, ***he was in the world***, showing that from the beginning of creation he was always in the world, causing and preserving all things; because if God for even a moment were to withhold his power from the things he established, all would return to nothing and cease to be.

Hence Origen uses an apt example to show this, when he says that as a human vocal sound is to a human word conceived in the mind, so is, the creature to the divine Word;[7] for as our vocal sound is the effect of the word conceived in our mind, so the creature is the effect of the Word conceived in the divine mind. *He spoke, and they were made* (Ps. 148:5 DRB). Hence, just as we notice that as soon as our inner word vanishes, the sensible vocal sound also ceases, so, if the power of the divine Word were withdrawn from things, all of them would immediately cease to be at that moment. And this is because he is *upholding the universe by his word of power* (Heb. 1:3).

136 So it is plain that a lack of divine knowledge in minds is not due to the absence of the Word, because ***he was in the world***; nor is it due to the invisibility or concealment of the Word, because he has produced a work in which his likeness is clearly reflected, that is, the world, *for from the greatness and beauty of created things comes a corresponding perception of their Creator* (Wis. 13:5). *His invisible nature . . . has been clearly perceived in the things that have been made* (Rom. 1:20). And so the Evangelist at once adds, ***and through him the world was made***, in order that that light might be manifested in it. For as a work of art manifests the art of the artisan, so the whole world is nothing else than a certain representation of the divine wisdom conceived within the mind of the Father: *He poured her out upon all his works* (Sir. 1:9).

Now it is clear that the lack of divine knowledge is not due to the Word, because he is efficacious, being ***the true light***; and he is at hand, since ***he was***
137 ***in the world***; and he is knowable, since ***through him the world was made***. The Evangelist indicates the source of this lack when he says, ***and the world did not know him***, as if to say: 'it is not due to him, but to the world, who ***did not know him***.' He says ***him*** in the singular, because earlier he had called the Word not only the ***light of men*** (John 1:4), but also ***God*** (John 1:1); and so when he says ***him***, he means God. Again, he uses ***world*** for man. For the angels knew

7. John Scotus Eriugena, *The Voice of the Eagle* 18.

him by their understanding, and the elements by their obeying him; but ***the***
138 ***world***, i.e., man, who lives in the world, ***did not know him***. We attribute this lack of divine knowledge either to the nature of man or to his guilt.

To his nature, indeed, because although all the aforesaid aids were given to man to lead him to the knowledge of God, human reason in itself lacks this knowledge. *Man beholds it from afar* (Job 36:25), and immediately after, *God is great beyond our knowledge*. But if some have known him, this was not insofar as they were in the world, but insofar as they were above the world; and the kind for whom the world was not worthy, because ***the world did not know him***. And this is a certain kind of reason why God is not known by man. And also as the world has an inordinate love of the world; thus it is said ***the world did not know him***. Hence if they mentally perceived anything eternal, that was insofar as they were not of this world.

But if this lack is attributed to man's guilt, then the phrase ***the world did not know him*** is a kind of reason why God was not known by man; in this sense ***world*** is taken for inordinate lovers of the world. It is as though it said, '***the world did not know him***, because they were lovers of the world.' For the love of the world, as Augustine says, is what chiefly withdraws us from the knowledge of God, because love of the world makes one an enemy to God (James 4:4);[8] *the sensual man does not perceive the things that pertain to the Spirit of God* (1 Cor. 2:14).

139 From this we can answer the question of the gentiles who futilely ask this: if it is only recently that the Son of God is set before the world as the savior of men, does it not seem that before that time he scorned human nature?

We should say to them that he did not scorn the world but was always in the world, and on his part is knowable by men; but it was due to their own fault that some have not known him, because they were lovers of the world.
140 We should also note that the Evangelist speaks of the incarnation of the Word to show that the incarnate Word and that which ***was in the beginning with God*** (John 1:1), and God, are the same.

He repeats what he had said of him earlier. For above he had said that the Word ***was the light of men*** (John 1:4);[9] here he says he was ***the true light***. Above, he said that ***all things were made through him*** (John 1:3);[10] here he says that ***through him the world was made***. Earlier he had said, ***Without him was made nothing*** (John 1:3), that is, according to one explanation, he conserves all things; here he says, ***He was in the world***, creating and conserving the world

8. Augustine, *Tractates on the Gospel of John* 2.11.

9. See Thomas Aquinas, *On John* 1.3. (not included in this collection).

10. See Thomas Aquinas, *On John* 1.2 (included in chapter 2 above).

and all things. There he had said, ***The darkness did not comprehend it*** (John 1:5);[11] here he says, ***the world did not know him***. And so, all he says after he was the ***true light*** is an explanation of what he had said before.

141 We can gather three reasons from the above why God willed to become incarnate. *One* is because of the perversity of human nature which, because of its own malice, had been darkened by vices and the obscurity of its own ignorance. And so he said before, ***The darkness did not comprehend it*** (John 1:5). Therefore, God came in the flesh so that the darkness might apprehend the light, i.e., obtain a knowledge of it. *Those who dwelt in a land of deep darkness, on them has light shined* (Isa. 9:2).

The *second* reason is that the testimony of the prophets was not enough. For the prophets came and John had come; but they were not able to give sufficient enlightenment, because ***he was not the light*** (John 1:8). And so, after the prophecies of the prophets and the coming of John, it was necessary that the light itself come and give the world a knowledge of itself. And this is what the Apostle says: *In many and various ways God spoke of old to our fathers by the prophets; but in these last days he has spoken to us by a Son* (Heb. 1:1–2). *We have the prophetic word made more sure. You will do well to pay attention to this, as to a lamp shining in a dark place, until the day dawns* (2 Pet. 1:19).

The *third* reason is because of the shortcomings of creatures. For creatures were not sufficient to lead to a knowledge of the Creator; hence he says, ***Through him the world was made, and the world did not know him***. Thus it was necessary that the Creator himself come into the world in the flesh and be known through himself. And this is what the Apostle says: *since in the wisdom of God the world did not know God by its wisdom, it pleased God to save those who believe by the foolishness of our preaching* (1 Cor. 1:21).

11. See Thomas Aquinas, *On John* 1.3 (not included in this collection).

Hebrews 1:1–2

Christ, the Ultimate Revelation

On Hebrews 1.1 (6–23)

1:1 ***God, who, in many ways and in diverse manners, speaking in times past to the fathers in the prophets,***

1:2 ***last of all, in these days, has spoken to us by his Son, whom he has appointed heir of all things, by whom also he made the world.***

6 He wrote this epistle against the errors of those converts from Judaism who wanted to preserve the legal observances along with the Gospel, as though Christ's grace were not sufficient for salvation. Hence it is divided into two parts.

In the *first,* he extols Christ's grandeur in order to show the superiority of the New Testament over the Old; in the *second* part, he discusses what unites the members to the head, namely, faith, at ***now, faith is the substance*** (Heb. 11:1).

He intends to show the New Testament's superiority over the Old by proving Christ's pre-eminence over three sacred persons of the Old Testament, namely, the angels, by whom the law was handed down: *The law . . . was ordained by angels through an intermediary* (Gal. 3:19); Moses, by whom or through whom it was given: *The law was given through Moses* (John 1:17); *there arose no more a prophet in Israel like unto Moses* (Deut. 3:10); and the priesthood, by which it was administered: ***Into the first tabernacle, the priests indeed always entered, accomplishing the offices of sacrifices*** (Heb. 9:6).

First, therefore, he favors Christ over the angels; *second,* over Moses, at ***wherefore, holy brethren*** (Heb. 3:1); *third,* over the priesthood of the Old Testament, at ***for every high priest*** (Heb. 5:1).

In regard to the *first,* he does two things: *first,* he favors Christ over the angels in this chapter; *second,* he defines what kind of reverence should be given to the new law, at ***We must pay the closer attention to what we have heard*** (Heb. 2:1).

Concerning the *first* he does two things: *first,* he shows the excellence of
Christ; *second,* he proves that this is true of Christ, and thus, that the angels
7 fall short of that excellence, at ***being made so much better*** (Heb. 1:4). Moreover,
it is unique in this epistle that every word has a separate meaning and keeps
its order.

In regard to the *first*, he indicates Christ's excellence in four matters: *first*, as to his unique origin, by calling him the true natural Son of God, when he says that he ***has spoken to us by his Son***; *second*, as to the extent of his rule, at ***whom he has appointed heir of all things***; *third*, as to the power of his activity, at ***by whom also he made the world***; *fourth*, as to the sublimity of his glory, at ***who being the brightness of his glory*** (Heb. 1:3).

But because he intends to extol Christ so that it redounds to the glory of
8 the New Testament, this favors the New Testament over the Old. About which
he mentions five things: *first*, how it was promulgated, ***in many ways and in diverse manners***; *second*, the time, when he says ***once***; *third*, the author or giver, ***God***; *fourth*, to whom it was given, ***to the fathers***; *fifth*, by which ministers, ***in the prophets***.

9 He says, therefore, ***in many ways***, referring *first* of all to various persons, because God spoke not to one person but to many, namely, Abraham, Noah, and others.

Second, he refers to the various times and always with the same certitude: *[He] went out early in the morning. . . . And going out about the third hour* (Matt. 20:3). Likewise, this is also in regard to the matters treated, namely, divine things: *I am who am* (Exod. 3:14 DRB); and future events: *She has foreknowledge of signs and wonders and the outcome of seasons and times* (Wis. 8:8); and promises of future benefits, at least in figure: *Matters too great for human understanding have been shown you* (Sir. 3:23).

In many ways also in the variety of figures; because at one time he uses the figure of a lion, at another the figure of a stone: *A stone was cut out by no human hand* (Dan. 2:34); *he is manifold in understanding* (Job 11:6).

And in diverse manners. This refers to the three kinds of vision: *first*, ocular vision: *Immediately the fingers of a man's hand appeared and wrote on the plaster of the wall of the king's palace, opposite the lampstand* (Dan. 5:5); *second*, imaginary vision: *I saw the Lord sitting upon a throne high and lifted up* (Isa. 6:1); *third*, intellectual vision, as to David: *I have had understanding above ancients* (Ps. 119:100 DRB). Hence, Hosea includes all of these: *It was I who multiplied visions* (12:10).

It refers also to the various ways he spoke, because sometimes he spoke plainly and sometimes obscurely. In fact, there is not a manner of speaking that has not been employed in the writings of the Old Testament: *I have described it to you three manner of ways, in thoughts and knowledge* (Prov. 22:20 DRB). *Third*, because he spoke by rebuking the wicked, by enticing the just, and by instructing the ignorant: *All Scripture is inspired of God and profitable for teaching, for reproof, for correction, and for training in righteousness* (2 Tim. 3:16).

10 Then he touches upon the time when this teaching was delivered, i.e., the past, because he spoke of old, i.e., not suddenly, because the things that were spoken about Christ were so great as to be incredible unless they had been taught bit by bit as time went on. Hence, as Gregory says: *As time went on, the knowledge of divine things grew.*[12] Isaiah 48:3: *The former things I declared of*
11 *old, they went out from my mouth and I made them known*. Thus, he mentions the author, namely, ***God***, who speaks: *Let me hear what God the Lord will speak* (Ps. 85:8). For he does not lie: *God is not a man that he should lie* (Num. 23:19).

These, then, are the first three things which commend the Old Testament: authorship, because it is from God; *second*, subtlety and sublimity, because ***in many ways and in diverse manners***; *third*, duration, because ***in times past***.

12 *Fourth*, he shows to whom it is delivered, namely, to our ***fathers***. This is why it is familiar and known to us: *We declare unto you the promise which was made to our fathers* (Acts 13:32 DRB); *as he spoke to our fathers* (Luke 1:55).

13 *Fifth*, he indicates the ministers, because it was delivered not by jesters but ***by prophets***: *He promised beforehand by his prophets* (Rom. 1:2); *to him all the prophets bear witness* (Acts 10:43).

14 Then when he says ***in these days***, he describes the doctrine of the New Testament and mentions five properties. Four of these are differences from those of the Old, and one is the same. For when he had said, ***in many ways and in diverse manners***, he was indicating that every ordered multitude should be referred to one thing. Therefore, although the manner is manifold, all is ordained to the last thing: *Continue in the fear of the Lord all the day* (Prov. 23:17); *Though your people Israel be as the sand of the sea, only a remnant of them will return . . . overflowing with righteousness. For the Lord . . . will make a full end, as decreed, in the midst of all the earth* (Isa. 10:22–23). Likewise, ***in times past*** referred to the time of waiting and of darkness, but ***in these days*** refers to our days, i.e., to the time of grace: *The night is far gone; the day is at hand* (Rom. 13:12).

15 It should be noted that in regard to the Old Testament he says ***speaking***, but here he says ***has spoken***, in order to designate that the speech of the New Testament is more perfect than that of the Old.

To understand this, it should be noted that three things are required for our speech: *first*, the conception of a thought whereby we preconceive in our mind that which is to be spoken by the mouth; *second*, the expression of the conceived thought to enable us to indicate what has been conceived; *third*, the manifestation of the thing expressed, so that it becomes evident.

God, therefore, when speaking, first conceived, so that there was but one conception and that from all eternity: *God speaks once* (Job 33:14). This eternal

12. Gregory the Great, *Homilies on the Book of the Prophet Ezekiel* 2.4.

conception is the engendering of the Son of God, concerning whom it says: *He said to me, "you are my son, today I have begotten you"* (Ps. 2:7).

Second, he expressed his concept in three ways: *first*, in the production of creatures, namely, when the conceived Word, existing as the likeness of the Father, is also the likeness according to which all creatures were made: *God said, "Let there be light"; and there was light* (Gen. 1:3). *Second*, through certain notions, for example, in the minds of the angels, in whom the forms of all things, which were concealed in the Word, were infused, and in the minds of holy men: and this by sensible or intellectual or imaginary revelations. Hence, every such manifestation proceeding from the eternal Word is called a speaking: *The word of the Lord came to me, saying* . . . (Jer. 1:4). *Third*, by assuming flesh, concerning which it says: *The Word became flesh* (John 1:14). Hence, Augustine says that the incarnate Word is related to the uncreated Word as the voice's word is related to the heart's word.[13]

But the *first* expression, namely, in creation, is not for the purpose of manifesting. For it is clear that that expression cannot be called a speaking; hence, it is never said that God speaks when making creatures, but that he is known: *Ever since the creation of the world his invisible nature . . . has been clearly perceived in the things that have been made* (Rom. 1:20). But the *second* expression, which is the infusion of forms in the minds of angels or of men, is directed only to the knowledge of divine wisdom; hence, it can be called a speaking. The *third* expression, namely, the assuming of flesh, took place for the purpose of existing and of knowing, and for expressly manifesting, because by assuming flesh the Word was made man and brought us to a complete knowledge of God: *for this was I born, that I should give testimony of the truth* (John 18:37). And he clearly manifests himself to us: *He was seen upon earth and conversed with men* (Bar. 3:38 DRB).

Thus, therefore, although God speaks in the New and the Old Testaments, he speaks more perfectly in the New, because in the Old he speaks in the minds of men, but in the New through the Son's incarnation. Furthermore, the Old Testament was handed down to the fathers looking on from afar and seeing God from a distance; the New has been handed down to us, namely, to the apostles, who have seen him in his very person: *That which was from the beginning, which we have heard, which we have seen with our eyes . . . and touched with our hands concerning the word of life* . . . [we] proclaim to you (1 John 1:1); *not with our fathers did the Lord make this covenant, but with us, who are all of us here alive this day* (Deut. 5:3). Hence, it is clear that that speaking was a promise: *The promises were made to Abraham* (Gal. 3:16); but the New was a manifestation: *Grace and truth came by Jesus Christ* (John 1:17). Also, in

13. Augustine, *The Trinity* 15.11.20.

the Old Testament, he spoke in the prophets; in the New Testament, in his Son, who is the Lord of the prophets: *The only Son, who is in the bosom of the Father, he has made him known* (John 1:18).

16 Does this mean that all the ones through whom God spoke were prophets? I answer that five things are required of a true prophet: *first*, the revealing of things which transcend human knowledge; otherwise, he would not be called a prophet but a sage, as Solomon, whose mind was enlightened in regard to things within the ken of human reason. Hence, not even the Jews called him a prophet but a sage.

Second, the understanding of the things revealed; otherwise, he would not be a prophet: *There is need of understanding in a vision* (Dan. 10:1 DRB). That is why Nebuchadnezzar, not understanding the revelation made to him, is not called a prophet, but Daniel, who did understand it, was called a prophet.

Third, it is required that he not be captivated by the things he sees, which are absent from him, as with real things. He must regard them as figures. Otherwise, he would not be a prophet but a lunatic, who apprehends imaginary things as though they were real: *Let the prophet who has a dream tell the dream, but let him who has my word speak my word faithfully* (Jer. 23:28).

Fourth, it is required that he perceive the things revealed with certitude, as though known through demonstration; otherwise, it would be a dream and not a prophecy: *The Lord God has opened my ear and I was not rebellious; I turned not backward* (Isa. 50:5).

Fifth, it is required that he has the will to announce the thing revealed; accordingly, some claim that Daniel was not a prophet because he did not receive the thing revealed in an expressible way. Hence, it is not said that the word of the Lord was made to Daniel, as is said of the other prophets: *The word of the Lord has become for me a reproach and derision all day long. If I say, 'I will not make mention of him, or speak any more in his name,' there is in my heart as it were a burning fire* (Jer. 20:8).

17 But another question arises: why does he say ***in the prophets***, when he might better have said 'through the prophets'? The answer is that he did this because he wished to exclude certain errors: *first*, the error of Porphyry, who claimed that prophets invented their statements and were not inspired by the Holy Spirit.[14] To counter this the Apostle says that he spoke ***in the prophets***. As if to say: 'they were not speaking of themselves, but God was speaking in

14. Porphyry was a Neoplatonist philosopher from the late third century who criticized the Christian movement in his book *Against the Christians*, of which only fragments survive in the writings of the apologists. Jerome, in his *Commentary on Daniel* (the likely source by which Thomas knew of his repudiation of the prophets), relates several of Porphyry's attacks against the legitimacy of the person and book of Daniel.

them': *No prophecy ever came by the impulse of man, but men moved by the Holy Spirit spoke from God* (2 Pet. 1:21).

Second, he writes ***in the prophets*** to exclude the error of those who maintained that prophecy is something natural and can be possessed by one's natural disposition, as a melancholy person might have a very strong imagination: so strong, indeed, that he considers the things he imagines to be real. Hence, it says he spoke ***in the prophets***. As if to say: 'prophecy does not come about through a natural disposition but by an inward utterance of God': *The Spirit breathes where he will* (John 3:8 DRB).

Third, he writes ***in the prophets*** against the error of those who claim that prophecy can be possessed like a habit, as science is possessed, so that whenever a person decides to do so, he can prophesy. But this is not true because the spirit of prophecy is not always present in the prophet, but only when their minds are enlightened by God; hence, Elisha says: *She is in bitter distress, and the Lord has hidden it from me* (2 Kings 4:27). Therefore, the Apostle says, ***in the prophets***. As if to say: 'not that prophecy is possessed by all or always, as habits are, but only in those in whom it pleases God to speak.'

Fourth, he writes ***in the prophets*** to exclude the error of Priscilla and Montanus, who maintained that prophets do not understand their utterances.[15] But this is not true; hence: *The word of the Lord came by the hand of Haggai, the prophet* (Hag. 1:3); and: *The spirits of prophets are subject to the prophets* (1 Cor. 14:32). And therefore he says ***in the prophets***, i.e., in the understanding and power of the prophets.

Thus, therefore, Christ's unique property is clear, namely, that he is the
18 natural Son: *I am in the Father and the Father is in me* (John 14:10). But is he one of those sons of whom it is said, *"You are gods, sons of the Most High, all of you"* (Ps. 82:6)? No; because these are called sons in a general sense, but he is the Son who was appointed heir and lord of all things.

Is he one of those sons of whom it is said: *He gave [them] power to become children of God* (John 1:12)? No; those are said to become the children, but Christ is the Son ***by whom also he made the world***. Is he one of those sons who *rejoice in [the] hope of sharing the glory of God* (Rom. 5:2)? No, because they are sons through the hope they have of God's glory, but he is the splendor of that glory. Others are called sons because they were made to the image of this Son: *Those whom he foreknew he also predestined to be conformed to the image of his*

15. Priscilla and Montanus were 2nd-century founders of the heretical, charismatic, and apocalyptic Christian sect (Montanists) in Phrygia (modern-day Turkey). The Montanists embraced a form of prophecy that, per Eusebius' description, in some ways resembled Dionysian or Orphic rites and featured a sequence of ecstatic states including terror, vacancy, and madness (see Eusebius, *Church History* 5.17.2–3). The Montanist prophets were excommunicated shortly after the emergence of the movement (c. 177) and subsequently established their own church institution.

Son (Rom. 8:29), but he is the image itself and *the very stamp of his nature* (Heb. 1:3). Others are called sons inasmuch as they contain within themselves the Word of God: *Be blameless and sincere children without reproof in the midst of a crooked and perverse generation, among whom you shine as lights in the world, holding fast the word of life* (Phil. 2:15–16). But he is the true Son who carries all things by the word of his power.

Therefore, Christ's supereminence is clear from his unique origin and from his relationship to other sons of God. It is these things which make the New
19 Testament greater than the Old. Yet in regard to both Testaments, he says ***speaking*** or ***has spoken***, in order to indicate that both have the same author. This is against the Manicheans: *Through him we both have access in one Spirit to the Father* (Eph. 2:18); *is God the God of Jews only? Is he not the God of gentiles also?* (Rom. 3:29).

Again, the Old was given to our fathers, but the New ***to us***, i.e., to the apostles, we who saw Christ in his very person: *Not with our fathers did the Lord make this covenant, but with us, who are all of us here alive this day* (Deut. 5:3).

Again, the Old was given through the prophets, but the New ***by his Son***, i.e., through his Son, who is the Lord of the prophets: *The only Son, who is in the bosom of the Father, he has made him known* (John 1:18).

20 Then he shows the greatness of Christ's power when he says, ***whom he has appointed heir of all things***; for as it says: *If a son, then an heir also* (Gal. 4:7). But in Christ are two natures, namely, the divine and the human. Insofar as he is the natural Son, he is not an appointed heir, but he is so naturally; but inasmuch as he is man, he has become the Son of God *who was descended from David according to the flesh* (Rom. 1:3). Indeed, as a man, he has been appointed heir of all things, just as he has become a true son of the Father: *All authority in heaven and on earth has been given to me* (Matt. 28:18), and it extends to every creature that he has taken under his rule. It extends, therefore, not only to one type of man, but to ***all***, i.e., both Jews and gentiles: *Ask of me and I will give you the gentiles for your inheritance* (Ps. 2:8 DRB).

21 Having shown Christ's excellence as to his unique origin, he now shows his excellence as to the majesty of his dominion. It is suitable that these two be joined: he ***has spoken to us by his Son***, whom he appointed the heir of all things: if a son, then an heir (Rom. 8:17).

But it should be noted that in Christ are two natures, namely, the divine and the human. But according to the divine nature, since he was not appointed Son, since he is the natural Son from all eternity, so neither was he appointed heir, but he is the natural heir from all eternity. But according to his human nature, just as he was made Son of God, *who was descended from David according to the flesh* (Rom. 1:3), so he was made heir to all things: ***whom he has***

appointed heir, that is, the Lord, ***of all things***: *This is the heir, come, let us kill him* (Matt. 21:38). *I will again bring an heir to you that dwell in Maresa: even to Odolam shall the glory of Israel come* (Mic. 1:15).

Indeed, according to his divine nature it belongs to Christ to be the begotten heir of the Lord. *First*, because he is *the power . . . and the wisdom of God* (1 Cor. 1:24) through whom the Father makes all things. Therefore, if the Father is called the God of all by reason of creation, the Son also, through whom all things were brought into existence, is called Lord: *I was with him forming all things* (Prov. 8:30 DRB). *Second*, because the Son is the Father's wisdom, by which he governs all things. It is said of wisdom: *She reaches mightily from one end of the earth to the other and she orders all things well* (Wis. 8:1). Therefore, if the Father is called Lord by reason of governing: *You*, the Father, *rule all things* (Wis. 12:15), the Son, too, has dominion. Furthermore, the Father is Lord inasmuch as all things are ordained to him as to the first principle and end of all things. So, too, the Son, who is the wisdom of God preceding all things, is Lord: *Wisdom was created before all things. Who can search them out?* (Sir. 1:3). *The Lord has made all things for himself* (Prov. 16:4 DRB).

But according to his human nature it also belongs to Christ to be heir and Lord of all things. *First*, by reason of the union, i.e., from the fact that that man was assumed in the person of the Son of God: *The Lord God exalted him . . . as Savior* (Acts 5:31); *he. . . made him sit at his right hand . . . far above all rule and authority and power and dominion* (Eph. 1:19). *Second*, by reason of power, because all things obey and serve him: *All authority in heaven and on earth has been given to me* (Matt. 28:18). *Third*, by reason of subjection: *At the name of Jesus every knee should bow, in heaven and on earth and under the earth* (Phil. 2:10).

But he says, ***of all things***, which refers to the totality of all nature, in which he obtains dominion: *You have subjected all things under his feet* (Ps. 8:6 DRB). It also refers to the whole human race, so that the sense would be: of all things, i.e., not only the Jews but also other men: *Ask of me and I will make the nations your heritage and the ends of the earth your possession* (Ps. 2:8). And of this it is said: *You are Lord of all* (Esther 13:11 DRB).

22 Then when he says, ***by whom also he made the world***, he shows the power of Christ's activity, i.e., why he has been appointed heir of all things. It was not because he was born at a certain moment of time and merited this by leading a good life, as Photinus says, but because all things were originally made by him, as they were made by the Father. For through him the Father made the world.

But it should be noted that the grammatical object of the preposition 'by' or 'through' designates the cause of an act: in one way, because it causes a making on the part of the maker. For the making is midway between the maker and the thing made. In this usage the object of 'by' can designate the final cause motivating the maker, as an artisan works by gain; or the formal cause, as fire warms by heat; or even the efficient cause, as a bailiff acts through the king. But the Son is not the cause making the Father act through him in any of these ways any more than he is the cause of his proceeding from the Father.

But sometimes the object of 'by' designates the cause of the action, taken from the viewpoint of the thing made, as an artisan acts through a hammer; for the hammer is not the cause of the artisan's action, but it is the cause why an artifact made of iron should proceed from the artisan, i.e., why iron be worked on by the artisan. This is the way the Son is the cause of things made and the way the Father works through the Son.

23 But is the Son inferior to the Father? It seems so, because that which is the cause of a thing's being made seems to be an instrument.

The answer is that if the power in the Father and in the Son were not the same numerically, and the activity not the same numerical activity, the objection would hold. But the fact is that the power and activity, as well as the nature and the being of the Father and of the Son are the same. Therefore, the Father is said to make the world through him, because he begot him forming the world: *Whatever [the Father] does, that the Son does likewise* (John 5:19).

Here, ***world*** means the temporal span of a created thing. ***Worlds***, i.e., *saecula*, therefore, are successions of times. Therefore, he made not only sempiternal times (in the sense in which philosophers say that God alone made eternal things, and angels created temporal things), but also temporal things, which the Apostle calls worlds: ***By faith we understand that the world was framed by the word of God*** (Heb. 11:3); *all things were made through him* (John 1:3).

Thus he removes the Manichean error in two ways: *first*, in calling God the author of the Old Testament; *second*, in saying that he made temporal things.

Chapter 8
CHRIST'S GRACE

John 1:16–17
Christ's Fullness: The Source of All Grace
On John 1.10 (200–207)

1:16 ***And of his fullness we have all received, indeed grace upon grace:***

1:17 ***For the law was given through Moses; grace and truth came through Jesus Christ.***

200 He follows with, ***Of his fullness we have all received.*** These words and those that follow: ***This is the testimony of John*** (John 1:19), are taken in two ways. According to Origen, these are the words of John the Baptist and are added by him to support what he had said previously.[1] It is as though he said: 'truly, ***he was before me*** (John 1:15), because ***of his fullness***, i.e., of his grace, not only I but ***we all***, including the prophets and patriarchs, ***have received***, because all had the grace they possessed by faith in the incarnate Word.' According to this explanation, John the Baptist began weaving the story of the incarnation at ***John bore witness to him*** (John 1:15).

But according to Augustine and Chrysostom, the words from ***John bore witness to him*** (John 1:15) are those of John the Evangelist.[2] And they are connected with the previous words, ***full of grace and truth*** (John 1:14), as though he were saying: 'above, the Evangelist gave the evidence for the Word, which was learned through sight and by hearing, but here he explains each.' *First*, how he was made known to the apostles through sight, which was tantamount to receiving the evidence from Christ. *Second*, how John bore witness to him, at ***this is the testimony of John*** (John 1:19).

As to the *first* he does two things. *First*, he shows that Christ is the origin, as a fountain, of every spiritual grace. *Second*, he shows that grace is dispensed to us through him and from him, at ***grace upon grace.***

201 He says first of all: we know from our own experience that we have seen him ***full of grace and truth*** (John 1:14), because ***of his fullness we have all received.*** Now one fullness is that of sufficiency, by which one is able to per-

1. Origen, *Commentary on John* 6.6.33.

2. Augustine, *Tractates on the Gospel of John* 3.8. John Chrysostom, *Commentary on Saint John* 14.1.

form acts that are meritorious and excellent, as in the case of Stephen. Again, there is a fullness of superabundance, by which the Blessed Virgin excels all the saints because of the eminence and abundance of her merits. Further, there is a fullness of efficiency and overflow, which belongs only to the man Christ as the author of grace. For although the Blessed Virgin superabounds her grace into us, it is never as authoress of grace. But grace flowed over from her soul into her body: for through the grace of the Holy Spirit, not only was the mind of the Virgin perfectly united to God by love, but her womb was supernaturally impregnated by the Holy Spirit. And so after Gabriel said, *Hail, full of grace*, he refers at once to the fullness of her womb, adding, *The Lord is with you* (Luke 1:28).

And so the Evangelist, in order to show this unique fullness of efficiency and overflow in Christ, said, ***of his fullness we have all received***, i.e., all the apostles and patriarchs and prophets and just men who have existed, do now exist, and will exist, and even all the angels.

202 Note that the preposition *de* [in English as either, of, or from,] sometimes signifies efficiency, as in an originative cause, as when it is said that a ray is or proceeds from the sun. In this way it signifies the efficiency of grace in Christ, i.e., authorship, because the fullness of grace in Christ is the cause of all graces that are in intellectual creatures. *Come to me, you who desire me, and eat your fill of my produce* (Sir. 24:19), that is to say, share in the fullness of those fruits which come from me.

But sometimes this preposition *de* signifies consubstantiality, as when it is said that the Son is from the Father [*de Patre*]. In this usage, the fullness of Christ is the Holy Spirit, who proceeds from him, consubstantial with him in nature, in power, and in majesty. For although the habitual gifts in the soul of Christ are other than those in us, nevertheless it is one and the same Holy Spirit who is in him and who fills all those to be sanctified. *All these are inspired by one and the same Spirit* (1 Cor. 12:11); *I will pour out my Spirit upon all flesh* (Joel 2:28); *anyone who does not have the Spirit of Christ does not belong to him* (Rom. 8:9). For the unity of the Holy Spirit produces unity in the Church: *The Spirit of the Lord has filled the whole world* (Wis. 1:7).

In a *third* way, the preposition *de* can signify a portion, as when we say *take from this bread or wine*, i.e., take a portion and not the whole. Taken in this way it signifies that those who take a part derive it from the fullness. For Christ received all the gifts of the Holy Spirit without measure, according to a perfect fullness; but we participate, through him, of some portion of his fullness; and this is according to the measure which God grants to each. *Grace was given to each of us according to the measure of Christ's gift* (Eph. 4:7).

203 Then when he says, ***grace upon grace***, he shows the distribution of graces into us through Christ. Here he does two things. *First*, he shows that we receive grace from Christ, as its author. *Second*, that we receive wisdom from him, at ***No one has ever seen God*** (John 1:18).

As to the *first* he does two things. *First*, he shows that we have received of his fullness. *Second*, our need to receive it: ***The law was given through Moses;***
204 ***grace and truth came through Jesus Christ***. *First*, he says that we have received of the fullness of Christ what is described as ***grace upon grace***.

In the light of what is said, we are forced to understand that of his fullness we have received grace, and that upon that grace we have received another. Accordingly, we must see what that first grace is upon which we have received a second one, and also what that second grace is.

According to Chrysostom, the first grace, which was received by the whole human race, was the grace of the Old Testament received in the law.[3] And this was indeed a great grace: *I will give you a good gift* (Prov. 4:2 DRB). For it was a great benefit for idolatrous men to receive precepts from God, and a true knowledge of the one true God. *What advantage has the Jew? Or what is the value of circumcision? Much in every way. To begin with, the Jews are entrusted with the oracles of God* (Rom. 3:1). Upon that grace, then, which was first, we have received a second far better. *He shall give equal grace to the grace thereof* (Zech. 4:7 DRB). But was not the first grace sufficient?

I answer that it was not, because the law gives only a knowledge of sin, but does not take it away. *The law brought nothing to perfection* (Heb. 7:19). Hence it was necessary that another grace come that would take away sin and reconcile one with God.

205 And so he says, ***for the law was given through Moses; grace and truth came through Jesus Christ***. Here the Evangelist ranks Christ above Moses the lawgiver, whom the Baptist ranked above himself. Now Moses was regarded as the greatest of the prophets: *There has not arisen a prophet since in Israel like Moses* (Deut. 34:10).

But he ranks Christ above Moses in excellence and in dignity of works, ***for the law was given through Moses***; and between these two, the one excels the other as the reality excels the symbol and the truth the shadow: *The law has but a shadow of the good things to come* (Heb. 10:1). Further, Christ excels him in the way he works, because the law was given by Moses as by one proclaiming it, but not originating it; for *the Lord is our lawgiver* (Isa. 33:22 DRB). But ***grace and truth came through Jesus Christ***, as through the Lord and author of truth and grace, as was explained above.

---

3. John Chrysostom, *Commentary on Saint John* 14.1.

206 According to Augustine, however, the first grace is justifying and prevenient grace, which is not given to us because of our works:[4] *If it is by grace, it is no longer on the basis of works* (Rom. 11:6). Upon that grace, then, which is imperfect, we have received another grace which is perfect, i.e., the grace of eternal life. And although eternal life is in some way acquired by merits, nevertheless, because the principle of meriting in everyone is prevenient grace, eternal life is called a grace: *The grace of God is eternal life* (Rom. 6:23 DRB). To be brief, whatever grace is added to prevenient grace, the whole is called ***grace upon grace.***

The need for this second grace arises from the insufficiency of the law, which showed what was to be done and what avoided; but it gave no help to fulfill what was commanded. Indeed, what seemed to have been directed to life was the occasion for producing death. Hence the Apostle says that the law was a minister of death: *If there was splendor in the dispensation of condemnation, the dispensation of righteousness must far exceed it in splendor* (2 Cor. 3:9). Also, it promised the help of grace but did not fulfill, because *the law brought nothing to perfection* (Heb. 7:19). Again, it prefigured the truth of the new grace by its sacrifices and ceremonies; indeed, its very rites proclaimed that it was a figure. Hence is was necessary that Christ come, who by his own death would destroy other deaths and grant the help of new grace, in order that we might both fulfill his precepts with ease and joy, and die to our sins and our old way of life: *Our old self was crucified with him* (Rom. 6:6), and in order that the truth of the figures contained in the law might be revealed and the promises made to the fathers be fulfilled (2 Cor. 1:20). This can be explained in another way: ***Truth came through Jesus Christ***, as to the wisdom and truth which was hidden for centuries, and which he openly taught when he came into the world: ***For this I was born, and for this I came into the world, that I should give testimony to the truth*** (John 18:37).

207 But if Christ is the truth, as it says below: ***I am . . . the truth*** (John 14:6),[5] how did truth come to be made through him, because nothing can make itself?

I answer that by his essence he is the uncreated truth, which is eternal and not made, but is begotten of the Father; but all created truths were made through him, and these are certain participations and reflections of the first truth, which shines out in those souls who are holy.

4. Augustine, *Tractates on the Gospel of John* 3.9.

5. See Thomas Aquinas, *On John* 14.2 (not included in this collection).

Titus 2:11–15

Christ's Grace for the Sanctification of All

On Titus 2.3 (67–76)

2:11 ***For the grace of God our Savior has appeared to all men:***

2:12 ***instructing us, that, denying ungodliness and worldly desires, we should live soberly and justly and godly in this world,***

2:13 ***looking for the blessed hope and coming of the glory of the great God and our Savior Jesus Christ:***

2:14 ***who gave himself for us, that he might redeem us from all iniquity and might cleanse for himself a people acceptable, in pursuit of good works.***

2:15 ***These things speak and exhort and rebuke with all authority. Let no man despise you.***

67 Above, the Apostle instructed Titus how to teach slaves and free men,[6] and he concluded about the account, that namely the doctrine of Christ be honored. Here he assigns the full reason for all he has said, explaining what he means by a good life. *First*, he mentions the grace and doctrine of Christ; *second*, he urges him to preach grace, at ***these things speak***.

Thus, *first*, he states that grace has appeared; *second*, its instruction, at
68 ***instructing us***; *third*, its operation, at ***who gave himself***. It should be noted that grace implies mercy, because grace is of that which is freely granted; and what is freely granted is conferred out of mercy.

Moreover, mercy has always been present in God; yet for some time it was hidden to men: *O Lord, your mercy is in heaven* (Ps. 36:5 DRB). For before Christ's coming, all men, no matter how holy, were under condemnation, but in Christ the Son of God assuming flesh, ***The grace of God our Savior has appeared***. *Great indeed . . . is the mystery of our religion: He was manifested in the flesh* (1 Tim. 3:16). *You who are enthroned upon the cherubim, shine forth* (Ps. 80:1).

But the more powerful a person is, the more his grace is desired. Hence, God's grace must be desirable; and this is why he says ***the grace of God***. And this is given for our salvation; hence he says, ***our Savior***: *My salvation will be*

6. See Titus 2:1–10 and Thomas Aquinas, *On Titus* 2.1–2 (not included in this collection).

forever (Isa. 51:6). But this grace is not offered only to the Jewish people alone, as formerly, but ***to all men***: *All flesh shall see it together for the mouth of the Lord has spoken* (Isa. 40:5); *all the ends of the earth shall see the salvation of our God* (Isa. 52:10); *God our Savior, who desires all men to be saved* (1 Tim. 2:4).

And we might say that in Christ's birth this grace appeared in two ways: in the *first* way, because Christ has been given as God's greatest gift. Hence his conception, although it was a work of the entire Trinity, is attributed particularly to the Holy Spirit, who is the giver and source of all graces. And this grace appeared to all men but especially to the man Christ, *full of grace and truth* (John 1:14).

Second, it appeared as an instruction to the human race, because before the coming of Christ, the world languished in ignorance and heresy: *Those who dwelt in a land of deep darkness, on them has light shined* (Isa. 9:2). Hence
69 he says, ***instructing us***, as a father instructs his son. But he instructs us about two things, because all men are in need of two things, namely, good works and a right intention. *First*, he shows how Christ instructed us in regard to good works; *second*, in regard to a right intention, at ***looking for the blessed hope***.

70 He says, therefore: ***denying ungodliness and worldly desires***. But notice that he says, ***ungodliness and worldly desires***, because all sins are involved either with matters directly against God, and are therefore sins of ungodliness: for godliness, or piety, is a virtue which inclines us to show proper respect toward parents and fatherland. But because God is our principal Father, godliness consists in paying worship to God. *Behold, the fear of the Lord, that is wisdom* (Job 28:28), but another version reads *behold godliness, that is wisdom*. Consequently, sins against God are called acts of ungodliness: *The wrath of God is revealed from heaven against all ungodliness* (Rom. 1:18), where ungodliness refers to idolatry.

Or sins consist in misusing temporal things, and these sins are ***worldly desires*** [*saecularia desideria*]. But a world [*saeculum*] is a span of time that measures how long things exist. Hence by ***worldly*** [*saecularia*] is meant secular things and all sins committed against our neighbor, or against things by misusing them.

71 Then when he says, ***live soberly***, he indicates what good we should do. And he says, ***soberly***, in relation to ourselves; ***justly***, in relation to our neighbor; and ***godly*** in relation to God. He says, ***soberly***, i.e., with due measure; but a limit is a measure, and this limit is observed if a man uses external goods and controls his passions with the limits set by reason. Hence, soberness means any moderate use of external things or of one's passions: *Righteousness . . . teaches self-control and prudence, justice and courage; nothing in life is more profitable for men than these* (Wis. 8:7). He says, ***justly***, in dealings with one's neighbor; *for the Lord*

is righteous, he loves righteous deeds (Ps. 11:7). And ***godly*** in one's dealings with God: *Train yourself in godliness* (1 Tim. 4:7).

72 Then when he says, ***looking for the blessed hope***, he instructs him about the end, which consists in two things, namely, in the soul's glory after death and in the body's glory at Christ's coming: *The hour is coming when all who are in the tombs will hear his voice and come forth, those who have done good, to the resurrection of life, and those who have done evil, to the resurrection of judgment* (John 5:28–29).

In regard to the *first* he says, ***looking for the blessed hope***, against those who place man's end in virtuous acts performed in this life. But this is not true because even if we live soberly and justly and godly, we are still awaiting something else like hirelings awaiting a day of rest (Job 7:1, 14:6); *blessed are all those who wait for him* (Isa. 30:18). Therefore, he says, ***looking for the blessed hope***, which can be understood in two ways: either because it is the hope for happiness, or because the very waiting makes us happy.

In regard to the *second* he says, ***and coming of the glory of the great God and our Savior Jesus Christ***, through whom our bodies will rise. For one who loves a friend looks for him with desire: *There is laid up for me the crown of righteousness, which the Lord . . . will award . . . not only to me, but also to all who have loved his appearing* (2 Tim. 4:8); *be like men who are waiting for their master* (Luke 12:36). And he says, ***the coming of the glory***, because his first coming was in humility: *He humbled himself and became obedient unto death* (Phil. 2:8); *learn from me, for I am gentle and humble of heart* (Matt. 11:29). But this time he will come in ***glory***, because his divinity will be recognized by all, *and then they will see the Son of man coming in a cloud with power and great glory* (Luke 21:27). And he says, ***of the great God***, against Arius, who said that the Son is not equal to the Father. Well does he say, ***great***, because *Christ is God over all . . . blessed forever* (Rom. 9:5); *This is the true God and eternal life* (1 John 5:20).

He is also the ***Savior***: *This is good, and it is acceptable in the sight of God our Savior, who desires all men to be saved* (1 Tim. 2:3–4). He came as Savior, as his name suggests: *He will save his people from their sins* (Matt. 1:21). And he adds, ***Christ***, namely, who was anointed; for in this anointing the union of divinity to human nature is understood. For some persons are united, but not in such a way as to have the essence of the godhead united to them, but because they partake of it. But the godhead was united to Christ: *God, has anointed you with the oil of gladness above your fellows* (Ps. 45:7).

73 Then when he says, ***who gave himself***, the workings of grace are revealed: *first*, he shows the benefits derived from the grace of his passion; *second*, the
74 fruit of his passion, at ***that he might redeem us***. He says, therefore: I say that he

is our Savior. But how? Because he ***gave himself for us***: *Walk in love, as Christ
loved us and gave himself up for us, a fragrant offering and sacrifice to God* (Eph.
75 5:2). Its fruit is deliverance and sanctification.

Deliverance, when he says, ***redeem us from all iniquity***: *Everyone who commits sin is a slave to sin* (John 8:34). For the first man, as a result of his sin, became a slave to sin, and this slavery inclined him to other sins. But Christ made satisfaction through his passion; consequently, we are redeemed from slavery: *Fear not, for I have redeemed you* (Isa. 43:1). And not only from original sin, but from all the sins which a person adds by his own will.

Sanctification unto good is mentioned when he says, ***and might cleanse for himself a people***, i.e., that he might sanctify the people in such a way that they become his people, i.e., consecrated to him: *Once you were no people but now you are God's people* (1 Pet. 2:10). ***Acceptable*** to God by reason of their right faith and intention: *A servant who deals wisely has the king's favor* (Prov. 14:35). Or, ***acceptable***, i.e., special: *The Lord your God has chosen you to be a people for his own possession, out of all the peoples that are on the face of the earth* (Deut. 7:6). But it is proper that they perform their good works outwardly; hence he says, ***in pursuit of good works***: *Do what is good, and you will receive his approval* (Rom. 13:3); *let us not grow weary in well-doing* (Gal. 6:9).

76 Then, he urges him to preach grace. In regard to this he does two things: *first*, he exhorts him to preach; *second*, he describes the way he should preach. He says, therefore: ***speak*** what is to be believed, ***and exhort*** what is to be done, *for our appeal does not spring from error or uncleanness, nor is it made with guile* (1 Thess. 2:3). ***Rebuke*** those who do evil: *as for those who persist in sin, rebuke them in the presence of all* (1 Tim 5:20).

And this ***with all authority***, because he speaks as an instrument and minister of God, and therefore with confidence in God's authority. Yet when he exhorts, he must sometimes entreat, considering his own weakness: *The poor use entreaties* (Prov. 18:23). At other times he must speak with authority, considering the authority entrusted to him: *Do you seek a proof of Christ who speaks in me?* (2 Cor. 13:3 DRB). Or, with gentleness to the good and with authority to the obstinate. The Apostle had to exhort him to speak with authority, because Titus was gentle by nature: *Let no one despise your youth* (1 Tim. 4:12).

Ephesians 2:8–10

Our Salutary Virtues Are Christ's Gifts

On Ephesians 2.3 (92–100)

2:8 ***For by grace you are saved through faith: and that not of yourselves, for it is the gift of God.***

2:9 ***Not of works, that no man may glory.***

2:10 ***For we are his workmanship, created in Christ Jesus in good works, which God has prepared that we should walk in them.***

92 When the Apostle was recounting above the blessing of God by which we have been freed from sin, he inserted that we had been saved by Christ's grace.[7] Now he intends to prove this. He makes two points concerning it: *first*, he sets down his intention; *second*, he clarifies the point in question, at ***and that not of yourselves.***

93 'I rightly declared,' he says of the *first*, 'by whose grace you were saved; and indeed, I still confidently say ***for***, in place of *because*, ***by grace you are saved.***' *By the grace of God I am what I am* (1 Cor. 15:10), *justified by his grace as a gift* (Rom. 3:24). For to be saved is the same as to be justified. Salvation implies a freedom from dangers; hence, man's perfect salvation will be in eternal life when he will be immune from all dangers, as a ship is said to be safe when it has arrived at port. *You shall call your walls Salvation and your gates Praise* (Isa. 60:18). Men receive the hope of this salvation when they are justified from sin in the present and are thus referred to as saved: *We are saved by hope* (Rom. 8:24 DRB).

But this salvation of grace is ***by faith*** in Christ. In the justification of an
adult who has sinned, the movement of faith towards God coincides with the
infusion of grace. *Your faith has saved you. Go in peace* (Luke 8:48). *Since we are*
justified by faith, we have peace with God through our Lord Jesus Christ (Rom.
94 5:1). When he next says ***and that not of yourselves***, he clarifies what he had
spoken of: *first*, regarding faith, which is the foundation of the whole spiritual
edifice; *second*, regarding grace, at ***for we are his workmanship.***

95 He eliminates two errors concerning the first point. The *first* of these is that, since he had said we are saved by faith, anyone can hold the opinion that

7. See Thomas Aquinas, *On Ephesians* 2.2 (not included in this collection).

faith itself originates within ourselves and that to believe is determined by our own wishes. Therefore to abolish this he states ***and that not of yourselves.***

Free will is inadequate for the act of faith since the contents of faith are above human reason. *Matters too great for human understanding have been shown to you* (Sir. 3:23). *No one comprehends the thoughts of God except the Spirit of God* (1 Cor. 2:11). That a man should believe, therefore, cannot occur from himself unless God gives it, according to what is written: *Who has learned your counsel unless you have given wisdom and sent your Holy Spirit from on high?* (Wis. 9:17). For this reason he adds ***for it is the gift of God***, namely, faith itself. *For you have been granted, for the sake of Christ, not only to believe in him, but also to suffer for him* (Phil. 1:29). *To another, faith [is given] by the same Spirit* (1 Cor. 12:9).

96 He rejects a *second* error: someone could think that faith is given by God to us on the merit of our prior actions. To exclude this he adds that it is ***not of works***—prior works, that is—that we at some point merit to be saved; for this is by grace, as was mentioned above, and according to what is written: *If it is by grace, it is no longer on the basis of works; otherwise grace would no longer be grace* (Rom. 11:6).

He follows with the reason why God saves man by faith without any preceding merits, ***that no man may glory*** in himself but refer all the glory to God. *Not to us, O Lord . . . but to your name give glory for the sake of your steadfast love and your faithfulness* (Ps. 115:1)*; that no human being should glory in the presence of God. He is the source of your life in Jesus Christ, whom God made our wisdom, our righteousness and sanctification and redemption* (1 Cor. 1:29–30).

97 Next, at ***for we are his workmanship***, he clarifies what he had said regarding grace. Concerning this he does two things: *first*, he clarifies the infusion of grace; *second*, he declares the predestination of grace, at ***which God has prepared.***

98 There are two essential characteristics of grace, which have already been spoken of.[8] The *first* of these is that what exists through grace is not present in man through himself or by himself, but from the gift of God. In reference to this he states ***for we are his workmanship***, because whatever good we possess is not from ourselves but from the action of God. *Know that the Lord is God! It is he that made us, and we are his* (Ps. 100:3). *Is he not your father, who created you, who made you and established you?* (Deut. 32:6). This is immediately linked with what went before: ***that no man may glory, for we are his workmanship.*** Or, it can be joined with what was said above: ***for by grace you are saved.***

99 The *second* essential characteristic of grace is that it is not from previous works; this is expressed when he adds ***created.*** To create anything is to produce it from nothing; hence, when anyone is justified without preceding merits, he

8. See *On Ephesians* 1.2.15.

can be said to have been created as though made from nothing. This creative action of justification occurs through the power of Christ communicating the Holy Spirit. On this account he adds ***in Christ Jesus***, that is, through Christ Jesus. *For in Christ Jesus neither circumcision nor uncircumcision avails anything, but a new creation* (Gal. 6:15 DRB). *When you send forth your Spirit, they are created* (Ps. 104:30).

Moreover, not only are the habits of virtue and grace given to us, but we are inwardly renewed through the Spirit in order to act uprightly. Whence he goes on ***in good works*** since the good works themselves are made possible to us by God. *For you have wrought for us all our works* (Isa. 26:12).

100 Since *those whom he predestined he also called* (Rom. 8:30) through grace, therefore he adds something concerning predestination, saying, ***which*** good works ***God has prepared.*** For predestination is nothing else than the pre-arrangement of God's blessings, among which blessings our good works themselves are numbered. God is said to prepare something for us insofar as he disposes himself to give it to us. *You provide their grain, for so you have prepared it* (Ps. 65:9).

Lest anyone imagine that good works are prepared for us by God in such a way that we do not cooperate in their realization through our free will, he annexes ***that we should walk in them.*** As though he said: 'thus has he prepared them for us, that we might perform them for ourselves through our free will.' *For we are God's fellow workers* (1 Cor. 3:9). For this reason the Apostle said of himself: *By the grace of God, I am what I am, and his grace in me has not been in vain. On the contrary, I worked harder than any of them, though it was not I, but the grace of God which is with me* (1 Cor. 15:10). He expressly says ***we should walk*** to designate a progress in good works, in line with that saying: *Walk while you have the light, lest the darkness overtake you* (John 12:35); ***walk then as children of light*** (Eph. 5:8).

Chapter 9

APPLICATION OF CHRIST'S GIFTS IN THE SACRAMENTS

Hebrews 6:1–6

The Spiritual Pedagogy of Christ

On Hebrews 6.1 (275–292)

6:1 ***Wherefore, leaving the word of the beginning of Christ, let us go on to things more perfect: not laying again the foundation of penance from dead works and of faith towards God,***

6:2 ***of the doctrine of baptisms and imposition of hands, and of the resurrection of the dead, and of eternal judgment.***

6:3 ***And this will we do if God permit.***

6:4 ***For it is impossible for those who were once illuminated, have tasted also the heavenly gift and were made partakers of the Holy Spirit,***

6:5 ***have moreover tasted the good word of God and the powers of the world to come,***

6:6 ***and are fallen away: to be renewed again to penance, crucifying again to themselves the Son of God and making him a mockery.***

275 Having mentioned the priesthood of Christ according to the order of Melchisedech and scolded the slowness of those to whom he was writing,[1] the Apostle now returns to his theme. In regard to which he does three things: *first*, he discloses his intention; *second*, its difficulty, at ***and this will we do***; *third*, he declares his intention, at ***but, my dearly beloved*** (Heb. 6:9).

In regard to the *first*, he does two things: *first*, he discloses his intention;
276 *second*, he explains what he says, at ***not laying again***. His intention is that passing over the things which pertain to the beginning of Christian doctrine, he may go on to loftier matters; hence he says: I have stated that solid food is for the perfect: ***wherefore, leaving the word of the beginning*** of the doctrine ***of Christ***, through which Christ begins to exist in us, which is by the doctrine

1. See Hebrews 5:10–12 and Thomas Aquinas, *On Hebrews* 5.2.

of faith: *that Christ may dwell by faith in your hearts* (Eph. 3:17), ***let us go on to things more perfect***, i.e., to things which look toward the perfection of Christ's doctrine: *When I became a man, I put away childish ways* (1 Cor. 13:11).

According to a gloss this can refer to two things, namely, either to the intellect, so that as a person advances in age, he should put away childish things and devote himself to what is perfect: *We speak wisdom among the perfect* (1 Cor. 2:6 DRB), or to the will, and then the sense is that one should not remain a beginner, but tend to the state of the perfect: *Walk before me and be perfect* (Gen. 17:1 DRB).

277 Here two objections arise: the *first* is based on his saying, ***leaving the word of the beginning***. For the beginning should never be forsaken: *I said, "now have I begun"* (Ps. 77:11 DRB); *my justification, which I have begun to hold* (Job 27:6 DRB).

I answer that there are two ways of forsaking a beginning: one is according to evaluation, and in this way a man should always be a beginner tending to what is higher: *Not that I have already obtained this or am already perfect; but I press on to make it my own* (Phil. 3:12). The other is according to progress toward perfection, and in this way a man should always strive to pass to the perfect state, *forgetting what lies behind and straining forward to what lies ahead* (Phil. 3:13). For, as Bernard says, not to progress in the way of God is to fall behind.[2]

278 The other objection is concerned with the invitation, ***let us go on to things more perfect***. For perfection consists in the counsels: *If you would be perfect, go and sell what you have and give to the poor* (Matt. 19:21). But not all are bound by the counsels.

I answer that there are two kinds of perfection: one is external and consists in external acts, which are signs of what is internal, such as virginity and voluntary poverty. To this perfection not all are bound. The other is internal and consists in the love of God and neighbor: *Put on love, which binds everything together in perfect harmony* (Col. 3:14). Not all are bound to a perfection of this kind, but all are bound to tend toward it; because if a person no longer desired to love God more, he would not be doing what charity requires.

But he says, ***let us go on***, and this by following the impulse of the Holy Spirit: *All who are led by the Spirit of God are sons of God* (Rom. 8:14). Or they are as though carried by God, who bears our infirmities: *Hearken unto me, O house of Jacob, all the remnant of the house of Israel, who have been borne by me from your birth, carried from the womb* (Isa. 46:3); or, as carried by one another: *Bear one another's burdens* (Gal. 6:2).

279 Then when he says, ***not laying again***, he explains what he has said. Here he intends to show what the things are which make for the beginning of Christ's

2. Bernard of Clairvaux, *Sermons on the Feast of the Purification of Holy Mary* 2.3.

doctrine. For this he uses a simile. For it is by faith that a soul is built into a spiritual edifice. Therefore, just as in a material building the foundation is laid first, so here the first rudiments of Christ's doctrine are, as it were, the foundation.

But this seems to conflict with what he teaches below (Heb. 11:1), where faith is set down as the foundation: for faith is one: *one Lord, one faith, one baptism* (Eph. 4:5).[3] But here he mentions six foundations. I answer that faith is the foundation of the virtues, but the things he mentions are the foundations of Christ's doctrine.

He says, ***not laying again the foundation of penance***, as though it were laid so firmly that there is no need to lay it again. Or, because you have just laid it, and it should not be laid again.

280 But the Apostle lists them quite clearly. For just as in the process of generation and of any motion, there is first of all the departure, so too here; because penance is a departure from sin and is, as it were, the foundation of that life. For, according to Augustine, no one who is master of his own will can begin a new life without repenting of the past.[4] Hence, at the beginning of his preaching the Lord says: *Do penance* (Matt. 4:17 DRB). Therefore, he says, ***of penance from dead works***. For works are called dead either because they are dead in themselves, or because they become dead. A thing is said to be alive, when it functions on its own power, so that wherever it fails, it is said to be dead. For our works are ordained to happiness, which is man's end; therefore, when they do not lead to happiness or cannot be ordained to happiness, they are said to be dead: and these are works performed in mortal sin: ***The blood of Christ, who by the Holy Spirit offered himself unspotted unto God***, shall ***cleanse our conscience from dead works*** (Heb. 9:14). But works performed in charity are made dead by sin; hence, they do not have the power to merit eternal life: *None of the righteous deeds which he has done shall be remembered* (Ezek. 18:24). But penance makes them revive; hence they are then once more counted for eternal life.

281 But in approaching the desired terminus, faith is first; hence, he says, the foundation ***of faith towards God***. For it is proper to faith that man believe and assent to things unseen by him, on the authority of another. But this testimony is either from man alone, and then it does not pertain to the virtue of faith, because man can deceive and be deceived; or that testimony is from God's judgment, and then it is most true and firm, because it comes from the truth itself, which cannot deceive or be deceived. Hence, he says, ***towards God***, i.e., the assent is made to what God says: *Believe in God, believe also in me* (John 14:1).

3. See Thomas Aquinas, *On Hebrews* 11.1 (included in chapter 15 of this collection).

4. Augustine, *Sermon 351: On the Value of Repentance* 2.

282 Second in that process are the sacraments of faith. But these are the two sacraments of those entering: for those are the only ones the Apostle is discussing here. The *first* is baptism, by which we are reborn; the *second* is confirmation, by which we are strengthened.

283 In regard to the *first* he says, ***of baptisms***. But this seems contrary to what is stated in Ephesians: *one faith, one baptism* (4:5). Therefore, there are not several baptisms.

I answer that there are three kinds of baptism, namely, of water, of desire, and of blood. But the last two have no force unless they are referred to the first because the first one must be intended, if it cannot be actually received by a person with the use of freedom. Hence, there are not three sacraments, but one sacrament, by which we are reborn unto salvation: *One is born of water and the Spirit* (John 3:5).

Of the other two, baptism of blood produces more of baptism's effects, provided that the first is desired, or the opposite is not present in the mind, as is clear in the case of the holy innocents, who were not of an opposite mind. For baptism has its power from the merit of Christ's passion: *All of us who have been baptized into Christ Jesus were baptized into his death* (Rom. 6:3). Therefore, just as one who is baptized is conformed sacramentally to Christ's death, so the martyr is conformed really. Therefore, the baptism of blood produces the total effect of baptism in the sense of washing away all guilt and punishment for sin; but it does not imprint a character. Therefore, if one who had undergone martyrdom without baptism of water were to rise, he would have to be baptized.

Penance, however, does not produce as many of baptism's effects, because it does not take away all punishment, although it takes away all guilt. But just as a martyr conforms himself to Christ's passion by external suffering, so does a penitent by internal suffering: *Those who belong to Christ Jesus have crucified the flesh with its passions and vices* (Gal. 5:24). Therefore, penance can be so great that it would remove all guilt and punishment, as happened to the good thief and to Magdalene. Hence, penance is called baptism, inasmuch as it performs the function of baptism. And because baptism cannot be repeated, penance was instituted.

Therefore, the others are called baptisms, because they produce the effect of baptism; but there is only one baptism, because the others produce no effect, unless the first is intended.

284 The second sacrament of those who are entering is imposed by the laying on of hands; hence, he says, ***and imposition of hands***. But this is twofold: one is productive of miracles, as when Christ cured the sick by laying his hands on them: *He laid his hands on every one of them and healed them* (Luke 4:40). And this is not sacramental.

But the other is sacramental and is found in two sacraments: *first*, in the sacrament of orders: *Do not be hasty in the laying on of hands* (1 Tim. 5:22); *second*, in the sacrament of confirmation unto renovation *by the washing of regeneration and renewal in the Holy Spirit* (Titus 3:5). For in confirmation the Holy Spirit is given for strength to enable a man to boldly confess Christ's name before men. For just as in the natural order a man is first born and then grows and becomes strong, so too, in the order of grace.

285 *Third*, there follows the terminus of motion, at which the motion is terminated. This is twofold: the first is the resurrection of bodies, which is the foundation of faith, because without it our faith is in vain (1 Cor. 15:14). Therefore, he says, ***of the resurrection of the dead***.

Second, we expect a reward, which is conferred by the judge: *God will bring every deed into judgment* (Eccles. 12:14); therefore, he says, ***and of eternal judgment***: not that that judgment will last a thousand years, as Lactantius taught, because it will last but a moment.[5] But it is called eternal because the sentence passed then will last forever: *They will go away into eternal punishment, but the righteous into eternal life* (Matt. 25:46).

It should be noted that all the things he says he desires to treat here are, as it were, the rudiments of the faith; hence he preaches them to newcomers, as is recorded in Acts 17:18 and in other places.

286 Then when he says ***and this will we do***, he shows how difficult it is to carry out his intention. For it is difficult both in itself and in relation to his hearers. Hence he does three things. *First*, he suggests that in this he especially needs divine help; *second*, he mentions their weakness, at ***for it is impossible***; *third*, he proposes a simile, at ***for the earth*** (Heb. 6:7).

287 He says, therefore: ***Let us go on to things more perfect . . . and this we will do, if God permit***. He says less than he means, for it is not only necessary that God permit, but he must do all things: *Both we and our words are in his hand* (Wis. 7:16). Therefore, he must place all things under the confidence of divine help. *Apart from me you can do nothing* (John 15:5); *you ought to say, "If the Lord will, and if we shall live and we shall do this or that"* (James 4:15).

288 Then when he says, ***it is impossible***, he shows their weakness. For they were ***weak to hear*** (Heb. 5:11). For just as in material things no state is so dangerous as that of those who fall back, so in spiritual things one who falls into sin after grace rises with more difficulty.

In regard to this he does three things: *first*, he lists the good things they had received; *second*, the difficulty caused in them from being received, at ***and***

5. Lactantius, *The Epitome of the Divine Institutes* 72. Lactantius was a lay, Christian author who lived in the third and fourth centuries. He wrote several theological and apologetic works and served as adviser to Emperor Constantine.

289 ***are fallen away***; *third*, he assigns the reason, at ***crucifying again***. Some of the goods are present, and some future.

But in the present they had spiritual rebirth; in regard to this he says ***illuminated***, namely by baptism. And baptism is fittingly called an enlightenment because it is the beginning of spiritual rebirth, in which the intellect is enlightened by faith: *Once you were darkness, but now you are light in the Lord* (Eph. 5:8). They are also partakers of God's goods; hence he says, who ***have tasted also the heavenly gift***. That gift is grace and is called heavenly, because God gave it from heaven: *He gave gifts to men* (Eph. 4:8); *every perfect gift is from above, coming down from the Father of lights* (James 1:17).

They are also partakers of the divine goodness: *He has granted to us precious and very great promises* (2 Pet. 1:4). Therefore, he says, ***and were made partakers of the Holy Spirit***. For all gifts are given from love; therefore, he attributes that participation to the Holy Spirit. For to participate is to take a part. But Christ alone had the Holy Spirit in fullness: *It is not by measure that he gives the Spirit* (John 3:34). For the other saints received of his fullness and were made partakers not of his substance, but of his distributions: ***gifts of the Holy Spirit distributed according to his will*** (Heb. 2:4). *There are varieties of gifts, but the same Spirit* (1 Cor. 12:4).

Also in the present day they had instruction of his doctrine; hence, he says, ***have moreover tasted the good word of God***. That word is called good, because it is the word of eternal life: *Lord, to whom shall we go? You have the words of eternal life* (John 6:69); *how sweet are your words to my taste* (Ps. 119:103). But he says, ***tasted***, because it not only enlightens the intellect, but also refreshes the affections, in which there is a certain savoring: *Taste and see that the Lord is good* (Ps. 34:8).

290 *We are saved by hope* (Rom. 8:24 DRB). Therefore, he says, ***and the powers of the world to come***. But some of these they have not only in hope, but also in an inchoate way, and these are the endowments of the soul, namely, vision, possession, and fruition, and these are possessed inchoatively inasmuch as faith, hope, and charity, which correspond to them, are possessed in the present. But the others are goods possessed only in hope, as the endowments of the body, namely, subtility, agility, impassability, and clarity.

291 Then when he says, ***and are fallen away***, he shows the difficulty in rising after one has fallen. Here it should be noted that he does not simply say ***fallen***, but ***fallen away***, i.e., completely fallen, because if they had merely fallen, it should not be difficult to rise: *A righteous man falls seven times and rises again* (Prov. 24:16).

But if the Apostle had said it is impossible for those who have ***fallen away*** to rise again, then it might be said that in this he was signifying how extremely difficult it is to rise, both because of sin and because of pride, as in the demons. But because he says that those who have once fallen away cannot ***be renewed again to penance***, and there is no sin in this world that man cannot repent of, there must be another explanation.

Hence, it should be noted that a certain Novatian, who was a priest of the Church in Rome, made this the occasion of his error.[6] For he declared that no one could rise to penance after baptism. But this opinion is false, as Athanasius says in a letter to Serapion, because Paul himself received the incestuous Corinthians, as shown in 2 Corinthians 2; and likewise in Galatians (4:19), because he says: *my little children, with whom I am again in travail until Christ be formed in you.*[7] Therefore, it must be understood, as Augustine says, that he does not say that it is impossible to repent, but that it is impossible to be renewed again, i.e., baptized, *by the washing of regeneration and renewal in the Holy Spirit* (Titus 3:5).[8] For a man could never repent in such a way that he could be baptized again. The Apostle says this because according to the law, the Jews were baptized frequently (Mark 7:3–4). Consequently, it was in order to remove that error that the Apostle says this.

292 Then when he says, ***crucifying again to themselves the Son of God and making him a mockery***, he gives the reason why baptism cannot be repeated, namely because baptism is a configuration to Christ's death, as is clear from Romans: *All of us who have been baptized into Christ Jesus were baptized into his death* (6:3). But this death is not repeated, because *Christ being raised from the dead will never die again* (Rom. 6:9). Therefore, those who are repeatedly baptized crucify Christ again.

Or, another way, it denotes that it is repugnant to Christ's grace for people to sin frequently and then be baptized again. Then the emphasis is not on the repetition of baptism, but on the falling away of the sinner, who, as far as in him lies, crucifies Christ again: *Christ also died for sins once for all* (1 Pet. 3:18). Therefore, when you sin after baptism, then, inasmuch as it is you, you

---

6. Novatian was a Roman priest and theologian in the third century who took a rigorist position in the debate, following the Decian Persecution (250), as to whether penance could be offered as a path of reconciliation and return to communion for Christians who had lapsed and denied their faith or performed pagan sacrifice during the persecution. Novation can be seen to have denied the legitimacy of the sacrament of Penance in his denial of the Church's right to offer it as an avenue by which to restore Christians to communion who had committed idolatry or otherwise betrayed their faith under duress. He ultimately parted ways with the Church over the issue and led a schismatic sect that lasted for several centuries.

7. Athanasius, *Epistola IV ad Serapionem* 13 (PL: 26:654). Although traditionally treated as part of the fourth letter to Serapion, the second half of the letter (sections 8–23), which contains the passage cited by St. Thomas here, is excluded from English translations and thought to be in fact a separate work of commentary on Matthew 12:32. Consequently, there is no English translation of this second half of the letter.

8. Augustine, *Baptism* 1.2.2.

give occasion for Christ to be crucified again; and in this way hold him up to contempt and stain yourself, washed in his blood: *[He] loved us and washed us from our sins in his own blood* (Rev. 1:15 DRB).

Romans 6:1–5

Baptism: Dying and Rising with Christ

On Romans 6.1 (468–477)

6:1 ***What shall we say, then? Shall we continue in sin, that grace may abound?***

6:2 ***God forbid! For we that are dead to sin, how shall we live any longer therein?***

6:3 ***Know you not that all we who are baptized in Christ Jesus are baptized in his death?***

6:4 ***For we are buried together with him by baptism into death: that, as Christ is risen from the dead by the glory of the Father, so we also may walk in newness of life.***

6:5 ***For if we have been planted together in the likeness of his death, we shall be also in the likeness of his resurrection.***

468 After showing that it is through Christ's grace that we are freed from the sin of our first parent and from that which abounded by reason of the law, the Apostle now shows that Christ's grace gives us the power to resist further sin.[9] In regard to this he does two things: *first*, he raises a question suggested by the foregoing; *second*, he answers it, at ***God forbid! For we that are dead.***

469 Above he had said that ***where sin increased, grace abounded all the more*** (Rom. 5:20). This could be misinterpreted by supposing that an increase of sin causes grace to abound all the more. That is why he asks: ***What shall we say, then? Shall we continue in sin, that grace may abound?*** One would have to say, yes, if increase of sin were the cause and not merely the occasion of grace abounding. Hence he had stated above: ***Why not do evil that good may come?—as some people slanderously charge us with saying*** (Rom. 3:8). *Why does the way of the wicked prosper? Why do all who are treacherous thrive?* (Jer. 12:1).

470 Then when he says ***God forbid***, he answers the question. *First*, he states why we should not continue in sin; *second*, he ends with an exhortation, at ***let not sin therefore reign*** (Rom. 6:12).

9. See Romans 5:15–21 and Thomas Aquinas, *On Romans* 5.5–6 (not included in this collection).

In regard to the *first* he does two things. *First*, he shows why we should not continue in sin; *second*, he shows that we have the power not to continue in sin, at ***knowing this*** (Rom. 6:6).

In regard to the *first* he presents the following argument: if we are dead to sin, we ought not live in sin. But we are dead to sin. Therefore, we ought not live in sin. Therefore, in regard to this he does four things. *First*, he states the conditional proposition; *second*, he proves the antecedent, at ***know you not***; *third*, he concludes the consequent, at ***that as Christ is risen***; *fourth*, he proves that the consequent necessarily follows, at ***for if we have been planted***.

471 *First*, therefore, he says, ***God forbid*** that we to continue in sin ***that grace may abound***, because *God has not given anyone permission to sin* (Sir. 15:20). And the reasoning is this: ***for we that are dead to sin***, inasmuch as sin has been put to death in us, ***how shall we live any longer therein?*** For it is not the natural order of things to return from death to life: *They are dead, they will not live* (Isa. 26:14); *I had bathed my feet, how could I soil them?* (Song of Sol. 5:3).

472 Then when he says, ***know you not***, he proves the antecedent, namely, that the faithful are dead to sin: *first*, he presents the fact he uses to prove his point; *second*, he proves it, at ***for we are buried together***.

473 *First*, therefore, he says: ***know you not***, as if to say: 'what I am about to propose to you is so obvious that you cannot fail to see it.' *If anyone does not recognize this, he is not recognized* (1 Cor. 14:38)—namely, ***that all we who are baptized in Christ Jesus***: which can be interpreted in three ways. *First*, as indicating that baptism was instituted by Jesus Christ: *Make disciples of all nations, baptizing them* (Matt. 28:19); *second*, as indicating that it is conferred in the name of Christ: *In the name of Jesus Christ they were baptized* (Acts 8:12); *third*, ***in Christ Jesus***, i.e., as indicating baptism into some likeness of Christ Jesus: *As many of you as were baptized into Christ have put on Christ* (Gal. 3:27).

Are baptized in his death, i.e., into a likeness of his death as re-presenting in ourselves the very death of Christ, *always carrying in the body the death of Jesus* (2 Cor. 4:10); *I bear on my body the marks of Jesus* (Gal. 6:17). Or ***in his death***, i.e., by virtue of his death: *He freed us from our sins by his blood* (Rev. 1:5).

Hence, from the side of Christ hanging on the cross flowed blood and water after his death (John 19:34). Therefore, just as we are configured to his death, inasmuch as we have died to sin, so he has died to his mortal life, in which there was the likeness of sin, although no sin was there. Therefore, all we who are baptized are dead to sin.

474 Then when he says, ***for we are buried together***, he proves that we are all baptized in conformity with the death of Christ, saying, ***we are buried together with him by baptism into death***. As if to say: 'burial is only for the dead.' *Leave the dead to bury their their own* (Matt. 8:22).

By baptism, however, men are buried with Christ, i.e., conformed to his burial. For just as a buried man is put under the earth, so one being baptized is submerged under water. Hence, there are three immersions in baptism not only to indicate belief in the Trinity but also to represent the three days of Christ's burial. And just as the three days of burial were one burial, so the triple immersion constitutes one baptism. That is also why solemn baptism is celebrated in the Church on Holy Saturday, when the burial of Christ is commemorated, and on the vigil of Pentecost in honor of the Holy Spirit, from whom the water of baptism derives its power to cleanse: *Unless one is born of water and the Spirit he cannot enter the kingdom of heaven* (John 3:5).

475 Yet it must be noted that in the body one dies before he is buried, but in the spiritual order the burial of baptism causes the death of sin, because the sacraments of the new law bring about what they signify. Hence, since the burial which occurs through baptism is a sign of the death of sin, it produces such a death in the baptized. And this is what he says, namely, that ***we are buried . . . into death***, so that in receiving in ourselves the sign of Christ's burial we might obtain death to sin.

476 Then when he says, ***that, as Christ***, he infers the consequent, namely, that we should not live in sin. To this end he adduces a likeness to the resurrection of Christ, saying ***that, as Christ is risen from the dead by the glory of the Father***, i.e., by the Father's power, whereby the Father himself is glorified: *Let your glory be over all the earth* (Ps. 57:11), ***so we also may walk in newness of life***, i.e., advance in the spiritual life through good works.

For the life of sin carries with it the weakness of old age, because it leads to dissolution: *what is becoming obsolete and growing old is ready to vanish away* (Heb. 8:13); hence it is said: *Why is it, O Israel . . . that you are in the land of your enemies* (Bar. 3:10); but whatever leads to restoration, i.e., to being without sin, is called newness of life: *Your youth is renewed like the eagle's* (Ps. 103:5); *be renewed in the spirit of your minds* (Eph. 4:25).

477 Then when he says, ***for if we***, he shows how the consequence follows necessarily. For after he died, Christ arose; hence it is fitting that those who are conformed to Christ's death in baptism should be conformed also to his resurrection by leading a blameless life. And that is what he says: ***for if we have been planted together in the likeness of his death***, i.e., if we are incorporated into his death as a branch is grafted to a tree, then, as we are united with Christ in his passion, ***we shall be also in the likeness of his resurrection***, so as to live blamelessly in our present life and to attain to a glory similar to his in the future life: *[He] will change our lowly body to be like his glorious body* (Phil. 3:21); *if we have died with him, we shall also live with him* (2 Tim. 2:11).

Thus, after using our likeness to the death of Christ to prove that we are dead to sin, the Apostle uses our likeness to the resurrection of Christ to show that we should not live in sin, which he introduces above as a consequence.

John 3:1–6

Spiritual Rebirth and the Necessity of Baptism

On John 3.1 (423–448)

3:1 ***And there was a man of the Pharisees, named Nicodemus, a member of the Sanhedrin.***

3:2 ***This man came to Jesus at night and said to him, "Rabbi, we know that you are a teacher come from God; for no man can do these signs which you do, unless God is with him."***

3:3 ***Jesus answered and said to him, "Amen, amen I say to you, unless a man is born again, he cannot see the kingdom of God."***

3:4 ***Nicodemus said to him, "How can a man be born when he is old? Can he enter a second time into his mother's womb and be born again?"***

3:5 ***Jesus answered, "Amen, amen I say to you, unless a man is born again of water and the Holy Spirit, he cannot enter into the kingdom of God.***

3:6 ***That which is born of the flesh, is flesh; and that which is born of the Spirit, is spirit."***

423 Above, the Evangelist showed Christ's power in relation to changes affecting nature;[10] here he shows it in relation to our reformation by grace, which is his principal subject. Reformation by grace comes about through spiritual generation and by the conferring of benefits on those regenerated.

First, then, he treats of spiritual generation. *Second*, of the spiritual benefits divinely conferred on the regenerated, at ***After these things was a festival day of the Jews*** (John 5:1). As to the *first* he does two things. *First*, he treats of spiritual regeneration in relation to the Jews. *Second*, of the spreading of the fruits of this regeneration even to foreign peoples, at ***when Jesus therefore understood that the Pharisees had heard*** (John 4:1).

Concerning the *first* he does two things. *First*, he explains spiritual regeneration with words. *Second*, he completes it with deeds, at ***After these things Jesus and his disciples came into Judean territory*** (John 3:22).

10. This is an allusion to the miracle at Cana, where Jesus transformed water into wine. See John 2:1–11 and Thomas Aquinas, *On John* 2.1 (not included in this collection).

As to the *first* he does three things. *First*, he shows the need for a spiritual regeneration. *Second*, its quality, at ***Nicodemus said to him, "How can a man be born when he is old?"*** *Third*, its mode and nature, at ***Nicodemus answered and said to him, "How can these things be done?"*** (John 3:9).

As to the *first* he does two things. *First*, he mentions the occasion for showing this need. *Second*, the need itself for this regeneration, at ***Jesus answered, and said to him, "Amen, amen I say to you, unless a man be born again."***

The occasion was presented by Nicodemus; hence he says, ***and there was a man of the Pharisees named Nicodemus.*** And he describes him as to his person, from the time, and from his statements.

424 He describes his person in three ways. *First*, as to his religion, because he was a Pharisee, hence he says, ***there was a man of the Pharisees.*** For there were two sects among the Jews: the Pharisees and the Sadducees. The Pharisees were closer to us in their beliefs, for they believed in the resurrection, and admitted the existence of spiritual creatures. The Sadducees, on the other hand, disagreed more with us, for they believed neither in the resurrection to come nor in the existence of spirits. The former were called Pharisees, as being separated from the others. And because their opinion was the more credible and nearer to the truth, it was easier for Nicodemus to be converted to Christ. *According to the strictest party of our religion I have lived as a Pharisee* (Acts 26:5).

425 As to his name he says, ***named Nicodemus***, which means *victor*, or *the victory of the people*. This signifies those who overcame the world through faith by being converted to Christ from Judaism. *This is the victory that overcomes the world, our faith* (1 John 5:4).

426 *Third*, as to his rank he says, ***a member of the Sanhedrin.*** For although our Lord did not choose the wise or powerful or those of high birth at the beginning, lest the power of the faith be attributed to human wisdom and power—*Not many of you were wise according to worldy standards, not many powerful, not many of noble birth; but God chose what is foolish in the world to shame the wise* (1 Cor. 1:26–27)—still he willed to convert some of the wise and powerful to himself at the very beginning. And he did this so that his doctrine would not be held in contempt, as being accepted exclusively by the lowly and uneducated, and so that the number of believers would not be attributed to the rusticity and ignorance of the converts rather than to the power of the faith. However, he did not will that a large number of those converted to him be powerful and of high birth, lest, as has been said, it should be ascribed to human power and wisdom. And so it says, ***Many even of the authorities believed in him*** (John 12:42), among whom was this Nicodemus. *The princes of the peoples gather* (Ps. 47:9).

427 Then he describes him as to the time, saying, ***this man came to Jesus at night***. In regard to this, it might be noted that in Scripture the quality of the time is mentioned as to certain persons in order to indicate their knowledge or the condition of their actions. Here an obscure time is mentioned, when it says he ***came at night***. For the night is obscure and suited to the state of mind of Nicodemus, who did not come to Jesus free of care and anxiety, but in fear; for he was one of those of whom it is said that they ***believed in him; but for fear of the Pharisees they did not confess it, lest they should be put out of the synagogue*** (John 12:42). For their love was not perfect; so it continues, ***They loved the praise of men more than the praise of God*** (John 12:43).

Further, night was appropriate to his ignorance and the imperfect understanding he had of Christ: *The night is far gone; the day is at hand. Let us then cast off the works of darkness* (Rom. 13:12); *they have neither knowledge nor understanding, they walk about in darkness* (Ps. 82:5).

428 Then he is described from his statements, when he says that Nicodemus said to Jesus: ***Rabbi, we know that you are a teacher come from God***. Here he affirms Christ's office as teacher when he says, ***Rabbi***, and his power of acting, saying, ***for no man can do these signs which you do, unless God is with him***. And in both remarks he says what is true, but he does not affirm enough.

He is right in calling Jesus ***Rabbi***, i.e., Teacher, because, ***you call me Master, and Lord; and you say well, for so I am*** (John 13:13). For Nicodemus had read what was written: *Sons of Zion be glad and rejoice for the Lord has done great things* (Joel 2:23).

But he says too little, because he says that Jesus came as a teacher from God but is silent on whether he is God. For to come as a teacher from God is common to all good prelates: *I will give you shepherds after my own heart, who will feed you with knowledge and understanding* (Jer. 3:15). Therefore, this is not unique to Christ even though Christ taught in a manner unlike other men. For some teachers teach only from without, but Christ also instructs within, because he was ***the true light that enlightens every man*** (John 1:9); thus he alone gives wisdom: *I will give you a mouth and wisdom, which none of your adversaries will be able to withstand or contradict* (Luke 21:15), and this is something that no mere man can say.

429 He affirms his power because of the signs he saw. As if to say: 'I believe that ***you are a teacher come from God, for no man can do these signs which you do***.' And he is speaking the truth, because the signs which Christ did cannot be worked except by God, and because God was with him: ***He who sent me is with me*** (John 8:29). But he says too little, because he believed that Christ did not perform these signs through his own power, but as relying on the power of another; as though God were not with him by a unity of essence but merely

by an infusion of grace. But this is false, because Christ performed these signs not by an exterior power but by his own; for the power of God and of Christ is one and the same. It is similar to what the woman says to Elijah: *By this I know that you are a man of God* (1 Kings 17:24 DRB).

430 Then when he says that ***Jesus answered, "Amen, amen, I say to you,"*** he sets down the necessity for spiritual regeneration, because of the ignorance of Nicodemus. And so he says, ***amen, amen***. Here we should note that this word ***amen***, is a Hebrew word frequently employed by Christ; hence out of reverence for him no Greek or Latin translator wanted to translate it. Sometimes it means the same as true or truly; and sometimes the same as so be it. Thus we have, in the Psalms *so be it* and the Hebrew has *amen, amen* (Ps. 72:19, 89:52).

But John is the only Evangelist who duplicates or makes a twin use of this word. The reason for this is that the other Evangelists are concerned mainly with matters pertaining to the humanity of Christ, which, since they are easier to believe, need less reinforcement; but John deals chiefly with things pertaining to the divinity of Christ, and these, since they are hidden and remote from men's knowledge and experience, require greater formal declaration.

431 Next we should point out that at first glance this answer of Christ seems to be entirely foreign to Nicodemus' statement. For what connection is there between Nicodemus' statement, ***Rabbi, we know that you are a teacher come from God***, and the Lord's reply, ***unless a man is born again, he cannot see the kingdom of God***?

But we should note, as has already been stated, that Nicodemus, having an imperfect opinion about Christ, affirmed that he was a teacher and performed these signs as a mere man. And so the Lord wishes to show Nicodemus how he might arrive at a deeper understanding of him. And as a matter of fact, the Lord might have done so with an argument, but because this might have resulted in a quarrel—the opposite of which was prophesied about him: *He will not cry or lift up his voice* (Isa. 42:2)—he wished to lead him to a true understanding with gentleness. As if to say: 'it is not strange that you regard me as a mere man, because one cannot know these secrets of the divinity unless he has achieved a spiritual regeneration.' And this is what he says: ***Unless a man is born again, he cannot see the kingdom of God.***

432 Here we should point out that since vision is an act of life, then according to the diverse kinds of life there will be diversity of vision. For there is a sentient life which some living things share in common, and this life has a sentient vision or knowledge. And there is also a spiritual life, by which man is made like God and other holy spirits; and this life enjoys a spiritual vision. Now spiritual things cannot be seen by the sentient: *The unspiritual man does not receive the gifts of the Spirit of God* (1 Cor. 2:14), but they are perceived by

the spiritual vision: *No one comprehends the thoughts of God except the Spirit of God* (1 Cor. 2:11). So the Apostle says: *You did not receive the spirit of slavery to fall back into fear but you have received the spirit of sonship* (Rom. 8:15). And we receive this spirit through a spiritual regeneration: *He saved us . . . by the washing of regeneration and renewal in the Holy Spirit* (Titus 3:5).

Therefore, if spiritual vision comes only through the Holy Spirit, and if the Holy Spirit is given through a cleansing of spiritual regeneration, then it is only by a cleansing of regeneration that we can see the kingdom of God. Thus he says, ***Unless a man is born again of water and the Holy Spirit, he cannot enter the kingdom of God***. As if to say: it is not surprising if you do not see the kingdom of God, because no one can see it unless he receives the Holy Spirit, through whom one is reborn a son of God.

433 It is not only the royal throne that pertains to a kingdom, but also the things needed for governing the kingdom, such as the royal dignity, royal favors, and the way of justice by which the kingdom is consolidated. Hence he says, ***He cannot see the kingdom of God***, i.e., the glory and dignity of God, i.e., the mysteries of eternal salvation which are seen through the justice of faith: *The kingdom of God is not food and drink* (Rom. 14:17).

Now in the old law there was a spiritual regeneration; but it was imperfect and symbolic: *All were baptized into Moses in the cloud and in the sea* (1 Cor. 10:2), i.e., they received baptism in symbol. Accordingly, they did see the mysteries of the kingdom of God, but only symbolically, *having seen it . . . from afar* (Heb. 11:13). But in the new law there is an evident spiritual regeneration, although imperfect, because we are renewed only inwardly by grace, but not outwardly by incorruption: *Though our outward nature is wasting away, our inward nature is being renewed every day* (2 Cor. 4:16). And so we do see the kingdom of God and the mysteries of eternal salvation, but imperfectly, for as it says, *Now we see in a mirror dimly* (1 Cor. 13:12). But there is perfect regeneration in heaven because we will be renewed both inwardly and outwardly. And therefore we shall see the kingdom of God in a most perfect way: *Then [we will see] face to face* (1 Cor. 13:12); and *when he appears we shall be like him, because we will see him as he is* (1 John 3:2).

434 It is clear, therefore, that just as one does not have bodily vision unless he is born, so one cannot have spiritual vision unless he is reborn. And according to the threefold regeneration, there is a threefold kind of vision.

435 Note that the Greek reading is not ***again***, but *another*, i.e., from above, which Jerome translated as ***again***, in order to suggest addition.[11] And this is the way Jerome understood the saying, ***unless one is born again***. It is as if he were saying: unless one is reborn once more through a supernatural generation.

11. Thomas is referring here to Jerome's Vulgate translation of the Bible.

Chrysostom, however, says that to be born from above is peculiar to the Son of God, because he alone is born from above: ***He who came from above is above all*** (John 3:31).[12] And Christ is said to be born from above both as to time (if we may speak thus), because he was begotten from eternity: *Before the daystar I begot you* (Ps. 110:3 DRB), and as to the principle of his generation, because he proceeds from the heavenly Father: ***I came down from heaven, not to do my own will, but the will of him who sent me*** (John 6:38). Therefore, because our regeneration is in the likeness of the Son of God, according to Romans: *Those whom he foreknew he predestined to become conformed to the image of his Son* (8:29), and because that generation is from above, our generation also is from above, as to the time, because of our eternal predestination, *He chose us in him before the foundation of the world* (Eph. 1:4), and as to its being a gift of God, ***No man can come to me, unless the Father, who has sent me, draws him*** (John 6:44); and *by grace you have been saved* (Eph. 2:5).

436 Then when he says, ***Nicodemus said to him, "How can a man be born when he is old?"*** he gives the manner of and the reason for this spiritual regeneration. *First,* the doubt of Nicodemus is set forth. *Second,* Christ's response, at ***Jesus answered, "Amen, amen I say to you."***

437 As to the first we should note that *the sensual man does perceives not these things that are of the Spirit of God* (1 Cor. 2:14 DRB). And so because Nicodemus was yet carnal and sensual, he was unable to grasp, except in a carnal manner, the things that were said to him. Consequently, what the Lord said, to him about spiritual regeneration, he understood of carnal generation. And this is what he says: ***How can a man be born when he is old?***

We should note here, according to Chrysostom, that Nicodemus wanted to object to what was said by the Savior.[13] But his objection is foolish, because Christ was speaking of spiritual regeneration, and he is objecting in terms of carnal regeneration. In like manner, all the reasons brought forth to attack the things of faith are foolish, since they are not according to the meaning of Sacred Scripture.

438 Nicodemus objected to the Lord's statement that a man must be born again according to the two ways in which this seemed impossible. In one way, on account of the irreversibility of human life; for a man cannot return to infancy from old age. Hence we read, *I shall go the way,* namely, this present life, *whence I shall not return* (Job 16:23). And it is from this point of view that he says, ***How can a man be born when he is old?*** As if to say: 'shall he become a child once more so that he can be reborn?' *He will not return again to his home, and his place will not know him any more* (Job 7:10).

12. John Chrysostom, *Commentary on Saint John* 26.1.

13. John Chrysostom, 25.1.

In the *second* way, regeneration seemed impossible because of the mode of carnal generation. For in the beginning, when a man is generated, he is small in size, so that his mother's womb can contain him; but later, after he is born, he continues to grow and reaches such a size that he cannot be contained within his mother's womb. And so Nicodemus says, ***Can he enter a second time into his mother's womb and be born again***? As if to say: 'he cannot, because the womb cannot contain him.'

439 But this does not apply to spiritual generation. For no matter how spiritually old a man might become through sin: *When I declared not my sin, my body wasted away* (Ps. 32:3), he can, with the help of divine grace, become new: *Your youth will be renewed like the eagle's* (Ps. 103:5). And no matter how enormous he is, he can enter the spiritual womb of the Church by the sacrament of baptism. And it is clear what that spiritual womb is; otherwise it would never have been said: *From the womb, before the daystar, I begot you* (Ps. 110:3 DRB).

Yet there is a sense in which his objection applies. For just as a man, once he is born according to nature, cannot be reborn, so once he is born in a spiritual way through baptism, he cannot be reborn, because he cannot be baptized again: *one Lord, one faith, one baptism* (Eph. 4:5).

440 When it says ***Jesus answered***, the response of Christ is given. Concerning this he does three things. *First*, he answers the arguments of Nicodemus by showing the nature of regeneration. *Second*, he explains this answer with a reason, at ***That which is born of the flesh, is flesh***. *Third*, he explains it with an example, at ***Do not wonder that I said to you, you ought to be born again*** (John 3:7).

441 He answers the objections by showing that he is speaking of a spiritual regeneration, not a carnal one. And this is what he says: ***Unless a man is born again of water and the Holy Spirit, he cannot enter into the kingdom of God.*** As if to say: 'you are thinking of a carnal generation, but I am speaking of a spiritual generation.'

Note that above he had said, ***he cannot see the kingdom of God***, while here he says, ***he cannot enter into the kingdom of God***, which is the same thing. For no one can see the things of the kingdom of God unless he enters it; and to the extent that he enters, he sees. *I will give him a white stone with a new name written on the stone which no one knows except him who receives it* (Rev. 2:17).

442 Now there is a reason why spiritual generation comes from the Spirit. It is necessary that the one generated be generated in the likeness of the one generating; but we are regenerated as sons of God, in the likeness of his true Son. Therefore, it is necessary that our spiritual regeneration come about through that by which we are made like the true Son. And this comes about by our having his Spirit: *Anyone who does not have the Spirit of Christ does not belong to*

him (Rom. 8:9); *by this we know that we abide in him, and he in us: because he has given us of his Spirit* (1 John 4:13). Thus spiritual regeneration must come from the Holy Spirit. *You did not receive the spirit of slavery to fall back into fear, but you have received the spirit of sonship* (Rom. 8:15); ***it is the Spirit that gives life*** (John 6:63).

443 Water, too, is necessary for this regeneration, and for three reasons. *First*, because of the condition of human nature. For man consists of soul and body, and if the Spirit alone were involved in his regeneration, this would indicate that only the spiritual part of man is regenerated. Hence in order that the flesh also be regenerated, it is necessary that, in addition to the Spirit through whom the soul is regenerated, something bodily be involved, through which the body is regenerated; and this is water.

Second, water is necessary for the sake of human knowledge. For, as Dionysius says, divine wisdom so disposes all things that it provides for each thing according to its nature.[14] Now it is natural for man to know; and so it is fitting that spiritual things be conferred on men in such a way that he may know them, *that we might understand the gifts bestowed on us by God* (1 Cor. 2:12). But the natural manner of this knowledge is that man know spiritual things by means of sensible things, since all our knowledge begins in sense knowledge. Therefore, in order that we might understand what is spiritual in our regeneration, it was fitting that there be in it something sensible and material, that is, water, through which we understand that just as water washes and cleanses the exterior in a bodily way, so through baptism a man is washed and cleansed inwardly in a spiritual way.

Third, water was necessary so that there might be a correspondence of causes. For the cause of our regeneration is the incarnate Word: ***He gave power to become children of God*** (John 1:12). Therefore it was fitting that in the sacraments, which have their efficacy from the power of the incarnate Word, there be something corresponding to the Word, and something corresponding to the flesh, or body. And spiritually speaking, this is water when the sacrament is baptism, so that through it we may be conformed to the death of Christ, since we are submerged in it during baptism as Christ was in the womb of the earth for three days: *We were buried with him by baptism* (Rom. 6:4).

Further, this mystery was suggested in the first production of things, when the Spirit of God hovered over the waters (Gen. 1:2). But a greater power was conferred on water by contact with the most pure flesh of Christ; because in the beginning water brought forth crawling creatures with living souls, but since Christ was baptized in the Jordan, water has yielded spiritual souls.

14. Pseudo–Dionysius, *The Divine Names* 4.33.

444 It is clear that the Holy Spirit is God, since he says, ***unless a man is born again of water and the Holy Spirit.*** For he says: ***Children of God . . . are born not of blood, nor of the will of the flesh, nor of the will of man, but of God*** (John 1:12–13). From this we can form the following argument: he from whom men are spiritually reborn is God; but men are spiritually reborn through the Holy Spirit, as it is stated here; therefore, the Holy Spirit is God.

445 Two questions arise here. *First*, if no one enters the kingdom of God unless he is born again of water, and if the fathers of old were not born again of water, for they were not baptized, then they have not entered the kingdom of God.

The other is since baptism is of three kinds, that is, of water, of desire, and of blood, and many have been baptized in the latter two ways, who we say have entered the kingdom of God immediately (even though they were not born again of water), it does not seem to be true to say that ***unless a man is born again of water and the Holy Spirit***, he cannot enter the kingdom of God.

The answer to the *first* is that rebirth or regeneration from water and the Holy Spirit takes place in two ways: in truth and in symbol. Now the fathers of old, although they were not reborn with a true rebirth, were nevertheless reborn with a symbolic rebirth, because they always had a sense-perceptible sign in which true rebirth was prefigured. So according to this, thus reborn, they did enter the kingdom of God, after the ransom was paid.

The answer to the *second* is that those who are reborn by a baptism of blood and desire, although they do not have regeneration in deed, they do have it in desire. Otherwise neither would the baptism of blood mean anything nor could there be a baptism of the Spirit. Consequently, in order that man may enter the kingdom of heaven, it is necessary that there be a baptism of water in deed, as in the case of all baptized persons, or in desire, as in the case of the martyrs and catechumens, who are prevented by death from fulfilling their desire, or in symbol, as in the case of the fathers of old.

446 It might be remarked that it was from this statement, ***unless a man is born again of water and the Holy Spirit***, that the Pelagians derived their error that children are baptized not in order to be cleansed from sin, since they have none, but in order to be able to enter the kingdom of God.

But this is false, because as Augustine says in his book *The Baptism of Children*, it is not fitting for an image of God, namely, man, to be excluded from the kingdom of God except for some obstacle, which can be nothing but sin.[15] Therefore, there must be some sin, namely, original sin, in children who are excluded from the kingdom.

447 Then when he says, ***that which is born of flesh, is flesh***, he proves by reason that it is necessary to be born of water and the Holy Spirit. And the reasoning

15. Augustine, *The Punishment and Forgiveness of Sins and the Baptism of Little Ones* 30.

is this: no one can reach the kingdom unless he is made spiritual; but no one is made spiritual except by the Holy Spirit; therefore, no one can enter the kingdom of God unless he is born again of the Holy Spirit.

So he says, ***that which is born of flesh, is flesh***, i.e., birth according to the flesh makes one be born into the life of the flesh: *the first man was from the earth, a man of dust* (1 Cor. 15:47); and ***that which is born of the Spirit***, i.e., from the power of the Holy Spirit, ***is spirit***, i.e., spiritual.

448 Note, however, that this preposition 'of' sometimes designates a material cause, as when I say that a knife is made of iron; sometimes it designates an efficient cause, as when I say that the house was built of a carpenter. Accordingly, the phrase, ***that which is born of flesh, is flesh***, can be understood according to either efficient or material causality. As efficient cause, indeed, because a power existing in flesh is productive of generation; and as material cause, because some carnal element in animals makes up the animal generated. But nothing is said to be made out of spirit in a material sense, since spirit is unchangeable, whereas matter is the subject of change; but it is said in the sense of efficient causality.

According to this, we can discern a threefold generation. One is materially and effectively from the flesh and is common to all who exist according to the flesh. Another is according to the Spirit effectively, and according to it we are reborn as sons of God through the grace of the Holy Spirit and are made spiritual. The third is midway, that is, only materially from the flesh but effectively from the Holy Spirit. And this is true in the singular case of Christ: because he was born deriving his flesh materially from the flesh of his mother, but effectively from the Holy Spirit: *That which is conceived in her is of the Holy Spirit* (Matt. 1:20). Therefore, he was born holy: *The Holy Spirit will come upon you, and the power of the Most High will overshadow you; therefore the child to be born, will be called holy, the Son of God* (Luke 1:35).

1 Corinthians 11:23–24

Christ's Institution of the Eucharist

On 1 Corinthians 11.5 (644–671)

11:23 ***For I have received of the Lord that which also I delivered unto you, that the Lord Jesus, the same night in which he was betrayed, took bread,***

11:24 ***and giving thanks, broke it and said, "Take, and eat: this is my body, which shall be delivered for you. Do this for the commemoration of me."***

644 After rebuking the Corinthians for their unbecoming behavior, when they came together to take the Eucharist, the Apostle now deals with the sacrament itself. *First,* he discusses the dignity of this sacrament; *second,* he urges the faithful to receive it reverently, at ***whoever eats the bread*** (1 Cor. 11:27).

In regard to the *first* he does two things. *First,* he commends the authority of the doctrine he is about to deliver; *second,* he presents the doctrine about the dignity of this sacrament, at ***that the Lord Jesus.***

645 In regard to the *first* he does two things. *First,* he commends the authority of the doctrine on the part of the author, who is Christ, saying: *It is not the Lord's supper that you eat* (1 Cor. 11:20), ***for I have received of the Lord***, namely, Christ, who is the author of this doctrine and not any mere man: *Paul, an apostle—not from men nor through men but through Jesus Christ* (Gal. 1:1); *it was declared at first by the Lord* (Heb. 2:3).

Second, he commends the authority of the doctrine on the part of the minister, who is Paul himself, when he adds, ***that which also I delivered unto you***: *What I have heard from the Lord of hosts, the God of Israel, I announce to you* (Isa. 21:10); *I learned without guile and I impart without grudging* (Wis. 7:13).

646 Then when he says, ***that the Lord Jesus***, he commends the dignity of this sacrament, describing its institution. *First,* he mentions the institution; *second,* the time of the institution, at ***the same night***; *third,* the manner of instituting, at ***took bread.***

647 The one who institutes this sacrament is Christ. Hence he says, ***that the Lord Jesus***, for it was stated above, when the sacrament of baptism was discussed, that Christ has in the sacraments the excellence of power, to which pertain four things: *first,* that his virtue and merit operate in the sacraments; *second,* that the sacraments are sanctified in his name; *third,* that he can pro-

duce the effect of a sacrament without the sacrament; *fourth*, the institution of a new sacrament.[16]

Yet it was especially suitable that he institute in his own person this sacrament, in which his body and blood are communicated. Hence he himself says: *The bread that I shall give for the life of the world is my flesh* (John 6:52).

648 Then when he says, ***the same night in which he was betrayed***, he describes the time of the institution of this sacrament. It was fitting to do this: *first*, as to the quality of the time. For it was night. For the soul is enlightened by virtue of this sacrament. Hence is it said that Jonathan *put forth the tip of his staff and dipped it in the honeycomb and put his hand to his mouth, and his eyes became bright* (1 Sam. 14:27); on which account it is said: *The night is as bright as the day* (Ps. 139:12).

Second, as to the negotiations carried on at that time, namely, it was when he was delivered over to the passion, by which he passed to the Father, that he instituted this sacrament, which is a memorial of the passion: *Come here, stranger, and prepare the table, and if you have anything at hand, let me have it to eat* (Sir. 29:26).

649 Then when he says, ***took bread***, he shows the manner of the institution. *First*, he relates what Christ said and did in instituting this sacrament; *second*, he explains, at ***as often as you eat*** (1 Cor. 11:26).

In regard to the *first* he does two things. *First*, he deals with the institution of this sacrament as to the body of Christ; *second*, as to his blood, at ***in like manner also the chalice*** (1 Cor. 11:25).

650 In regard to the *first*, before explaining the text one must first consider the need for instituting this sacrament. So it should be noted that the sacraments were instituted on account of a need in the spiritual life. And because bodily things are likenesses of spiritual things, it is fitting that the sacrament be proportionate to things which are necessary to bodily life, in which generation comes *first*, to which baptism is proportionate and through which one is reborn into the spiritual life.

Second, for bodily life is required growth, by which one is brought to perfect size and power. To this is proportionate the sacrament of confirmation, in which the Holy Spirit is given for strength.

Third, for the spiritual life is required food, by which man's body is sustained, and likewise the spiritual life is fed by the sacrament of the Eucharist: *He makes me lie down in green pastures. He leads me beside still waters* (Ps. 23:2).

651 It should be known that the cause of generation is not joined according to its substance to the one generated, but only according to its power; but food is joined according to its substance to the fed. Hence in the sacrament of

16. See Thomas Aquinas, *On 1 Corinthians* 1.2 (not included in this collection).

baptism, by which Christ regenerates us to salvation, it is not Christ according to his substance but only according to his power. But in the sacrament of the Eucharist, which is spiritual food, Christ is there according to his substance.

652 He is contained under another appearance for three reasons: *first*, indeed, it would be horrifying for the faithful to receive this sacrament, if they ate the flesh of a man under its ordinary appearance and drank his blood; *second*, so that it would not be a source of derision to unbelievers; *third*, in order that the merit of faith grow, which consists in believing something not seen.

653 This sacrament is presented under two species for three reasons: *first*, indeed, on account of its perfection, because, since it is spiritual refreshment, ought to be spiritual food and spiritual drink. For even bodily refreshment is not complete without food and drink. Hence he also says above: ***All ate the same supernatural food and all drank the same supernatural drink*** (1 Cor. 10:3–4).

Second, on account of its signification. For it is the memorial of the Lord's passion, through which the blood of Christ was separated from his body; that is why in this sacrament the blood is offered separately from the body.

Third, on account of the salutary effect of this sacrament, for it avails for the health of the body, and so the body is offered; and it avails for the health of the soul, and so the blood is offered. *For the soul is in the blood* (Lev. 17:11).

654 This sacrament is offered specifically under the appearance of bread and wine: *first* of all, because men generally use bread and wine for their refreshment. Therefore, these are used in this sacrament, as water in baptism. *Second*, on account of the power of this sacrament: for bread strengthens the heart of man, but wine gladdens it.

Third, because the bread, which is made up of many grains, and the wine, which is made from many grapes, signify the unity of the Church, which is made up of many believers. Furthermore, this Eucharist is especially the sacrament of unity and charity, as Augustine says.[17]

655 Having seen these matters relating to the explanation of the text: *first*, what
656 Christ did must be explained; *second*, what he said, at ***and said***. But he does three things: the *first* is designated when he says, ***took bread***. Two things can be signified by this: *first*, that he voluntarily accepted the passion, of which this sacrament is the memorial: *He was offered because it was his own will* (Isa. 53:7 DRB). *Second*, that he received from the Father the power of completing this sacrament: *All things have been delivered to me by my Father* (Matt. 11:27).

He touches on the *second*, when he says, ***and giving thanks***. In which is given to us an example of giving thanks for all that is given to us by God: *Give thanks in all circumstances* (1 Thess. 5:18).

17. Augustine, *Tractates on the Gospel of John* 26.

He touches on the *third*, when he says, ***broke***: *Share your bread with the*
657 *hungry* (Isa. 58:7). But this seems contrary to the practice of the Church, according to which the body of Christ is first consecrated and then broken, whereas here it is said that he first broke it and then said the words of consecration. For this reason, some have said that Christ first consecrated with other words and later said the words with which we consecrate. But this cannot be, because the priest, while he is consecrating, does not pronounce those words as from his own person, but as from the person of Christ consecrating. Hence it is clear that Christ consecrated with the same words with which we consecrate.

Therefore, it should be noted that what is said here, ***and said***, is not to be taken successively, as though Christ took bread and giving thanks broke it, and later said the words which follow; rather, they are taken concomitantly, namely, that while he took bread, giving thanks he broke it and said. Therefore with Matthew it should be stated that *Jesus took bread and blessed and broke it* (26:26). The Apostle here did not care to mention about the blessing, understanding that the blessing was nothing else than what the Lord said: ***this is my body.***

658 Then when he says, ***and said***, he shows what Christ said when instituting this sacrament. *First*, he enjoined the use of the sacrament; *second*, he expressed the truth of the sacrament; *third*, he taught the mystery.

659 He enjoined the use of the sacrament, saying, ***take.*** As if not from any human power or merit is it proper for you to use this sacrament, but from an eminent gift of God: *You did give your people the food of angels* (Wis. 16:20); *what have you that you that you did not receive?* (1 Cor. 4:7). And he determines the kind of use when he says, ***and eat***: *Unless you eat the flesh of the Son of man* . . . (John 6:54); *if the men of my tent have not said, "Who is there that has not been filled with his meat?"* (Job 31:31).

660 It should be noted, however, that these words are not from the form of consecration. For there is this difference between this and other sacraments, that the latter are completed not in the consecration of the matter but in the use of consecrated matter, as in the washing with water or in the anointing with oil or chrism. The reason is that in the matter of the other sacraments, it is not some rational nature which is receptive of sanctifying grace; and for this reason, in the form of other sacraments mention is made of the use of the sacrament, as when it is stated: *I baptize you in the name of the Father and of the Son and of the Holy Spirit.* But this sacrament is completed in the very consecration of the matter, in which Christ himself is contained, who is the end of all sanctifying grace.

Therefore, the words which pertain to the use of the sacrament are not of the substance of the form, but only those containing the truth and content
661 of the sacrament, which he mentions last, adding, ***this is my body.*** In regard

to these words three things should be considered: *first*, the reality signified by these words, namely, that the body of Christ is there; *second*, the truth of this statement; *third*, whether this is a suitable form for this sacrament.

662 In regard to the *first* it should be noted that some have said that the body of Christ is not truly present in this sacrament, but only as in a sign explaining what is said here: ***This is my body***, i.e., this is a sign and figure of my body, just as it was said above: ***The rock was Christ*** (1 Cor. 10:4), i.e., as a figure of Christ. But this is heretical, since the Lord expressly says: *My flesh is food indeed, and my blood is drink indeed* (John 6:56).

Hence others say that the body of Christ is truly there but along with the substance of bread. This is impossible, as was shown above.[18] Therefore, others said that only the body of Christ is there, the substance of bread not remaining because either it is annihilated or reduced to prejacent matter.[19] But this cannot be, because, as Augustine says: *God is not the author of tending to non-existence.*[20] *Second*, because even this position takes away the fact that the substance of bread is converted into the body of Christ. Moreover, if the body of Christ does not begin to be in this sacrament by the conversion of something else into it, the only remaining option is that he begins to be there by local motion: but that is impossible, as was shown above. Therefore, one must say that the body of Christ is truly in this sacrament by the conversion of bread into it.

663 Yet it should be noted that this conversion differs from all conversions that occur in nature. For the action of nature presupposes matter, and therefore its action does not extend beyond changing something according to its form, either substantial or accidental. Hence every natural conversion is said to be formal. But God, who makes this conversion, is the author of form and of matter, and therefore the entire substance of bread, the matter not remaining, can be converted into the entire substance of the Body of Christ. And because matter is the principle of individuation, this whole signated individual, which is a particular substance, is converted into another particular substance. For this reason it is called a substantial conversion or transubstantiation.

18. See Thomas Aquinas, *On 1 Corinthians* 11.4 (not included in this collection).

19. The "prejacent" matter (Lat. *praeiacens*: lying or standing before) is the antecedent and elementary material of a thing considered in whatever form it would have prior to its being a component of a particular thing. For instance Thomas explains the doctrine of *creatio ex nihilo* by reference to prejacent matter, denying that God formed the universe out of prejacent matter (see *Summa contra Gentiles* 2.16). In this context, prejacent matter comes to be equivalent to "prime matter" which is matter conceived as absolutely void of form. In other contexts, as here, prejacent matter is not synonymous with prime matter but conceived in terms of elements or the simple bodies that combine together to compose more complex or mixed bodies and substances. He compares these two construals in his *Commentary on the Sentences* 4.11.1.2.

20. Augustine, *Eighty-Three Different Questions*, 21.

In this conversion, therefore, occurs the contrary of what happens in natural conversions, in which, the subject remaining, a change sometimes occurs affecting the accidents. But here the substance is changed, while the accidents remain intact without a subject. This is done by divine power, which as the first cause sustains them without a material cause, which is the substance caused in order that the body of Christ and the blood be consumed under a different appearance, for the reasons given above. And because accidents are referred to their substance in a definite order, the dimensions remain without a subject and the other accidents remain in those dimensions as in a subject.

664 But if no substance remained under those dimensions except the body of Christ, there could be doubt about the breaking of the consecrated host, since the body of Christ is glorified and, therefore, unbreakable. Hence he cannot subsist under this particle, nor can it be pretended that he subsists so, because the sacrament of truth is incompatible with any pretense. Hence nothing is perceived by the senses in this sacrament which is not there in truth. For the *per se* sensibles are qualities, which indeed remain as they previously existed, in this sacrament, as we have stated.

Therefore, others have said that a certain breaking without a subject occurs there; hence nothing is broken there. But this cannot be said either, because, since breaking is in the category of 'being acted upon,' which is a weaker category than quality, it cannot exist in this sacrament without a subject any more than quality can.

Hence it must be said that the breaking is founded, as on a subject, on the dimensions of bread and wine which remain. But the body of Christ is not affected by such breaking, because the whole body remains under each part of the divided dimensions.

This indeed can be considered in this way. For the body of Christ is in this sacrament from the conversion of the substance of bread into it. But the conversion does not come about by reason of the dimensions. For the dimensions of the bread remain, but only by reason of the substance. Hence, too, the body of Christ is there by reason of its own substance, but not by reason of its own dimensions, although its dimensions are there by way of consequence, inasmuch as they are not separated from his substance. But as far as the nature of the substance is concerned, it is entire under each part of the dimensions. Hence, just before the consecration the whole truth of the substance and nature of bread was under each part of its dimensions, so after the consecration the whole body of Christ is under each part of the divided bread.

665 The division of the consecrated host signifies, *first* of all, the passion of Christ through which his body was broken by wounds: *They have pierced my hands and my feet* (Ps. 22:16).

Second, the distribution of the gifts of Christ from his own, as it says below: ***There are varieties of gifts*** (1 Cor. 12:4).

Third, the various parts of the Church. For among Christ's members some are still pilgrims in this world, some may be in glory with Christ, both as to the soul and as to the body, but some await the final resurrection at the end of the world, and this is signified by the division of the host into three parts.

666 *Second*, one should consider the truth of this statement. For the statement, ***this is my body***, seems to be false. For the conversion of bread into the body of Christ occurs at the time of the pronouncing of these words. For it is then that the signification of these words is completed. For the forms of the sacrament effect by signifying; therefore, it follows that in the beginning of the statement, when it is stated that the body of Christ is not there but only the substance of the bread, which is pointed out by the pronoun, ***this***, when it points out a substance. It is the same, therefore, to say, ***this is my body***, as to say: 'the substance of bread is my body,' which is obviously false.

667 Therefore, some have said that the priest pronounces these words materially and recitatively from the person of Christ and, therefore, this pronoun's function of pointing out is not referred to the matter present, such that as a result the statement should be rendered false as the objection supposed.

But this cannot stand. *First* of all, because if this statement is not applied to the material present, it will do nothing in regard to it, which is false. For Augustine says: *The word comes to the element and the sacrament comes to be.*[21] Hence it is necessary to say that the words are taken formally as referring to the material present. But the priest, in the person of Christ, from whom he has obtained power, says them from the same efficacy now, as when Christ spoke them. For the power conferred on these words does not vanish either by the difference of time or by the variety of ministers.

Second, because the same difficulty remains in regard to the first time these
668 words were spoken, namely, by Christ. Therefore, others say that the sense of these words is, ***this is my body***, i.e., this bread designates my body, so that ***this*** designates that which is present at the beginning of the statement. But even this cannot be, because since the sacraments effect what they signify, these words effect nothing except what they signify.

Second, because it would follow from this that nothing would be effected by these words, except that the body of Christ would be there, as under a sign, which was disproved earlier. Therefore, others say that the ***this*** points out something to the intellect and indicates that which will be at the end of the utterance, namely, the body of Christ. But neither does this seem to be suitable, because according to this the sense would be: 'my body is my body,'

21. Augustine, *Tractates on the Gospel of John* 80.3.

which is not brought about by these words. Since this was true before the words of consecration.

669 Therefore, there must be another explanation, namely, that the forms of the sacraments not only signify, but also make: for by signifying they make. But in every instance of making, something common must be subject as a principle. But in this conversion the common factor is not a substance but the accidents, which were present in the beginning and continue to remain. Therefore, on the part of the subject in this statement no noun is used, which signifies a definite species of substance, but a pronoun, which signifies a substance without naming its species.

The sense, therefore, is, ***this***, i.e., which is contained under these accidents, ***is my body***. And this is what occurs through the words of consecration. For before the consecration that which was contained under these accidents was not the body of Christ, but it is made the body of Christ through consecration.

670 *Third*, it is important to consider how this is a suitable form for this sacrament. For this sacrament, as has been said, does not consist in the use of the matter but in its consecration. But the consecration does not occur by the consecrated matter merely receiving some spiritual power, but by the fact that it is transubstantiated according to its being into the body of Christ. Therefore, no other word was to be used except a substantive, so as to say, ***this is my body***. For by this is signified that which is at the end, which is effected by signifying.

671 Then when he says, ***which shall be delivered for you***, he touches on the mystery of this sacrament. For this sacrament represents the Lord's passion, through which his body was delivered over to death for us: *I gave my back to the smiters* (Isa. 50:6), and: *Christ . . . gave himself up for us* (Eph. 5:2).

And to show the reason for making frequent use of this mystery, he adds: ***do this for the commemoration of me***, by recalling this to mind, namely, such a great blessing, for which I gave myself in death. Hence it is said: *He has filled me with bitterness; he has sated me with wormwood* (Lam. 3:15), and: *He has caused his wonderful works to be remembered; the Lord is gracious and merciful. He provides food for those who fear him* (Ps 111:4–5).

Matthew 26:27–29

Christ's Consecration of the Chalice

On Matthew 26.4 (2190–2203)

26:27 ***And taking the chalice, he gave thanks, and gave to them, saying, "Drink, all of you, of this.***

26:28 ***For this is my blood of the New Testament, which will be shed for many unto the remission of sins.***

26:29 ***And I say to you, from this time forward, I will not drink of this fruit of the vine, until that day when I will drink it with you new in the kingdom of my Father."***

2190 Above, he treated of the institution of the new sacrament with regard to the sacrament of the Lord's body;[22] here he treats of the institution of the same sacrament with regard to the sacrament of the blood. And concerning this he does two things: *first*, Christ's deeds are set down; *second*, his words, at ***drink, all of you, of this.***

Concerning the *first*, three deeds are set down: *first*, that he took the
2191 chalice; *second*, that he gave thanks; *third*, that he gave to the disciples. Hence
it says, ***and taking the chalice***, which indicates that it was not instituted that the sacrament be done under one appearance, but under two.

And what is the reason for this? One reason is that there are three things in this sacrament: one which is a sacrament only, another which is a reality only, and another which is both sacrament and reality. The appearances of bread and wine are a sacrament only, the spiritual effect is a reality only, and the body contained is both reality and sacrament. If therefore we consider that which is a sacrament only, in this way it is quite fitting that the body be signified under the appearance of bread, and the blood under the appearance of wine, for it is signified as indicating spiritual refreshment; but refreshment is found properly in food and drink. Likewise, if it be taken as both reality and sacrament, it pertains to this that the sacrament is commemorative of the Lord's passion. And it could not signify better than in this way, that it signify the blood as poured out and separated from the body. It is likewise with regard to that which is taken as reality only, for the blood pertains to the soul, not because the blood is the soul, but because life is preserved in the blood. Hence

22. See Matthew 26:1–16 and Thomas Aquinas, *On Matthew* 26.2 (not included in this collection).

it signifies that, since this sacrament is for the health of the faithful, the bread is offered for the health of the body, and the blood for the health of the soul. *Come, eat my bread, and drink of the wine I have mixed* (Prov. 9:5), for this refreshment is with bread and wine. Likewise another reason, that the whole Christ is contained in the body.

2192 What need then is there that the blood be by itself? Hence one should consider what was said above, that one thing is there directly, by the strength of the sacrament, and another by a natural concomitance. The body of Christ is contained under the appearance of bread by the strength of the sacrament, and the blood by concomitance. But it is the other way around with the blood contained under the appearance of wine, for the blood is there by the strength of the sacrament, and the body by concomitance. Hence when the blood of Christ was poured out on the ground, if the sacrament had been celebrated, the blood would only have been present separately. So, since some had not understood this, they said that this form is continued. Hence they say that when the body is consecrated, the blood is not there until the wine has been consecrated. But this is not so, because if the priest were to die before he consecrated the wine, both the body and the blood would be present in the host.

2193 Likewise, it says, ***taking the chalice***, and does not say, *taking the wine*, and because of this some have said that the sacrament should be performed with water. And this is ruled out, because there follows, ***I will not drink of this fruit of the vine***. *Second*, it is clear that it was wine mixed with water. And one reason for this is on the side of the sacrament, for it was going to be celebrated as the Lord instituted. But it is customary in hot regions that wine is not drunk without water; so one should not believe that he confected the sacrament with pure wine. It also befits the thing contained, for this sacrament is commemorative of the Lord's passion; but from Christ's side flowed out blood and water, as is said in John (19:34). Likewise, to signify the effect of the sacrament, and this in two ways: for it signifies the memory of Christ's passion, so it produces in us the effect of Christ's passion. Now, there are two effects, to purify and to redeem. He redeemed us through his blood: *By your blood did [you] ransom men for God* (Rev. 5:9). Similarly, he purified the unclean, *who has loved us and washed us from our sins in his own blood* (Rev. 1:5 DRB). And these things were necessary, that he should purify and redeem. And the purification is signified by the water, the redemption by the wine. Likewise, the water signifies the people; *a great multitude . . . many waters* (Rev. 19:6). And through this sacrament, the people is united to Christ; so this mixing together of water and wine signifies that the people is united to Christ.

2194 But what happens to the water? Some say that it remains. Others say that it is turned into wine, because when a very little is put in, the species is changed, and thus the whole is converted; and in this way it has to do with a mystery, that the Church's unity is contained in this sacrament.

2195 Likewise, when it says ***taking***, it signifies that he endured the passion voluntarily; hence, *I will lift up the cup of salvation and call on the name of the Lord* (Ps. 116:13).

2196 Likewise, ***he gave thanks***. And for what? For the sign, and for the thing signified. For the sign, ***he gave thanks*** for the effect; for the thing signified, ***he gave thanks*** for the passion. Which indicates that we should not only give thanks for good things, but for evils and adversities as well; *give thanks in all circumstances* (1 Thess. 5:18); *in everything God works for good with those who love him* (Rom. 8:28). Likewise, he gave thanks for the institution of this sacrament, because he brought this about by the divine power; hence, *I can do nothing on my own authority* (John 5:30). This is why he gives thanks to God the Father: *Father, I give you thanks that you have heard me* (John 11:41). Which gives us an example, that if Christ gave thanks, who was equal to the Father, we should give thanks. Likewise, he gives thanks for the effect, because the effect is the salvation of the whole world. And he could only have brought this about by the divinity; *it is the Spirit that gives life: the flesh is of no avail* (John 6:63).

2197 There follows, ***and gave***, that they might receive him in the sacrament. And by this he signified that the fruit of his passion should be ministered to others through others. Hence the Apostles can be compared to an eagle's young, of whom it says, *as the eagle enticing her young to fly, and hovering over them* (Deut. 32:11 DRB).

2198 Then he enjoins its use. And *first*, he sets out the use; *second*, the words
2199 of the consecration of the blood; *third*, he foretells the resurrection. He says
therefore, ***Drink, all of you, of this***. *Drink deeply, O lovers* (Song of Sol. 5:1).
Hence it is signified that Christians can communicate in time and place.

2200 ***For this is my blood***. These are the words of consecration. And notice that there is a difference between these words and those which the Church uses. The Church adds, *this is the chalice*. Likewise, where he says, ***of the new testament***, the Church adds, *of the new and eternal testament*. And where he says, ***for many***, the Church adds *for you*. So where does the Church get this form from? One should say that, as Dionysius says, the Evangelists did not intend to hand down the forms of the sacraments but kept them as secrets;[23] hence they meant only to recount the history. So where does the Church get it from? From the apostles' ordinance. Hence Paul said, *About the other things I will give directions when I come* (1 Cor. 11:34).

2201 But there is a question: why does he say, ***This is my body*** (Matt. 26:26), or ***This is my blood***? Why does he not say, 'this is converted into a body, or into

23. Pseudo-Dionysius, *The Ecclesiastical Hierarchy* 3.10.

blood'? But there are two reasons. The first is that the forms of the sacraments should signify what they effect. What they effect is that the bread be changed into the body of Christ; but the ultimate effect is that the body comes to be, and so the ultimate effect is what should be signified. Therefore, what should be signified is that this is the body, and not that the bread is converted into the body.

2202 Now, in this form there is one thing similar to the old, and another thing dissimilar. They are similar in that, as is written, when Moses had written the law, he sacrificed bulls, and took the blood, and said: *Behold the blood of the covenant which the Lord has made with you* (Exod. 24:8). Thus this blood was offered for the salvation of the people. Hebrews says, *the high priest alone, once a year: not without blood, which he offers for his own, and the people's ignorance* (9:7).

But a difference shows up with regard to four things. *First*, in the fact that that was the blood of bulls, and this the blood of Christ; therefore this blood is efficacious for the remission of sins. *For if the blood of goats and of oxen, and the ashes of a heifer being sprinkled, sanctify such as are defiled, to the cleansing of the flesh: how much more will the blood of Christ . . . cleanse our conscience from dead works, to serve the living God?* (Heb. 9:13–14). Likewise, that blood was called the blood of the testament, but this is called the testament. Again, 'testament' is taken commonly and properly. Commonly, it is taken to mean any given deed, because it used to be that witnesses were brought in for everything done. 'Testament' is said properly when something is written at death, in accord with what the Apostle says, that a testament is confirmed at the death of the one who made it (Heb. 9:16). Either way of speaking fits here, for a covenant was made there, and it was made with blood, for in ancient times when they made a covenant of peace, they showed blood, and this is why it was called *the blood of the covenant*. Similarly, according as it is said with reference to the dead, in this way there was a certain pact between God and men in the old and in the new law, but in different ways. For the first one, namely the old law, was about temporal things, as it is clear that he promised them the land of the Amorites; this is why it was old, for it did not renew men, but rather aged them. But this testament is about heavenly things, and about lofty things. Hence above, ***Do penance, for the kingdom of heaven is at hand*** (Matt. 4:17 DRB). This is why he says, ***of the New Testament***, while it was said, *Behold the blood of the covenant which the Lord has made with you in accordance with these words* (Exod. 24:8). *I will make a new covenant with the house of Israel and the house of Judah* (Jer. 31:31). Hence, ***for this is my blood of the New Testament***, in which you should have confidence; *we have confidence to enter the sanctuary by the blood of Jesus* (Heb. 10:19). Likewise, it befits the meaning of testament regarding the dead; for the promise was confirmed through Christ's death.

Likewise there is another difference, for this adds ***of the New and eternal Testament***, which can be referred either to the eternal inheritance, or to Christ, who is eternal. Another difference is that in that one it says, *which the Lord has made with you*; hence that testament was restricted to those only, but this testament is also with the nations; *he will sprinkle*, namely with his blood, *many nations* (Isa. 52:15). ***For many*** and for all, because if its sufficiency is considered: *He is the expiation for our sins, and not for ours only but also for the sins of the whole world* (1 John 2:2). But if we consider the effect, it has effect only on those who are saved, and this is due to men's fault. But the Church adds *for you*, i.e., the apostles, because they are the ministers of this blood, and it passes on through them to the nations. Likewise, there is set down ***unto remission of sins***, because the blood of the Old Testament could not remit sins.

2203 ***And I say***. Here a consolation is set down, according to Chrysostom.[24] For he had mentioned his blood being poured out, by which he indicated the passion, and so he consoles them, and foretells his glory. And it can be explained in four ways. Chrysostom explains it this way, that the Lord had foretold the passion, and so wanted to cheer them. ***From this time forward, I will not drink of this fruit of the vine***, i.e., of wine, ***until that day***. This ***kingdom*** names the day of the resurrection. At that time he received a new kingdom, i.e., in a new way. That he drank with them afterward is clear (John 21).

But why does it say, in a ***new*** way? Because he ate differently before and after: for before he ate out of necessity, but after the resurrection he ate not out of necessity but to demonstrate the truth of the resurrection.

Jerome says that the vine signifies the Jewish people;[25] *for the vineyard of the Lord of hosts is the house of Israel* (Isa. 5:7); *yet I planted you a choice vine, wholly of pure seed* (Jer. 2:21). ***And I say to you, from this time forward, I will not drink of this fruit of the vine***, i.e., my soul will not rejoice over this people, ***until that day when I will drink it with you new in the kingdom of my Father***. The kingdom signifies the present Church; ***new***, i.e., renewed through faith, because then they will be converted, and then I will rejoice with them. For many have converted, and many will be converted.

Remigius explains that this should be referred to the Paschal ceremonies, that is to say: 'I will not celebrate the other ceremonies of this sort until the establishment of the Church, when I will rejoice over the renewal of the Church.'[26]

---

24. John Chrysostom, *Homilies on the Gospel of Saint Matthew* 82.

25. Jerome, *Commentary on Matthew* 26.29.

26. See Thomas Aquinas, *Catena Aurea on Matthew* 26.8.

Augustine, explains that when he says, ***new***, it is opposed to the old.[27] Now, there are two sorts of oldness: that of punishment, and that of guilt, and this is passed down from Adam, as is said in Romans 5:12. Now, Christ had the oldness of punishment, not of guilt. Hence his simple unbound our double. He says therefore, ***I will not drink*** of the oldness of punishment ***until that day when I will drink it with you new***, because he was going to lay aside that body, and take up the body glorified in the resurrection, and he promised the apostles that they also would take up their bodies again. And this signifies that they are not of a different nature, because the body which he will take up will be of the same nature, but of a different glory.

27. Augustine, *Questions on the Gospels* 1.43.

PART IV

THROUGH HIM

Participation in the Triune Life through Christ

For God's Blessing

A PRAYER OF THOMAS AQUINAS

I praise, glorify, and bless you, my God
for the immeasurable blessings
shown to me who am unworthy of them.

I praise
your compassion
extended to me for so long a time
and your gentleness
appearing in the guise of correction.

I praise
your tenderness
calling out to me,
your kindness
welcoming me,
and your mercy
forgiving my sins.

I praise
your goodness
given to me beyond what I deserve
and your forbearance
that does not remember grievances.

I praise
your humility
that consoles me,
your patience
that shelters me,
your eternity
that preserves me,
and your truth
that rewards me.

What can I proclaim, my God,
about your ineffable generosity?

For you call the fugitive back.
You welcome the one who returns.
You sustain the faltering.
You gladden the despondent.
You prod the negligent.
You arm the warrior.
You crown the victor.
You spurn not the repentant sinner.
You do not remember his wrongdoing.
You free him from many perils.
You soften his heart for penitence.
You frighten him with chastisement.
You entice him with promises.
You castigate him with rods.
You guard him with ministering angels.

For you supply us with all temporal goods.
You reserve for us an eternal good.
You inspire us with the beauty of creation.
You appeal to us with the mercy of redemption.
You promise us blessings in reward.

For all these I am incapable of sufficient praise.

I thank your majesty
for the abundance of your immense goodness.
May you always increase your grace in me,
preserve that increase,
and reward what you have preserved.

Amen

Chapter 10

CHRIST'S GIFT OF HIS SPIRIT

John 14:15–17

Receiving the Spirit of Love and Truth

On John 14.4 (1907–1920)

14:15 ***If you love me, keep my commandments.***

14:16 ***And I will ask the Father, and he will give you another Paraclete, that he may abide with you forever.***

14:17 ***The Spirit of truth, whom the world cannot receive, because it sees him not, nor knows him: but you will know him; because he will abide with you and will be in you.***

1907 Above, our Lord consoled his disciples over his leaving by promising that they would be able to approach the Father.[1] But because it might seem that this was in the distant future, and in the meantime they would still be in sorrow without their Teacher, he here soothes their sorrow by promising them the Holy Spirit.

First, we see the preparation needed to receive the Holy Spirit; *second*, the Holy Spirit is promised, ***he will give you another Paraclete***. *Third*, this promise is clarified, ***that he may abide with you forever***.

Preparation for receiving the Holy Spirit was necessary both for the dis-
1908 ciples and for Christ. The disciples needed a twofold preparation: love in their hearts and obedience in their work. Our Lord assumes they have one of these, for he says, ***if you love me***. And it is clear that you do because you are sad over my leaving: ***You will give testimony, because you have been with me from the beginning*** (John 15:27). The other he commands for the future, ***keep my commandments***. This is like saying: 'you do not express your love for me by tears but by obedience to my commands, for this is a clear sign of love': ***If a man loves me, he will keep my word*** (John 14:23).

Thus, two things prepare one to receive the Holy Spirit. Since the Holy Spirit is love, he is given only to those who love: *I love those who love me* (Prov. 8:17). Likewise, he is given to the obedient: *To this we are witnesses* (Acts 3:15); *I have put my Spirit upon him* (Isa. 42:1).

1. See Thomas Aquinas, *On John* 14.1 (not included in this collection).

1909 Yet is it true that it is the obedience of the disciples and their love for Christ that prepare them for the Holy Spirit? It seems not, because the love by which we love God is from the Holy Spirit: *God's love has been poured into our hearts through the Holy Spirit who has been given to us* (Rom. 5:5). Further, our obedience is from the Holy Spirit, *for all who are led by the Spirit of God are sons of God* (Rom. 8:14); *I will run in the way of your commandments when you enlarged my understanding* (Ps. 119:32).

One might answer that it is by loving the Son that we deserve to receive the Holy Spirit, and having him, we love the Father. But this is false because our love for the Father and the Son is the same love.

Accordingly, we should say that it is characteristic of the gifts of God that if one makes good use of a gift granted to him, he deserves to receive a greater gift and grace. And one who badly uses a gift, has it taken from him. For we read in Matthew that the talent which the lazy servant received from his master was taken from him because he did not use it well, and it was given to the one who had received five talents (25:24). It is like this with the gift of the Holy Spirit. No one can love God unless he has the Holy Spirit: because we do not act before we receive God's grace, rather, the grace comes first: *He has first loved us* (1 John 4:10 DRB). We should say, therefore, that the apostles first received the Holy Spirit so that they could love God and obey his commands. But it was necessary that they make good use, by their love and obedience, of this first gift of the Holy Spirit in order to receive the Spirit more fully. And so the meaning is, ***if you love me***, by means of the Holy Spirit, whom you have, and obey my commandments, you will receive the Holy Spirit whom you will have with greater fullness.

1910 Another preparation was needed for Christ, and as to this he says, ***and I will ask the Father***, and so forth. Note that our Lord Jesus Christ, as a human being, is the mediator between God and humankind (1 Tim. 2:5). And so as a human being he approaches God and asks heavenly gifts for us and, coming to us, he lifts us up and leads us to God. And so, because he had already come to us, and by giving us the commandments of God had led believers to God, he still had to return to the Father and ask for spiritual gifts: *approaching God by himself he is able to save forever* (Heb. 7:25). He does this by asking the Father; and he says this, ***I will ask the Father***: *When he ascended on high, he led a host of captives and he gave gifts to men* (Eph. 4:8).

Note that it is the same person who asks that the Paraclete be given and who gives the Paraclete. He asks as a human being; he gives as God. And he says ***I will ask*** in order to banish their sorrow over his leaving them, because his very leaving is the reason they can now receive the Holy Spirit.

1911 Now we see the promise of the Holy Spirit. The word 'paraclete' is Greek and means 'consoler.' He says, ***he will give you another Paraclete***, that is, the Father, although not without the Son, will give the Holy Spirit, who is the Consoler, since he is the Spirit of love. It is love that causes spiritual consolation and joy: *The fruit of the Spirit is love, joy* (Gal. 5:22). The Holy Spirit is our advocate, *for we do not know how to pray as we ought, but the Spirit himself intercedes for us with sighs too deep for words* (Rom. 8:26). The fact that he says, ***another***, indicates a distinction of persons in God, in opposition to Sabellius.

1912 An objection is that the word 'paraclete' suggests an action of the Holy spirit. Therefore, by saying ***another Paraclete***, a difference in nature seems to be indicated, because different actions indicate different natures. Thus the Holy Spirit does not have the same nature as the Son.

I reply that the Holy Spirit is a consoler and advocate, and so is the Son. John says that the Son is an advocate: *We have an advocate with the Father, Jesus Christ* (1 John 2:1). In Isaiah we are told he is a consoler: *The Spirit of the Lord . . . has sent me . . . to comfort all that mourn* (61:1–2 DRB). Yet the Son and the Holy Spirit are not consolers and advocates in the same way if we consider the appropriation of persons. Christ is called an advocate because as a human being he intercedes for us to the Father; the Holy Spirit is an advocate because he makes us ask. Again, the Holy Spirit is called a consoler because he is formally love. But the Son is a consoler because he is the Word. The Son is a consoler in two ways: because of his teaching and because he gives the Holy Spirit and incites love in our hearts. Thus the word ***another*** does not indicate a different nature in the Son and in the Holy Spirit. Rather, it indicates the different way each is an advocate and a consoler.

1913 Now the promise of the Holy Spirit is given: *first*, we see how it is given; *second*, what the gift itself is; *third*, those who receive it, ***If you know these things, you will be blessed if you do them*** (John 13:17).

1914 The Spirit is truly given because it is given forever. Thus he says, ***that he may abide with you forever; the Spirit of truth.*** When something is given to a person only for a time, this is not a true giving; but there is a true giving when something is given to be kept forever. And so the Holy Spirit is truly given because he is to remain with them forever. He is with us forever: in this life he enlightens and teaches us, bringing things to our mind; and in the next life he brings us to see the very reality: *The Spirit of the Lord came mightily upon David from that day forward* (1 Sam. 16:13). Although Judas had received him, the Spirit did not remain with him forever, because he did not receive him to remain with him forever, but only for a temporary righteousness.

According to Chrysostom, one could say that our Lord said these things to dispel a certain physical interpretation they might have.[2] They could have imagined that this Paraclete, which was to be given to them, would also leave them after a while by some kind of suffering, like Christ. He rejects this when he says, ***that he may abide with you forever***. This is like saying: 'the Spirit will not suffer death as I do, nor will he leave you.'

1915 We saw above that it was said to John the Baptist: ***He on whom you see the Spirit descend and remain, this is he who baptizes with the Holy Spirit*** (John 1:33). It seems from this that it is peculiar to Christ that the Holy Spirit remain with him forever. Yet this is not true if he also remains with the disciples forever.

According to Chrysostom, the solution is that the Holy Spirit is said to remain in us by his gifts.[3] Certain gifts of the Holy Spirit are necessary for salvation; these are found in all the saints and always remain in us, as charity, which *never ends* (1 Cor. 13:8), since it will continue into the future. Other gifts are not necessary for salvation but are given to the faithful so they can manifest the Spirit: *To each is given the manifestation of the Spirit for the common good* (1 Cor. 12:7). With this in mind, the Holy Spirit is with the disciples and the saints forever by the first type of gift. But it is peculiar to Christ that the Spirit is always with him by the second type of gift, for Christ always has a plenitude of power to work miracles and to prophesy, and so on. This is not true of others, because, as Gregory says, the spirits of the prophets are not under the control of the prophets.[4]

1916 The Spirit is a most excellent gift because he is the ***Spirit of truth***. He is called the Spirit to show the subtlety or fineness of his nature, for the word 'spirit' is used to indicate something which is undiscoverable and invisible. And so what is invisible is usually referred to as a spirit. The Holy Spirit also is undiscoverable and invisible: ***The wind blows where it wills; and you hear the sound of it, but you do not know whence it comes or whither it goes*** (John 3:8). He is also called the Spirit to indicate his power, because he moves us to act and work well. For the word 'spirit' indicates a certain impulse, and that is why the word 'spirit' can also mean the wind: *All who are led by the Spirit of God are sons of God* (Rom. 8:14); *let your good Spirit lead me on a level path* (Ps. 143:10).

He adds, ***of truth***, because this Spirit proceeds from the truth and speaks the truth, for the Holy Spirit is nothing else than love. When a person is impelled to love earthly things and the world, he is impelled by the spirit of the world: *We have received not the spirit of the world, but the Spirit which is from God* (1 Cor. 2:12); and when one is impelled to works of the flesh, he

2. John Chrysostom, *Commentary on Saint John* 75.

3. John Chrysostom, 75.

4. Gregory the Great, *Moralia in Job* 2.56.90–92.

is not impelled by the Holy Spirit: *Woe to the foolish prophets who follow their own spirit* (Ezek. 13:3).

But the Holy Spirit leads to the knowledge of the truth, because he proceeds from the truth, who says, ***I am the way, and the truth, and the life*** (John 14:6). In us, love of the truth arises when we have conceived and considered truth. So also in God, love proceeds from conceived truth, which is the Son. And just as love proceeds from the truth, so love leads to knowledge of the truth: ***He will glorify me, for he will take what is mine and declare it to you*** (John 16:14). And therefore Ambrose says that any truth, no matter who speaks it, is from the Holy Spirit.[5] *No one can say, "Jesus is Lord," except by the Holy Spirit* (1 Cor. 12:3); ***when the Paraclete comes, whom I will send you from the Father, the Spirit of truth*** (John 15:26). It is a characteristic of the Holy Spirit to reveal the truth because it is love which impels one to reveal his secrets: ***I have called you friends; because all things whatsoever I have heard from my Father, I have made known to you*** (John 15:15); *he showed it*, the truth, *to his friend* (Job 36:33 DRB).

1917 The ones who receive the Holy Spirit are those who believe; he says, ***whom the world cannot receive.*** *First*, he shows to whom the Spirit is not given; *second*, to whom he is given, ***you will know him***.

First, he shows that he is not given to the world; *second*, he mentions why, ***if you know these things, you will be blessed if you do them*** (John 13:17).

1918 As to the *first* he says, ***whom the world cannot receive.*** Our Lord is here calling those who love the world, the ***world.*** As long as they love the world they cannot receive the Holy Spirit, for he is the love of God. And no one can love, as his destination, both God and the world: *If anyone loves the world, love for the Father is not in him* (1 John 2:15). As Gregory says: *The Holy Spirit inflames everything he fills with a desire for invisible things. And because worldly hearts love only visible things, the world does not receive him, because it does not rise to the love of what is invisible. For worldly minds, the more they widen themselves with their desires, the more they narrow the core of their hearts to the Spirit.*[6] Wisdom of Solomon says, *The Holy Spirit of discipline will flee from the deceitful* (1:5 DRB).

1919 In regard to the *second*, why he is not given to the world, he says, ***because it sees him not, nor knows him***. For spiritual gifts are not received unless they are desired: *She*, divine Wisdom, *hastens to make herself known to those who desire her* (Wis. 6:14).

Now there are two reasons why they are not known. *First*, because one does not want to know them; and *second*, because one is not capable of such knowledge. These two reasons apply to the worldly. In the first place, they do

5. This quote, in fact, belongs to Ambrosiaster, *Commentary on 1 Corinthians* 12.

6. Gregory the Great, *Moralia in Job* 5.28.50.

not desire this, and as to this he says, ***because it sees him not***, that is, does not want to know him: *They have set their eyes bowing down to the earth* (Ps. 17:11 DRB). Further, they are not capable of knowing him, and as to this he says, ***nor knows him***. As Augustine says: *Worldly love does not have invisible eyes which alone can see the invisible Holy Spirit.*[7] As is written: *The unspiritual man does not receive the gifts of the Spirit of God . . . and he is not able to understand them* (1 Cor. 2:14). Just as a tainted tongue does not taste sweet flavors, so a soul tainted by the corruption of the world does not taste the sweetness of heavenly things.

Here is the interpretation of Chrysostom.[8] I say that ***he will give you another Paraclete . . . the Spirit of truth***, but he will not assume flesh, ***because it sees him not, nor knows him***, that is, it will not receive him, but only you will.

1920 Now he mentions, *first* of all, to whom the Spirit is given; *second*, he gives the reason. The Holy Spirit is given to believers: he says, ***you***, who are moved by the Holy Spirit, ***will know him***: *We have received not the spirit of the world, but the Spirit which is from God* (1 Cor. 2:12). This is because you scorn the world: *We look not to the things that are seen but to the things that are unseen* (2 Cor. 4:18).

The reason for this is, ***for he will abide with you***. Note, *first*, the familiarity of the Holy Spirit with the apostles, ***for he will abide with you***, that is, for your benefit: *Let your good Spirit lead me on a level path!* (Ps. 143:10); *O, how good . . . is your Spirit, O Lord, in all things* (Wis. 12:1 DRB). *Second*, note how intimate his indwelling is, ***will be in you***, that is, in the depths of your heart: *I will . . . put a new Spirit within them* (Ezek. 11:19).

7. Augustine, *Tractates on the Gospel of John* 74.4.

8. John Chrysostom, *Commentary on Saint John* 75.

John 14:22–26

The Son's Spirit of Love

On John 14.6 (1938–1960)

14:22 ***Judas said to him (not the Iscariot), "Lord, how is it, that you will manifest yourself to us, and not to the world?"***

14:23 ***Jesus answered and said to him, "If anyone love me, he will keep my word, and my Father will love him, and we will come to him, and will make our abode with him.***

14:24 ***He who does not love me, does not keep my words. And the word which you have heard, is not mine; but the Father's who sent me.***

14:25 ***These things have I spoken to you, abiding with you.***

14:26 ***But the Paraclete, the Holy Spirit, whom the Father will send in my name, he will teach you all things, and bring all things to your mind, whatsoever I will have said to you."***

1938 Above, our Lord promised the disciples that he would come to them; here he clears up a perplexity for one of the disciples.[9] *First*, we see the bewildered disciple; *second*, Christ's answer: ***Jesus answered, and said to him.***

1939 With respect to the *first*, when those who are humble and saintly hear great things about themselves, they are usually astonished and bewildered. Now the disciples had just heard our Lord say, ***Yet a little while, and the world will see me no more. But you will see me*** (John 14:19), and so on. So it seemed that he was preferring the apostles to the entire world. Thus Judas, the brother of James, whose letter is part of Holy Scripture, was bewildered and astonished, and said, ***Lord, how is it that you will manifest yourself to us, and not to the world?*** It is like saying: 'why will you do this? Are we superior to the whole world?' David said something like this: *Who am I, O Lord God, and what is my house, that you have brought me thus far?* (2 Sam. 7:18). And the righteous also say: *Lord, when did we see you hungry and feed you?* (Matt. 25:37).

1940 Then at ***Jesus answered, and said to him***, Christ's answer is given: *first*, Christ states the reason why he will manifest himself to the disciples and not to the world; *second*, he explains something he had said: ***And the word which you have heard, is not mine.***

9. See Thomas Aquinas, *On John* 14.5 (not included in this collection).

He shows, *first*, why he will manifest himself to his disciples; *second*, why he will not manifest himself to the world, at ***he who does not love me, keeps not my words.***

As to the *first*, we see the fitness of the disciples to have Christ manifest himself to them; *second*, we see the manner and order of this manifestation, at ***and my Father will love him.***

In regard to the *first*, he mentions two things which make a person fit to receive God's manifestation. The *first* is charity, the *second* is obedience.

1941 As to charity, he says, ***if anyone love me.*** Three things are necessary for a person who wants to see God. *First*, one must draw near to God: *They that approach to his feet shall receive his doctrine* (Deut. 33:3 DRB). *Second*, one must lift up his eyes in order to see God: *Lift up your eyes on high and see who created these things* (Isa. 40:26). And *third*, one must take time to look, for spiritual things cannot be seen if one is absorbed by earthly things: *Taste and see that the Lord is good* (Ps. 34:8). Now it is charity which accomplishes these three things. Charity joins our soul to God: *He who abides in love abides in God, and God abides in him* (1 John 4:16). It also makes us look at God, *for where your treasure is, there will your heart be also* (Matt. 6:21). As the saying goes: *where your love is, there your eyes are.* Charity also frees us from worldly matters: *If anyone loves the world, love for the Father is not in him* (1 John 2:15). Thus, to turn it about, one who perfectly loves God, does not love the world.

1942 Obedience follows from charity; and so he says, ***he will keep my word.*** Gregory says: *The proof of love is one's actions. Love for God is never lazy: if it is present, it accomplishes great things; if it refuses to work, it is not love.*[10] For the will, especially when it is concerned with an end, moves the other powers to their actions: for a person does not rest until he does those things which will bring him to his intended end, especially if it is intensely desired. And so, when a person's will is intent on God, who is its end, it moves all powers to do those things which obtain him. Now it is charity which makes one intent on God, and thus it is charity which causes us to keep the commandments: *The love of Christ controls us* (2 Cor. 5:14); *its flashes are flashes of fire* (Song of Sol. 8:6). And through obedience a person is rendered fit to see God: *Through your precepts*, that is, as kept by me, *I get understanding* (Ps. 119:104). Again, *I have more understanding than the aged* (Ps. 119:100).

1943 Then when he says, ***and my Father will love him***, we see the manner and order of this manifestation. Three things are needed so a divine manifestation can be made to us.

The *first* is divine love; and he refers to this when he says, ***and my Father will love him.*** We explained above why the future tense is used, ***will love***, which

10. Gregory the Great, *Forty Gospel Homilies* 30.1.

is that he is referring to the effect of love, although from the point of view of his willing to do good, God loves us from eternity: *I have loved Jacob but I have hated Esau* (Mal. 1:2). Jesus does not say here, 'I will love him,' because he had already made that clear to them before: *I love those who love me* (Prov. 8:17). It remained for him to say that the Father would love them: *He loved his people; all those consecrated to him were in his hand* (Deut. 33:3).

1944 The *second* thing needed is that the divine come to us; referring to this, he says, ***and we will come to him.*** An objection to this is that for a thing to come, it has to change its place. But God does not change.

Therefore, I answer that God is said to come to us not because he moves to us, but because we move to him. Something comes into a place in which it previously was not: but this does not apply to God since he is everywhere: *Do I not fill heaven and earth?* (Jer. 23:24). Rather, God is said to come to someone because he is there in a new way, in a way he had not been there before, that is, by the effect of his grace. It is by this effect of grace that he makes us approach him.

1945 According to Augustine, God comes to us in three ways, and we go to him in the same three ways.[11] *First,* he comes to us by filling us with his effects; and we go to him by receiving them: *Come to me, you who desire me, and eat your fill of my produce* (Sir. 24:19). *Second,* God comes to us by enlightening us; and we go to him by thinking of him: *Come to him . . . and be enlightened* (Ps. 34:6 DRB). *Third,* he comes to us by helping us; and we go to him by obeying, because we cannot obey unless helped by Christ: *Come, let us go up to the mountain of the Lord* (Isa. 2:3).

1946 Why does he not mention the Holy Spirit? Augustine says that we do not read here that the Spirit will be excluded when the Father and Son come, because we read above ***to be with you forever*** (John 14:16).[12] Since in the Trinity there is a distinction of persons and a unity of essence, sometimes the three persons are mentioned to indicate the distinction of the persons. And sometimes only two of the three persons are mentioned to indicate the unity of essence.

Or again, one could say that since the Holy Spirit is nothing other than the love of the Father and the Son, when the Father and Son are mentioned, the Spirit is implied.

1947 The *third* thing required for the manifestation of God is the continuation of each of the above, that is, of the love of God and of his coming to us. In regard to these he says, ***and make our abode with him.*** Two things are indicated here. *First,* when he says, ***abode***, he indicates the stability with which we cling to God. God comes to some by faith but does not remain because *they*

11. Augustine, *Tractates on the Gospel of John* 76.2–3.

12. Augustine, 76.4.

believe for a while and in time of temptation fall away (Luke 8:13). He comes to others through their sorrow for sin; yet he does not stay with them because they return to their sins: *Like a dog that returns to his vomit is a fool that repeats his folly* (Prov. 26:11). But he remains forever in his predestined: *I am with you always, to the close of the age* (Matt. 28:20).

Second, these words indicate the intimacy of Christ with us: ***with him***, that is, with the one who loves and obeys him, since he takes pleasure in us, and has us take pleasure in him, *delighting in the sons of men* (Prov. 8:31). *And your God will rejoice over you* (Isa. 62:5).

1948 Chrysostom gives this a different meaning.[13] He says that when Judas heard ***I will not leave you orphans*** (John 14:18), again, ***but you see me*** (John 14:19), he thought that after his death Christ would come to them like the dead appear to us in a dream. So he asks, ***how is it, that you will manifest yourself to us, and not to the world?*** This was like saying: 'how unfortunate for us! You will die and can only help us as the dead do.' To exclude this Christ says, I and the Father ***will come to him***, that is, as the Father manifests himself, so I do also, ***and make our abode with him***, which is not done in dreams, in which there is no prolonging of time.

1949 Now he gives the reason why he will not manifest himself to the world: this reason is the lack of those things on account of which he says that he will manifest himself. For when the cause is absent, the effect is absent. Now the causes for a divine manifestation to be made to the worldly are not found in them. And so God will not manifest himself to the world and the worldly.

It is clear that they do not have the cause, because the world ***does not love him***. Referring to this he says, ***he who does not love me***. Further, they do not obey him; and so he says, ***keeps not my words***. As Gregory says: *To love God it is necessary to use our words, our minds, and our lives*.[14] The reason is obvious why God will manifest himself to his own, and not to the world. It is because his own really have love, and it is love which distinguishes the saints from the world: *In his hands he hides the light. He shows his friend concerning it* (Job 36:32 DRB); *the deep says, "it is not in me," and the sea*, that is, one who is disordered, *says, "it is not with me"* (Job 28:14).

1950 Then when he says, ***and the word which you have heard, is not mine***, he clears up what he had just said, ***If anyone loves me, he will keep my word, and my Father will love him***. For someone could say that there was no reason for this statement: ***If anyone love me, he will keep my word, and my Father will love him***, and it would be more reasonable to have said: *I will love him, and I will come to him*. To exclude this idea he says, ***and the word which you have***

13. John Chrysostom, *Commentary on Saint John* 75.3.

14. Gregory the Great, *Forty Gospel Homilies* 30.2.

heard is not mine, that is, it is not mine as coming from myself, but it is mine as coming from another, from the Father, who sent me. It is like saying: 'one who does not hear this word does not love only me, he also does not love the Father.' And therefore, one who loves both Christ and the Father deserves a manifestation of each. So he says: ***and the word which you have heard***, spoken by me, as a human being, is indeed mine insofar as I speak it, and yet it ***is not mine***, insofar as it is mine from another: ***My teaching is not mine*** (John 7:16); ***the words that I say to you I do not speak on my own authority*** (John 14:10).

1951 Augustine remarks that when our Lord refers to his own words he uses the plural, ***my words***, but when he speaks of the utterance of the Father, he uses the singular form, ***the word which you have heard is not mine***, because he wants us to understand that the word of the Father is he himself, the unique Word of the Father.[15] Thus he says he is from the Father, and not from himself, because he is neither his own image nor his own son, but the Son and Image of the Father. Yet all the words in our heart are from this unique Word of the Father.

1952 Here our Lord promises gifts to his disciples. He had promised them both the Holy Spirit and himself; and so now he *first* mentions what they will receive when the Holy Spirit comes; and *second*, what they will receive from himself: ***Peace I leave with you, my peace I give to you*** (John 14:27).

From the coming of the Holy Spirit they will receive great things, namely an understanding of all the words of Christ. In regard to this he *first* mentions what he taught them, and *second* he promises they will understand them: ***but the Paraclete, the Holy Spirit . . . he will teach you all things.***

1953 He says, in regard to the *first*, ***these things***, what I have said, ***have I spoken to you***, by the instrument of my human nature, ***abiding with you***, as bodily present. It is indeed a very great favor that the Son himself should speak to us and teach us: *In many and various ways God spoke of old to our fathers by the prophets; but in these last days he has spoken to us by a son* (Heb. 1:1–2); *what is all flesh that it should hear the voice of the living God?* (Deut. 5:26 DRB).

1954 He promises them that they will understand his teachings through the Holy Spirit, who will give himself to them; he says, ***The Paraclete . . . will teach you all things***. He does three things concerning the Holy Spirit: he describes him, mentions his mission, and his effect.

1955 He describes the Holy Spirit in several ways: as the Paraclete, as Spirit, and as Holy. He is the Paraclete because he consoles us. He consoles us in our sorrows which arise from the troubles of this world: *fighting without and fear within* (2 Cor. 7:5); *who comforts us in all our affliction* (2 Cor. 1:4). He does this because he is love and causes us to love God and give him great honor. For this reason we endure insults with joy: *Then they left the presence of the council*

15. Augustine, *Tractates on the Gospel of John* 76.5.

rejoicing that they were counted worthy to suffer dishonor for the name of Jesus (Acts 5:41); *rejoice and be glad, for your reward is great in heaven* (Matt. 5:12). He also consoles us in our sadness over past sins; Matthew refers to this in *Blessed are those who mourn, for they shall be comforted* (5:4). He does this because he gives us the hope of forgiveness: ***Receive the Holy Spirit. If you forgive the sins of any, they are forgiven*** (John 20:22): *to grant to those who mourn in Zion* (Isa. 61:3).

He is the Spirit because he moves hearts to obey God: *He will come like a rushing stream, which the Spirit of the Lord drives* (Isa. 59:19 DRB); *all who are led by the Spirit of God are sons of God* (Rom. 8:14).

He is Holy because he consecrates us to God, and all consecrated things are called holy: *Do you not know that your body is a temple of the Holy Spirit within you?* (1 Cor. 6:19); *there is a river whose streams make glad the city of God* (Ps. 46:4).

1956 Then when he says, ***whom the Father will send in my name***, he refers to the mission of the Spirit. We should not think the Spirit comes by a local motion, but rather by being in them in a new way in which he was not before: *When you send forth your Spirit, they are created*, that is, with a spiritual existence (Ps. 104:30).

Notice that the Holy Spirit is sent by the Father and the Son. To show this Christ sometimes says that the Father sends him, as he does here; and he sometimes says that he himself sends him, ***I will send him to you*** (John 16:7). Yet Christ never says that the Spirit is sent by the Father without mentioning himself. So he says here, ***whom the Father will send in my name***. Nor does Christ say that the Spirit is sent by himself, the Son, without mentioning the Father: ***the Paraclete . . . whom I will send to you from the Father*** (John 15:26).

1957 Why does he say, ***in my name***? Will the Holy Spirit be called the Son? One could answer that this was said for the reason that the Holy Spirit was given to the faithful when they invoked the name of Christ. But it is better to say that just as the Son comes in the name of the Father, ***I have come in my Father's name*** (John 5:43), so the Holy Spirit comes in the name of the Son. Now the Son comes in the name of the Father not because he is the Father, but because he is the Son of the Father. In a similar way, the Holy Spirit comes in the name of the Son not because he was to be called the Son, but because he is the Spirit of the Son: *Anyone who does not have the Spirit of Christ does not belong to him* (Rom. 8:9); *God has sent the Spirit of his Son into our hearts* (Gal. 4:6), because he is the Spirit of his Son, and not because he was to be called the Son: *He predestined to be conformed to the image of his Son* (Rom. 8:29). The basis for this is the consubstantiality of the Son with the Father and of the Holy Spirit with the Son. Likewise, as the Son comes in the name of the Father, so his faithful are subject to the Father: *[You] have made them a kingdom and priests* *to our God* (Rev. 5:10): so the Holy Spirit conformed us to the Son, insofar as he adopts us to be sons of God, *you have received the spirit of sonship. When we cry, "Abba! Father!" it is the Spirit himself bearing witness . . . that we are children of God* (Rom. 8:15–16).

1958 Next he mentions the effect of the Holy Spirit, saying, ***he will teach you all things.*** Just as the effect of the mission of the Son was to lead us to the Father, so the effect of the mission of the Holy Spirit is to lead the faithful to the Son. Now the Son, because he is begotten Wisdom itself, is truth itself: ***I am the way, and the truth, and the life*** (John 14:6). And so the effect of this kind of mission is to make us sharers in the divine wisdom and knowers of the truth. The Son, since he is the Word, gives teaching to us; but the Holy Spirit enables us to grasp it.

He says, ***he will teach you all things***, because no matter what a person may teach by his exterior actions, he will have no effect unless the Holy Spirit gives an understanding from within. For unless the Spirit is present to the heart of the listener, the words of the teacher will be useless: *The breath of the Almighty . . . makes him understand* (Job 32:8). This is true even to the extent that the Son himself, speaking by means of his human nature, is not successful unless he works from within by the Holy Spirit.

1959 We read before that ***Everyone who has heard and learned from the Father comes to me*** (John 6:45).[16] Here he is expanding on this, because one does not learn without the Holy Spirit teaching. He is saying in effect: 'one who receives the Holy Spirit from the Father and the Son knows the Father and the Son and comes to them.' The Spirit makes us know all things by inspiring us from within, by directing us and lifting us up to spiritual things. Just as one whose sense of taste is tainted does not have a true knowledge of flavors, so one who is tainted by love of the world cannot taste divine things: *The unspiritual man does not receive the gifts of the Spirit of God* (1 Cor. 2:14).

1960 But if to remind a person of something is the task of an inferior, for instance of the officiants in divine rites, will we say that the Holy Spirit, who brings things to our mind, is inferior to us?

According to Gregory, we should say that the Holy Spirit is said to bring things to our remembrance not as though he brought us knowledge from below, but because in a hidden way he aids our ability to know.[17] Or, one could say the Spirit teaches because he makes us share in the wisdom of the Son; and he brings things to our remembrance because, being love, he incites us. Or, the Spirit ***will bring all things to your mind, whatsoever I will have said to***

16. See Thomas Aquinas, *On John* 6.5 (not included in this collection).

17. Gregory the Great, *Forty Gospel Homilies* 30.3.

you, that is, he will recall them to your memory: *All the ends of the earth shall remember and turn to the Lord* (Ps. 22:27).

We should notice that of all the things Christ said to his disciples, some were not understood, and others were not remembered. Thus our Lord says, ***he will teach you all things***, which you cannot now understand, and ***bring all things to your mind*** that you cannot remember. How could John the Evangelist after forty years have remembered all the sayings of Christ he wrote in his Gospel unless the Holy Spirit had brought them to his mind?

Galatians 4:6–7

Christ's Spirit of Adoption

On Galatians 4.3 (210–217)

4:6 ***And because you are sons, God has sent the Spirit of his Son into your hearts, crying, "Abba, Father."***

4:7 ***Therefore, now he is not a servant, but a son. And if a son, an heir also through God.***

210 Above, the Apostle revealed the gift bestowed on the Jews;[18] here he shows that this gift pertains also to the gentiles. *First*, he mentions the gift; *second*, the means of obtaining it, at ***God has sent the Spirit***; *third*, he discloses the fruit of this gift, at ***therefore, now he is not a servant.***

211 He says therefore that the gift of adoption of sons pertains not only to those who were under the law but to the gentiles as well. Hence he says: ***because you are sons of God***, i.e., you are the sons of God, because not only the Jews but all others who believe in the Son of God are adopted as sons: *To all who received him, who believed in his name, he gave power to become children of God* (John 1:12).

212 The manner in which that gift is obtained is by the sending of the Spirit of the Son of God into your hearts. Augustine says, however, that Christ, existing in the flesh, preached in a principal manner to the Jews, but to the gentiles as a matter of course:[19] *Christ became a servant to the circumcised to show God's truthfulness, in order to confirm the promises given to the patriarchs, and in order that the gentiles might glorify God* (Rom. 15:8). Accordingly, whatever pertains to the condition of the Jews is fittingly adapted to Christ.

And because they might have said that the Galatians had not been adopted as sons of God, since Christ did not assume flesh from them or preach to them, for that reason the Apostle, elucidating the manner of this adoption, says that although they were not related to Christ according to the flesh, i.e., according to race, or by reason of preaching, yet they were united to him through the Spirit and thereby adopted and made sons of God. Hence the conversion of the gentiles is in a special way attributed to the Holy Spirit. Consequently, Peter, when he was blamed by the Jews for going to preach to the gentiles, excused himself through the Holy Spirit, saying that he could not resist the Holy Spirit

18. See Thomas Aquinas, *On Galatians* 4.2 (not included in this collection).

19. Augustine, *Tractates on the Gospel of John* 31.11.

by whose inspiration he had done this (Acts 11). And so, because ***God*** the Father ***sent the Spirit of his Son into*** our ***hearts***, i.e., the hearts of the Jews and gentiles, we are united to Christ and by that fact are adopted as sons of God.

213 But it should be noted that if in certain passages of Scripture the Holy Spirit is said to be sent by the Father—*The Counselor, the Holy Spirit, whom the Father will send in my name* (John 14:26)—and in others to be sent by the Son: *When the Counselor comes, whom I shall send to you from the Father* (John 15:26). The Holy Spirit is nonetheless common to Father and Son and proceeds from both and is sent by both. Accordingly, wherever it is said that the Father sends the Holy Spirit, mention is made of the Son, as in the aforesaid passage: ***whom the Father will send in my name***; and where he is said to be sent by the Son, mention is made of the Father; hence he says, *whom I will send to you from the Father* (John 15:26). Even here, when he says, ***God*** the Father ***has sent the*** Holy ***Spirit***, mention is made at once of the Son, for he adds, ***of his Son.***

Nor does it matter that at times the Holy Spirit is only said to proceed from the Father, for the fact that the Son sends him shows that he proceeds from him. Accordingly, the Holy Spirit is called the Spirit of the Son as of the one sending and as of the one from whom he proceeds, as well as of the one from whom the Holy Spirit has whatever he has, just as of the Father: *He will glorify me, for he will take what is mine and declare it to you* (John 16:14).

214 But he says, ***into your hearts***, because there is a twofold generation: one is carnal and comes about through fleshly seed sent to the place of generation. This seed, small as it is, contains in effect the whole.

The other is spiritual, which comes about by spiritual seed transmitted to the place of spiritual generation, i.e., man's mind or heart, because they are born sons of God through a renewal of the mind. Furthermore, the spiritual seed is the grace of the Holy Spirit: *Anyone born of God does not sin, but he who was born of God keeps him, and the evil one does not touch him* (1 John 5:18). This seed contains, in effect, the whole perfection of beatitude; hence it is called the pledge and deposit of beatitude (Eph. 1:14); *I will put a new spirit within you* (Ezek. 36:26).

215 ***Crying***, i.e., making us cry, ***Abba, Father***, not with a loudness of voice but with a great fervor of love. For we cry, ***Abba, Father***, when our affections are kindled by the warmth of the Holy Spirit to desire God: *You did not receive the spirit of slavery to fall back into fear, but you have received the spirit of sonship. When we cry, "Abba! Father! . . ."* (Rom. 8:15).

Abba, Father. *Abba* in Hebrew and *pater* in Latin and *patēr* in Greek all have the same meaning. And he makes mention of both languages [Hebrew and Greek] to show that the grace of the Holy Spirit, as such, is related in a common way to both peoples.

216 Then when he says, ***therefore, now he is not a servant, but a son***, he mentions the fruit of this gift. *First*, as to removing all evil, from which we are freed through adoption by the Holy Spirit. This is freedom from bondage. With respect to this he says: ***therefore***, i.e., because the Spirit cries ***Father*** in us, ***now***, from the time of grace, ***he***, i.e., each one of us who believes in Christ, ***is not a servant***, i.e., serving in fear—*I will not now call you servants but friends* (John 15:15); *you did not receive the spirit of slavery to fall back into fear, but you have received the spirit of sonship* (Rom. 8:15)—***but a son***: *It is the Spirit himself bearing witness with our spirit that we are children of God* (Rom. 8:16).

For although we be in the condition of servants, because it is said in Luke: *You also, when you have done all that is commanded you, say, "We are unworthy servants"* (17:10), we are not ill-disposed servants, i.e., serving in fear—for such a servant is deserving of torture and chains—but we are good and faithful servants, serving out of love. For that reason we obtain freedom through the Son: *I the Son makes you free, you will be free indeed* (John 8:36).

217 *Second*, he mentions the fruit as to its effect of attaining every good. With regard to this he says: ***and, if a son, an heir also through God***: *and if sons, heirs also; heirs indeed of God and joint heirs with Christ* (Rom. 8:17 DRB). Now this inheritance is the fullness of all good, for it is nothing other than God himself, according to a psalm: *The Lord is the portion of my inheritance* (16:5 DRB). He said to Abraham: *I am your protector and your reward, exceedingly great* (Gen. 15:1 DRB).

He says, ***through God***, because as the Jews obtained the inheritance through the promise and justice of God, so the gentiles too received it through God, i.e., through the mercy of God, *that the gentiles might glorify God for his mercy* (Rom. 15:9). Or, ***through God***, i.e., through the working of God: *You have wrought all our works for us, O Lord* (Isa. 26:12).

Chapter 11

CHRIST'S GIFT OF DIVINE SONSHIP

Romans 8:14–17

Adoptive Sonship in Christ

On Romans 8.3 (634–651)

8:14 ***For whosoever are led by the Spirit of God, they are the sons of God.***

8:15 ***For you have not received the spirit of slavery again in fear: but you have received the spirit of adoption of sons, in whom we cry, "Abba, Father."***

8:16 ***For the Spirit himself gives testimony to our spirit that we are the sons of God.***

8:17 ***And if sons, heirs also; heirs indeed of God and joint heirs with Christ: yet so, if we suffer with him, that we may be also glorified with him.***

634 After stating that the life of glory, which will exclude all mortality from our bodies, will be given to us through the Holy Spirit, the Apostle now proves this.[1] *First,* he shows that this glorious life is given by the Holy Spirit; *second,* why it is deferred, at ***yet so, if we suffer with him.***

In regard to the *first* he presents this argument: all who are sons of God obtain the inheritance of a glorious life; but those who are ruled by the Holy Spirit are sons of God. Therefore, all who are ruled by the Holy Spirit obtain the inheritance of a glorious life.

First, therefore, he posits the minor premise of this proof; *second,* the major, at ***and if sons, heirs also.***

In regard to the *first* he does two things. *First,* he states his proposition; *second,* he proves it, at ***for you have not received.***

635 In regard to the *first* there are two things to consider. *First,* how some are led by the Spirit of God. This can be understood in the following way: ***for whosoever are led by the Spirit of God,*** i.e., ruled as by a leader and director, which the Spirit does in us, inasmuch as he enlightens us inwardly about what

1. See Thomas Aquinas, *On Romans* 8.2 (not included in this collection).

we ought to do: *Let your good spirit lead me* (Ps. 143:10). But because one who is led does not act on his own, whereas the spiritual man is not only instructed by the Holy Spirit regarding what he ought to do, but his heart is also moved by the Holy Spirit, it is necessary to get a better understanding of what is meant by ***whosoever are led by the Spirit of God.***

For those are led who are moved by a higher instinct. Hence we say that animals do not act but are led, because they are moved to perform their actions by nature and not from their own impulse. Similarly, the spiritual man is inclined to do something not as though by a movement of his own will chiefly, but by the prompting of the Holy Spirit, as it says in Isaiah: *He will come like a rushing stream, which the wind of the Lord drives* (59:19 DRB); and in Luke: *Jesus . . . was led by the Spirit . . . in the wilderness* (4:1).

However, this does not mean that spiritual men do not act through will and free choice, because the Holy Spirit causes the very movement of the will and of free choice in them, as it says in Philippians: *God is at work in you both to will and to work* (2:13).

636 *Second*, we must consider how those who ***are led by the Spirit of God . . . are the sons of God.*** This is clarified by a likeness to natural children, who are produced by the natural seed coming from the father. But the spiritual seed proceeding from the Father is the Holy Spirit. Therefore, through this seed some men are born as sons of God: *No one born of God commits sin, because God's nature abides in him* (1 John 3:9).

637 Then he proves that men who receive the Holy Spirit are sons of God, when he says ***for you have not received***; and this in three ways. *First*, by distinguishing the gifts of the Holy Spirit; *second*, by our own testimony, at ***whereby we cry***; *third*, by the testimony of the Spirit, at ***for the Spirit himself.***

638 In regard to the *first* it should be noted that the Holy Spirit produces two effects in us: one is fear: *His delight shall be in the fear of the Lord* (Isa. 11:3); the other is love: *God's love has been poured into our hearts through the Holy Spirit who has been given to us* (Rom. 5:5). But fear makes slaves; love does not.

To realize this it is necessary to consider that fear bears on two things, namely, the evil from which someone flees through fear, and whatever seems to be the source of that evil. For a person is said to fear being killed and the king who has the power to kill. But sometimes it happens that the evil from which someone recoils is contrary to a bodily or temporal good which a person sometimes loves inordinately and recoils from having it injured or destroyed by a mere man. This is human or worldly fear and is not from the Holy Spirit. Indeed, the Lord forbids such fear: *Do not fear those who kill the body* (Matt. 10:28).

639 There is a *second* type of fear which recoils from an evil contrary to created nature, namely, the evil of being punished, and shrinks from having this evil inflicted by a spiritual cause, namely, by God. Such fear is praiseworthy in at least one respect, namely, that it fears God: *Oh that they had such a mind as this always, to fear me and to keep all my commandments* (Deut. 5:29). In this respect it is from the Holy Spirit.

But insofar as such fear does not recoil from an evil opposed to one's spiritual good, namely, sin, but only punishment, it is not praiseworthy. It has this shortcoming not from the Holy Spirit but from man's guilt; just as deformed faith, inasmuch as it is faith, is from the Holy Spirit, but not its deformity. Hence, even if a person does something good under the influence of such fear, he does not act well, because he does not act spontaneously but compelled by fear of punishment—and this is characteristic of slaves. Therefore, this fear is properly called servile, because it makes a man act as a slave does.

640 There is a *third* type of fear which recoils from evil opposed to a spiritual good, namely, from sin or separation from God, which a person fears to incur from the just vengeance of God. Thus it bears on spiritual goods, but with an eye on punishment.

This is called initial fear, because it is usually found in men at the beginning of their conversion. For it fears punishment due to past sins and it fears separation from God through sin because of grace infused with charity. This is the fear mentioned in the Psalm: *The fear of the Lord is the beginning of wisdom* (Ps. 111:10).

641 The *fourth* type of fear has its eye entirely on spiritual things, because it fears nothing except separation from God. This is holy fear: *The fear of the Lord is holy, enduring forever and ever* (Ps. 19:10 DRB). But just as initial fear is caused by imperfect love, so this fear is caused by perfect love: *Perfect love casts out fear* (1 John 4:18). Therefore, initial fear and chaste fear are not distinguished against charity's love, which is the cause of both, but the fear of punishment is; because just as this fear produces slavery, so charity's love produces the freedom of sons. For it makes a man act voluntarily for the honor of God—which is characteristic of sons.

642 Now the old law was given in fear, which was signified by the thunder and things of that sort which occurred when it was given, as it says in Exodus 19:16. And therefore it says in Hebrews: *So terrifying was the sight that Moses said, "I tremble with fear"* (12:21). So the old law, which induced men to obey God's commandments by inflicting punishments, was given in a spirit of slavery; hence it says in Galatians: *One is from Mount Sinai, bearing children for slavery* (4:24).

643 Therefore, he says here: it was correct to say that *whosoever are led by the Spirit of God, they are the sons of God.* For ***you have not received the spirit of slavery again***, in the new law as was in the old law, ***in fear***, namely, of punishments, which fear the Holy Spirit was causing; ***but you have received the spirit***, namely, of charity, which is ***of adoption of sons***, by which we are adopted as children of God *that we might receive adoption as sons* (Gal. 4:5).

This does not mean that there is one spirit and another spirit, but that it is the same Spirit, who in some produces servile fear, as imperfect, and in others, produces love, as a certain perfection.

644 Then he manifests the same thing by our confession, when he says ***in whom we cry***. For we confess that we have God as our Father, when we follow the Lord's instruction to pray: *Our Father, who art in heaven* (Matt. 6:9). And since it is suitable not only for the Jews but also for gentiles to say this, he uses two words to signify Father, namely, ***Abba***, which is Hebrew, and ***Pater***, which can be Latin or Greek. Even the Lord himself says: *Father, all things are possible to you* (Mark 14:36); *you would call me, My Father* (Jer. 3:19).

We say this not so much with the sound of our voice as with the intention of our heart, an intention so strong that it is called a cry, as with Moses to whom it was said: *Why do you cry to me?* (Exod. 14:15), namely, with the intention of your heart. But the great strength of this intention comes from the feeling of filial fear which he produces in us. Therefore, he says ***in whom***, namely, in the Holy Spirit, ***we cry, "Abba, Father."*** Hence it says in Isaiah that the seraphim, burning with the fire of the Holy Spirit, *called to [one] another: "Holy, holy, holy"* (6:3).

645 Then he manifests the same thing through the testimony of the Holy Spirit, to show that we are not deceived in our confession; hence he says: the reason I say that ***we cry, "Abba, Father"*** in the Holy Spirit is that ***the Spirit himself gives testimony to our spirit that we are the sons of God***. He bears this testimony not with external words that reach men's ears, as the Father gave testimony to his own Son in Matthew (3:17), but through the effect of filial love he produces in us. Therefore, he says that ***he gives testimony*** not to our ears ***but to our spirit***: *We are witnesses of these things and so is the Holy Spirit* (Acts 5:32).

646 Then he posits the major premise, at ***and if sons***. *First*, he shows that to children is owed the inheritance, saying: If some are children, namely, through the Spirit, it follows that they are heirs, because the inheritance is owed not only to the natural child but also to the adopted: *We have been born anew . . . to an inheritance which is imperishable* (1 Pet. 1:4); *I have a goodly heritage* (Ps.
647 16:6). *Second*, he shows what that inheritance is.

First, he describes it in relation to God the Father, saying, ***heirs indeed of God***. Now one's heir is a person who receives or gets his chief goods and not some small gifts, as we read in Genesis that Abraham gave all his possessions to Isaac, but to the sons of his concubines he bestowed gifts (25:5–6). Now the chief good by which God is rich is himself. For he is rich of himself and not in virtue of something else, because he does not need the goods others have: *You have no need of my goods* (Ps. 16:2 DRB). Hence the children of God obtain God himself as their inheritance: *The Lord is my chosen portion* (Ps. 16:5); *the Lord is my portion, says my soul* (Lam. 3:24).

648 But since the child does not obtain the inheritance unless the father dies, it seems that man cannot be an heir of God, who never dies. The answer is that this applies to temporal goods which cannot be possessed by many at the same time; hence one must die if another is to inherit. But spiritual goods can be held by many at the same time; therefore, it is not necessary that the Father die in order that the children become heirs. Yet it can be said that God dies for us inasmuch as he is in us by faith: but he will be our inheritance, insofar as we will see him through a form.

649 *Second*, he describes this inheritance on the part of Christ, saying, ***joint heirs with Christ***, because just as he is the chief Son with whom we share sonship, so he is the chief heir, to whom we are united in the inheritance: *This is the heir* (Matt. 21:38); *yet will I bring an heir to you* (Mic. 1:15).

650 Then he shows why this glorious life is delayed, when he says, ***yet so, if we suffer with him***. *First*, he gives the reason concerned with suffering; *second*, the pre-eminence of glory over suffering, at ***for I consider*** (Rom. 8:18).

651 In regard to the first it must be recalled that Christ, the principal heir, attained to the inheritance of glory through suffering: *Was it not necessary that the Christ should suffer these things and so enter his glory?* (Luke 24:26). But we must not expect to obtain the inheritance by an easier way. Therefore, it is necessary that we attain to that inheritance through suffering: *Through many tribulations we must enter the kingdom of God* (Acts 14:21). For we do not receive an immortal and unsuffering body at once, in order that we might suffer along with Christ.

Hence he says, ***yet so, if we suffer with him***, i.e., along with Christ endure the tribulations of this world patiently, ***in order that we may be also glorified*** with Christ: *If we have died with him . . . we shall also reign with him* (2 Tim. 2:11–12).

John 15:9–13

"That They Would Be Gods"

Participation in Divine Love

On John 15.2 (1997–2009)

15:9 ***As the Father has loved me, I also have loved you. Abide in my love.***

15:10 ***If you keep my commandments, you will abide in my love; as I also have kept my Father's commandments and abide in his love.***

15:11 ***These things I have spoken to you, that my joy may be in you, and your joy may be filled.***

15:12 ***This is my commandment, that you love one another, as I have loved you.***

15:13 ***Greater love than this no man has, that a man lay down his life for his friends.***

1997 Above, our Lord urged his disciples to remain united with him; here he shows what this involves.[2] He makes three points: *first*, to abide in him is to abide in his love; *second*, to abide in his love is to keep his commandments: ***If you keep my commandments, you will abide in my love***; *third*, that his commandment is to love: ***This is my commandment, that you love one another.***

He does two things about the *first*: *first*, he recalls the benefit granted to
1998 the disciples; *second*, he urges them to persevere: ***Abide in my love.*** He says that
the fact that we abide in Christ is due to his grace; and this grace is the effect
of his love: *I have loved you with an everlasting love* (Jer. 31:3).

It is clear from this that all our good works are ours due to the benefit of divine love. For they would not be ours unless faith acted through love, and we would not love unless we were first loved. And so he reminds them of this benefit by saying, ***As the Father has loved me, I also have loved you.***

1999 The word 'as' sometimes indicates an equality of nature, and at other times a similarity in acting. The Arians, who erred about this passage, wanted the ***as*** to indicate an equality, and because of this they concluded that the Son was inferior to the Father. But this is false. We must say, then, according to

2. See Thomas Aquinas, *On John* 15.1 (not included in this collection).

Augustine, that the word ***as*** indicates a likeness in grace and love;[3] for the love with which the Son loves his disciples is a certain likeness of that love with which the Father loves the Son. Since, however, to love someone is to will his good, the Father loves the Son according to his divine nature, insofar as he wills his infinite good, that he himself has, sharing with him the same nature in number which he himself has; ***the Father loves the Son and shows him all that he himself is doing*** (John 5:20). He loves him also according to his human nature, *When Israel was a child, and I loved him, and out of Egypt I called my son* (Hos. 11:1). And from this, that God and man would be similar.

But the Son did not love the disciples in either of these ways. For he did not love them to the point of their being God by nature, nor to the point that they would be united to God so as to form one person with him. But he did love them up to a similar point: he loved them to the extent that they would be gods by their participation in grace: *I say, "you are gods"* (Ps. 82:6); *he has granted to us precious and very great promises, that through these you may . . . become partakers of the divine nature* (2 Pet. 1:4), and he loved them to the extent that they would be united to God in affection: *He who is united to the Lord becomes one spirit with him* (1 Cor. 6:17); *for those whom he foreknew he also predestined to be conformed to the image of his Son* (Rom. 8:29). Thus the Father communicated to the Son a greater good, with respect to each nature of the Son, than the Son did to his disciples; yet there is a similarity, as was said.

2000 ***Abide in my love.*** This is like saying: 'because you have received such a great benefit from my love, ***abide*** in it so that you love me.' Or it could mean: '***abide in my love*** because I love you, that is, abide in my grace so you will not be excluded from the good things I have prepared for you.' This meaning is the more apt, so that the thought is: persevere in this state so that you will be loved by me through the effect of grace: *Everyone should remain in the state in which he was called* (1 Cor. 7:20). *He who abides in love abides in God, and God abides in him* (1 John 4:16).

2001 Now he shows what it means to abide in his love. *First*, he shows that it means to keep his commandment; *second*, he illustrates it with an example, ***as I also have kept my Father's commandments***; *third*, he eliminates an assumption:
2002 ***These things I have spoken to you, that my joy may be in you.*** He says, ***abide in my love***, and you will do this ***if you keep my commandments***, for this is the way you will abide in my love.

Keeping the commandments is an effect of divine love, not only of the love by which we love, but also of the love by which God loves us. For from the fact that God loves us, he influences us and helps us to fulfill his commandments,

3. Augustine, *Tractates on the Gospel of John* 82.4.

which we cannot do without grace: *In this is charity, not as though we had loved God, but because he has first loved us* (1 John 4:10 DRB).

2003 He adds an example when he says, ***as I also have kept my Father's commandments and abide in his love.*** For just as the love which the Father has for him is the model or standard of Christ's love for us, so Christ wants his obedience to be the model of our obedience. By saying this Christ shows that he abided in the Father's love because in all things he kept the Father's commandments. For he submitted to death: *He humbled himself and became obedient unto death, even death on a cross* (Phil. 2:8); and refrained from all sin: *He committed no sin; no guile was found on his lips* (1 Pet. 2:22). These things are to be understood of Christ in his human nature: ***He has not left me alone, for I always do what is pleasing to him*** (John 8:29). And so he says, ***I . . . abide in his love,*** because there is nothing in me, as a human being, opposed to his love.

2004 Now, so that they do not think he is urging them to keep his commandments for his own benefit and not for their benefit, he says, ***these things I have spoken to you***, that you keep my commandments, for your own good, so ***that my joy may be in you.*** Now love is the cause of joy, for everyone takes joy in what he loves. But God loves himself and creatures, especially rational creatures, to whom he grants an infinite good. So Christ rejoices in two things from all eternity: *first*, in his own good and that of the Father: *I was daily his delight, rejoicing before him always* (Prov. 8:30); *second*, he delights in the good of the rational creature: *delighting in the sons of men* (Prov. 8:31), that is, in the fact that I am shared in by the children of men. He rejoices in these things from eternity: *As the bridegroom rejoices over the bride, so will your God rejoice over you* (Isa. 62:5).

Consequently, our Lord wants us to become sharers of his joy by our observing his commandments. He says, ***that my joy***, the joy I take in my divinity and that of my Father, ***may be in you.*** This is nothing else than eternal life, which as Augustine says, is joy in the truth.[4] ***That my joy may be in you*** means, in effect, that you may have eternal life: *You will delight yourself in the Almighty* (Job 22:26). ***And that your joy***, which I take in my own humanity, ***may be full.*** The goods in which we rejoice are either imperfect or imperfectly possessed; and so in this life our joy cannot be full. But it will be full when perfect goods are perfectly possessed: *Enter into the joy of your Master* (Matt. 25:21).

2005 Now our Lord states what his precepts are: *first*, he states his commandment; *second*, he presents an example: ***as I have loved you***; *third*, he recalls a benefit: ***you are my friends, if you do the things that I command you.***

2006 The commandment he gives is the commandment of charity, which he wants us to keep: ***this is my commandment, that you love one another.*** Since

4. Augustine, *Tractates on the Gospel of John* 83.1.

there are many other commandments of the Lord in the sacred writings, why does he say that his commandment is only the practice of charity?

The answer, according to Gregory, is that charity is the root and end of all the virtues.[5] It is the root, because it is from charity, firmly rooted in the human heart, that we are led to accomplish all the other commandments: *He who loves his neighbor has fulfilled the law* (Rom. 13:8). Therefore, all the commandments are, in a way, directed to this: that we do good to our neighbor, and not harm him; and this is done best through charity. Charity is the end because all the commandments are directed to it and by it alone are given strength: *The aim of our charge is love* (1 Tim. 1:5). So he says, ***This is my commandment, that you love one another***, since everything comes from charity as its source, and all things are directed to charity as their end. As Gregory puts it: *Just as many branches of a tree spring from one root, so the many virtues are produced from one root; and the branch of a good work has no life if it is not united to the root of charity.*[6]

2007 Since we read in Matthew that the law and the prophets depend not only on love for God, but also on love for neighbor, why does Christ mention here only love for neighbor (22:40)?

The answer is that one is included in the other: for a person who loves God must love his neighbor and things which belong to God; and the person who loves his neighbor for the sake of God must love God. Now although the objects of these acts are different, yet the outcomes are the same.

There are two reasons why he mentions love of neighbor rather than the love of God. By doing this he wants to teach and lead them to help their neighbor, and to help them to become strong enough to endure sufferings from those who will persecute them. To do both of these, charity for our neighbor is necessary.

2008 Here he shows by an example how we should love our neighbor, which is, as Christ loved us. Now Christ loved us in the correct order and efficaciously. His love was orderly because he loved nothing in us but God and in relation to God: *I am the mother of fair love* (Sir. 24:18 DRB), and efficacious because he loved us so much that he delivered himself for us: *Christ loved us and gave himself up for us, a fragrant offering and sacrifice to God* (Eph. 5:2). So we should love our neighbor, in a holy way, for his good, and efficaciously, by showing our love by our actions: *Let us not love in word or speech but in deed and in truth* (1 John 3:18).

2009 ***Greater love than this no man has, that a man lay down his life for his friends***. Here he shows the efficacy of love, which is that one undergo death

5. Gregory the Great, *Forty Gospel Homilies* 27.1.

6. Gregory the Great, 27.1.

for his friends; this is a sign of the greatest love. Yet one could object that it is considered to be a sign of a greater love when someone lays down his life for his enemies, as Christ did: *God shows his love for us in that while we were yet sinners Christ died for us* (Rom. 5:8).

We should answer that Christ did not lay down his life for his enemies so that they would remain his enemies, but to make them his friends. Or, one could say, that he lay down his life for his friends, not in the sense that they were friends who loved him, but rather were those whom he loved. It is clear that the sign of the greatest love is to lay down one's life for one's friends. This is so because there are four lovable things to be put in order: God, our soul, our neighbor, and our body. We should love God more than ourselves and our neighbor, so that for the sake of God we ought to give ourselves, body and soul, for our neighbor. We should lay down our body, but not give it, for the sake of our soul. For our neighbor, we should expose our body and our physical life for his salvation. Consequently, since our physical life is the best thing we have after our soul, it is the greatest thing to expose it for the sake of our neighbor, and a sign of greater love: *In this the love of God was made manifest among us, that God sent his only Son into the world, so that we might live through him* (1 John 4:9).

John 16:23–24

Prayer to the Father in Christ's Name

On John 16.6 (2135–2146)

16:23 ***And in that day you will not ask me anything. Amen, amen I say to you: if you ask the Father anything in my name, he will give it to you.***

16:24 ***Hitherto you have not asked anything in my name. Ask, and you will receive; that your joy may be full.***

2135 Above, our Lord enlarged on two things which would comfort his apostles, the promise of the Paraclete and his own return.[7] Here he mentions a third reason by which he comforts them, promising them access to the Father.

First, he promises them an intimate relationship with the Father; *second*, he gives a reason for this intimacy: ***These things I have spoken to you in proverbs*** (John 16:25).

He does two things about the *first*: he gives them that security that comes from confidence; *second*, he encourages them to act on their confidence: ***Hitherto you have not asked anything in my name.***

He does two things with the *first*: *first*, he rejects a need for an intercessor; *second*, he promises them an opportunity to ask: ***Amen, amen I say to you: if you ask the Father anything in my name, he will give it to you.***

2136 He says, ***In that day you will not ask me anything.*** According to Augustine, where we have ***ask***, the Greeks have a word which means two things: to ask for something, or to pose a question.[8] Consequently, ***In that day you will not ask me anything*** can mean two things: you will not ask me for anything, or you will not question me about anything.

In that day: what that day is can be seen from what he said before: ***I will see you again*** (John 16:22). This can be understood to be the day of his resurrection, or the day when we have the vision of his glory.

2137 Chrysostom understands this passage the first way.[9] Thus, ***in that day***, when I arise from the dead, ***you will not ask me anything***, that is, you will not say such things as ***Show us the Father*** (John 14:8). Augustine objects to this interpretation because after the resurrection the disciples did say: *Lord, will*

7. See Thomas Aquinas, *On John* 16.2, 5 (neither lecture included in this collection).

8. Augustine, *Tractates on the Gospel of John* 101.4.

9. John Chrysostom, *Commentary on Saint John* 79.1.

you at this time restore the kingdom to Israel? (Acts 1:6); and Peter poses the question: ***Lord, what about this man?*** (John 21:21).

Yet one can uphold Chrysostom's explanation by saying that our Lord calls ***that day*** not only the day of his resurrection, but also that day the disciples were to be taught by the Holy Spirit: ***When he, the Spirit of truth, has come, he will teach you all truth*** (John 16:13). And so by speaking in a vague manner of that time, our Lord also includes the coming of the Holy Spirit. It is like saying: '***in that day***, once the Holy Spirit has been given, ***you will not ask me anything***, because you will know all things by the Holy Spirit': *His anointing teaches you about everything* (1 John 2:27). Again, according to Chrysostom, ***in that day***, when the Holy Spirit comes, ***you will not ask me anything***, that is, you will have no need to ask me.

2138 But after the resurrection did not the apostles pray to Christ for things? It seems so, for the Apostle says: *Three times I besought the Lord*, that is, Christ (2 Cor. 12:8).

I answer that there are two natures in Christ: his human nature, by which he is the mediator between God and us (1 Tim. 2:5), and his divine nature, by which he is one God with the Father. Christ, considered as having a human nature, was not a mediator who never united us to God, like some mediators who never unite extremes. So, Christ joins us to the Father. Now to join God the Father and to join Christ as God are the same. Thus he says: it is not necessary for you to use my mediation as man. Thus, ***in that day you will not ask me anything*** as mediator, because you will have access to God by yourselves, but you will ask me as God. Although Christ intercedes for us, as the Apostle says (Rom. 8:34), still the Church does not ask him as an intercessor. Thus we do not say, 'Christ, pray for us'; but we do ask him as God, adhering to him as God by faith and love.

2139 Augustine explains this passage as referring to the day of the vision of glory in this way:[10] ***in that day***, when I see you in glory, ***you will not ask me anything***, that is, you will not ask me for anything because there will be nothing left to desire, since all goods will be ours in superabundance in our homeland: *You will fill me with joy with your face* (Ps. 16:11 DRB); and again, *I will be satisfied when your glory appears* (Ps. 17:15). Also, you will ask no questions because you will be filled with the knowledge of God: *In your light do we see light* (Ps. 36:9).

2140 An objection can be raised against both. The saints do pray in our homeland: *Call now, is there anyone who will answer you? To which of the holy ones will you turn* (Job 5:1); and in 2 Maccabees we see that a saint prayed for the entire Jewish people (15:12). Nor can one say that the saints pray just for others

10. Augustine, *Tractates on the Gospel of John* 102.2.

and not for themselves, for we read: *How long before you will judge and avenge our blood on those who dwell upon the earth?* (Rev. 6:10).

Further, the saints ask questions, for they will be equal to the angels (Matt. 22:30), and the angels question: *Who is the King of glory?* (Ps. 24:8), and, according to Dionysius, it is the angels who ask, *Who is this that comes from Edom?* (Isa. 63:1).[11] Therefore, the saints also question.

Two points can be made in answer to this. The time of glory can be considered in two ways: the time of the beginning of glory, and the time of its full completion. The time of the beginning of glory lasts until the day of judgment: for the saints receive glory in their soul, but something still remains to be received, that is, the glory of the body for each one, and the completion of the number of the elect. Consequently, till the day of judgment the saints can both ask for things and question, but not about what pertains to the very essence of beatitude. The time of fully complete glory is after the day of judgment, and after this nothing is left to be asked for, and nothing left to be known. It is about this that he says, ***in that day***, of consummated glory, ***you will not ask me anything.***

The observation about the angels asking questions is true in this way: they do ask about the mysteries of the humanity of Christ and the incarnation, but they do not question about the divinity.

2141 Now he promises them an opportunity to ask. This is related to the above in two ways. According to Chrysostom, this refers to the time of the resurrection and the coming of the Holy Spirit.[12] It is like saying: 'it is true that in that day of the resurrection and of the Holy Spirit that you will not ask me; yet you will have my help, because you will ask the Father, to whom you have access through me, ***in my name.***'

Augustine explains it the other way.[13] ***In that day***, of my glory, ***you will not ask me anything***; but in the meantime, during your sorrowful pilgrimage, ***if you ask the Father anything . . . he will give it to you.*** So according to this explanation, ***if you ask the Father anything***, does not refer to ***in that day***, but to what precedes that day.

2142 Our Lord lays down seven conditions for good prayer. The *first* is that spiritual goods should be sought, when he says, ***if . . . anything.*** For what is entirely earthly, even though it is something good in itself, is nothing when compared to spiritual goods: *I accounted wealth as nothing in comparison with her* (Wis. 7:8); *I looked on the earth, and lo, it was waste and void* (Jer. 4:23).

11. Pseudo-Dionysius, *The Celestial Hierarchy* 7.3.

12. John Chrysostom, *Commentary on Saint John* 79.1.

13. Augustine, *Tractates on the Gospel of John* 102.2.

But an objection: in Matthew, our Lord teaches us to ask for temporal goods: *Give us this day our daily bread* (6:11). I answer that a temporal good asked for in relation to a spiritual good is then something.

The *second* is that it be made with perseverance; as to this he says, ***if you ask***, with perseverance: *They ought always to pray and not lose heart* (Luke 18:1); *pray constantly* (1 Thess. 5:17).

Third, we should pray in harmony with others; he says, ***if you***, in the plural, ***ask***: *If two of you agree on earth about anything they ask, it will be done for them by my Father in heaven* (Matt. 18:19). Thus the *Gloss* says, about the final chapter of Romans, *that it is impossible for the prayers of many not to be heard.*

Fourth, it should arise from an affection like that of a child for its parents, as he says, ***the Father***. One who asks out of fear does not ask a father, but a master or an enemy: *If you . . . who are evil, know how to give good gifts to your children, how much more will your Father who is in heaven give good things to those who ask him?* (Matt. 7:11).

The *fifth* condition is that it be made with piety, that is, with humility: *He has had regard to the prayer of the humble: he has not despised their petition* (Ps. 102:17 DRB); with confidence that it will be granted: *Let him ask in faith, with no doubting* (James 1:6); and it should be made correctly: *You ask and do not receive, because you ask wrongly* (James 4:3). In regard to this he says, ***in my name***, which is the name of the Savior, in which name one asks when asking for things pertaining to salvation, and when asking in that way by which one can attain salvation: *There is no other name under heaven given among men by which we must be saved* (Acts 4:12).

The *sixth* condition is that prayer be made for an appropriate time, so he says, ***he will give***. One should not stop praying if one does not immediately receive; it will be given to us even if it is postponed till a better time, so as to increase our desire: *You give them their food in due season* (Ps. 145:15).

Seventh, one should ask for himself. Thus he says, ***to you***, because sometimes prayers for others are not heard because the demerits of those we ask for stand in the way: *Do not pray for this people* (Jer. 7:16); *though Moses and Samuel stood before me, yet my heart would not turn toward this people* (Jer. 15:1).

2143 Now he encourages them to act with the confidence he has given them:
first, he reminds them of what they lacked in the past; *second*, he encourages
2144 them to advance in the future: ***ask, and you will receive***. What they lacked in
the past was not asking; thus he says, ***hitherto you have not asked anything in my name***.

But this seems to conflict with Luke where it says that Christ gave the twelve *power and authority over all demons and to cure diseases* (9:1). Now they did these things by praying. Therefore, they did ask something in the name of

Christ, especially because the disciples said: *Lord, even the demons are subject to us in your name!* (Luke 10:17).

We must say, then, that this can be explained in two ways. *First, **hitherto you have not asked anything***, that is nothing great, ***in my name***. For to ask for cures for the body is a small matter compared to the great things they would accomplish by their prayers; nor had they yet received the Spirit of adoption to make them aspire to spiritual and heavenly things. And if you object that they did ask for something great when they asked before, ***Lord, show us the Father*** (John 14:8), I answer that they were not asking the Father, which is what Christ is talking about here, but only Christ as man, trusting that as a mediator he would show them the Father.

Another explanation of ***if you ask the Father anything in my name*** is that up to now, they had not asked in his name because they did not have a complete knowledge of the name of Christ.

2145 When he says, ***ask, and you will receive***, he is urging them to make progress, that is, they are now to ask: *Ask, and it will be given you* (Matt. 7:7). ***Ask***, I say, ***and you will receive***, that is, what you are asking for, that your joy may be full: *The seventy returned with joy, saying, "Lord, even the demons are subject to us in your name!"* (Luke 10:17). The phrase ***that your joy may be full*** can be taken to indicate the reason why their prayers are heard. Or, it can point to what they are praying for, so the meaning is: ***ask, and you will receive***, and what you should ask for is ***that your joy may be full***.

2146 Note that the object of joy is a good that is desired. Since desire is a kind of movement toward a good, and joy is rest in that good, a person has joy when he rests in a good, now possessed, to which his desire was moved. And one's joy is proportionate to the good possessed. There cannot be full joy in a created good because it does not give complete rest to man's desires and yearnings. Our joy will be full when we possess that good in which all the goods we can desire are found superabundantly. This good is solely God *who satisfies you with good* (Ps. 103:5). Therefore he says, ***ask*** this, ***that your joy may be full***, that is, ask to enjoy God and the Trinity, as Augustine says, and no joy is greater:[14] *You will fill me with joy with your face* (Ps. 16:11). And why is this? Because *all good things came to me along with her*, that is, with the contemplation of divine wisdom (Wis. 7:11).

14. Augustine, *The Trinity* 1.10.20.

John 16:25–28

Christ's Promise of Intimacy with the Father

On John 16.7 (2147–2163)

16:25 ***These things I have spoken to you in proverbs. The hour comes, when I will speak no more to you in proverbs but will show you plainly of the Father.***

16:26 ***In that day you will ask in my name; and I say not to you, that I will ask the Father for you:***

16:27 ***For the Father himself loves you, because you have loved me, and have believed that I came out from God.***

16:28 ***I came forth from the Father and have come into the world: again I leave the world, and I go to the Father.***

2147 Above, our Lord promised his disciples an access and intimacy with the Father.[15] Now he gives the reason for this intimacy. There are two things that make a person intimate with another and foster confidence when asking for something: knowledge and love. Thus our Lord gives these two reasons here. The *first* is taken from their clear knowledge of the Father; the *second*, from his special love for them: ***in that day, you will ask in my name.***

2148 He does two things about the *first*: *first*, he reminds them of their previous imperfect knowledge of the Father; *second*, he promises them complete knowledge, ***the hour comes when I will speak no more to you in proverbs.*** Indeed, their knowledge was imperfect; so he says, ***these things I have spoken to you in proverbs.*** A 'proverb,' strictly speaking, is a maxim, a common expression, as *Train up a child in the way he should go, and when he is old he will not depart from it* (Prov. 22:6). Now because proverbs are sometimes not clear and are metaphorical, the word 'proverb' is sometimes used to indicate a parable, which states one thing while actually meaning something else. This is the case here, and ***proverb*** should be taken to mean parable.

2149 The statement, ***I have spoken to you in proverbs***, can be taken in four ways. The *first* is literal and refers to what he had said immediately before this. Then the sense is: I said to you that ***hitherto you have asked nothing in my name***, and that ***you will ask in my name***, and ***I have spoken to you in proverbs***, and obscurely. But ***the hour comes*** when what I said obscurely, I will say plainly.

15. See John 16:23 and Thomas Aquinas, *On John* 16.6 (the preceding lecture in this collection).

Thus he adds: ***the Father himself loves you***, and ***I came forth from the Father and have come into the world.*** This seems to be the way the apostles understood it because when they heard him say these things they said, ***behold, now you speak plainly, and speak no proverbs*** (John 16:29).

2150 In the *second* way, ***I have spoken to you in proverbs***, refers to everything which is read in this Gospel about the teaching of Christ. Then the next statement, ***the hour comes when I will speak no more to you in proverbs***, would refer to the time of glory. For now we see in a mirror, in an obscure manner, since what we are told about God is presented to us in proverbs. But in our homeland we will see *face to face* (1 Cor. 13:12). Therefore, we will then be plainly told of the Father, and not in proverbs. He says, ***of the Father***, because no one can see the Father in that glory unless the Son reveals him: *No one knows the Father except the Son and anyone to whom the Son chooses to reveal him* (Matt. 11:27). For the Son is the true light and gives us the light by which we can see the Father: ***I am the light of the world*** (John 8:12).

2151 But the next statement, ***in that day you will ask in my name***, does not fit this explanation. For if that hour is the time of glory, we will not ask for anything because our desires will be satisfied with good. Accordingly, there are two other meanings. According to Chrysostom the sense is this: ***I have spoken to you***, that is, what I have just said, ***in proverbs***, that is, in veiled language, not entirely expressing all that you should know about me and the Father, because ***I have yet many things to say to you, but you cannot bear them now*** (John 16:12).[16] But ***the hour comes***, that is, when I have arisen from the dead, ***when I will speak no more to you in proverbs***, that is, obscurely and in figures, ***but show you plainly of the Father.*** Indeed, during those forty days during which he appeared to them, he taught them many mysteries and told many things about himself and the Father. Further, they had been raised to higher things by their faith in the resurrection, firmly believing that Christ was the true God. So we read that Christ was *speaking of the kingdom of God* to them (Acts 1:3), and that *He opened their minds to understand the Scriptures* (Luke 24:45).

2152 The other reading is given by Augustine and is this. When Christ said ***I have spoken to you in proverbs***, our Lord is promising to make them spiritual.[17] There is a difference between one who is spiritual and one who is sensual: a sensual person understands spiritual words as proverbs, not because they were spoken as proverbs, but because the mind of such a person cannot rise above material things, and spiritual things are hidden, *but the sensual man perceives not these things that are of the Spirit of God* (1 Cor. 2:14 DRB). But one who is spiritual understands spiritual words as spiritual. At the beginning, the disci-

16. John Chrysostom, *Commentary on Saint John* 79.2.

17. Augustine, *Tractates on the Gospel of John* 102.4.

ples themselves were sensual, and what was told them they found obscure, and took as proverbs. But after they were made spiritual by Christ and had been taught by the Holy Spirit, they clearly understood spiritual words as spiritual. And so Christ says, ***I have spoken to you in proverbs***, that is, you understood what I said as proverbs. But ***the hour comes, when I will speak no more to you in proverbs***: *We all, with unveiled face, beholding the glory of the Lord, are being changed into his likeness, as by the Spirit of the Lord* (2 Cor. 3:18).

2153 Now we see the *second* reason why they should have confidence, and it is based on the Father's love for the disciples: *first*, he shows the Father's love for them; *second*, the intimacy of the Father with the Son: ***I came forth from the Father and have come into the world.*** He does two things with the *first*: *first*, he repeats a promise he made to them; *second*, he gives the reason for what was promised, ***for the Father himself loves you.***

2154 He does two things with the *first*: *first*, he repeats one of his promises; *second*, he promises that they will have confidence when they pray. He says, ***in that day***, when I tell you plainly of the Father, ***you will ask in my name***; for when you plainly know the Father you will know that I am equal to him and of the same essence, and that it is through me that you can approach or have access to him. To have this hope of approaching or having access to the Father through Christ is what is meant by asking in the name of Christ: *Some boast of chariots, and some of horses; but we boast of the name of the Lord our God* (Ps. 20:7). But Christ is silent about asking the Father for them; he says, ***I say not to you, that I will ask the Father for you.***

2155 But does not Christ pray for us? Certainly: *We have an advocate with the Father, Jesus Christ the righteous* (1 John 2:1); *he is able for all time to save those who draw near to God through him* (Heb. 7:25).

According to Augustine, Christ says this so the disciples will not think that Christ, since he is a man, is limited to interceding for them.[18] So in that day when ***but will show you plainly***, and not only ***you will ask in my name***, but you will know that I am one with the Father, and not just an intercessor, but in addition to interceding, I, as God, will hear your prayer.

According to Chrysostom, however, Christ probably says this so the disciples will not believe that they are to ask through the Son as if they could not approach the Father directly.[19] He is saying in effect: 'at present you come to me to intercede for you. But in that day you will have such confidence in the Father that you will be able to ask the Father in my name, without needing another to intercede for you.'

18. Augustine, *Tractates on the Gospel of John* 102.4.

19. John Chrysostom, *Commentary on Saint John* 79.2.

2156 But the apostles did need Christ, as man, to intercede, did they not? If not,
then since he does intercede, his intercession is superfluous. We should say that
Christ intercedes for them not as though they were strangers and had no access
2157 to the Father, but he makes their prayers more effective. Here he gives the reason
for the promise, which is the Father's love for them: and *first*, he mentions the
Father's love; *second*, the proof of this love, ***because you have loved me.***

2158 He says: ***I say not to you, that I will ask the Father for you***, for then it
might seem that the Father did not love them. Assuredly, ***the Father himself***,
who loves all things by willing them the goods of nature loves you, apostles
and saints, with an exceptional love, by willing you the highest good, that is,
himself: *You love all things that exist, and have loathing for none of the things*
which you have made (Wis. 11:24). *He loved his people; all those consecrated to*
him were in his hand (Deut. 33:3), because he loved them that much. *The souls*
2159 *of the righteous are in the hand of God* (Wis. 3:1). He proves this from two facts,
from the love of the disciples for Christ, and from their faith.

With regard to the *first* he says, ***because you have loved me.*** This proof does not give the cause, for we read, *not as though we had loved God, but because he has first loved us* (1 John 4:10 DRB). Rather, it gives a sign, for the fact that we love God is a sign that he loves us, for our being able to love God is a gift from God: *God's love has been poured into our hearts through the Holy Spirit who has been given to us* (Rom. 5:5); ***he who loves me, will be loved by my Father*** (John 14:21).

Referring to the *second* he says, ***and have believed that I came out from the Father***: *Without faith it is impossible to please him* (Heb. 11:6). Our faith is due to God's love for us, for *it is the gift of God* (Eph. 2:8). Now a gift is not given except through the love of the giver. To believe in and to love Christ insofar as he comes forth from God is a clear sign of one's love for God, since that in virtue of which something is such is itself even more so. Therefore, when one loves Christ, who came forth from God, this love is particularly traced back to God the Father; but this is not so when one loves Christ precisely as human.

2160 Because he had mentioned his coming forth from the Father, he now
comments more fully on it, saying, ***I came forth from the Father and have***
come into the world. This shows his intimacy with the Father. He *first* men-
tions his coming forth from the Father; and *second*, his return to the Father:
2161 ***Again, I leave the world, and I go to the Father***. The Son proceeds or comes
from the Father in two ways: one is eternal, the other temporal. He refers to
the eternal procession when he says, ***I came forth from the Father***, eternally
begotten from him.

Everything which comes forth from another was first in it. There are three ways one thing can be in something else. *First*, as what is contained is in its container; *second*, as a part in some whole; *third*, as an accident in its subject and as an effect in its cause. What comes forth is in that from which it comes forth in one of these ways. In the first two ways, what comes forth remains the same individual it was. For example, what comes from the cask is the very same wine that was in the cask; and the very same part that was in the whole comes from the whole. In the other two ways what comes forth is not the same individual.

Now none of these ways apply to God: for since God is entirely simple, and is in some place only metaphorically speaking, we cannot say that the Son is in God like some part, or that the Son is contained in a container. Rather, the Son is in the Father by a oneness of essence: ***I and the Father are one*** (John 10:30). For the entire essence of the Father is the entire essence of the Son, and vice versa. Consequently, the Son does not come forth from the Father in the previously mentioned ways. For when a part comes from the whole, it is distinct from the whole in essence: for when a part comes from the whole it becomes a being in act, while in the whole it was only a being in potency. Likewise, what comes from being contained in some container now occupies a different place than it did. But the Son does not come forth from the Father to occupy a different place because he fills all things, *Do I not fill heaven and earth?* (Jer. 23:24). Nor is the Son split off from the Father because the Father is indivisible. Rather, the Son comes forth by reason of a distinction in person. Thus, insofar as the coming forth of the Son presupposes some kind of existing in another, this indicates a unity of essence; while insofar as there is a certain coming forth, a distinction in person is indicated. *His going out is from the end of heaven*, that is, from God the Father (Ps. 19:6 DRB); *before the daystar I begot you* (Ps. 110:3 DRB). In material things, what comes forth from another is no longer in it, since it comes from it by a separation from it in place or in essence. This is not the kind of coming forth we have here, for the Son came forth from the Father from all eternity in such a way that the Son is still in the Father from all eternity. And so when the Son is in the Father, he comes forth, and when the Son comes forth he is in the Father: so the Son is always in the Father and always coming forth from the Father.

2162 He mentions his temporal coming when he says, ***I . . . have come into the world.*** As the Son's coming forth from the Father from eternity does not involve a change of place, neither does his coming into the world imply a change of place. Since the Father is in the Son and the Son is in the Father, then just as the Father fills all things, so does the Son; nor is there any place to go. Thus the Son is said to have come into the world because he assumed a human nature, which had its origin from the world as far as its body was concerned. But the Son did not move to a new place. ***He came to his own home, and his own people received him not*** (John 1:11).

2163 Then when he says, ***again, I leave the world, and I go to the Father***, he speaks of his return to the Father. *First*, he mentions his leaving the world, ***again, I leave the world***, but not ceasing to govern us by his providence, because he is always governing the world together with the Father, and he is always with the faithful by the help of his grace: *I am with you always, to the close of the age* (Matt. 28:20). Rather, he left the world by withdrawing from the physical sight of the worldly.

Second, he mentions his return to the Father when he says, ***and I go to the Father***, whom he had never left. He goes insofar as he offered himself to the Father in his passion: *Christ . . . gave himself up for us, a fragrant offering and sacrifice to God* (Eph. 5:2). Again, he goes to the Father insofar as by his resurrection his human nature became like the Father in its immortality: *The life he lives he lives to God* (Rom. 6:10). Further, he goes to the Father by ascending into the heavens where he shines in a special way with divine glory: *The Lord Jesus, after he had spoken to them, was taken up into heaven, and sat down at the right hand of God* (Mark 16:19); ***but now I go to him who sent me; and none of you ask me: where do you go?***

Chapter 12
THE VISION OF GOD

1 Timothy 6:15–16
The Incomprehensible Infinity of God
On 1 Timothy 6.3 (262–271)

6:15 ***Which in his times he shall show, who is the Blessed and only Mighty, the King of kings and Lord of lords:***

6:16 ***Who alone has immortality and inhabits light inaccessible: whom no man has seen, nor can see: to whom be honor and empire everlasting. Amen.***

262 Above, the Apostle gave certain orders to Timothy, commanding him to observe the foregoing until the coming of Christ;[1] therefore, he now discusses Christ's coming, about which he discloses three things: *first*, that it will occur at a suitable time; *second*, that it will be evident; *third*, he reveals the author of this coming.

263 In regard to the *first*, he says, ***which in his times he shall show who is the Blessed and only Mighty, the King of kings***: *Scoffers will come in the last days with scoffing, following their own passions and saying, "Where is the promise of his coming?"* (2 Pet. 3:3). Therefore, he wishes to show that even though his coming seems to be delayed, it will nevertheless be shown in his time: *For everything there is a season* (Eccles. 3:1); *every matter has its time and way* (Eccles. 8:6). The suitable time will be the end of the world, because that is the time of harvest and of collecting the fruits; consequently, it must come at the end of the world.

264 In regard to the *second* he says, ***he shall show***, i.e., will manifest. For although he is visible in the flesh, his power is hidden; but then, even his divinity will be manifest to the saints: but the wicked will see only the glory of his body.

265 In regard to the *third* he says that he who is God and the Trinity shall show him. In regard to this he does two things: *first*, he describes the coming of Christ; *second*, bursting out in praise of Christ, he applauds him, at ***to whom be honor and empire everlasting.***

1. See 1 Tim. 6:11–14 and Thomas Aquinas, *On 1 Timothy* 6.2 (not included in this collection).

In regard to the *first* he does three things: *first*, he describes the author of this coming in terms of his perfect action; *second*, in terms of his singular power; *third*, in terms of his incomprehensible nature.

266 He describes the *first* when he says, ***Blessed***; for blessedness is a perfect action, which is distinctive of the supreme active power disposed in the best way: and this is our blessedness, whereas God's blessedness is that by which he knows himself: for if God did not know himself, he would not be blessed. As Gregory says: *So long as God enjoys himself, he is perfectly glorious.*[2] And it is fitting that the author of this coming be described as ***Blessed***, because the purpose of Christ's coming is to lead us to blessedness: *Happy shall I be if there shall remain of my seed to see the glory of Jerusalem* (Tob. 13:20 DRB).

267 In regard to the *second* he says, ***the only Mighty***: *You are mighty* (Ps. 89:8 DRB). But why does he say, ***the only***? Do not all things have might? Yes, by participation, but God alone is mighty of himself and essentially. Hence he says, ***King of kings and Lord of lords***. As Ambrose says, *Lord is a name of power, so also king.*[3] Therefore, one who has a lord and king over him is subject to power, and such a one is not powerful of himself, but purely of another. Therefore, if Christ is the ***King of kings and Lord of lords***, then he alone has power not from someone else, but all others from him.

And two of God's powers are mentioned, namely, his governance of the world, when he says, ***King of kings***: *A king who sits on the throne of judgment winnows all evil with his eyes* (Prov. 20:8); and his creative power, when he says, ***Lord of lords***: *Know that the Lord is God! It is he that made us, and we are his* (Ps. 100:3); *On his robe and on his thigh he has a name inscribed, King of kings and Lord of lords* (Rev. 19:16).

268 In regard to the *third* he says, ***who alone has immortality and inhabits light inaccessible***. God's incomprehensibility is clear from two things: *first*, because he transcends whatever is comprehensible in creatures; *second*, because, being God, he is too great for anyone's comprehension.

He shows the *first* when he says, ***alone***: for in every change something is lost, because whatever is changed ceases to be what it was. Therefore, that is properly and truly incorruptible which is altogether unchangeable. But every creature considered in itself undergoes some change, and God alone is altogether unchangeable. Therefore, if any creature is unchangeable, this is the result of grace. But this shows that God's nature transcends everything in created nature: ***To the King of ages, immortal, invisible, the only God, be honor and glory*** (1 Tim. 1:17).

---

2. Gregory the Great, *Moralia in Job* 32.8.

3. Ambrose, *Exposition of the Christian Faith* 1.1.7.

As to the *second* he says, ***inhabits light inaccessible***. For in material things light is the principle of seeing; hence that by which something is known in any way whatsoever is called a light. But that by which each thing is known is its form, insofar as that form is actual; hence to the extent that a thing's form is actual, to that extent it has light. Therefore, things which are acts, but not pure act, are said to be lucent, but not light. But the divine essence, which is pure act, is light itself: *He was not the light, but came to bear witness to the light. The true light . . . was coming into the world* (John 1:8). But God abides with himself, and this light is inaccessible, i.e., not visible to a bodily eye, but to the intellectual eye. Yet no created intellect can approach to it.

269 But it should be noted that there are two ways in which an intellect can approach to a knowledge of some nature; namely, by knowing it and by comprehending it. But it is impossible for our intellect to arrive at a comprehension of God because that requires knowing all that can be known about God. But God is perfectly knowable, insofar as he is being and light. But these are infinite. Therefore God is infinitely knowable. But a created intellect is finite. Therefore, not even Christ's human intellect comprehended God.

But there is another way of knowing God, namely, by attaining to God; yet even in this way no created intellect, utilizing only its own power, attains to a knowledge of what God is: the reason being that no cognitive faculty can transcend its object, just as sight cannot go beyond seeing color. Now the appropriate object of our intellect is the essence of a thing; hence, whatever is over and above the essence of a thing exceeds the power of any intellect. But in God there is nothing other than his essence.

Then how can he be known? We arrive at knowing him in this life through grace, and in the future life through glory: *Come to him . . . and be enlightened*
270 (Ps. 34:6 DRB). But then how does God inhabit ***light inaccessible***? For it is said: *Clouds and darkness are round about him* (Ps. 97:2), and in Exodus: *Moses went into the thick darkness where God was* (20:21).

I answer with Dionysius: *Every dark cloud is an inaccessible light*; therefore, what is light here is a dark cloud there: but it is a dark cloud inasmuch as it is invisible, and a light inasmuch as it is visible.[4]

But something is invisible for two reasons: *first*, by reason of itself, as something opaque; *second*, by reason of its excessive brilliance, as the sun is invisible to the eye of an owl. Hence, some things are not visible to us on account of a deficiency within themselves, and others on account of their richness, which is the way God is inaccessible to us.

Whom no man has seen: if this refers to being comprehended, it is absolutely true, even for the angels, because God alone comprehends himself. But

4. See Pseudo-Dionysius, *The Celestial Hierarchy* 1.3 and 15.6.

if it refers to the vision by which he is reached bodily, then it is true in three ways: *first,* because no one sees him with his bodily eyes; *second,* according to the essence in the mind's eye. Then no one living in the flesh, except Christ, can see him: *You cannot see my face: for man shall not see me and live* (Exod. 33:20); *third,* no one sees what God is in himself: *No one knows the Father except the Son and anyone to whom the Son chooses to reveal him* (Matt. 11:27); *flesh and blood have not revealed it to you* (Matt. 16:17).

271 Then he bursts forth in praise of God, saying, ***to whom be honor and empire everlasting***; and he mentions two things: the *first* pertains to showing reverence, saying, ***honor***, which is to show reverence: *If I am a father, where is my honor?* (Mal. 1:6); the *second,* to governance, when he says, ***and empire everlasting.***

1 Corinthians 13:12–13

The Beatific Vision

On 1 Corinthians 13.4 (799–806)

13:12 We see now through a glass in a dark manner: but then face to face. Now I know in part: but then I shall know even as I am known.

13:13 And now there remain faith, hope, and charity, these three: but the greatest of these is charity.

799 Here he speaks of the vision, which is knowledge of God. Hence, all the preceding gifts must be understood as destined to be eliminated inasmuch as they are directed to knowledge of God.[5] In regard to this he does two things: *first*, he proves what he proposes in general; *second*, in detail about himself, at ***now I know in part.***

800 He says, therefore: I have said that we know imperfectly, because ***we see now through a glass in a dark manner***, but then, namely, in heaven, we shall see ***face to face***. The *first* consideration concerns what it is to see ***through a glass in a dark manner***; the *second* concerns what it is to see ***face to face***.

It should be noted, therefore, that something sensible can be seen in three ways, namely, by its presence in the one seeing, as light itself, which is present in the eye; or by the presence of its likeness in the sense and immediately derived from the thing, as whiteness in a wall is seen, even though the whiteness does not exist in the eye, but its likeness (although the likeness is not seen by the eye); or by the presence of a likeness not immediately derived from the thing itself but from a likeness of the thing in something else, as when a man is seen through a mirror. For the likeness of the man is not immediately in the eye, but the likeness of the man reflected in a mirror.

Therefore, speaking in this way about the vision of God, I say that by natural knowledge God alone sees himself, because in God essence and intellect are the same. Therefore, his essence is present to his intellect. But in a *second* way the angels perhaps see God by natural knowledge, inasmuch as a likeness of the divine essence immediately shines back on them. But in a *third* way we know God in this life, inasmuch as we know the invisible things of God

5. In this section, St. Thomas' discussion of "gifts" centers on the theological virtues (faith, hope, charity) and charity in particular, but in his commentary on 1 Corinthians 12:7–11 he discusses a number of other "gifts" of the Holy Spirit as well. See Thomas Aquinas, *Commentary on 1 Corinthians* 12.2.

through creatures. And thus it is said that all creation is a mirror for us (Rom. 1:20) because from the order and goodness and multitude which are caused in things by God, we come to a knowledge of his power, goodness, and eminence. And this knowledge is called seeing in a mirror.

801 It should be further noted that a likeness of this sort, which is of a likeness gleaming back on someone else, is twofold: because sometimes it is clear and open, as that which appears in a mirror; sometimes it is obscure and secret, and then that vision is said to be enigmatic, as when I say: 'me a mother begot, and the same is born from me.' That is secret by a simile. And it is said of ice, which is born from frozen water and the water is born from the melted ice. Thus, therefore, it is clear that vision through the likeness of a likeness is in a mirror, by a likeness hidden in an enigma, but a clear and open likeness makes another kind of allegorical vision.

Therefore, inasmuch as we know the invisible things of God through creatures, we are said to see through a mirror. Inasmuch as those invisible things are secrets to us, we see in an enigma. Or another way, ***we see now through a glass***, i.e., by our reason, and then ***through*** designates the power only. As if to say: ***We now see through a glass***, i.e., by a power of our soul.

802 In regard to the *second* it should be noted that God as God does not have a face, and therefore the expression ***face to face*** is metaphorical. For when we see something in a mirror, we do not see it, but its likeness; but when we see someone by face, then we see him as he is. Therefore, the Apostle wishes to say nothing else, when he says: in heaven we shall see ***face to face***, then that we shall see the very essence of God: *We shall see him as he is* (1 John 3:2).

But opposed to this it is said: *I have seen God face to face and yet my life is preserved* (Gen. 32:30). But it is evident that he did not at that time see the essence of God; therefore, to see face to face is not to see the essence of God.

The answer is that that vision was imaginary; but an imaginary vision is of a higher degree, namely, seeing what appears: in the image in which he appears is another lowest grace, namely, only to hear words. Hence Jacob, to indicate the excellence of the imaginary vision showed to him says: *I have seen the Lord face to face*, i.e., I have seen the Lord through my imagination in his own image and not through his essence. For then it would not have been an imaginary vision.

803 But still some say that in heaven the divine essence will be seen through a created likeness. This, however, is entirely false and impossible, because something can never be known through its essence by a likeness, which does not agree with that thing in species. For a stone cannot be known as it is except through the stone's species, which is in the soul. For no likeness leads to knowledge of a thing's essence if it differs from that according to species; and much

less if they differ in genus. For the essence of a man, much less than the essence of an angel, cannot be known through the species of a horse or of whiteness. Much less, then, can the divine essence be seen through any created species, whatever it be, since any created species in the soul is more distant from the divine essence than the species of a horse or whiteness from the essence of an angel. Hence, to suppose that God is seen only by a likeness or through some brilliance of his clarity is to suppose that the divine essence is not seen.

Furthermore, since the soul is a certain likeness of God, that vision would not be more mirror-like or enigmatic, which it is in this life, than clear and open vision, which is promised to the saints in glory and in which will consist our beatitude. Hence Augustine says in a gloss that a vision of God through a likeness pertains to a vision in a mirror and enigma.[6]

It would also follow that man's final beatitude would be in something other than God; which is alien to the faith. Even man's natural desire, which is to arrive at the first cause of things and of knowing him in himself, would be in vain.

804 He continues: ***now I know in part***. Here he proves in particular what he had proved in general about knowledge of himself, saying: ***now***, i.e., in the present life, I, Paul, ***know in part***, i.e., obscurely and imperfectly, ***but then***, namely, in heaven, ***I shall know even as I am known***. Just as God knows my essence, so I shall know God through his essence, so that the ***as*** does not imply equality of knowledge but only similarity.

805 Then he infers the principal conclusion, when he says: ***and now there remain***. But the reason he does not mention all the gifts but only three is that these three join to God; the others do not join to God, except through the mediation of those three; also the other gifts dispose for the birth of those three in the hearts of men. Hence, too, only those three, namely, faith, hope, and charity, are called theological virtues, because they have God for their imme-
806 diate object. But since the gifts exist for perfecting the affections or intellect, and charity perfects the affections, and faith the intellect, it does not seem that hope is necessary but superfluous. The answer is that love is a unitive force, and all love consists in some union. Hence according to the various unions, the various species of friendship are distinguished by the Philosopher.[7]

Now we have a twofold union with God: one refers to the goods of nature, which we partake of here from him; the other refers to beatitude, inasmuch as through grace we partake here of heavenly felicity, as far as it is possible here. We also hope to arrive at the perfect attainment of that eternal beatitude and become citizens of the heavenly Jerusalem. According to the first communi-

6. Augustine, *The Trinity* 15.9.15.

7. Aristotle, *Nicomachean Ethics* 8.2–3.

cation with God there is a natural friendship, according to which each one, inasmuch as he is, seeks and desires as his end God as first cause and supreme being. According to the second communication there is the love of charity, by which only an intellectual creature loves God.

But because nothing can be loved unless it is known, for the love of charity a knowledge of God is first required. And because this is above nature, there is required, first of all, faith which is concerned with things not seen. *Second*, in order that a man not fail or fall away, hope is required through which he tends to that end as pertaining to himself. Concerning these three it is said: *You who fear the Lord, believe in him*, as to faith; *you who fear the Lord, hope in him*, as to hope; *you who fear the Lord, love him* (Sir. 2:8–10 DRB), as to charity.

Therefore, these three remain now, but charity is greater than the others for the reasons indicated above.

2 Corinthians 12:1–2

The Rapture of Saint Paul

On 2 Corinthians 12.1 (440–457)

12:1 ***If I must glory (it is not expedient indeed) still I will come to visions and revelations of the Lord.***

12:2 ***I know a man in Christ: over fourteen years ago (whether in the body, I do not know, or out of the body, I do not know: God knows), such a one was caught up to the third heaven.***

440 Having commended himself for the evils he suffered, the Apostle continues to commend himself and shows the pre-eminence of his dignity in regard to good things received from God.[8] For he first gloried in his weaknesses, but now in his good things. In regard to this he does two things. *First*, he commends himself on the good things received from God; *second*, he begs pardon for this commendation, alleging that he is compelled to do this, at ***I have become foolish*** (2 Cor. 12:11).

In regard to the *first* he does two things. *First*, he extols the greatness of the things conferred on him by God; *second*, he discloses the remedy given to him against the danger of pride, at ***and lest the greatness*** (2 Cor. 12:17).

In regard to the *first* he does two things: *first*, he mentions a good divinely conferred; *second*, he shows how he behaved in regard to glorying in it, at ***for such a one, I will glory*** (2 Cor. 12:5).

In regard to the *first* he does two things. *First*, he shows in general that this was divinely bestowed; *second*, in particular, at ***I know a man***.

441 The good divinely bestowed on the Apostle are revelations made to him by God; it is of these that he wishes to glory. Hence he says: ***if I must glory***, i.e., because I must glory for your sake, although in itself there is nothing to be gained by it, because a person who glories in a good he has received runs the risk of losing what he has: *Through this*, i.e., by vain glory, *are the treasures* of the virtues *opened, and the clouds fly out like birds.* (Sir. 43:14 DRB). And this is signified in Hezekiah, when he showed the treasures of the Lord's house to the messengers of the king in Babylon (Isa. 39:2).

And although, absolutely speaking, it is not expedient to glory, nevertheless, for some special reason a man may glory, as is clear from what has been

8. See 2 Corinthians 11:21–26 and Thomas Aquinas, *On 2 Corinthians* 11.5 (not included in this collection).

stated above. Therefore he says: because I must boast, I will leave off commending myself on my infirmities and ***I will come*** by commending myself ***to visions and revelations of the Lord.***

442 Here it should be noted the difference between a vision and a revelation. For a revelation includes a vision, but not vice versa. For sometimes things are seen, the understanding and significance of which are hidden from the beholder; in that case it is only a vision, as in the visions of Pharaoh and Nebuchadnezzar (Dan. 2:1; Gen. 41:1). But when the significance of the understanding of those things which are seen is had with the vision, then it is revelation; whence in regard to Pharoah and Nebuchadnezzar, the vision of ears of corn and of the statue was only a vision. But in regard to Joseph and Daniel, who understood the meaning of what was seen, it was a revelation and a prophecy.

Both, however, namely vision and revelation, are sometimes produced by God. *There is a God in heaven who reveals mysteries* (Dan. 2:28); *it was I who multiplied visions* (Hos. 12:10); *open my eyes, that I may behold wondrous things out of your law* (Ps. 119:18); but sometimes by an evil spirit: *They prophesied by Baal and led my people Israel astray* (Jer. 23:13). To the Apostle were made both vision and revelation because he fully understood the secret things he saw. They were produced by the Lord and not by an evil spirit. Hence he says: ***I will come to visions and revelations of the Lord.***

Now a revelation is a removing of a veil.[9] But a veil can be of two kinds: one on the part of the beholder, and this is unbelief or sin or hardness of heart. Of this veil he said above: ***To this day whenever Moses is read a veil lies over their minds*** (2 Cor. 3:15); the other is on the part of the object seen, namely, when spiritual things are proposed to someone under the figures of sense-perceptible objects. Concerning this it is said that the priests delivered the vessels of the sanctuary veiled to the Levites because weaker persons cannot grasp spiritual things as they are in themselves (Num. 4:15). This is why the Lord spoke to the multitudes in parables (Matt. 13:13).

443 Then the Apostle describes these visions and revelations in particular, speaking of himself as though of another person; hence he says, ***I know a man in Christ.*** He mentions two visions: the *first* begins here; the *second* begins at ***and I know such a man.***

444 When speaking of the first vision, the Apostle makes use of a distinction, for he says in regard to this revelation that he knew certain things but not others. But he knew three things, namely, the condition of the beholder; hence he says: ***I know a man in Christ***; the time of the vision, that is, ***over fourteen***

9. St. Thomas here is defining 'revelation' in terms of the etymology of the term. The Latin *revelare* comprises the prepositional prefix *re-*, here with the force of the English "un-," and *velare* (to veil or cover with a veil). Thus, most literally *revelare* means to remove a veil, as St. Thomas says here.

years ago; and the high point of the vision, because he ***was caught up to the third heaven***. And he says that he did not know the disposition of the beholder,
445 ***whether in the body, I do not know, or out of the body, I do not know***. Therefore let us see what he knew, so that through what is known we may more easily attain to what was not known.

First of all, the condition of the beholder, which is praiseworthy, because he was ***in Christ***, i.e., conformed to Christ. But on the contrary, no one is in Christ, unless he has charity, because *he who abides in love abides in God* (1 John 4:16). Therefore, he knew that he had charity, which is contrary to what is stated in Ecclesiastes: *The righteous and the wise and their deeds are in the hand of God; whether it is love or hate man does not know* (9:1).

I answer that being in Christ can be taken in two ways: in one way by faith and the sacrament of faith according to Galatians: *As many of you as were baptized into Christ have put on Christ* (3:27), namely, by faith and the sacrament of faith. This is the sense in which the Apostle knew that he was in Christ.

In another way a person is said to be in Christ through charity, and in this way no one knows for certain that he is in Christ, except by certain tests and signs, inasmuch as he feels himself disposed and joined to Christ in such a way that he would not permit himself to be separated from him for any reason including death. This the Apostle experienced in regard to himself, when he said: *I am sure that neither death, nor life, nor angels, nor principalities, nor things present, nor things to come, nor powers, nor height, nor depth, nor anything else in all creation, will be able to separate us from the love of God in Christ Jesus our Lord* (Rom 8:38). Hence, he could have had such signs that he was in the charity of Christ.

446 *Second*, the time of the vision, which was fitting, because it was ***over fourteen years ago***; for fourteen years had elapsed from the time he saw the vision, until he wrote this epistle, because when he wrote this epistle he had not yet been cast into prison. Hence it seems to have been written at the beginning of Nero's reign, by whom he was killed much later.[10] Hence if we go back fourteen years from the beginning of Nero's reign, it is clear that the Apostle had these visions at the beginning of his conversion.

For he had been converted to Christ in the same year that the Lord suffered. But Christ suffered near the end of Tiberius Caesar's reign, who was succeeded at death by the emperor Caius, who lived four years, after which Nero became emperor. Therefore, between Tiberius and Nero there were four

10. Nero (37–68), the fifth emperor of Rome, famously persecuted Christians following the Great Fire of Rome (64), for which he blamed the Christians (although he is believed to have lit the fire himself in order to clear land for the construction of a palace). It is during this first persecution of the Christian movement that both Peter and Paul are thought to have been martyred.

years. Adding two years from Tiberius's reign, because he was not yet dead, when Paul was converted, and from Nero's reign the eight years which had passed until he wrote this epistle, there were fourteen years between the time of his conversion to the time he wrote this epistle. Therefore, some say quite probably that the Apostle had these visions during those three days after he was struck down by the Lord, when he remained neither seeing nor eating nor drinking (Acts 9:9).

But he recalls the time of his conversion to show that if he was so pleasing to Christ from the time of his conversion that he revealed such things to him, then how much more pleasing was he after fourteen years, when he had grown in charity before God and in the virtues and graces?

447 *Third*, let us see the high point of the vision, because he ***was caught up to the third heaven***. But it should be noted that it is one thing to be the victim of thievery and another to be rapt. Properly speaking, the former takes place when something is taken away from another in a secret way, hence, Joseph said: *I was indeed stolen out of the land of the Hebrews* (Gen. 40:15). A person is, properly speaking, rapt when something is taken suddenly and by force: *as the torent that passes swiftly*, i.e., suddenly and rapidly, *in the valleys* (Job 6:15 DRB). Hence it is that plunderers who despoil violently are called ravagers [*raptores*].

But note that a man is said to be rapt from men, as Enoch: *He was caught up lest evil change his understanding or guile deceive his soul* (Wis. 4:11); sometimes the soul is rapt from the body: *Fool! This night your soul is required of you* (Luke 12:20). Sometimes a person is said to be rapt from himself, when for some reason he is made to be outside himself; and this is the same as ecstasy.

But a man is made to be outside himself both by his appetitive power and by his cognitive power. For by the former a person is in himself when he cares only for things that are his own; but he is made to be outside himself when he does not care about things that are his own, but about things that pertain to others; and this is the work of charity. *Love does not insist on its own way* (1 Cor. 13:5). Concerning this ecstasy Dionysius says: *Ecstasy is produced by divine love not permitting one to be a lover of self but of the beloved*, i.e., of the things loved.[11] But a person is made to be outside himself according to the cognitive power when he is raised up above the human mode to see something. This is the rapture about which the Apostle is speaking here.

448 But it should be noted that a mode natural to human knowing is that a man know simultaneously with his mental power, which is the intellect, and with a bodily one, which is a sense. This is why a man, in knowing, has a free judgment of the intellect when the senses are well disposed in their vigor and not hindered by a fettering, as happens during sleep. Therefore a man is made

11. Pseudo-Dionysius, *The Divine Names* 4.

to be outside himself when he is removed from this natural disposition for knowing, namely, when the intellect, being withdrawn from the use of the senses and sense-perceptible things, is moved to see certain things.

This occurs in two ways: *first*, by a lack of power, no matter how it is produced. This happens in insane persons and those suffering psychosis, so that this withdrawal from the senses is not a state of being elevated, but of being cast down, because their power has been weakened.

But the other way is by divine power, and then it is, properly speaking, an elevation, because since the agent makes its patient to be like itself, a withdrawal produced by divine power and above men is something higher than man's nature.

449 Therefore, a rapture of this sort is defined as 'an elevation from that which is according to nature into that which is above nature, produced in virtue of a higher nature.' In this definition are mentioned its genus, when it is called an elevation; the efficient cause, because it is by the power of a higher nature; and the two termini of the change, namely, the terminus *from which* and *into which*, when it is described as being from that which is according to nature into what is above nature. Thus it is clear what rapture is.

450 Then he mentions the terminus reached by the rapture, when he says, ***to the third heaven***. But it should be noted that the third heaven is taken in three ways: in one way according to the things below the soul; in another way according to the things in the soul; and in a *third* way according to things above the soul.

Below the soul are all bodies, as Augustine says.[12] And so we can think of a threefold heaven: the ethereal, sidereal, and empyrean.[13] In this way the Apostle is said to have been rapt to the third heaven, i.e., to see things in the empyrean heaven; not to exist there, because then he would have known whether he was in the body or out of the body. Or according to Damascene, who does not admit an empyrean heaven, we can say that the third heaven, to which the Apostle was rapt, is above the eighth sphere, so that he could clearly see the things which exist above all corporeal nature.[14]

12. Augustine, *True Religion* 41.77.

13. The "empyrean heaven" (or "fiery heaven") mentioned here is the highest of the three heavens or celestial spheres that St. Thomas, with many of his contemporaries, believed to exist as part of the physical world (see *Summa theologiae* 1.68.4). On the authority of the fathers and scriptural allusion (especially the passage of this commentary), St. Thomas understood the empyrean heaven to be a motionless, luminous, physical realm that moved the lower heavens. Most importantly, however, it was where the angels and the blessed enjoy the contemplation of God.

14. John of Damascus, *An Exact Exposition of the Orthodox Faith* 2.

451 But if we take heaven according to the things in the soul itself, then we should call heaven some altitude of mind which transcends natural human knowledge.

Now there are three kinds of sight, namely, bodily, by which we can see and know bodies; spiritual or imaginary, by which we see likenesses of bodies; and intellectual, by which we know the nature of things in themselves. For the proper object of the intellect is the *what it is* of things. But such a sight of things, if it takes place according to the natural mode (e.g., if I see something visible, if I imagine something previously seen, or if I understand through phantasms), cannot be called heaven.

But each of these is called heaven when they are above the natural faculty of human knowledge. For example, if you see something with your bodily eyes above the faculty of nature, then you are rapt into the first heaven. This is the way Belshazzar was rapt, when he saw the handwriting on the wall (Dan. 5:5). But if you are raised up by the imagination or spirit to know something supernaturally, then you are rapt to the second heaven. This is the way Peter was rapt, when he saw the linen sheet descending from heaven (Acts 10:11). But if a person were to see intelligible things themselves and their nature, not through sense-perceptible things nor through phantasms, he would be rapt to the third heaven.

452 But it should be noted that to be rapt to the first heaven is to be alienated from the bodily senses. Hence, since no one can be totally withdrawn from the bodily senses, it is obvious that no one can be rapt in the strict sense to the first heaven, but only in a qualified sense, inasmuch as it sometimes happens that a person is so engrossed in one sense that he is withdrawn from the act of the others.

One is rapt to the second heaven when he is alienated from sense to see imaginable things; hence, such a person is always said to be in ecstasy. And so when Peter saw the linen sheet, it is said that he was in ecstasy (Acts 10:11).

But Paul is said to have been rapt to the third heaven, because he was so alienated from the senses and lifted above all bodily things that he saw intelligible things naked and pure in the way angels and separated souls see them. What is more, he saw God in his essence, as Augustine expressly says in *The Literal Meaning of Genesis*, in a gloss, and in *A Book on Seeing God*.[15]

Furthermore, it is improbable that Moses, the minister of the Old Testament to the Jews, should have seen God while [Paul] the minister of the New Testament and teacher of the gentiles, be deprived of this gift. Hence he says above: ***If there was splendor in the dispensation of condemnation, the dispensation of righteousness must far exceed it in splendor*** (2 Cor. 3:9).

15. Augustine, *The Literal Meaning of Genesis* 12.27; *A Book on Seeing God* 8.20.

Concerning Moses, moreover, it is clear that he may have seen the essence of God for he himself asked the Lord *show me your face* (Exod. 33:13 DRB). And although it was denied him at that time, it is not stated that the Lord denied him ultimately. Hence, Augustine says that it was granted him by reason of what is said: *If there is a prophet among you, I the Lord make myself known to him in a vision, I speak with him in a dream. Not so with my servant Moses; he is entrusted with all my house* (Num. 12:5).[16] For he saw God openly and not in a dark manner.

453 But would it have been possible for Paul to see God without being rapt? I answer: no, for it is impossible for God to be seen in this life by a man not alienated from his senses because no image or phantasm is a sufficient medium for showing God's essence; therefore, he must be removed and alienated from the senses.

454 In a *third* way, by taking heaven according to things above the soul; in this way the three heavens are the three hierarchies of angels. According to this the Apostle was rapt to the third heaven, i.e., to see God's essence as clearly as the angels of the higher and first hierarchy see him, because they see God in such a way as to receive illumination in God himself and to know the divine mysteries. This is the way Paul saw. Thus therefore he saw the essence of God as do the angels of the higher hierarchy.

455 But if he saw God as the angels of the higher and first hierarchy do, then it seems that the Apostle was beatified and, consequently, was immortal. I answer that although he saw God in his essence, he was not absolutely beatified, but only in a qualified sense.

Yet it should be noted that the vision of God's essence takes place by means of a certain light, namely, the light of glory, of which it is said: *In your light do we see light* (Ps. 36:9). But light is communicated to some things after the manner of a passing quality and to others after the manner of an inhering form, as the light of the sun is found in a carbuncle and in the stars as an inhering form, i.e., connaturally produced;[17] but it is found in the air as a passing form and not as a permanent form, because it vanishes when the sun is absent.

Similarly, the light of glory is infused in the mind in two ways: in one way, after the manner of a form connaturally made and permanent and then it makes a mind beatified in the strict sense. This is the way it is infused in the beatified in heaven. Hence they are called comprehenders and, so to say, seers. In another way the light of glory affects a human mind as a passing quality; this is the way Paul's mind in rapture was enlightened by the light of glory. Hence, the very name, 'rapture,' suggests that this was done in a pass-

16. Augustine, *The Literal Meaning of Genesis* 12.27.

17. A "carbuncle" (Lat. *carbunculus*), as used here, most likely refers to a small ember.

ing manner. Consequently, he was not glorified in the strict sense or had the mark of glory, because that brightness was not produced as a property. As a result it was not derived from the soul in the body, nor did he remain in this state permanently. Hence, when he was in rapture, he had only the act of the beatified, but he was not beatified.

Thus it is clear what the Apostle saw in his rapture, namely, the condition
456 of the beholder, the time of the vision, and the high point of the vision. Then he tells what he did not know, namely, whether he was in the body or out of the body, although he says that God knew. Hence he says, ***whether in the body, I do not know, or out of the body, I do not know: God knows.*** Some interpret this as meaning that the rapture referred to his body, saying that the Apostle did not say he did not know whether the soul was joined to the body in that rapture, but whether he was rapt according to the soul and body simultaneously, so as to have been transported bodily into heaven as Habakkuk was transported (Dan. 14:35–39), or whether it was according to the soul only that he enjoyed the vision of God, as it is said: *He brought me in visions of God to Jerusalem* (Ezek. 8:3).

This was the way a certain Jew understood, as Jerome mentions in the prologue to Daniel, where he says: *Finally, he says that even our Apostle does not dare to say that he was rapt in the body, but he said: whether in the body or out of the body I do not know, God knows.*[18]

But Augustine disproves this interpretation because it does not agree with the other words of the Apostle.[19] For the Apostle says that he was rapt to the third heaven; hence he knew for certain that it was the third heaven. Consequently, he knew whether that heaven was corporeal or incorporeal, i.e., an incorporeal thing. But if it was incorporeal, he knew that he could not have been rapt there bodily, because a body cannot exist in an incorporeal thing. But if it had been corporeal, he knew that the soul was not there without the body, because the soul joined to the body cannot be in a place where there is no body, unless the incorporeal heaven is called a likeness of the bodily heaven. But if that were the case, the Apostle would not have said that he knew he was rapt to the third heaven, i.e., to a likeness of heaven, because by that same token it could be said that he was rapt in the body, i.e., in the likeness of a body.

457 Therefore it must be admitted according to Augustine that no one set in this life and living this mortal life can see the divine essence.[20] Hence, the Lord says: *Man shall not see me and live* (Exod. 33:20), i.e., no man will see me, unless he is entirely separated from the body, namely, in such a way that his soul is not

18. Jerome, "Prologue to Daniel."

19. Augustine, *The Literal Meaning of Genesis* 12.3–5.

20. Augustine, *The Literal Meaning of Genesis* 12.27.

in the body as a form, or if it is as a form, nevertheless his mind is totally and altogether alienated from the sense in such a vision. Therefore, it must be said that the Apostle says he does not know whether the soul was entirely separated from the body in that vision. Hence he says, ***or out of the body***, or whether his soul existed in the body as a form, but his mind was alienated from the bodily senses; hence, he says, ***whether in the body***. Even others concede this.

John 17:24–26

Christ's Prayer for the Glory of the Faithful

On John 17.6 (2252–2270)

17:24 ***Father, I will that where I am, they whom you have given me may be with me: that they may see my glory which you gave me, because you loved me before the creation of the world.***

17:25 ***Just Father, the world has not known you; but I have known. And these have known that you sent me.***

17:26 ***And I have made known your name to them and will make it known that the love wherewith you loved me may be in them, and I in them.***

2252 Above, our Lord prayed for the perfect unity of his disciples;[21] here he is asking the vision of glory for them. *First*, he mentions the persons for whom he is praying; *second*, he shows the way he is praying; *third*, he states what he is asking for.

2253 He is praying for those given to him; he says, ***Father . . . whom you have given me.*** That is given to a person which is subject to his will, so he can do with it as he wills. We can distinguish two wills in Christ: a will to mercy and a will to justice. His will to mercy is fundamental and absolute, because *his compassion is over all that he has made* (Ps. 145:9); *who desires all men to be saved* (1 Tim. 2:4). But his will for a punishing justice is not fundamental, as it presupposes sin: *God . . . does not delight in the death of the living* (Wis. 1:13); *I do not desire the death of the sinner* (Ezek. 18:32), absolutely; but he wills it as a consequence of sin.

All men have been given to the Son: ***You have given him power over all flesh*** (John 17:2), that is, over all men, to accomplish his will in their regard: his will for mercy, leading to salvation, or his will for justice, leading to punishment: *He is the one ordained by God to be judge of the living and the dead* (Acts 10:42). But those were given to him absolutely who were given to him so that he might accomplish his will of mercy for their salvation; he says of these people, ***whom you have given to me***, that is, in your predestination from all eternity, *I and the children whom the Lord has given me* (Isa. 8:18).

2254 The way he asks is given when he says, ***I will.*** This can indicate authority or merit. It indicates authority if we refer this to Christ's divine will, which is

21. See John 17:20–21 and Thomas Aquinas, *On John* 17.5 (not included in this collection).

the same as the will of the Father: for by his will he justifies and saves men: *He has mercy upon whomever he wills* (Rom. 9:18).

If we refer this to Christ's human will, it indicates merit, for Christ's human will merits our salvation. For if the wills of the just, who are the members of Christ, have merit entitling them to be heard: ***ask whatever you will, and it will be done unto you*** (John 15:7), then much more so does the human will of Christ, who is the head of all the saints.

2255 He mentions what he is asking for when he says, ***where I am, they . . . may be with me.*** *First*, he asks that the members be united to the head; *second*, that his glory be shown to his members, ***that they may see my glory.***

2256 He says, ***I will***, namely, ***where I am, they . . . may be with me.*** This can be understood in two ways. In the *first* way it can be understood of Christ in his human nature. Christ, in his human nature, is soon to ascend and to be in heaven: ***I ascend to my Father and your Father*** (John 20:17). Then the meaning is: ***I will***, as in heaven, ***where I am***, about to ascend, ***they***, namely, the faithful, ***may be with me***, also in that place: *Wherever the body is, there the eagles*, that is, the saints, *will be gathered together* (Matt. 24:28). For this is what Christ promised: *Rejoice and be glad, for your reward is great in heaven* (Matt. 5:12).

2257 There is a difficulty with this meaning. Since Christ was not yet in heaven, he should have said, 'where I will be,' and not ***where I am.*** And besides, he also said, ***No one has ascended into heaven but he who descended from heaven*** (John 3:13).

I reply to the *first* that Christ, who was speaking, was both God and man. And although he was not yet in heaven in his human nature, he was there in his divine nature. And so, while present on earth, he was in heaven; and thus he says, ***where I am.***

As to the *second* objection, when we read that ***No one has ascended into heaven but he who descended from heaven*** (John 3:13), we should understand that the Son is in heaven by reason of his divinity, and descended by taking on a human nature, and then ascended by reason of his human nature, now glorified. But now we have been made one with him. Thus, he alone comes, in himself, by descending from heaven, and he alone returns there, now one with us, by ascending into heaven. This is the observation of Gregory.[22]

He says, ***where I am***, using the present tense instead of the future, either because he would very soon be there, or because he was referring to Christ as
2258 God. But since God is everywhere: *Do I not fill heaven and earth?* (Jer. 23:24),
it seems to follow that the saints also will be everywhere.

We should reply to this that God is related to us like light is to men. When the sun is over the earth, the light spreads everywhere. And although

22. Gregory the Great, *Moralia in Job* 27.15.30.

the light is with all, yet all are not in the light, but only those who see it. So, since God is everywhere, he is with all, wherever they are; yet not all are with God, but only those joined to him by faith and love; and they will be finally joined in complete joy: *I am continually with you* (Ps. 73:23); *we shall always be with the Lord* (1 Thess. 4:17). Thus the meaning is this: ***where I am***, that is, in your divinity, Father, which I have by nature, ***they . . . may be with me***, by participating in grace: ***He gave power to become children of God*** (John 1:12); *he who abides in love abides in God, and God abides in him* (1 John 4:16).

2259 He speaks of manifesting his glory to his members when he says, ***that they may see my glory***. *First*, he makes his request; *second*, he mentions the source of this glory, ***which you have given me***; *third*, he gives the reason for this glory, ***because you loved me before the creation of the world***.

2260 He says: ***I will*** not only ***that they . . . may be with me but that they may see***—namely, with a beatifying vision: *When he appears we will be like him, for we will see him as he is* (1 John 3:2). This can be understood to refer to the glory of his human nature after the resurrection: *[He] will change our lowly body to be like his glorious body* (Phil. 3:21), or to the glory of his divine nature, for he is the brightness of the Father's glory and *the very stamp of his nature* (Heb. 1:3), and *a reflection of eternal light* (Wis. 7:26). The saints in glory will see both of these glories. We read about the *first*: *Your eyes will see the king in his beauty* (Isa. 33:17). The wicked will see this glory only at the judgment, *and then they will see the Son of man coming in a cloud with power and great glory* (Luke 21:27); and Mark adds *and glory* (13:26). But the sight of this glory will be taken away from them after the judgment: *The wicked . . . shall not see the glory of the Lord* (Isa. 26:10), as we read in one version. Yet the saints will see the second glory forever: *In your light*, that is, of grace, *do we see light* (Ps. 36:9), that is, of glory, which the wicked will never see. *In his hands*, that is in the proud, *he hides the light. . . . He shows his friend concerning it, that it is his possession, and that he may come up to it* (Job 36:32–33 DRB).

2261 The source of this glory is the Father: so he says, ***which you gave me***. He gave him the glory of his body at the resurrection. Although this still remained to be done, it had already been done in the divine decree; and this is why he says, ***gave***: *You . . . crown him with glory* (Ps. 8:5). But he gave him divine glory from all eternity, because the Son is from the Father from all eternity, like radiance from light.

2262 He gives the explanation for the glory given to him when he says, ***because you loved me before the creation of the world***. If we refer this to Christ in his human nature, then the ***because*** indicates the cause. For just as love and predestination are the cause why we have the radiance of grace in the present life and of glory in the future, for *he chose us in him before the foundation of* *the world* (Eph. 1:4), so also it is the cause of the radiance which Christ has in his human nature, *who was predestinated the Son of God in power* (Rom. 1:4 DRB). So the meaning is this: 'I say that you have given me this radiance: and the cause of this is that you have loved me, ***because you loved me before the creation of the world***.' The result being that this man is united to the Son of God to form one person: *Blessed is he whom you choose and bring near, to dwell in your courts* (Ps. 65:4).

If we refer this to Christ as God, then the ***because*** indicates a sign. For then the Father did not give because he loved: for when we say the Father gave to the Son we are referring to the eternal generation of the Son. If love is taken essentially, it indicates the divine will; if it is taken notionally, it indicates the Holy Spirit. Now it was by nature that the Father gave radiance to the Son, not by his will, because the Father begot the Son by nature. And so he also did not give to the Son because he brought forth the Holy Spirit.

2263 Now he gives the reason why his prayer should be heard. Before, our Lord had included the faithful in his petition when he said, ***Not for them only do I pray, but for those also who through their word will believe in me*** (John 17:20). He also excluded the world and unbelievers when he said, ***I pray for them; I pray not for the world*** (John 17:9). Now he gives the reason for this: *first*, he mentions the failure of the world; *second*, the progress of the disciples: ***but I have known you***.

2264 Note that when he prayed for their sanctification he called the Father ***holy Father*** (John 17:11). But now, calling for retribution, he refers to the Father as just: *God is a just judge* (Ps. 7:12 DRB). This eliminates the old error which said that there was a just God, the God of the Old Testament, and another God who was good, the God of the New Testament.

The failure of the world concerned its knowledge of God. He says, ***the
world***, not as reconciled, but damned, ***has not known you***, as above: ***The world
2265 was made through him, yet the world knew him not*** (John 1:10). But this seems
to conflict with Romans: *What can be known about God is plain to them . . . Ever since the creation of the world his invisible nature, namely, his eternal power and deity, has been clearly perceived in the things that have been made* (1:19–20).

We should say to this that knowledge is of two kinds: one is speculative, and the other affective. Through neither of these ways did the world know God completely. Although some gentiles knew God as having some of those attributes which are knowable by reason, they did not know God as the Father of an only begotten and consubstantial Son, and our Lord is talking about knowledge of these things. Again, if they did have some speculative knowledge of God, this was mixed with many errors: some denied his providence over all things; others said he was the soul of the world; still others worshipped other gods along with him. For this reason they are said not to know God. Composite things can be known in part, and unknown in part, while simple things are unknown if they are not known in their entirety. Thus, even though some erred only slightly in their knowledge of God, they are said to be entirely ignorant of him. Consequently, since these people did not know the special excellence of God, they are said not to know him: *Although they knew God, they did not honor him as God or give thanks to him, but they became futile in their thinking and their senseless minds were darkened* (Rom. 1:21); *nor did they recognize the craftsman while paying heed to his works* (Wis. 13:1).

Furthermore, the world did not know God by an affective knowledge, because it did not love him, *like heathen who do not know God* (1 Thess. 4:5). So he says, ***the world has not known you***, that is, without error, and as a Father, through love.

2266 Then the progress of the disciples is mentioned: ***I have known you: and these have known.*** *First*, their progress in knowledge; *second*, the fruit of this knowledge: ***that the love wherewith you loved me, may be in them, and I in them.***

As regards the disciples' progress in knowledge he does three things: *first*, he gives the root and fountain of this knowledge of God; *second*, the branches and streams that flow from it; *third*, we see their origin in the root or fountain.

2267 The root and fountain of our knowledge of God is the Word of God, that is, Christ: *The Word of God . . . is the fountain of wisdom* (Sir. 1:5 DRB). Human wisdom consists in knowing God. But this knowledge flows to us from the Word, because to the extent that we share in the Word of God, to that extent do we know God. Thus he says, ***the world has not known you*** in this way, ***but I***, the fountain of wisdom, your Word, ***have known you***, eternally and fully: ***If I said I do not know him I should be a liar like you*** (John 8:55).

2268 From this knowledge of the Word, which is the fountain and root, springs, like streams and branches, all the knowledge of the faithful. Accordingly he says, ***and these have known that you sent me.*** Augustine understands the word ***that*** [*quia*] as meaning ***because***, and it then indicates the reason for their knowledge.[23] The meaning is then: ***I have known you***, by nature, ***and these have known*** you by grace. Why? ***Because you sent me***, so that they may know you: ***For this was I born, and for this I have come into the world, to bear witness to the truth*** (John 18:37); ***I have manifested your name*** (John 17:6).

23. Augustine, *Tractates on the Gospel of John* 111.5. Note that the Latin conjunction *quia* can be used to introduce an object clause in the way that we use 'that' in English (e.g. *these have known* ***that*** *you sent me*), but its more predominant use parallels 'because' and introduces an explanatory clause (e.g. *these have known* ***because*** *you sent me*).

If we understand the word ***quia*** as meaning ***that***, it then refers to what is known. The meaning is: ***and these have known***. What do they know? ***That you sent me*** because he who sees the Son also sees the Father (John 14:9).

2269 They did not know this by themselves; they learned it from me because *no one knows the Father except the Son and anyone to whom the Son chooses to reveal him* (Matt. 11:27). So he says, ***I have made known your name to them, and will make it known***. He is indicating the two types of knowledge which the faithful have through him. *First*, is that of doctrine, and he refers to this by saying, ***I have made known to them your name***, teaching them by my external words: ***No one has ever seen God; the only Son, who is in the bosom of the Father, he has made him known*** (John 1:18); *it was declared at first by the Lord, and it was attested to us by those who heard him* (Heb. 2:3).

The other knowledge is from within, through the Holy Spirit. Referring to this he says, ***and I will make it known*** by giving them the Holy Spirit: ***When he, the Spirit of truth, has come, he will teach you all truth*** (John 16:13). Or, alternatively, ***I have made known your name to them*** by the knowledge of faith, *for now we see in a mirror dimly*, ***and will make it known*** through the vision of glory in their homeland, where they will see *face to face* (1 Cor. 13:12).

2270 The fruit of this knowledge is ***that the love wherewith you loved me, may be in them, and I in them***. This can be explained in two ways. The first and better way is that since the Father loves the Son, as is shown by the glory he gave him, consequently, he loves all those in whom the Son is present, and the Son is in them insofar as they have knowledge of the truth. So the meaning is this: ***I will make it***, your name, ***known to them***; and by the fact that they know you, I, your Word, will be in them; and by the fact that I am in them, ***the love wherewith you loved me may be in them***, that is, will be given to them, and you will love them as you have loved me.

Here is the other explanation: ***that the love wherewith you loved me, may be in them***, that is, as you have loved me, so they, by sharing in the Holy Spirit, may love. And by that fact I will be in them as God in a temple, and they in me, as members of the head: *He who abides in love abides in God, and God abides in him* (1 John 4:16).

PART V

WITH HIM

Christian Discipleship and the Mystical Body of Christ

For the Attainment of Heaven

A PRAYER OF THOMAS AQUINAS

God of all consolation,
you who see nothing in us
but what you have given us,
I invoke your help:
after this life has run its course,
grant me
knowledge of you, the first Truth,
and enjoyment of your divine majesty.

O most bountiful rewarder, endow my body
with beauty of splendor,
with swift responsiveness to all commands,
with complete subservience to the spirit,
and with freedom from all vulnerability.

Add to these
an abundance of your riches,
a river of delights,
and a flood of other goods,

So that I may enjoy
your solace above me,
a delightful garden beneath my feet,
the glorification of body and soul within me,
and the sweet companionship
of men and angels around me.

With you, most merciful Father,
may my mind attain
the enlightenment of wisdom,
my desire
what is truly desirable,
and my courage
the praise of triumph.

There, with you, is
refuge from all dangers,
multitude of dwelling places,
and harmony of wills.

There, with you, resides
the cheerfulness of spring,
the brilliance of summer,
the fruitfulness of autumn,
and the gentle repose of winter.

Give me, O Lord my God,
that life without death
and that joy without sorrow,
where there is
the greatest freedom,
unconfined security,
secure tranquility,
delightful happiness,
happy eternity,
eternal blessedness,
the vision of truth,
and praise, O God.

Amen

Chapter 13

THE BEING AND MISSION OF CHRIST'S CHURCH

Matthew 16:13–19

"Upon This Rock"

Christ Founds His Church

On Matthew 16.2 (1368–1393)

16:13 ***And Jesus came into the regions of Caesarea Philippi and he asked his disciples, saying, "Who do men say that the Son of man is?"***

16:14 ***But they said, "Some John the Baptist, and others Elijah, and others Jeremiah, or one of the prophets."***

16:15 ***Jesus says to them, "But who do you say that I am?"***

16:16 ***Simon Peter answered and said, "You are the Christ, the Son of the living God."***

16:17 ***And Jesus answering, said to him, "Blessed are you, Simon Bar-Jonah, because flesh and blood have not revealed this to you, but my Father who is in heaven.***

16:18 ***And I say to you that you are Peter; and upon this rock I will build my Church, and the gates of hell will not prevail against it.***

16:19 ***And I will give to you the keys of the kingdom of heaven. And whatever you bind on earth will be bound also in heaven, and whatever you loose on earth will be loosed also in heaven."***

1368 Above, the Lord taught that the evangelical teaching is to be preserved pure from the leaven of the Jews; and here he teaches the loftiness of the teaching.[1] And *first*, as regards faith in both natures, namely the deity and the humanity; *second*, as regards faith in the passion, at ***From that time Jesus began to show to his disciples*** (Matt. 16:20); *third*, as regards faith in the judiciary power, at ***The Son of man will come in the glory of his Father*** (Matt 16:27).

1. See Matthew 16:6 and Thomas Aquinas, *On Matthew* 16.1 (not included in this collection).

Concerning the *first*: *first*, the crowds' opinion about Christ is sought out; *second*, the disciples' faith, at ***Who do you say that I am?***

Concerning the *first*: *first*, the place is set down; *second*, Christ's questioning, at ***Who do men say that the Son of man is?***; *third*, Peter's response, at ***but they said.***

1369 It says then, ***Jesus came into the quarters of Caesarea Philippi***; and not only this, but he added ***Philippi***, because there were two Caesareas, namely Caesarea Traconis, where Peter was sent to Cornelius, and this other one, which is otherwise called Paneas. The first was established by Herod, in honor of Caesar Augustus; Philip constructed this one in honor of Tiberius.

But why did the Lord ask this question here? One should say that this city was situated on the borders of the Jews; so before he wished to ask for faith, he took them out from the Jews. A similar thing is written that the Lord, when he was leading the Jews from Egypt, did not lead them through the land of the Philistines (Exod. 13:17).

1370 Next, the questioning is set down: ***He asked his disciples.*** When the wise man asks, he teaches, as Jerome says.[2] Hence we are instructed in many places that we should be concerned about what is said about us: so that if it is bad, we may correct it, and if it is good, we may preserve and multiply it. Hence, *Have regard for your name, since it will remain for you longer than a thousand great stores of gold* (Sir. 41:12). Hence Christ asked what was said about him. Likewise, those who know the divinity are called gods, *I say, "you are gods"* (Ps. 82:6), but those who know the humanity are called men; hence he says, ***Who do men say that the Son of man is?*** But, as Hilary says, Christ seemed to be only a man, so he willed that they should know that he was something other than a simple man.[3] Hence he himself gives one to understand by this that there is something else in him. Also, Christ's humility is shown, because he confesses himself to be the Son of man, in accord with that above, ***Learn from me, because I am meek, and humble of heart*** (Matt. 11:29).

1371 Next, the opinion of the crowds is set down: ***They said, "Some John the Baptist."*** Different ones felt different things about Christ. The Pharisees blasphemed Christ, but the crowds said he was a prophet; hence, *a great prophet is risen up among us* (Luke 7:16). For they called him John by reason of authority, since John preached penance: ***Do penance, for the kingdom of heaven is at hand*** (Matt. 3:2). So they thought he was John, since Christ began in a similar way: ***Do penance, for the kingdom of heaven is at hand*** (Matt. 4:17).

---

2. This appears to be a misattribution. Elsewhere (*Summa theologiae* 3.12.3 and *Catena Aurea on Luke* 2.13) St. Thomas ascribes a similar quote to Origen (*Homilies on Luke* 19.6), who says of Christ, "He interrogated the teachers not to learn anything, but to teach them by his questions."

3. Hilary of Poitiers, *Commentary on Matthew* 16.6.

Likewise, they held Elijah the Prophet in reverence; *I will send you Elijah the prophet before the great and terrible day of the Lord comes* (Mal. 4:5). Hence they thought him to be Elijah, because of the power of his word and the virtue of his preaching; *the prophet Elijah arose like a fire, and his word burned like a torch* (Sir. 48:1). And it is said of Christ, above, that ***he was teaching them as one having power*** (Matt. 7:29).

Also, on account of loftiness of life, they thought him to be Jeremiah, of whom the Lord said, *Before I formed you in the womb I knew you, and before you were born I consecrated you* (Jer. 1:5). And in the same book, it says that he was honored among the gentiles (Jer. 40). In this same way, Christ was held in reverence by outsiders, but was blasphemed by the Jews. So they compared him to Jeremiah.

But how did they call him Elijah? Because it is said that he was taken up, and that he was still alive (2 Kings 2:11) and was promised to the Jews for salvation (Mal. 4:5). For some posited transcorporation, and so according to this opinion it could have been that Elijah's soul entered another body.

1372 ***Jesus says to them, "But who do you say that I am?*** Here the disciples' faith is sought out. And *first*, the questioning is set down; *second*, the response; *third*, the approval. The *second* is at ***Simon Peter answered***; the *third*, at ***and Jesus answering.***

1373 ***Jesus says to them, "But who do you say that I am?"*** as though to say: 'so the crowds say, but since more is entrusted to you, more is required of you. You have seen miracles, so you should suppose more.'

But why did he ask? Did not he know? Indeed he knew, but he willed that they should merit by confession; *for with the heart, we believe unto justice; but with the mouth, confession is made unto salvation* (Rom. 10:10). For things are more meritorious the more they are separated off, and, as it were, the greater things are not suited to the crowd, which knows the lowest things.

1374 ***Simon Peter answered and said, "You are the Christ, the Son of the living God."*** He responds for himself and for the others; but he himself responds more frequently, and in this response perfect faith is touched upon, for faith in the humanity is touched upon. ***You are the Christ,*** i.e., the anointed one. And it is agreed that he is anointed with the oil of the Holy Spirit. Anointing does not belong to him according to the divinity, because it proceeds from it, but according to the humanity. So he says this that they might regard the humanity of Christ in a way different from the crowds.

But it is asked why they called him a prophet. A prophet was anointed, as is written of Elisha. Kings were anointed, as is written of Saul. Likewise, priests, as is written in Leviticus. And all these things are brought in by the name ***Christ***.[4] For he is called a king, as in Jeremiah: *He shall reign as king and deal wisely* (23:5). Also a priest: *You are a priest forever after the order of Melchisedech* (Ps. 110:4). And also a prophet: *The Lord your God will raise up for you a prophet like me from among you, from your brethren* (Deut. 18:15).

1375 And Peter did not just confess the humanity, but piercing through the outer shell, he climbed up even to the divinity, saying, ***you are . . . the Son of the living God***. For others said that he blasphemed; hence *It is not for a good work that we stone you but for blasphemy; because you, being a man, make yourself God* (John 10:33). But this man recognized the Son of God.

And he says, ***living***, to exclude the error of the gentiles, who called certain dead men gods, such as Jove. Likewise, some held as gods the elements and other dead things, like earth, fire, etc. (Wis. 13:2); but this man calls him ***the Son of the living God***.

But one should know that when he is called ***the living God*** and a living man, living is said of the man through participation in life, but it is said of God because he is the fount of life: *With you is the fountain of life* (Ps. 36:9). And, *I am the way, and the truth, and the life* (John 14:6).

1376 ***And Jesus answering***. Here *first*, he approves his confession; *second*, he commands silence, at ***He charged the disciples to tell no one that he was the Christ*** (Matt. 16:20).

Concerning the *first*: *first*, he approves this confession by praising the one who confessed; *second*, by a reward, at ***I say to you that you are Peter and upon***
1377 ***this rock I will build my Church***. Hence it says, ***Jesus answering, said to him, "Blessed are you, Simon Bar-Jonah."*** 'Bar' is the same as 'son'; 'Jonah' is the same as 'dove,' his name. Hence ***Bar-Jonah***, i.e., son of the dove.

And Christ's response seems to correspond to Peter's confession. For he had confessed him to be the Son of God, and Jesus calls him the son of the dove, namely of the Holy Spirit, for this confession could only have come about by the Holy Spirit. But it is thought that it was said ***Bar-Jonah*** at first, i.e., son of John, but then was said in this way by a corruption of the Scripture.

1378 But what is this? Did not others confess him to be the Son of God? Indeed, it is written of Nathaniel (John 1:49). Likewise, those who were in the boat, above (Matt. 9). Why then is Peter blessed here, and not the others? Because the others confessed him to be an adoptive son, but this man confessed him to be the natural Son; therefore this one is blessed before the others, because he first confessed the divinity.

4. A key to understanding the point that St. Thomas is making here is that each of these prophets, in some sense, were *christs* insomuch as "christ," from the Greek *christos*, simply means *anointed*.

Origen says, *It seems that it had not been confessed before.*[5] But how did he send them to preach? He responds that they did not preach that he was the Christ from the beginning, but preached penance. Also, it could be that they preached Christ, but this man first confessed that he was the Son of God. Therefore he rewards this man especially.

1379 ***Blessed are you, Simon***, because he is blessed in knowledge; *and this is eternal life: that they know you the only true God* (John 17:3). But there are two kinds of knowledge: there is one which comes through natural reason, and another which is above reason. The first does not make for blessedness, because there is doubt, and hence it does not satisfy the intellect; but blessedness should satisfy the natural appetite, and this shall be had in the homeland. *The eye has not seen, O God, besides you, what things you have prepared for those who wait for you* (Isa. 64:4). Therefore in this life, someone is more blessed to the degree that he is more able to perceive of this knowledge; *blessed is the man who finds wisdom* (Prov. 3:13 DRB). Hence he says, ***blessed are you***, because you begin to be blessed.

1380 ***Because flesh and blood have not revealed this to you.*** This can be explained in such a way that flesh and blood are taken for carnal friends; *I did not confer with flesh and blood* (Gal. 1:16). Hence ***flesh and blood has not revealed this to you***, i.e., you did not get it from the Jews' traditions, but from God's revelation. Likewise, in Christ there was flesh and blood and divinity; therefore, since Peter did not focus on the flesh and blood, it is said to him, ***blessed are you***, because you do not judge according as flesh and blood reveal, but according as my Father reveals. Or, you do not have this knowledge from natural diligence, but from my Father, for *no one knows who the Son is, except the Father* (Luke 10:22). For it is his to reveal, whose it is to know. Hence no one knows the Son except the one to whom the Father wills to reveal him; *there is a God in heaven who reveals mysteries* (Dan. 2:28).

1381 ***And I say to you that you are Peter.*** Here he gives a reward for the confession. He had confessed the humanity and the divinity, so the Lord gives a reward. *First*, he gives a name; *second*, a power.

Concerning the *first*: *first*, he gives a name; *second*, the reason for the name,
1382 at ***and upon this rock I will build my Church.*** And I came into the world for this, to found a church. *I am laying in Zion for a foundation a stone, a tested stone, a precious cornerstone, of a sure foundation* (Isa. 28:16). This was signified by the stone which Jacob put beneath his head and oiled (Gen. 28:18). This stone is Christ, and from this anointing all are called Christians; hence we are not only called Christians from Christ, but from the rock. For this reason, he specially imposes a name: ***You are Peter***, from the rock which is Christ.

5. Origen, *Commentary on Matthew* 12.15.

Although, according to Augustine, it might seem that it was not imposed now, but from the beginning: *You shall be called Cephas* (John 1:42).[6] Or it can be said that it was promised then and given here.

1383 As a sign of this thing, ***Upon this rock I will build my Church.*** It is a property of the rock that it is placed in the foundation; also, that it gives firmness. Above, ***Everyone . . . who hears these words of mine and does them will be like a wise man who built his house upon the rock*** (Matt. 7:24).

Hence it can be explained as about Christ: ***and upon this rock***, i.e., on Christ, that he might be the foundation, and that the thing founded might receive a support. Augustine says in the book of *Retractions* that he explained it in many ways and left it to the hearers to accept what they would.[7] Or, to demonstrate that ***this rock*** means Christ: *The rock was Christ* (1 Cor. 10:4). And in another place, *No other foundation can anyone lay, but that which is laid, which is Christ Jesus* (1 Cor. 3:11).

Another explanation: ***upon this rock***, i.e., upon you, Peter, because from me, the rock, you receive that you are a rock. And just as I am a rock, so upon
1384 you, Peter, I will build my Church. But what is this? Are both Christ and Peter the foundation?

One should say that Christ is the foundation through himself, but Peter insofar as he holds the confession of Christ, insofar as he is his vicar. *The household of God [is] built upon the foundation of the apostles and prophets, Jesus Christ himself being the chief corner stone* (Eph. 2:19–20). *And the wall of the city had twelve foundations, and on them the twelve names of the twelve apostles of the Lamb* (Rev. 21:14). So Christ is the foundation through himself, but the apostles are the foundation not through themselves, but by Christ's permission, and by the authority given by Christ; *the foundations thereof are in the holy mountains* (Ps. 87:1 DRB). But especially Peter's house, which is founded upon the rock, shall not be destroyed (Matt. 7:25). Thus it can be attacked but cannot be conquered.

1385 ***And the gates of hell will not prevail against it.*** *They will fight against you but they shall not prevail* (Jer. 1:19). And who are the gates of hell? Heretics, because just as one enters into a house through a gate, so one enters into hell through these. Also tyrants, demons, sins. And although other churches can be reproached for heretics, yet the Roman Church was not corrupted by heretics, because it was founded upon the rock. Hence there were heretics in Constantinople, and the apostles' labor was lost; only Peter's Church remained inviolate. Hence, *I have prayed for you, that your faith fail not* (Luke 22:32). And this does not only refer to Peter's Church, but to Peter's faith, and to the whole

6. Augustine, *Agreement among the Evangelists* 2.17.

7. Augustine, *Revisions* 1.21.1.

western Church. Hence I believe that those in the west owe more reverence to Peter than to the other apostles.

1386 ***And I will give to you the keys of the kingdom of heaven.*** Here is set down the second gift which Christ, according to his humanity, gave to Peter. For he founded a Church on earth, and established Peter as his vicar, that he might lead into heaven; *we have confidence to enter the sanctuary by the blood of Jesus* (Heb. 10:19). For Christ established Peter as his vicar, that he might lead others into heaven, for which reason he gave him that ministry; hence he gave the keys. For keys lead one in; hence Peter has the ministry of leading in. And he does two things: *first*, he entrusts the keys; *second*, he teaches their use: ***and whatever you bind on earth will be bound also in heaven***.

1387 But let us see what the keys are. When a house is locked, it obstructs entry; but a key removes the obstacle. The kingdom of heaven had an obstacle, but not on its own part; *I looked, and behold a door was opened in heaven* (Rev. 4:1 DRB), but the obstacle was on our part, namely, sin, because *nothing unclean shall enter it* (Rev. 21:27). Christ removed this impediment by his passion because *he freed us from our sins by his blood* (Rev. 1:5). And he communicated this so that sins might be removed through a ministry, which is completed by the strength of Christ's blood. Hence the sacraments have strength from the strength of Christ's passion. Hence I will give to you a ministry. *I will place on his shoulder the key of the house of David; he shall open, and none shall shut; he shall shut, and none shall open* (Isa. 22:22).

But he says, ***I will give to you***, for the keys were not yet made; and a thing cannot be given before it exists. Now, they were made in the passion, hence their efficacy came in the passion. Hence he promised them here, but gave them after the passion, when he said, *Feed my sheep* (John 21:17).

1388 But why does he say ***keys***? Because to absolve is to remove an obstacle. For there are two keys, since two things are required, power and knowledge. But what is this? Are there not some priests who do not have knowledge? Understand that they have knowledge, because no one has the key of knowledge except priests. Knowledge here does not mean a habit of the intellect, but the authority of discerning. Hence there is a judge who does not have knowledge in the first way, and yet has knowledge in the second way, because he has authority; and there is someone who has knowledge in the first way, and not the second way, because he has no authority. Hence knowledge here means the authority of discerning, and any priest has this, so he may discern in absolving.

1389 Next, he sets down the use of the keys: ***Whatever you bind on earth will be bound also in heaven.*** But it seems that this is set down unfittingly, because a key is not used to bind, but to open. I say that this is a fitting use of a key. For heaven itself is open: *I looked, and behold a door was opened in heaven* (Rev. 4:1 DRB).

Hence it is not necessary that it be opened; rather, the bond of him who should enter must be loosed.

1390 But here some errors should be avoided. The *first* is touched upon in the *Gloss*, for some have claimed that anyone who wished could absolve, and lead others into the kingdom of heaven. But this cannot stand, because it belongs to God alone to change desires.

Another error is that the priest does not bind, but merely points out that a sin is absolved. But this takes away from the strength of the sacrament, because the sacraments of the new law effect what they figure; but the sacraments of the old law did not. Hence if it effected nothing, it would not be a sacrament of the new law.

Third, some say that there are three things in sin: guilt, liability, and punishment. A man is absolved *per se* from two of these by contrition; but when a man is absolved from these, he remains bound to a temporal punishment, which a man cannot take away and avoid of himself. Therefore the keys are given, which reduce something of this punishment, and bind as regards some punishment.

Yet it seems to me that this is not well said, because a sacrament of the new law gives grace, and grace is not ordered against punishment but against guilt. Hence I say that in the sacrament of confession, just as in the sacrament of baptism, there is a spiritual, instrumental strength, according to which it cleanses from guilt. Hence Augustine: *What is water's strength, that it washes off the body and takes away guilt?*[8] Thus I say that in a priest there is a certain spiritual, instrumental strength, from which he is called a 'minister,' and thus he works the remission of sins ministerially, just as water works baptism.

1391 But here a difficulty arises, because at the present time only children come to baptism. And if an adult were to approach, he would come either falsely, or not: he would come falsely if he came without a renewal of the mind, and then guilt would not be remitted; he would not come falsely if he came with the intention of confession. Hence grace is required, or the intention of conversion, which is from grace. Now, grace takes away guilt. Hence in the sacrament of baptism, when an adult comes, if he prepares himself, he receives the remission of guilt. Thus in the sacrament of penance, to which only adults come, a man is not contrite unless he has the intention of subjecting himself to the discretion and judgment of a priest. If he is not contrite, the effect will not follow, just as neither in baptism. But it can happen that someone approaches not entirely contrite and is made contrite by virtue of the grace received in the perfect sacrament; therefore one should understand, ***whatever you loose***, i.e., if you use the ministry of absolution. And he says, ***whatever*** because not only

8. Augustine, *Tractates on the Gospel of John* 80.3.

guilt, but punishment is loosed. ***Will be loosed also in heaven***, i.e., it will be held as loosed in heaven, just as it is with baptism. Hence the priest should say, *I absolve you*, just as he says, *I baptize you*.

1392 But someone can ask how he binds. One should know that the priest is a minister of God, and the action of the minister depends on the Lord's action. Hence in the same way the Lord binds and looses, so the priests do ministerially. The Lord looses by pouring in grace and binds by not pouring in: in the same way, the priest looses by the sacrament, by administering the sacrament, but binds by not giving it.

In another way, it is said that the present Church is designated by the heavens; hence ***whatever you bind*** by excommunication, or ***loose***, will be loosed or bound as regards the administration of the Church's sacraments. Hence they would have it that this administration, this binding and loosing, is on earth, so that it does not extend to the dead.

But this is refuted, because it extends not only to the living, but even to the dead. Hence if it is referred to both, the sense is: ***whatever you bind upon earth***, at that time, I say, being on earth, ***will be bound also in heaven***.

1393 But there is another question, because it is written in another place, *whose sins you forgive, they are forgiven them* (John 20:23), but here he says this only to Peter.

One should say that he gave it to Peter immediately, but the others receive from Peter. For this reason, lest they believe that this is said only to Peter, he says, *whose sins you forgive* (John 20:23). And for this reason the Pope, who is in the place of holy Peter, has full power, but the others have power from him.

Colossians 1:18–23

Christ's Headship Over His Mystical Body

On Colossians 1.5 (45–57)

1:18 ***And he is the head of the body, the church, who is the beginning, the firstborn from the dead, that in all things he may hold the primacy:***

1:19 ***Because in him, it has well pleased the Father that all fullness should dwell:***

1:20 ***And through him to reconcile all things unto himself, making peace through the blood of his cross, both as to the things that are on earth and the things that are in heaven.***

1:21 ***And you, whereas you were some time alienated and enemies in mind in evil works:***

1:22 ***Yet now he has reconciled in the body of his flesh through death, to present you holy and unspotted and blameless before him:***

1:23 ***If you so continue in the faith, grounded and stable, and immoveable from the hope of the Gospel which you have heard, which is preached in all the creation that is under heaven, whereof I Paul am made a minister.***

45 After the Apostle commended Christ in his relationship to God and to all creatures, he here commends him in his relationship to the Church: *first*, in a general way;[9] *second*, in particular, in reference to the Colossians, at ***and you, whereas you were some time alienated***; and *third*, in reference to himself, at ***whereof I Paul am made a minister.***

In regard to the *first* he does two things: *first*, he mentions Christ's relationship to the entire Church; and *second*, he explains this relationship, at ***who is the beginning.***

46 He says, therefore, that Christ, the firstborn among creatures, is the one in whom we have our redemption.[10] But because he has been made the head of the Church, two things have to be explained: *first*, in what way the Church is a body; and *second*, how Christ is its head.

9. See Colossians 1:15–17 and Thomas Aquinas, *On Colossians* 1.4 (not included in this collection).

10. Thomas alludes here to Col. 1:15.

The Church is called a body because of its likeness to a single human being. This likeness is twofold: *first,* in that it has distinct members: *His gifts were that some should be apostles, some prophets, some evangelists, some pastors and teachers* (Eph. 4:11); *second,* because the members of the Church serve each other in ways that are different: *The members . . . have the same care for one another* (1 Cor. 12:25); *bear one another's burdens, and so fulfill the law of Christ* (Gal. 6:2). Again, just as a body is one because its soul is one, so the Church is one because the Spirit is one: *There is one body and one Spirit* (Eph. 4:4); *because there is one bread, we who are many are one body, for we all partake of the one bread* (1 Cor. 10:17). Next we have to consider the relationship of the members to the head of the Church, i.e., to Christ. For Christ is the head of the Church. *You, O Lord . . . are the lifter of my head* (Ps. 3:3).

47 He explains what it means to be a head, saying, ***who is the beginning, the firstborn from the dead.*** The head has three privileges over the other members of the body. *First,* it is superior in dignity, because it is a source and a ruler. *Second,* it has the fullness of the senses, which are all in the head. *Third,* it is the source of an inflow of sense and movement to the members of the body. So *first,* Paul shows how Christ is head because of his dignity; *second,* because of the fullness of his grace, at ***because in him, it has well pleased***; and *third,* because of an inflow from him, at ***and through him to reconcile.***

48 The Church exists in two states: the state of grace in the present time, and the state of glory in the future. But it is the same Church, and Christ is its head in both states, because he is the first in grace and the first in glory.

With respect to the *first* he says, ***who is the beginning,*** because he is not only first in grace insofar as he is a man, but all men are justified by faith in Christ: *By one man's obedience many will be made righteous* (Rom. 5:19). So he says, ***who is the beginning,*** that is, the beginning or source of justification and grace in the entire Church; because even in the Old Testament some were justified by faith in Christ: *[I am] the beginning, who also speak unto you* (John 8:25 DRB); *before the daystar I begot you* (Ps. 110:3).

Christ is also the beginning of the state of glory; and so he says, ***the firstborn from the dead.*** The reason for this is that the resurrection from the dead is a kind of second birth, because it restores us to eternal life: *In the regeneration, when the Son of man sits on the seat of his majesty* (Matt. 19:28 DRB); but Christ is the first of all; and thus he is ***the firstborn from the dead***, that is, the firstborn of those who are born by the resurrection.

49 But what about Lazarus (John 11)? I answer that he and some others did not rise to the above-mentioned immortal life, but to a mortal life; but *Christ, being raised from the dead, will never die again* (Rom. 6:9); *Jesus Christ . . . the firstborn of the dead, and the ruler of kings on earth* (Rev. 1:5); *Christ has been*

raised from the dead, the first fruits of those who have fallen asleep (1 Cor. 15:20). And this is so ***that in all things he might hold the primacy***: pre-eminent in the gifts of grace, because he is the beginning; and pre-eminent in the gifts of glory, because he is the firstborn: *In every people and nation I have gotten a possession* (Sir. 24:6).[11]

50 Then, he shows the dignity of the head with respect to the fullness of all graces. For some saints had particular graces, but Christ had all graces; and so he says, ***because in him, it has well pleased the Father that all fullness should dwell.***

Each word has its own force. ***Pleased*** indicates that the gifts Christ had as man were not the result of fate or merits, as Photinus says, but were due to the good pleasure of the divine will taking this man into a unity of person: *This is my beloved Son, with whom I am well pleased* (Matt. 3:17). He says, ***all,*** because some have one gift and others different ones; *the Father had given all things into his hands* (John 13:3).

He says, ***fullness,*** because one can have a gift without having the fullness of it or of its power, because perhaps one lacks something unwillingly. But John says that Christ was *full of grace and truth* (1:14); *my abode is in the full assembly of saints* (Sir. 24:12 DRB).

He says, ***to dwell,*** because some received the use of a grace for only a time; thus the spirit of prophecy was not always possessed by the prophets, but it is continuously present in Christ, because he always has control over this fullness to use it as he wishes: *He on whom you see the Spirit descend and remain, this is he who baptizes with the Holy Spirit* (John 1:33).

51 Then when he says, ***and through him***, he shows that Christ is the head of the Church because of an inflow from him. And this is the *third* characteristic of a head. *First,* he shows the inflow of grace; and *second*, he explains it, at ***making peace.***

52 He says, therefore: I say that it pleased God not only that this fullness exist in Christ, but that it also flow from Christ to us; and so he says, ***and through him to reconcile all things unto himself***: *In Christ God was reconciling the world to himself* (2 Cor. 5:19).

53 He mentions the nature of this reconciliation and how all things are reconciled. Now there are two things to be considered in a reconciliation. *First,* the matters in which the reconciled persons agree. For people at odds have conflicting wills, but when they have been reconciled, they agree in some things;

11. Given Thomas' emphasis on the Christ's character as firstborn (following the theme of Col. 1:15), it is possible that the passage he intended here was not Sir. 24:6 but Sir. 24:5 (which he quotes in his commentary on Col. 1:15) where divine wisdom is described as *the firstborn before all creatures* (DRB).

and so wills that were before in conflict are made to harmonize in Christ. For example, the wills of men, of God, and of the angels. The will of men, because Christ is a man; and the will of God, because Christ is God. There was also conflict between the Jews, who wanted the law, and the gentiles, who did not want the law. But Christ created harmony between the two, because he was from the Jews, and he freed us from the legal observances.

This harmony was accomplished ***through the blood of his cross***. The cause of discord between God and men was sin; the discord between the Jews and the gentiles was caused by the law. Now Christ destroyed sin by his cross and fulfilled the law; and thus he took away the causes of discord: *You have come to Mount Zion and to the city of the living God, the heavenly Jerusalem* (Heb. 12:22). Thus we are reconciled, and all things are set at peace, ***both as to the things that are on earth***, that is, Jews and gentiles, ***and the things that are in heaven***, that is, the angels and God. And so when Christ was born the angels sang: *Glory to God in the highest, and on earth peace among men* (Luke 2:14). Again, Christ said at his resurrection: *Peace be with you* (John 20:19); *for he is our peace, who has made us both one* (Eph. 2:14).

54 Then when he says, ***and you, whereas you were some time alienated***, Christ is commended because of the gifts he gave them. *First*, Paul recalls their past condition; *second*, Christ's gift, at ***yet now***; and *third*, what they have to do now, at ***if you so continue***.

55 Their past condition had three evils: in their intellect, they were ignorant; in their affections, they were enemies of justice; and in their actions, they committed many sins.

In regard to the *first* he says, ***alienated***. In regard to the *second*, ***and enemies in mind***, according to the reading of one version. This shows that there was a defect in that wisdom that the Jews proclaimed about the one God: *Men loved darkness rather than light* (John 3:19). But were the Jewish people bound to the law of Moses? Yes, they were, so far as it concerned the worship of the one God. Or, we could say the Jews were ***alienated in mind***, i.e., by choice, maliciously contradicting God: *They turned aside from following him* (Job 34:27). As to the *third* evil of their past condition he says, ***in evil works***: *Their deeds were evil* (John 3:19).

56 Then when he says, ***yet now***, he mentions the benefits coming from Christ. The *first* of these is reconciliation in his body. He says, ***in the body of his flesh***, not because his body and his flesh are not the same, but to show that Christ took a real body: *The Word became flesh and dwelt among us* (John 1:14). A body of flesh, that is, a mortal body: *God . . . sending his own Son in the likeness of sinful flesh and for sin, he condemned sin in the flesh* (Rom. 8:3). The *second* benefit coming from Christ is holiness; thus he says, ***to present you holy***: *So Jesus*

also suffered outside the gate in order to sanctify the people through his own blood (Heb. 13:12). The *third* benefit is their cleansing from sin; and as to this he says, ***and unspotted***: *The blood of Christ, who through the eternal Spirit offered himself without blemish to God, purifies your conscience from dead works* (Heb. 9:14).

Looking to the future he says, ***and blameless***: *Be zealous to be found by him without spot or blemish and at peace* (2 Pet. 3:14). And he adds, ***before him***: *Man looks on the outward appearance, but the Lord looks on the heart* (1 Sam. 16:7).

57 What God requires of us is that we be firm in faith and hope. And so Paul continues, ***if you so continue in the faith, grounded***. For faith is a foundation; if it is firm, the entire structure of the Church is firm. ***And stable*** in hope, not weakening themselves from within; ***and immoveable***, by not allowing others to shake that hope. ***From the hope***, I say, that is ***of the Gospel***, namely, the hope that the Gospel gives for the good things of the kingdom of heaven: *Repent, for the kingdom of heaven is at hand* (Matt. 4:17). And there is no excuse, because the Gospel has been ***preached***; and he uses the past tense here instead of the future tense because this future event is so certain. The Gospel has been preached, by the apostles that is, ***in all the creation that is under heaven***, that is, to every new creature, that is, to the faithful, for whom it had been prepared.

Romans 12:4–13

The Members of Christ's Mystical Body

On Romans 12.2 (972–995)

12:4 ***For as in one body we have many members, but all the members have not the same act:***

12:5 ***So we, being many, are one body in Christ; and everyone members one of another:***

12:6 ***And having different gifts, according to the grace that is given us, either prophecy, to be used according to the rule of faith;***

12:7 ***or ministry, in ministering; or he who teaches, in doctrine;***

12:8 ***he who exhorts, in exhorting; he who contributes, in simplicity; he who rules, in carefulness; he who does acts of mercy, in cheerfulness.***

12:9 ***Let love be without dissimulation. Hating evil, cleaving to good,***

12:10 ***loving one another with the charity of brotherhood; with honor anticipating one another;***

12:11 ***in carefulness, not slothful; in spirit, fervent; serving the Lord;***

12:12 ***rejoicing in hope; patient in tribulation; constant in prayer;***

12:13 ***communicating to the necessities of the saints; pursuing hospitality.***

972 After this admonition the Apostle assigns a reason based on the mystical body's likeness to a natural body.[12] *First*, he touches on three things in a natural body; *first*, its unity when he says: ***for as in one body***; *second*, the multiplicity of members when he says: ***We have many members***; for the human body is an organism consisting of various members; *third*, the variety of functions when he says: ***All the members do not have the same act***. For the variety of members would serve no purpose unless they were ordered to different functions.

973 Then he likens these three aspects to the mystical body of Christ, which is the Church: *He . . . has made him the head over all things for the Church, which is his body* (Eph. 1:22). Concerning which he touches on three things.

12. See Romans 12:1–2 and Thomas Aquinas, *On Romans* 12.1 (not included in this collection).

First, he touches on the number of members, i.e., of believers when he says: ***so we, being many***: *A man once gave a great banquet and invited many* (Luke 14:16); *many are the children of the desolate* (Isa. 54:1). For although they are few compared to the unfruitful multitude of the damned, according to Matthew, *The gate is narrow and the way is hard that leads to life, and those who find it are few* (7:14), yet absolutely speaking, they are many: *Behold, a great multitude which no man could number* (Rev. 7:9).

974 *Second*, he touches on the unity of the mystical body when he says ***we are one body***: *that he might create in himself one new man in place of the two, so making peace and might reconcile us both to God in one body through the cross* (Eph. 2:16). This mystical body has a spiritual unity through which we are united to one another and to God by faith and love: *There is one body and one spirit* (Eph. 4:4). And because the Spirit of unity flows into us from Christ—***anyone who does not have the Spirit of Christ does not belong to him*** (Rom. 8:9)—he adds ***in Christ***, who unites us to one another and to God by his Spirit whom he gives us: *That they may be one even as we are one* (John 18:22).

975 *Third*, he touches on the variety of functions, which are rooted in the common utility, when he says: ***and everyone members one of another***. For any given member has its own function and power. Therefore, inasmuch as the function and power of one member aids another, it is said to be the other's member; thus, the foot is called the eye's member, inasmuch as it carries the eye, and the eye is called the foot's member, inasmuch as it directs the foot: *The eye cannot say to the hand, 'I have no need of you'* (1 Cor. 12:21).

So, too, in the mystical body one who has received the gift of prophecy needs the one who has received the gift of healing, and so on for all the others. Hence, as long as each believer uses the grace given him to help another, he becomes the other's member: *Bear one another's burdens* (Gal. 6:2); *as each has received a gift, employ it for one another* (1 Pet. 4:10).

976 Then when he says, ***having gifts***, he explains in more detail the previous general admonition to use grace in a sober and moderate way. *First*, he sets out the variety of graces: ***we are***, I say, ***members one of another***, not on account of the same grace, but by ***having different gifts***; and this is not due to differing merits but ***according to the grace given to us***: *Each has his own special gift from God, one of one kind and another of another* (1 Cor. 7:7); *[he] called his servants and entrusted to them his property; to one he gave five talents, to another two, to another one* (Matt. 25:14).

977 *Second*, he touches on the use of different graces, and *first* with respect to knowledge of divine things, saying: ***if prophecy***, the one among us who has it should use it ***according to the rule of faith***.

978 ***Prophecy*** is a kind of apparition arising from the divine revelation of things far remote. Hence it is said in 1 Samuel: *He who is now called a prophet was formerly called a seer* (9:9). Among matters far remote from our knowledge some are remote of their very nature, as future contingents, which are not knowable, because their causes are indeterminate; but divine matters are remote from our knowledge not of their very nature, for they are knowable in the highest degree, because *God is light and in him is no darkness* (1 John 1:5), but on account of the weakness of our intellect, which is related to matters most evident as the eye of an owl to sunlight. And because something is said to be thus and so in a truer sense, when it is thus and so on its own account rather than on account of something else, future contingents are in a truer sense said to be far from our knowledge. For this reason they are the proper concern of prophecy: *Surely the Lord God does nothing without revealing his secret to his servants the prophets* (Amos 3:7). But prophecy in a general sense includes the revelation of any secret things.

This gift of prophecy existed not only in the Old Testament but in the New as well: *I will pour out my spirit on all flesh; your sons and daughters shall prophesy* (Joel 2:28). In the New Testament those who explained prophetic statements were also called prophets, because Sacred Scripture is explained in the same spirit as it is written: *I will again pour out teaching like prophecy* (Sir. 24:33).

979 The gift of prophecy, as all the other charismatic graces, is ordained to the building up of faith: *To each is given the manifestation of the Spirit for the common good* (1 Cor. 12:7); *it was declared*, i.e., the doctrine of faith, *by the Lord, while God also bore witness by signs and wonders and various miracles and by gifts of the Holy Spirit* (Heb. 2:3–4). Consequently, prophecy should be used ***according to the rule of faith***, i.e., not in vain but in order that faith be strengthened, not opposed, by it: *If a prophet arises among you . . . . and if he says, "let us go after other gods," . . . you shall not listen to the words of that prophet* (Deut. 13:1–3), because he is not prophesying in proportion to the faith.

980 In regard to administering the sacraments he adds: ***or ministry, in ministering***, i.e., if one has received the grace or office of the ministry, such as the bishop or priest who are called God's ministers—*You shall be called the priests of the Lord . . . the ministers of our God* (Isa. 56:6)—let him perform his office diligently ***in ministering***: *Fulfill your ministry* (2 Tim. 4:5).

981 *Second*, he touches on matters pertinent to human affairs in which one person can help another: *first*, with respect to knowledge both speculative and practical. With respect to speculative knowledge he says: ***or he who teaches***, i.e., who has the office or grace of teaching, let him use it ***in teaching***, i.e., teach diligently and faithfully: *You have instructed many* (Job 4:3); *go, therefore, and teach all nations* (Matt. 28:19 DRB).

With respect to practical knowledge he says: ***he who exhorts***, i.e., has the office and grace of exhorting, let him use it ***in exhorting***: *Our appeal does not spring from error or uncleanness, nor is it made with guile* (1 Thess. 2:3); *declare these things; exhort with all authority* (Titus 2:15).

982 Then he mentions those that pertain to external works in which a person sometimes helps another by giving a gift. In this regard he says, ***he who contributes***, i.e., has the power and grace to contribute, should do this ***in simplicity***, namely, with no evil ulterior motive, such as enticing men to evil with gifts, and with no intention of obtaining a great deal more from the small amount given: *A fool's gift will profit you nothing, for he has many eyes instead of one. He gives little and upbraids much* (Sir. 20:14–15); *the simplicity of the just shall guide them* (Prov. 11:3 DRB).

Sometimes one helps another because he has charge of him. In regard to this he says: ***he who rules***, i.e., has been entrusted with the office of prelate, should use that office ***in carefulness***: *Obey your leaders and submit to them; for they are keeping watch over your souls, as men who will have to give an account* (Heb. 13:17); *my anxiety for all the churches* (2 Cor. 11:28).

Again, sometimes one helps another by easing his misery. In regard to this he says: ***he who does acts of mercy***, i.e., has the means and a merciful heart, should do this ***in cheerfulness***, as doing it gladly, *not reluctantly or under compulsion, for God loves a cheerful giver* (2 Cor. 9:7); *with every gift show a cheerful face* (Sir. 35:9).

983 Then when he says, ***let love be without dissimulation***, he shows how to use a gift which is common to all, namely, charity. *First*, he states what pertains to charity in general; *second*, charity toward special classes of persons, at ***communicating to the necessities of the saints***.

With respect to the *first* he does three things: *first*, he describes the qualities of charity as it exists in the one possessing it; *second*, the qualities of charity toward one's neighbor, at ***loving one another with the charity of brotherhood***; *third*, toward God, at ***in carefulness, not slothful***.

984 In regard to the qualities of charity he teaches three things. *First*, that charity should be true. Hence he says: ***let love be without dissimulation***, so that it consist not in word or outward appearance but in a genuine affection of heart and in efficacious works: *Let us not love in word or speech, but in deed and in truth* (1 John 3:18); *there is nothing so precious as a faithful friend* (Sir. 6:15).

Second, he teaches that love should be pure when he says: ***hating evil***. Love is pure when a person does not consent to his friend in evil, but so loves him that he hates his vices: *It does not rejoice at wrong but rejoices in the right* (1 Cor. 13:6); *I hate the impious* (Ps. 119:113).

Third, he teaches that love should be honorable when he says: ***cleaving to good***, so that one adheres to another because of his virtuous goodness: *Be zealous for that which is good* (Gal. 4:18 DRB). This is fair love, about which it is said: *I am the mother of fair love* (Sir. 24:18).

985 Then when he says, ***loving one another with the charity of brotherhood***, he shows how charity should be shown to one's neighbor. And *first* as regards interior affection, when he says ***loving one another with the charity of brotherhood***, i.e., so that through charity we not only love the brethren but even love the very charity by which we love them and are loved by them. For if we regard charity as such a great treasure, we will not allow it to be dissolved so easily: *Let brotherly love continue* (Heb. 13:1); *if a man offered for love all the wealth of his house, it would be utterly scorned* (Song of Sol. 8:7).

986 *Second*, with respect to its outward effect when he says: ***with honor anticipating one another***. Three things are designated here.

First, that a person should hold the neighbor in reverence. This pertains to the very notion of honor, for no one can truly love a person he despises: *In humility, count others better than yourselves* (Phil. 2:3). This is realized when one considers his own shortcomings and the good qualities of his neighbor. Under the heading of honor are included not only honor but the provision of necessities, for when it is commanded in Exodus: *Honor your father and your mother* (20:12), the provision of necessities is commanded. This is clear from the fact that our Lord in Matthew rebuked the Pharisees for violating this precept by hindering children from helping their parents (15:5).

Second, it designates that the effect of love should be shown mutually, i.e., a person should desire not only to receive benefits but also to grant them: *Let not your hand be extended to receive and withdrawn when it is time to repay* (Sir. 4:31); *give and take* (Sir. 14:16). He refers to this when he says: ***one another***.

Third, he designates that the effect of love should be prompt and swift, when he says, ***anticipating***, so that one should anticipate a friend in doing favors: *Every friend will say, "I too am a friend"* (Sir. 37:1).

987 Then when he says, ***in carefulness***, he shows the qualities surrounding charity's love of God. *First*, he starts with reason's attentiveness when he says: ***in carefulness, not slothful***, when it is a question of worshiping God: *He has shown you, O man, what is good; and what does the Lord require of you*, and he continues: *but . . . to walk humbly with your God?* (Mic. 6:8); *do your best to present yourself to God as one approved* (2 Tim. 2:15).

988 *Second*, the affections when he says: ***be fervent in the spirit***, namely, in loving God. Being fervent comes from an abundance of heat; hence it is called fervor of spirit, because the whole person is fervent toward God on account of the abundance of his love: *Apollos . . . . being fervent in spirit . . . spoke and*

taught accurately of the things concerning Jesus (Acts 18:25); *do not quench the Spirit* (1 Thess. 5:19).

989 *Third*, the outward homage when he says: ***serving the Lord***, namely, with the worship of latria, which is paid to God alone: *You shall fear the Lord your God and shall serve him only* (Deut. 6:13 DRB); *serve the Lord with fear* (Ps. 2:11). Or according to another text, *serving the time*, namely that we should perform our service of God at the fitting time: *Every matter has its time and way* (Eccles. 8:6).

990 *Fourth*, the reward of serving when he says: ***rejoicing in hope***, namely of a reward which is the enjoyment of God: *I am your protector and your reward, exceedingly great* (Gen. 15:1 DRB); ***we rejoice in our hope of sharing the glory of God*** (Rom. 5:2). But hope rejoices a man by reason of its certainty, but it afflicts him by reason of its delay: *Hope deferred makes the heart sick* (Prov. 13:12).

991 *Fifth*, the difficulty a person endures in the service of God when he says: ***in tribulation***, which you endure for God, ***patient***: ***tribulation produces patience*** (Rom. 5:3).

992 *Sixth*, in the light of all the foregoing he says: ***constant in prayer***, in which is indicated continuance in prayer: *They ought always to pray and not lose heart* (Luke 18:1); *pray constantly* (1 Thess. 5:17). For by prayer carefulness is aroused in us and fervor kindled, we are stimulated to serve God, the joy of hope is increased, and we win help in tribulation: *In my distress I cry to the Lord that he may answer me* (Ps. 120:1).

993 Then when he says, ***communicating to the necessities of the saints***, he discusses charity with regard to certain particular persons. *First*, as regards the needy; *second*, as regards enemies, at ***bless those who persecute you*** (Rom. 12:14).

994 Concerning the *first* he does two things. *First*, he urges in general that the benefits of charity be afforded to the needy, when he says: ***communicating to the necessities of the saints***. Three things should be noted here: *first*, that alms be given out of charity to the poor and needy: *Let him labor, doing honest work with his hands, so that he may be able to give to others in need* (Eph. 4:28).

Second, that upright and saintly persons should be helped before others; hence he says: ***to the necessities of the saints***: *Give to the godly man, but do not help the sinner* (Sir. 12:4). This does not mean that sinners should not be helped in their needs, but that they should not be helped so as to nourish sin. Yet it is more useful to help the just, because such an alms is fruitful not only for the giver but also from the prayers of the recipient: *Make friends for yourselves by means of unrighteous mammon, so that when it fails they may receive you into the eternal habitations* (Luke 16:9), namely, by their prayers.

995 Then he urges them to be hospitable when he says: ***pursuing hospitality***, because the other works of mercy are included in this one. For a host offers not

only his home as a shelter but provides for other needs as well: *Do not neglect to show hospitality to strangers* (Heb. 13:2); *practice hospitality ungrudgingly to one another* (1 Pet. 4:9).

John 21:1–6

The Church's Toil in the Twilight of the Resurrection

On John 21.1 (2569–2590)

21:1 ***After this, Jesus showed himself again to the disciples at the Sea of Tiberias. And he showed himself in this manner.***

21:2 ***Simon Peter, and Thomas, who is called Didymus, and Nathanael, who was of Cana of Galilee, and the sons of Zebedee, and two others of his disciples were all together.***

21:3 ***Simon Peter said to them, "I am going fishing." They say to him, "We too will come with you." And they went out, and got into the ship, and that night they caught nothing.***

21:4 ***But when the morning arrived, Jesus stood on the shore, yet the disciples did not know that it was Jesus.***

21:5 ***Jesus therefore said to them, "Children, have you any meat?" They replied, "No."***

21:6 ***He said to them, "Cast the net on the right side of the ship, and you will find." They therefore cast; and they were not able to draw it up, because of the multitude of fish.***

2569 The Evangelist has just told of two appearances of Christ to his disciples.[13] Now he mentions a third appearance. If we consider the order and purpose of these appearances, it is evident that the *first* showed Christ's divine authority by his breathing the Holy Spirit upon them; the *second* showed that he was the same person as before, since he let them view his wounds; and the *third* showed the reality of his risen human nature, for he ate with them.

There are two parts in this. The Evangelist *first* mentions Christ's dealing with a group of the disciples; *second*, with two of them he especially loved: ***When therefore they had dined, Jesus said to Simon Peter, "Simon son of John, do you love me more than these?"*** (John 21:15).

As to the *first*, the Evangelist mentions the time and circumstance of his appearance, ***and he showed himself in this manner***, and then adds a short

13. See John 20 and Thomas Aquinas, *On John* 20.1–6 (20.1–3 are included in chapter 6 of this collection).

epilogue, ***This was now the third time that Jesus was manifested*** (John 21:14). In the title, however, three are designated, namely, time, way, and place.

2570 The time is ***after this***, that is, after what the Evangelist just narrated. It is significant that he says this for it shows that Christ was not with them continuously but appeared to them at intervals. The reason for this was that he had not risen with the same life as before, but with a glorious life, as the angels have and the blessed will have: *except the gods*, that is, the angels, *whose dwelling is not with flesh* (Dan. 2:11).

2571 Since the Evangelist seemed to be ending his Gospel before, when he wrote, ***these are written so that you may believe*** (John 20:31), why, then, does he add on this appearance?

Augustine gives a mystical reason for this, which is that this appearance signifies the glory of the future life, when Christ will appear to us *as he is* (1 John 3:2).[14] And so the Evangelist put this appearance after what seemed to be the end of his Gospel so that this could be better understood.

2572 The circumstance of his appearance was that ***Jesus showed himself again to the disciples at the Sea of Tiberias***. It is in the nature and power of a glorified body that it can be seen or not seen, as the person wishes, by non-glorified bodies. That is why he says, ***showed***, i.e., Christ made himself visible. In the same way he is said to appear, which means the same thing as to reveal, *appearing to them during forty days* (Acts 1:3). As Ambrose says, a thing is said to appear if it has the power to be seen or not seen.[15]

2573 The place is ***at the Sea of Tiberias***, which is the Sea of Galilee. It is called the Sea of Tiberias after the city of Tiberias, which was built in honor of Tiberius Caesar. The Evangelist mentions this, *first*, to show that our Lord had kept the promise made to the disciples: *He is going before you to Galilee* (Matt. 28:7). *Second*, he wanted to show that our Lord had banished the very great fear from the hearts of his disciples, so that they no longer remained shut up in their house, but even traveled as far as Galilee.

2574 In describing this appearance, ***and he showed himself in this manner***; he *first* mentions the persons to whom Christ appeared; what they were doing; ***Simon Peter said to them, "I am going fishing."*** And *third*, the circumstances of this appearance: ***When the morning arrived, Jesus stood on the shore.***

2575 Christ appeared to seven persons. The Evangelist says that there were together ***Simon Peter***, who had denied him, ***Thomas called Didymus***, who was not present at the first appearance, ***Nathanael of Cana in Galilee***, who is thought to be the brother of Philip, ***the sons of Zebedee***, that is, James and John, and ***two others of his disciples*** not explicitly named.

---

14. Augustine, *Tractates on the Gospel of John* 122.1.

15. Ambrose, *Commentary on Luke* 1.24.

In the mystical sense, this number signifies the state and appearance of future glory, which will be after the seventh age, that is, in the eighth, which is the age of those who arise: *From new moon to new moon, and from Sabbath to Sabbath, all flesh will come to worship before me* (Isa. 66:23).

2576 The work which occupied them was fishing; thus it says: ***Simon Peter said to them, "I am going fishing,"*** and *first* there is Peter's invitation to do this work; *second*, their assent; *third*, the execution of this duty.

2577 Peter asks them to go fishing, saying, ***I am going fishing.*** In the mystical interpretation, this signifies the work of preaching: *I will make you fishers of men* (Matt. 4:19). So when Peter said, ***I am going fishing***, the mystical sense is that he is taking the others to share in his concerns and preaching: *So it will be easier for you, and they will bear the burden with you* (Exod. 18:22).

2578 Their actual fishing seems to go against Luke: *No one who puts his hand to the plow and looks back is fit for the kingdom of God* (9:62). And it is clear that Peter had given up his work as a fisherman. Why then did he return to it and look back?

I answer, with Augustine, that if he had returned to this work of fishing before Christ's resurrection and before seeing Christ's wounds, we would think that he was acting out of despair.[16] But now, even after Christ returned from the grave, after they had seen his wounds, and had received the Holy Spirit by Christ's breathing on them, they became what they were before, fishers of fish. We can learn from this that a preacher can use his abilities to earn the necessaries of life and still preserve the integrity of his apostolate if he has no other means of sustenance. For if St. Paul learned an art he did not previously have in order to obtain the food he needed, so as to avoid being a burden to others, Peter could all the more do this by using his own skill.

2579 Augustine says that a preacher can do this when he cannot gain a living in any other way.[17] But in this case Peter did have another way, for our Lord promised: *Seek first his kingdom and his righteousness, and all these things will be yours as well*, that is, what is necessary for life (Matt. 6:33).

The answer is that it is true that these things will be added, with our cooperation. So our Lord did keep his promise here, with the cooperation of Peter. For who else but our Lord caused the fish that were caught to be within the range of their net?

2580 Gregory remarks that there are two kinds of work.[18] One absorbs the mind, and hinders our spiritual concerns, as tax collecting. No one should return to such work, even to provide food. So we do not read that Matthew returned

16. Augustine, *Tractates on the Gospel of John* 122.2.

17. Augustine, 122.4.

18. Gregory the Great, *Forty Gospel Homilies* 24.1.

to his tax collecting post. There is another kind of work which can be done without sin and without absorbing the mind, such as fishing and similar things. And it was not a sin for Peter to return to this kind of work after his conversion.

2581 The others agree to this: ***We too will come with you.*** This sets an example for preachers and prelates to encourage each other in their work of turning people to God: *A brother helped is like a strong city* (Prov. 18:19); *he was like a young cedar on Lebanon; and they surrounded him like the trunks of palm trees* (Sir. 50:12).

2582 Next, we see that they were working at this: ***they went out and got into the ship, and that night they caught nothing.*** Here he touches on three things that preachers ought to do. *First*, they should leave those places which are sunk in sin: *Come out from them*, the Chaldeans, *and be separate from them, says the Lord, and touch nothing unclean; then I will welcome you* (2 Cor. 6:17). And they should go out from their carnal affections: *Go from your country and your kindred and your father's house* (Gen. 12:1). And also leave the quiet of contemplation: *Let us go forth into the fields and lodge in the villages; let us go out early to the vineyards* (Song of Sol. 7:11–12).

Second, preachers should get into the ship, that is, go forward in charity within the unity of the Church, which is called a ship: *In the days of Noah, during the building of the ark, in which a few, that is, eight persons, were saved through water* (1 Pet. 3:20). They should also board the ship of the cross by depriving the flesh: *Far be it from me to glory except in the cross of our Lord Jesus Christ, by which the world has been crucified to me, and I to the world* (Gal. 6:14); *blessed is the wood by which righteousness comes* (Wis. 14:7).

Third, preachers should have total confidence in the help of Christ. All ***that night they caught nothing***, because as long as God's help and the interior preacher are not there, the words of the preacher have no effect. But when the light comes, enlightening hearts, the preacher makes a catch: *Send out your light and your truth* (Ps. 43:3). Here, night indicates the lack of divine help: ***Night comes, when no one can work*** (John 9:4). Or, one could say, ***that night***, during the time of the Old Testament, ***they caught nothing***, because they could not bring the gentiles to the faith: *The night has passed* (Rom. 13:12). According to Augustine, they were fishing at night because they were still afraid.[19]

2583 Now we see the way and stages in which Jesus appeared: ***When the morning arrived, Jesus stood on the shore***; *first*, he allows himself to be seen; *second*, he is recognized: ***Children, have you any meat?***; and *third*, he eats with the

19. No such comment appears in Augustine's *Tractates on the Gospel of John* nor in his other New Testament commentaries. The quote might belong, instead, to John Chrysostom, who commenting on John 21:3, says "they did this [fishing] at night because of being very fearful" (*Commentary on Saint John* 87).

disciples: ***Jesus said to them, "Bring here the fish which you have now caught"*** (John 21:10).

2584 The Evangelist says that the ***morning arrived.*** In the mystical interpretation, morning or the break of day indicates the glory of the resurrection: *Weeping may tarry for the night*, as with the weeping for eternal life, *but joy comes with the morning* (Ps. 30:5); *in the morning I will stand before you and I will see* (Ps. 5:5 DRB).

2585 Before his passion, on the occasion of a similar miracle, Jesus did not stand on the shore, but was in a boat. Why, after the passion, does he stand on the shore? The reason is that the sea signifies the troubles and tribulations of this present life, but all these end at the shore. *I placed the sand as the bound for the sea, a perpetual barrier which it cannot pass* (Jer. 5:22). So, before his passion, Christ stood on the sea, because he had a body subject to death; but after the resurrection, he had surmounted the corruption of the flesh and stood upon the shore.

2586 ***The disciples did not know that it was Jesus*** because of their own ignorance. We can see from this that on this turbulent sea of the present, we cannot know the hidden things of Christ: *The eye has not seen, O God, besides you, what things you have prepared for those who wait for you* (Isa. 64:4 DRB).

2587 Next, Jesus brings them to recognize him: ***Jesus therefore said to them, "Children, have you any meat?"*** *First*, the Evangelist shows how they came to recognize him; and *second* who was the first to do so: ***That disciple therefore whom Jesus loved, said to Peter, "It is the Lord"*** (John 21:7).

2588 The Evangelist does three things regarding the *first. First*, he shows our Lord asking for food, ***children, have you any meat?*** The disciples did not think it was Christ asking, but someone who wanted to buy fish, for he spoke like a customer. In the mystical interpretation, Christ asks us for food to refresh himself. And we do this for him by obeying the commandments: ***My food is to do the will of him who sent me, so that I may accomplish his work*** (John 4:34). ***They answered him, "No,"*** that is, not of themselves: *I can will what is right, but I cannot do it* (Rom. 7:18).

2589 *Second*, the Evangelist mentions Christ's order, ***Cast the net on the right side of the ship.*** In Luke there is a similar incident, but there Christ did not tell them to cast their nets to the right side, as he does here: ***Cast the net on the right side of the ship.*** The reason for this is that the fishing mentioned by John signifies that fishing by which the predestined are taken to eternal life, and it is only those children on the right who are brought there: *The Lord knows the ways that are on the right hand; those are perverse which are on the left hand* (Prov. 4:27 DRB); *the right hand of the Lord does valiantly* (Ps. 118:16). The fishing mentioned in Luke signified the call into the Church, and so the net is cast to all sides because people are caught and brought to Christ from all over: *Go out quickly to the streets and lanes of the city* (14:21).

2590 The obedience of the disciples is shown when the Evangelist says, ***they therefore cast*** the net; and the effect of this obedience, ***and now they were not able to draw it up, because of the multitude of fish***, that is, for the great number of those who would be saved: *By your descendants shall all the nations of the earth bless themselves, because you have obeyed my voice* (Gen. 22:18); *behold, a great multitude which no man could number* (Rev. 7:9).

This fishing differs from that mentioned by Luke because there (5:6) the nets broke; and in a like way the Church is rent by disagreements and heresies. But in the fishing mentioned by John the net does not break because there will be no lack of unity in the future life. Again, in the incident mentioned by Luke, the fish were taken into the boat. But here in John's incident, the fish are brought to the shore, because the saints destined for glory are hidden from us: *In the covert of your presence you hide them from the plots of men* (Ps. 31:20).[20]

20. Cf. Augustine, *Tractates on the Gospel of John* 122.7.

John 21:15–17

"Feed My Lambs"

Christ's Mandate to Church Leaders

On John 21.3 (2614–2627)

21:15 ***When therefore they had dined, Jesus said to Simon Peter, "Simon son of John, do you love me more than these?" He said to him, "Yes, Lord, you know that I love you." He said to him, "Feed my lambs."***

21:16 ***He said to him again, "Simon, son of John, do you love me?" He said to him, "Yes, Lord, you know that I love you." He said to him, "Feed my lambs."***

21:17 ***He said to him the third time, "Simon, son of John, do you love me?" Peter was grieved because he had said to him the third time: do you love me? And he said to him, "Lord, you know all things, you know that I love you." He said to him, "Feed my sheep."***

2614 The Evangelist just showed what the Lord did for the disciples in general;[21] here he shows him dealing with his two especially loved disciples: *first*, what he did for Peter; *second*, how he dealt with John: ***Peter, turning around, saw the disciple whom Jesus loved*** (John 21:20).

He does two things with the *first*: *first*, he lays on Peter the pastoral office; *second*, he predicts that he will be martyred: ***Amen, amen I say to you, when you were younger*** (John 21:18).

He imposes the pastoral office on Peter only after an examination. Thus, those who are to be raised to this office are first examined: *Do not be hasty in the laying on of hands* (1 Tim. 5:22). Christ examined him three times, and so this part is divided into three parts according to the three examinations.

The parts are obvious. In the *first* part we *first* see our Lord's question: *second*, we see Peter's answer, ***Yes, Lord, you know that I love you***; and *third*, we see the imposition of the office: ***He said to him: feed my lambs.***

Looking at the *first*, we can consider three things: the time of the examination; the tenor of the conversation; and on what Peter was examined.

2615 The order of this event is given as ***when therefore, they had dined.*** This signifies the spiritual meal by which the soul is refreshed with spiritual gifts, even when it is united to the body: *I will come in to him and eat with him* (Rev. 3:20).

21. See John 21:7–14 and Thomas Aquinas, *On John* 21.1 (featured above).

Therefore it is appropriate that one who is raised to this office be already refreshed with this joyous meal. Otherwise, how could he refresh the hungry ones that come to him: *I will feast the soul of the priests with abundance* (Jer. 31:14), with that abundance mentioned in the Psalm: *My soul is feasted as with marrow and fat* (Ps. 63:5).

2616 The tenor of the conversation is seen when he says, ***Jesus said to Simon Peter***. Three things are given here which are necessary for a prelate.

First, obedience, when he says, ***Simon***, which means *obedient*. A prelate needs to be obedient because one who does not know how to obey superiors does not know how to govern inferiors: *An obedient man will speak of victory* (Prov. 21:28 DRB).

Second, a prelate needs knowledge, indicated by ***Peter***, which means 'understanding.' A prelate needs understanding for he is the appointed watchman, and one who is blind is a poor watchman: *His watchmen are blind* (Isa. 56:10); *because you have rejected knowledge, I reject you from being a priest to me* (Hos. 4:6).

Third, a prelate needs grace, for he says ***son of John***. Prelates need grace because if they do not have grace they do not have anything: *By the grace of God I am what I am* (1 Cor. 15:10); *and when they perceived the grace that was given to me, James and Cephas and John, who were reputed to be pillars, gave to me and Barnabas the right hand of fellowship* (Gal. 2:9).

2617 The questions are about love; and Jesus asks, ***Do you love me more than these?*** This was a suitable question, for Peter had previously fallen, as we saw before, and it was not appropriate that he be preferred to the others until his sin was forgiven, which is only brought about by charity: *Love covers a multitude of sins* (1 Pet. 4:8); *love covers all offenses* (Prov. 10:12). So it was fitting that his charity be made known by this questioning, not indeed to him who looks into the depths of our hearts, but to others. So Christ said, but not as one who did not already know, ***Do you love me more than these?*** Now we read that *perfect love casts out fear* (1 John 4:18). Thus it was that when our Lord was about to die, Peter was afraid and denied him; but the risen Lord restored love and banished his fear. So Peter, who before had denied Christ because he was afraid to die, now, after our Lord has arisen, feared nothing. Why should he be afraid, since he now realized that death had died?

2618 This questioning was also appropriate for the office, since many who assume a pastoral office use it as self-lovers: *In the last days there will come times of stress. For men will be lovers of self* (1 Tim. 3:1–2). One who does not love the Lord is not a fit prelate. A fit prelate is one who does not seek his own advantage, but that of Christ; and he does this through love: *The love of Christ controls us* (2 Cor. 5:14).

Love also becomes this office because it benefits others: for it is due to the abundance of love that those who love Jesus will at times give up the quiet of their own contemplation to help their neighbor. Although the Apostle said, *I am sure that neither death nor life . . . will be able to separate us from the love of God* (Rom. 8:38–39), he added, *I could wish that I myself were accursed and cut off from Christ for the sake of my brethren* (Rom. 9:3). Thus a prelate should be questioned about his love.

2619 He adds, ***more than these***, for even as the Philosopher says in his *Politics*, it is the natural order of things that the one who cares for and governs others should be better.[22] Thus he says that just as the soul is to the body that it rules, and reason is to our lower powers, so man is related to the irrational animals. And there ought to be a similar relation between prelates and their subjects. Thus, according to Gregory, the life of a pastor should be such that he is related to his subjects as a shepherd to his sheep.[23] So Christ says, ***more than these***, because the more Peter loves the better he is: *Do you see him whom the Lord has chosen? There is none like him among all the people* (1 Sam. 10:24).

2620 But in selecting someone is it always necessary to choose the one who is unconditionally better, even if the laws say that it is enough to choose one who is merely good? To answer this, two distinctions must be made. Some things are sufficient according to human judgment which are still not sufficient according to the divine judgment. According to human judgment, if a person cannot be reproached for something, this is sufficient for his election to stand. For it is obvious that it would be difficult to have elections if they could be nullified because someone was found who was better than the one actually chosen. So, according to our human judgment, it is sufficient if an election is honest and a suitable person is chosen.

But, so far as concerns the divine judgment, and our own conscience, it is necessary to choose what is better. Now a person can be better simply; and this is the way a holier person is said to be better, for holiness makes one good. Yet such a person might not be better for the Church. For this purpose, that person would be better who is better educated, more competent, more discerning, and chosen more unanimously. But if other things are equal, such as the benefit and welfare of the Church, one would sin if he were to choose a person who was less unconditionally good than another. The reason for this is either the honor of God and the benefit of the Church, or some private motive. If the motive is the honor of God and the benefit to the Church, these goods will be regarded as linked to the one chosen, and will make him the better person, in these respects. If there is some private motive for the choice, such as carnal

22. Aristotle, *Politics* 1.12.

23. Gregory the Great, *Forty Gospel Homilies* 14.

love, the expectation of ecclesiastical advancement, or temporal advantage, the election is a fraud and there has been partiality.

2621 Now we see Peter's answer: ***Yes, Lord, you know that I love you.*** This is a clear sign that he had retracted his previous denial. And it shows that if the predestined fall, they are always better after they are corrected. Before his denial, Peter thought that he was better than the other apostles, saying, *Though they all fall away because of you, I will never fall away* (Matt. 26:33). And when Jesus said to him, *you will deny me three times*, Peter went against this and even boasted, *Even if I must die with you, I will not deny you* (Matt. 26:35). But now, Peter, having been conquered by his own weakness, does not presume to state his love unless it is attested to and confirmed by the Lord. He humbles himself before Christ, saying, ***you know that I love you***: *My witness is in heaven, and he that vouches for me is on high* (Job 16:19). He also humbles himself in respect to the apostles, for he does not say that he loves Jesus more than they do, but simply, ***I love you.*** This teaches us not to rank ourselves before others, but others before ourselves: *In humility count others better than yourselves* (Phil. 2:3).

2622 We can also notice, as Augustine points out, that when our Lord asks, ***do you love*** [*diligis*] ***me***, Peter does not answer with the same word, but says, ***I love*** [*amo*] ***you***, as if they were the same.[24] And they are the same in reality, but there is some difference in meaning. Love [*amor*] is a movement of our appetitive power, and if this is regulated by our reason it is the will's act of love, which is called delight [*dilectio*], because it presupposes an act of election, choice [*electio*]. This is why the brute animals are not said to love [*diligere*]. For if the appetitive movement is not regulated by reason, it is called *amor*.

2623 After this examination, Christ assigns Peter his office, saying, ***feed my lambs***, that is, my faithful, which I, the Lamb, call lambs: ***Behold the Lamb of God, who takes away the sin of the world!*** (John 1:29). Thus, one should not be called a Christian who says he is not under the care of that shepherd, that is, Peter: *they will all have one shepherd* (Ezek. 37:24); *they will appoint for themselves one head* (Hos. 1:11).

It was appropriate that this office be assigned to Peter, the others being passed over, because, according to Chrysostom, he was the extraordinary apostle, the voice of the disciples, and the head of the group.[25]

2624 Now is the *second* examination. In order to avoid repetition, note that Christ says three times, ***feed my lambs***, because Peter ought to feed them three ways. *First*, they are to be fed by being taught: *I will give you shepherds after my own heart, who will feed you with knowledge and understanding* (Jer. 3:15). *Second*, they are to be fed by example: *Set the believers an example in speech and*

24. Augustine, *Tractates on the Gospel of John* 123.5.

25. John Chrysostom, *Commentary on Saint John* 88.1.

conduct, in love, in faith, in purity (1 Tim. 4:12); *upon the mountain heights of Israel*, that is, in the excellence of great men, *will be their pasture* (Ezek. 34:14). *Third*, they are to be fed by being offered temporal help: *Woe, shepherds of Israel who have been feeding yourselves! Should not shepherds feed the sheep?* (Ezek. 34:2).

2625 The third time Christ says to him, ***feed my sheep***. This is because there are three types of people in the Church: beginners, those who have made some progress, and the perfect. The first two types are the lambs, since they are still imperfect. The others, since they are perfect, are called sheep: *The mountains*, that is, the perfect, *skipped like rams*, and *the hills*, the others, *like lambs* (Ps. 114:4). And so all prelates ought to guard their charges as Christ's sheep and not their own. But alas! As Augustine says in his Easter sermon: *we witness the appearance of certain unfaithful servants who have abandoned Christ's flock and by their thefts have made gold their flock. You hear them say: these are my sheep. What do you want with my sheep? I will not let you come to my sheep. But if we say: my sheep, and others talk about their sheep, then Christ has lost his own sheep.*[26]

2626 Note also that just as Peter was assigned his office three times, so he was examined three times. This was because he had denied Christ three times. As Augustine says: *A threefold profession was required so that Peter's tongue might show as much love as it had shown of fear, and that life gained would wrest more words than the threat of death.*[27]

Another reason for this was because Peter was obligated to love Christ for three things. *First*, because his sin was forgiven; *many sins are forgiven her, because she has loved much* (Luke 7:47). *Second*, because he was promised a great honor: *On this rock I will build my church* (Matt. 16:18). *Third*, because of the office entrusted to him, as here, when Christ says ***feed*** and entrusts the care of the Church to him. *You shall love the Lord your God with all your heart*, so that you will direct your entire intention to God, *and with all your soul*, so that your entire will might rest in God through love, *and with all your might* (Deut. 6:5), so that the performance of all your actions will serve God.

2627 Peter, because he was asked three times, became sad. As was seen, he was rebuked by our Lord before the passion when he so quickly asserted that he loved him. Now, seeing that he is questioned so many times about his love, he is afraid he will be rebuked again and becomes sad. Thus he says, ***Lord, you know all things, you know that I love you***. He is saying in effect: 'I do love you; at least I think I do. But you know all things, and perhaps you know of something else that will happen.' And so the final commitment of the Church is

26. Augustine, *Sermons* 147a.2.

27. Augustine, *Tractates on the Gospel of John* 123.5.

given to the humbled Peter. According to one of the Greek doctors, this is also the reason why catechumens are questioned three times during their baptism.[28]

28. Theophylact of Ochrid, *The Explanation of the Holy Gospel According to John* 21.15–19.

John 17:20–23

Christ's Prayer for the Unity of the Church

On John 17.5 (2232–2251)

17:20 ***Not for them only do I pray, but for those also who through their word will believe in me;***

17:21 ***that they all may be one, as you, Father, in me, and I in you; that they also may be one in us; that the world may believe that you sent me.***

17:22 ***And the glory which you gave me, I have given to them; that they may be one, as we also are one:***

17:23 ***I in them, and you in me; that they may be made perfect in one: and the world may know that you sent me, and loved them, as you also loved me.***

2232 After our Lord prayed for his disciples, he now prays in general for all the faithful.[29] *First,* we see his prayer; *second,* he states why he should be heard: ***Just Father, the world has not known you*** (John 17:25).

In his prayer he asks the Father two things for those who follow him: *first,* a perfect unity; *second,* the vision of glory: ***Father, I will that where I am, they whom you have given me may be with me*** (John 17:24).

He does two things about the *first*: *first,* he asks, as man, for a perfect unity; *second,* he shows that as God he gives them the ability to acquire this unity: ***The glory which you gave me, I have given to them.***

He does two things with the *first*: *first,* he mentions for whom he is asking; *second,* what he is asking for: ***that they all may be one.***

2233 He is praying for the entire community of the faithful. He says: I have asked that you protect my disciples from evil, and that you sanctify them in the truth; but ***not for them only do I pray, but for those also who through their word will believe me***, that is, for those whose faith will be strengthened, ***through their word***, the word of the apostles. It is right for him to ask this, because no one is saved except by the intercession of Christ. So that it would not only be the apostles who were saved, but also others, he also had to pray for these others: *He loved your fathers and chose their descendants after them* (Deut. 4:37); *their prosperity will remain with their descendants* (Sir. 44:11).

29. See John 17:11–16 and Thomas Aquinas, *On John* 17.3 (not included in this collection).

2234 The objection is made that he does not seem to be praying for all his faithful, because he is praying for those who would be converted by the word of the apostles. But the old fathers and John the Baptist were not converted by their word.

We should answer that these persons had already arrived at their destination; and although they were not enjoying the vision of God, since the price had not yet been paid, they went from this world with their merits, so that as soon as the gate was opened, they would enter. Thus, they did not need such prayer.

2235 Again, what of others who did not believe through the word of the apostles, but through Christ's, as Paul did: *I did not receive it from man, nor was I taught it, but it came through a revelation of Jesus Christ* (Gal. 1:12), or like the thief on the cross (Luke 23:43). It does not seem that Christ prayed for them.

The answer, according to Augustine, is that those are said to believe through the word of the apostles who not only listened to the apostles, but those also who believed through the word which the apostles preached, which is the word of faith (see Rom 10:8).[30] The word of faith is called the word of the apostles because they were especially commissioned to preach it. The same word was divinely revealed to Paul and the thief on the cross.

Or, one could say that those who were converted directly by and through Christ, like Paul and the thief on the cross, and others like these, are included in that part of the prayer in which our Lord prayed for his disciples. And so our Lord said: ***whom you have given me*** (John 17:6) or will give me.

2236 What about us, who do not believe through the Apostles? We should say that although we do not believe through the apostles, we do believe through their disciples.

2237 He prays for a perfect unity when he says, ***that they all may be one.*** *First,* he mentions the unity he is asking for; *second,* he gives an example of it, and its cause: ***as you, Father, in me***; *third,* he gives the fruit of unity: ***that the world may believe that you have sent me.***

2238 He says: I am praying ***that they all may be one.*** As the Platonists say, a thing acquires its unity from that from which it acquires its goodness. For that is good for a thing which preserves it; and a thing is preserved only if it remains one. Thus when our Lord prays that his disciples be perfect in goodness, he prays that they be one. Indeed, this was accomplished: *The company of those who believed were of one heart and soul* (Acts 4:32); *behold, how good and pleasant it is when brothers dwell in unity* (Ps. 133:1).

2239 He gives an example of this unity and its cause, saying, ***as you, Father, in me, and I in you.*** Others are one, but in evil. Our Lord is not asking for this kind of unity, but that which unites in good, that is, in God. And so he says,

30. Augustine, *Tractates on the Gospel of John* 109.2.

as you, Father, in me, and I in you, that is, let them be united by believing in me and in you: *We, though many, are one body in Christ* (Rom. 12:5); *eager to keep the unity of the Spirit . . . one Lord, one faith, one baptism* (Eph. 4:3). We are one or united in the Father and the Son, who are one; for if we were seeking different things to believe and desire, our affections would be scattered.

2240 Arius uses this passage to argue that the Son is in the Father and the Father in the Son in the same way that we are in God. However, we are not in God by a unity of essence, but by a conformity of will and love. Therefore, he says, like us, the Father is not in the Son by a unity of essence.

We should say to this that there is a twofold unity of the Father and the Son: a unity of essence and of love. In both of these ways the Father is in the Son and the Son is in the Father. ***As you, Father, in me, and I in you***, can be understood of the unity of love, according to Augustine, and then the meaning is: ***as you, Father, in me***, through love, because love, charity, makes one be with God.[31] It is like saying: 'as the Father loves the Son and the Son loves the Father, so the disciples love the Father and the Son.' Then the word ***as*** does not imply equality but a remote likeness.

Or, according to Hilary, this statement can refer to a unity of nature;[32] not indeed that the same numerical nature is in us and in the Father and the Son, but in the sense that our unity resembles that of the divine nature, by which the Father and the Son are one. In this case the word ***as*** indicates a certain imitation. That is why we are invited to imitate divine love: *Be imitators of God, as beloved children, and walk in love, as Christ loved us* (Eph. 5:1). And we are also to imitate the divine perfection or goodness: *You . . . must be perfect, as your heavenly Father is perfect* (Matt. 5:48).

2241 He indicates the fruit of this unity when he says, ***that the world may believe***: for nothing shows the truth of the Gospel better than the charity of those who believe: ***By this will all men know that you are my disciples, if you have love for one another*** (John 13:35). This will be the fruit of unity: because if my disciples are one, ***the world may believe*** that the teaching I gave to them is from you and know that ***you have sent me***. For God is a cause of peace, not of contentions.

2242 There is a problem here. If we will be perfectly one in our homeland, where we will not believe, it seems out of place to say, after mentioning unity, ***that the world may believe that you have sent me***. Our reply is that our Lord is speaking here of the unity which is taking shape and not of perfected unity.

31. Augustine, *Tractates on the Gospel of John* 110.1.

32. Hilary of Poitiers, *The Trinity* 8.10–11.

2243 There is another problem. Our Lord is praying that those who believe in him may be one; therefore, even the believing world is one. Therefore, how can he say, after the world has become one, ***the world may believe***?

One can answer by giving the mystical sense. Then our Lord is praying that all believers be one. Yet all would not believe at the same time; some would be the first to believe, and they would convert others. So when he says, ***that the world may believe***, it refers to those who did not believe at first, from the beginning, but when they did believe they did become one. And the same applies to those who would believe after them and continuing to the end of the world.

Hilary has another interpretation. The words ***the world may believe*** indicate the purpose of their unity and perfection.[33] It is like saying: 'you will perfect them so that they may be one,' for this purpose, ***that the world may believe that you sent me***. Here the word ***that*** indicates a final cause.

A third interpretation is by Augustine.[34] For him, ***that the world may believe*** is another petition. In this case the ***I pray*** has to be repeated, so that the sense is: *I pray that they may be one, and I pray that the world may believe.*

2244 Christ's part in establishing this unity is mentioned when he says, ***the glory which you gave me, I have given to them***, since what he is asking for as man he is accomplishing as God. *First*, he shows that he acted to make them one; *second*, he mentions the kind and degree of this unity, ***I in them and you in me***; and *third*, we see the purpose of this unity, ***that the world may know that you sent me***.

2245 He says: although, as man, I am asking for their perfection, still I am accomplishing this together with you, because ***the glory***, of my resurrection, ***which you***, Father, ***gave me***, by an eternal predestination, and which you will soon give me in reality, ***I have given to them***, my disciples. This glory is the immortality which the faithful will receive at the resurrection, an immortality even of the body: *[He] will change our lowly body to be like his glorious body* (Phil. 3:21); *it is sown in dishonor, it is raised in glory* (1 Cor. 15:43). And this is ***that they may be one***, because by the fact that they have glory they will be made one, ***as we also are one***.

2246 He seems to be distinguishing his own activity from that of the Father, for he says that the Father gave him glory, and Christ gave this to his faithful. If this is understood correctly, we see that he is not saying these things to distinguish their activities, but their persons. For the Son, as Son, together with the Father, gives glory to Christ in his human nature, and together with the Father Christ gives it to the faithful. But because Christ gave glory to his faithful especially through his own human nature, he attributes this giving to himself, while he

33. Hilary of Poitiers, *The Trinity* 8.12.

34. Augustine, *Tractates on the Gospel of John* 110.2.

attributes to the Father the giving of glory to his own human nature. This is the opinion of Augustine.[35]

Or, according to Chrysostom, ***the glory***, that is, the glory of grace, ***which you gave me***, in my human nature, giving me a superior knowledge, perfection, and power to accomplish miracles, ***I have given to them***, in a limited way, and will give it later more fully:[36] *We . . . are being changed into his likeness from one degree of glory to another* (2 Cor. 3:18); *you have given gifts to men* (Ps. 68:18). And this is in order ***that they may be one, as we also are one***, for the purpose of God's gifts is to unite us in a unity which is like the unity of the Father and the Son.

2247 The manner of this unity is added when he says, ***I in them and you in me.*** They arrive at unity, because they see that I am in them, as in a temple: *Do you not know that you are God's temple and that God's Spirit dwells in you?* (1 Cor. 3:16), by grace, which is a certain likeness of the Father's essence, by which you, Father, are in me by a unity of nature: ***I am in the Father and the Father in me*** (John 14:10). And this is in order ***that they may be made perfect in one.***

Above, he had said, ***that they may be one***, while here he says, ***perfect in one.*** The reason for this is that the first time he was referring to the unity brought about by grace, but here to its consummation. Hilary gives another interpretation: ***I in them***, that is, I am in them by the unity of human nature, which I have in common with them, and also because I give them my body as food; ***and you in me***, by a unity of essence.[37]

2248 Referring to the first explanation, since the Father also, as well as the Son, is in them by grace: ***We will come to him and make our home with him*** (John 14:23), why then does he say, ***I in them***, without mentioning the Father? According to Augustine, he does this not to mean that the Son is in them without the Father, but because they have access to the Father through the Son: *We have peace with God through our Lord Jesus Christ. Through him we have obtained access* (Rom. 5:1).[38]

Or, according to Chrysostom, above Christ said, ***We will come to him*** (John 14:23), to indicate that there is a plurality of divine persons, contrary to Sabellius;[39] but here he says, ***I in them***, to indicate the equality of the Father and the Son, contrary to Arius. We can understand from this that it is enough for the faithful if the Son alone dwells in them.

---

35. Augustine, *Tractates on the Gospel of John* 110.3.

36. John Chrysostom, *Commentary on Saint John* 82.2.

37. Hilary of Poitiers, *The Trinity* 8.13.

38. Augustine, *Tractates on the Gospel of John* 110.4.

39. John Chrysostom, *Commentary on Saint John* 82.2.

2249 The purpose of this unity is given when he says, ***that the world may know that you sent me***. If the ***perfect in one*** refers to the perfection of this life, then ***that the world may know*** is the same as what he said before, ***that the world may believe***. This would indicate just a beginning state. But here he is saying, ***know***, because complete knowledge, not faith, comes after imperfect knowledge.

He says, ***that the world may know***, not the world as it is now, but as it was, so that the meaning is: ***that the world***, now a believing world, ***may know***. Or, ***that the world***, that is, the lovers of the world, ***may know*** that you have sent me: for by that time those who are evil will know by clear signs that Christ is the Son of God: *Every eye will see him* (Rev. 1:7); ***they will look on him whom they pierced*** (John 19:37); *they will see the Son of man coming in a cloud with power and great glory* (Luke 21:27).

2250 The world will not only know this; it will also know the glory of the saints: ***and loved them***, that is, the faithful. At the present time we cannot know how great God's love for us is: this is because the good things that God will give us exceed our longings and desires, and so cannot be found in our heart: *No eye has seen, nor ear heard, nor the heart of man conceived, what God has prepared for those who love him* (1 Cor. 2:9).

Thus the believing world, that is, the saints, will now know by experience how much God loves us; but the lovers of the world, that is, the wicked, will know this by seeing in amazement the glory of the saints: *This is the man whom we once held in derision and made a byword of reproach* (Wis. 5:4); and it continues, *Why has he been numbered among the sons of God? And why is his lot among the saints?* (Wis. 5:5).

2251 He continues, ***as you also loved me***. This does not imply an equality of love, but a similarity and a reason. It is like saying: 'the love you have for me is the reason and cause why you love them: for by the fact that you love me, you love those who love me and are my members'; ***the Father himself loves you, because you have loved me*** (John 16:27).

God loves all the things he has made, by giving them existence: *You love all things that exist and have loathing for none of the things you have made* (Wis. 11:24). But above all he loves his only Son, to whom he has given his entire nature by an eternal generation. In a lesser way he loves the members of his only Son, that is, the faithful of Christ, by giving them the grace by which Christ dwells in them: *He loved his people; all those consecrated to him were in his hand* (Deut. 33:3).

Chapter 14

CHRIST'S MORAL TEACHING AND THE FRUIT OF HIS SPIRIT

Matthew 5:3–10

The Beatitudes

On Matthew 5.2 (403–443)

5:3 ***Blessed are the poor in spirit: for theirs is the kingdom of heaven.***

5:4 ***Blessed are the meek: for they will possess the land.***

5:5 ***Blessed are they who mourn: for they will be comforted.***

5:6 ***Blessed are they who hunger and thirst after justice: for they will have their fill.***

5:7 ***Blessed are the merciful: for they will obtain mercy.***

5:8 ***Blessed are the clean of heart: for they will see God.***

5:9 ***Blessed are the peacemakers: for they will be called children of God.***

5:10 ***Blessed are they who suffer persecution for justice's sake: for theirs is the kingdom of heaven.***

403 Above, the Evangelist set down a brief title, as it were, of the teaching of Christ;[1] now he sets down the teaching itself, and its effect, namely, the wonder of the crowds.

Now it should be considered that, according to Augustine, the whole perfection of our life is contained in this sermon of the Lord.[2] And he proves it by the fact that the Lord includes the end to which he leads us, that is, a promise. But that which man desires most of all is beatitude. Hence the Lord does three things.

1. The "brief title" to which he refers comprises the first two verses of Matthew 5. See Thomas Aquinas, *On Matthew* 5.1 (not included in this collection).

2. Augustine, *On the Lord's Sermon on the Mount* 1.1.1.

First, he promises a reward, which those who accept this teaching will obtain; *second*, he sets down the precepts, at ***Think not that I have come to abolish the law*** (Matt. 5:17); *third*, he teaches how someone can succeed in observing them, at ***Ask, and it will be given you*** (Matt. 7:7).

Concerning the *first*, he does two things, because some are only observers of this teaching, others ministers. *First*, therefore, he describes the beatitude of the one who observes the precepts; *second*, the beatitude of the ministers, at ***Blessed are you when men revile you*** (Matt. 5:11).

404 Now, one should note that many things are set down here about the beatitudes; but never could anyone speak so skillfully about the Lord's words that he could attain to the Lord's purpose. Yet one should know that all complete happiness is included in these words: for all men desire happiness, but they differ in their judgments about happiness, and for this reason some men desire this, others desire that.

But we find four opinions about happiness. For some believe that it consists only in exterior things: namely, in an abundance of temporal things; *happy the people to whom such blessings fall!* (Ps. 144:15). Others, that perfect beatitude consists in the fact that a man fulfills his own will; hence we say, 'blessed is he who lives as he wants.' *I know that there is nothing better for them than to be happy and enjoy themselves as long as they live* (Eccles. 3:12). Others say that perfect beatitude consists in the virtues of the active life. Others, that it consists in the virtues of the contemplative life, namely of divine and intelligible things, as Aristotle says.[3] But all these opinions are false, although not in the same way. Hence the Lord condemns all these.

405 He condemns the opinion of those who say that it consists in the abundance of exterior things: hence, he says, ***blessed are the poor***, as though to say
406 that the wealthy are not happy. And he condemns the opinion of those who place beatitude in the satisfaction of appetite when he says, ***blessed are the merciful***.

But one should know that there are three appetites in man. The irascible, which desires vengeance on enemies, and he condemns this when he says, ***blessed are the meek***. The concupiscible, whose good is to rejoice and be delighted; he condemns this when he says, ***blessed are they who mourn***. The will, which is twofold, according as it seeks two things: *first*, that the will be forced by no higher law; *second*, that it be able to bind others as subjects: hence it desires to command, and not to be under another. But the Lord shows the contrary regarding both. And regarding the *first*, he says, ***blessed are they who hunger and thirst after justice***. Regarding the *second*, he says, ***blessed are the merciful***.

3. See Aristotle, *Nicomachean Ethics* 10.

Therefore both those who place beatitude in the abundance of exterior things and those who place it in the satisfaction of appetite are wrong.

407 Those, however, who place beatitude in the actions of the active life, namely, in moral acts, are wrong, but less so, because that is the way to beatitude. Hence the Lord does not condemn them as though evil but shows the ordering to beatitude. Because the virtues of the active life are either ordered to oneself, such as temperance and others of this kind, and their end is cleanness of heart, because they enable one to conquer the passions; or they are ordered to another, and so their end is peace, and of this kind: *The effect of righteousness will be peace* (Isa. 32:17). And therefore these virtues are ways to beatitude, and not beatitude itself; and hence, ***blessed are the clean of heart: for they will see God.*** He does not say, 'they see,' because this would be beatitude itself. And similarly, ***blessed are the peacemakers***, not because they make peace, but because they tend toward something else: ***for they will be called children of God.***

408 Now, the opinion of those who say that beatitude consists in the contemplation of divine things is condemned by the Lord only as to the timing, for otherwise it is true; because the last happiness does consist in the vision of the best intelligible, namely God; hence he says, ***they will see.***

And one should note that, according to the Philosopher, two things are required for the contemplative act to make one happy: one has to do with the substance, namely, that it be the act of the highest intelligible, which is God; the other has to do with form, namely love and delight, for delight perfects happiness just as beauty perfects youth.[4] And therefore the Lord sets down two things, ***they will see God*** and ***they will be called children of God***, for this pertains to the union of love. *See what love the Father has given us, that we should be called children of God; and so we are* (1 John 3:1).

409 Likewise, one should note that in these beatitudes, certain things are set down as merits, and certain things as rewards: and this is clear in each case. ***Blessed are the poor in spirit***: here is a merit; ***for theirs is the kingdom of heaven***: here is the reward; and so on in the others.

410 And one should note also something about merit in general, and something about reward in general. About merit, one should know that the Philosopher distinguishes two kinds of virtue: one common, which perfects a man in a human manner; the other special, which he calls heroic, which perfects above the human manner.[5] For when a brave man fears where there is something to be feared, that is a virtue; but if he did not fear, it would be a vice. But if he feared nothing, trusting in the help of God, that would be a virtue above the human manner; and these virtues are called divine. Therefore, these acts are

4. See Aristotle, 10.4.

5. Aristotle, 7.1.

perfect, and virtue also is a perfect operation, according to the Philosopher.[6] So these merits are either acts of the gifts or acts of the virtues according as they are perfected by the gifts.

411 Likewise, note that the acts of the virtues are those about which the law commands; moreover, the merits of the beatitudes are acts of the virtues; and therefore all those things which are commanded and are contained below are referred back to these beatitudes. Hence just as Moses first set down the commandments, and afterwards said many things which were all referred back to the commandments given, so Christ in his teaching first sets forth these beatitudes, to which all the others are reduced.

412 Concerning the *first*, one should note that God is the reward of those who serve him; *the Lord is my portion, said my soul: therefore will I hope in him* (Lam. 3:24); *the Lord is my chosen portion and my cup* (Ps. 16:5); *I am the Lord who brought you from Ur of the Chaldees, to give you this land to possess* (Gen. 15:7). And as Augustine says: *When a soul turns away from you, it seeks goods outside of you.*[7] Now, men seek diverse things; but anything that can be found in any life, the Lord promises in its entirety in God. For some place the highest good in the abundance of riches, through which they can attain the greatest dignity; the Lord promises a kingdom which embraces both, but he says that one must arrive at this kingdom by the way of poverty, not of riches. Hence, ***Blessed are the poor.*** Others arrive at this honor through war; but the Lord says, ***Blessed are the meek.*** Others seek consolations through pleasure; the Lord says, ***Blessed are they who mourn.*** Some are unwilling to be subject to another; but the Lord says, ***Blessed are they who hunger and thirst after justice.*** Some wish to avoid evil by oppressing those subject to them; the Lord says, ***blessed are the merciful.*** Some place the vision of God in the contemplation of truth in this life; but the Lord promises this vision in the homeland; hence, ***Blessed are the clean of heart.***

413 And one should notice that these rewards, which the Lord touches upon here, can be had in two ways, namely perfectly and completely, and they are had in this way only in the homeland; or as a beginning and imperfectly, and they are had in this way in this life. Hence the saints have a certain beginning of that beatitude. And because these things cannot be explained in this life as they will be in the homeland, therefore Augustine explains them [the promised rewards] according as they are in this life; therefore, ***blessed are the poor in spirit***: not in hope only, but also in actuality.[8] *For lo, the kingdom of God*

6. Aristotle, 2.6.

7. Augustine, *Confessions* 2.

8. Augustine, *On the Lord's Sermon on the Mount* 1.4.12.

is within you (Luke 17:21). Hence, these things having been prefaced, let us proceed to the text.

414 The Evangelist does two things in these beatitudes. *First*, the beatitudes themselves are set down; *second*, a manifestation of the beatitudes, at ***Blessed are they who suffer persecution for justice's sake: for theirs is the kingdom of heaven***; for this expresses all the beatitudes.

Now, virtue does three things: for it removes one from evil, it works and makes one to work what is good, and it disposes one to what is best. *First*, then, he determines about the *first*, at ***Blessed are the poor***; about the *second*, at ***Blessed are they who hunger***; about the *third*, at ***Blessed are the clean of heart***.

Moreover, virtue removes one from three evils: greed, cruelty or disturbance, and harmful pleasure. The *first* is noted at ***Blessed are the poor***; the *second*, at ***Blessed are the merciful***; the *third*, at ***Blessed are they who mourn***.

415 He says then, ***Blessed are the poor***. It is read in two ways. *First*, in this way: ***Blessed are the poor***, i.e., the humble, who reckon themselves to be poor; for they are the truly humble who reckon themselves poor, not only in external things, but even in interior things; *I am poor and needy* (Ps. 40:17); on the other hand: *You say, "I am rich, I have prospered, and I need nothing"; not knowing that you are wretched, pitiable, poor, blind, and naked* (Rev. 3:17).

And then what is said, ***in spirit***, can be read in three ways. For the pride of a man is sometimes called the spirit; *cease therefore from the man, whose breath is in his nostrils, for he is reputed high* (Isa. 2:22 DRB); *the spirit of the mighty is like a whirlwind beating against a wall* (Isa. 25:4). And pride is called ***spirit*** because as breath inflates a bag, so pride inflates a man, *puffed up without reason by his sensuous mind* (Col. 2:18). Therefore, ***blessed are the poor***, namely those who have little of the spirit of pride. Or ***spirit*** is taken as the will of man. For some are humble by necessity, and these are not blessed, but rather those who put on humility. *Third*, it is taken as the Holy Spirit; hence, ***Blessed are the poor in the Spirit***, who are humble through the Holy Spirit. And these two come to the same thing, so to speak. And he says, ***the poor in spirit***, because humility gives one the Holy Spirit; *but for whom will I have respect, except him that is poor and little, and of a contrite spirit, and that trembles at my words?* (Isa. 66:2 DRB).

To these poor ones is promised the kingdom, in which is understood the highest excellence. And although this is bestowed upon any virtue, yet it is especially given to humility; because *he who humbles himself, will be exalted* (Luke 14:11). *Glory will uphold the humble of spirit* (Prov. 29:23 DRB).

416 Or in another way, according to Jerome. ***Poor in spirit***, literally, in renunciation of temporal things.[9] And he says, ***in spirit***, because some are poor by necessity, but beatitude is not due them, but rather to those who are poor by

9. Jerome, *Commentary on Matthew* 5.3.

will. And those who are poor by will are so called in two ways, because although some have riches, yet they do not have them in their heart; *if riches increase, set not your heart on them* (Ps. 62:10). Others neither have, nor desire, and this is more secure, because the mind is drawn from spiritual things by riches. And these are properly called ***poor in spirit***, because the acts of the gifts, which are above the human manner, are those of the blessed man: and that a man should reject all riches, so that he does not even desire them in some way, this is above the human manner.

417 To these is promised ***the kingdom of heaven***, in which is indicated not only loftiness of honor, but the abundance of riches; *has not God chosen those who are poor in this world to be rich in faith and heirs of the kingdom which he has promised to those who love him?* (James 2:5).

And note that Moses first promised riches: *The Lord your God will set you high above all the nations of the earth* (Deut. 28:1); and further down, *Blessed will you be in the city, and blessed in the field* (28:3). And therefore, that the Lord might distinguish the old law from the new, he first places beatitude in the contempt of temporal riches.

418 Likewise note, following Augustine, that this beatitude pertains to the gift of fear.[10] Because fear, most of all filial fear, makes one have reverence toward God; and out of this a man despises riches. Isaiah sets out the beatitudes in descending order: *There shall come forth a shoot from the stump of Jesse, and a branch shall grow out of his roots. And the Spirit of the Lord shall rest upon him, the spirit of wisdom and understanding, the spirit of counsel and might, the spirit of knowledge and the fear of the Lord* (11:1–3). Christ sets them out the other way around, from the gift of fear, namely from poverty, because Isaiah foretold the coming of Christ to earth, but Christ drew men up from the earth.

419 ***Blessed are the meek.*** This is the *second* beatitude; but lest someone say that poverty is enough for beatitude, he shows that it is not enough: rather gentleness is required, which restrains one with regard to anger, just as temperance restrains one with regard to concupiscence; for he is meek who does not grow angry. Now this could come about by virtue, namely that you are not angered except by a just cause; but if you are not provoked even when you have a just cause, this is above the human manner; and therefore he says, ***blessed are the meek***. For fighting is on account of an abundance of external things; and therefore there would be no disturbance if a man did not desire riches. And therefore those who are not meek are not poor in spirit. And this is why he immediately adds, ***blessed are the meek***.

And note that this consists in two things. *First*, that a man is not angered; *second*, that if he is angered, he restrains his anger. Ambrose speaks this way:

10. Augustine, *On the Lord's Sermon on the Mount* 1.4.11.

It belongs to the prudent man to moderate the motion of anger, nor is it called a lesser virtue to be angry with restraint, than not to be angered at all. I judge the latter much easier, the former much harder.[11]

420 Chrysostom says: *Among many eternal promises, he places one earthly promise.*[12] Hence, literally, the meek ***possess*** that ***land***. For many go to court to acquire possessions, but frequently they lose their life and all their things; but frequently the gentle have it all: *The meek shall possess the land* (Ps. 37:11).

But it is better explained as referred to the future. And then it can be explained in many ways. Hilary speaks this way: ***they will possess the land***, i.e., the glorified body of Christ, because they will be conformed to that brilliance in their own body;[13] *his eyes will see the king in his beauty, they will see the land far off* (Isa. 33:17); *the Lord Jesus Christ . . . will change our lowly body to be like his glorious body* (Phil. 3:21).

Or in another way. This land is the land of the dead for a while, because it is subjected to corruption, but it will be freed from corruption, according to the Apostle (Rom. 8:21). Therefore this land, when it is glorified and freed from the servitude of corruption, will be called the land of the living. Or, by ***the land*** is understood the fiery heaven, where the blessed are;[14] and it is called ***the land***, because just as the land is related to heaven, so is that heaven related to the heaven of the Holy Trinity. Or, ***they will possess the land***, i.e., their own glorified body.

Augustine explains this metaphorically, and he says that by this one should understand a certain solidity of the saints in the knowledge of the first truth;[15] *I believe that I shall see the goodness of the Lord in the land of the living* (Ps. 27:13).

421 This *second* beatitude is related to the gift of piety, because those get angry, properly speaking, who are not contented with the divine ordering of things.

422 ***Blessed are they who mourn.*** Two beatitudes were mentioned by which we are drawn away from the evils of desire and of cruelty; here a *third* is set down, by which we are drawn away from the evil of harmful pleasure or enjoyment. And this is ***Blessed are they who mourn.***

In the Old Testament, he promised earthly things, and earthly enjoyment: *They shall be radiant over the goodness of the Lord, over the grain, the wine, and the oil* (Jer. 31:12). Then after that, *Then shall the maidens rejoice in the dance,*

11. Ambrose, *Commentary on Luke* 5.54.

12. John Chrysostom, *Homilies on the Gospel of Saint Matthew* 15.5.

13. Hilary of Poitiers, *Commentary on Matthew* 4.3.

14. For more on this "fiery heaven" (or "empyrean heaven"), see *On 2 Corinthians* 12.1 (included above in chapter 12 of this collection).

15. Augustine, *On the Lord's Sermon on the Mount* 1.2.4.

and the young men and the old shall be merry (Jer. 31:13). But the Lord on the contrary places beatitude in mourning.

But one should notice that not just any lamenting can be called mourning, but that by which someone laments a dead one dear to him; for the Lord speaks here by way of excess. Just as above, ***blessed are the poor***, so here he mentions the greatest grief; for just as those who grieve the dead receive no consolation, so the Lord wishes our life to be in mourning; *make mourning as for an only son, a bitter lamentation* (Jer. 6:26).

And this mourning can be explained in three ways. *First*, for sins, not only personal, but another's as well, for if we mourn those who are dead in body, much more those who are dead spiritually; *how long will you grieve over Saul?* (1 Sam. 16:1); *O that my head were waters and my eyes a fountain of tears that I might weep day and night for the slain of the daughter of my people!* (Jer. 9:1). Now this beatitude is set down fittingly enough after the previous one. For someone could say, 'it is enough not to do evil,' and this is true in the beginning, before sin; but after a sin is committed, it is not enough unless you make satisfaction. *Second*, it can be taken as mourning for our dwelling in present misery; *woe is me, that my sojourning is prolonged!* (Ps. 120:5 DRB). This is *the watering above and below*, about which, *weep over your sins, and over the sojourning of the heavenly homeland* (Josh. 15:19).[16] *Third*, according to Augustine, for the mourning which men make over the joys of the world, which they abandon by coming to Christ; for some men die to the world, and the world dies to them;[17] *God forbid that I should glory, save in the cross of our Lord Jesus Christ; by whom the world is crucified to me, and I to the world* (Gal. 6:14). Now as we mourn over the dead, so these men mourn, because it cannot be but that they feel some sorrow in abandoning everything.

423 Moreover, to these three mournings correspond three consolations, because to the mourning for sins corresponds remission of sins, which David begged for, saying, *Restore to me the joy of your salvation* (Ps. 51:12). To the delay of the heavenly homeland and the dwelling in present misery corresponds the consolation of eternal life, about which it is said, *I will turn their mourning into joy; I will comfort them, and give them gladness for sorrow* (Jer. 31:13); and, *you will be comforted in Jerusalem* (Isa. 66:13). To the third mourning corresponds the consolation of divine love; for when someone sorrows over the loss of a thing loved, he takes consolation if he acquires another thing more loved. Hence men are consoled when instead of temporal things they receive spiritual and

16. It is unclear what passage(s) St. Thomas is citing here. Only part of the quotation matches Joshua 15:19: *Give me a blessing: you have given me a southern and dry land, give me also a land that is watered. And Caleb gave her the upper and the nether watery ground.*

17. Augustine, *On the Lord's Sermon on the Mount* 1.2.5.

eternal things, which is to receive the Holy Spirit, which is why he is called the Comforter (John 15:26). For men rejoice through the Holy Spirit, who is the divine love; *your sorrow will be turned into joy* (John 16:20).

424 And one should note that this beatitude is appropriated to the gift of knowledge, because they mourn who know the misery of others; hence it says about certain men who do not have such knowledge, *They live in great strife due to ignorance, and they call such great evils peace* (Wis. 14:22); on the other hand, *in much wisdom is much vexation* (Eccles. 1:18).

425 And one should notice that this reward is so ordained that the second is always added onto the first. For *first* he said, ***Blessed are the poor in spirit: for theirs is the kingdom of heaven***; afterward, ***for they will possess the land***: for it is more to possess than merely to have. Likewise, afterward, ***for they will be comforted***: for it is more to be consoled than to possess, for some possess things but do not take delight in them.

426 Next, those beatitudes being set down which pertain to the removal of evil; here the beatitude which pertains to the working of good is set down. And our good is twofold, namely the good of justice and the good of mercy. And so he sets out two things.

427 As regards the *first*, he says, ***Blessed are they who hunger and thirst after justice.*** Justice is taken in three ways, according to Chrysostom and the Philosopher.[18] For sometimes it is taken as every virtue: and every virtue is called legal justice, which commands concerning the acts of the virtues. Hence insofar as a man obeys the law, he fulfills the work of all the virtues. It is taken in another way as a particular virtue, one of the four cardinal virtues, to which is opposed greed, or injustice, and it concerns buying, selling, and renting.

So what he says here, ***who hunger after justice***, can be understood generally, or particularly. If it is understood as about the general meaning of justice, he says this for two reasons.

The *first* is Jerome's, who says that it is not enough that a man should work the work of justice, unless he works with desire;[19] *I will freely sacrifice to you* (Ps. 54:6 DRB). And in another place, *my soul thirsts for God . . . when shall I come and behold the face of God?* (Ps. 42:2). *I will send a famine on the land;*

18. This threefold distinction of justices appears to be an error in the manuscript as can be seen from the fact that he goes on to enumerate only two forms of justice along the lines of the universal-general distinction affirmed by both Aristotle (*Nicomachean Ethics* 5) and John Chrysostom (*Homilies on the Gospel of Saint Matthew* 4.7). See also the alternate Basel Manuscript of this lecture, in which the distinction is a twofold (*dupliciter*) rather than three as in this version of the manuscript (Anton ten Klooster, "Thomas Aquinas on the Beatitudes: Edition of the Basel Manuscript," *European Journal for the Study of Thomas Aquinas* 36, no 1. [December 2017]: 40–87) and other places in St. Thomas' corpus where he ascribes a twofold distinction of justice to Aristotle and Chrysostom (*Summa theologiae* 2–2.58.7, *On Matthew* 1.4).

19. Jerome, *Commentary on Matthew* 5.6.

not a famine of bread, nor a thirst for water, but of hearing the words of the Lord (Amos 8:11). Therefore it is a hunger when someone works with desire.

Another reason. Justice is twofold, perfect and imperfect. We cannot have perfect justice in this world, because *if we say that we have no sin, we deceive ourselves, and the truth is not in us* (1 John 1:8). *All our justices [are] as the rag of a menstruous woman* (Isa. 64:6 DRB). But we have this in heaven; *your people shall be all just, they shall inherit the land forever* (Isa. 60:21 DRB). But we can have a desire for justice here: and therefore, he says, ***Blessed are they who hunger and thirst after justice.*** And what Pythagoras did is similar.[20] For in the time of Pythagoras, those who studied were called *sophoi*, i.e., wise men; but Pythagoras did not wish to be called *sophos*, i.e., wise, but 'philosopher' [*philósophos*], that is, a lover of wisdom; in this way the Lord wills that his own be and be called lovers of justice.

But if it is understood as about particular justice, which is that a man render to each what is his own, then it is fittingly said, ***blessed are they who hunger***, because hunger and thirst properly belong to the greedy, since those who desire to possess another's goods unjustly are never satisfied. Hence the hunger about which the Lord speaks is opposed to this one, namely the hunger of the greedy. And the Lord wills that we pant after that justice in this way, because we will never be, as it were, satisfied in this life, just as the greedy man is never satisfied. ***Blessed are they who hunger and thirst after justice: for they will have their fill.***

428 A fitting reward is set forth, ***they will have their fill***, and it is first in the eternal vision, for they will see God through his essence; *I will be satisfied when your glory will appear* (Ps. 17:15). For there nothing remains to be desired; *who satisfies your desire with good things* (Ps. 103:5 DRB); *to the just their desire will be given* (Prov. 10:24 DRB).

Second, in the present. And this satisfaction is twofold. One is in spiritual goods, that is in the fulfillment of God's commands; *my meat is to do the will of him that sent me, that I may perfect his work* (John 4:34); and Augustine explains this. In another way, it is taken as concerning a plenitude of temporal things. Unjust men are never filled, but men who have as their end justice itself, do not go beyond it; *the just eats and fills his soul: but the belly of the wicked is never to be filled* (Prov. 13:25 DRB).

429 According to Augustine, this beatitude is reduced to the gift of fortitude, because it pertains to fortitude that a man works justly.[21] Likewise, he adds

20. Pythagoras was a philosopher and mathematician from the 6th century B.C. Elsewhere (*Commentary on the Metaphysics of Aristotle* 1.3) St. Thomas further explains that Pythagoras refused to be called a *sophos* because he felt this label to be presumptuous.

21. Augustine, *On the Lord's Sermon on the Mount* 1.4.11.

something to the reward set out above, because to be filled is to fulfill the desires entirely.

Likewise, note that first he says, ***blessed are they who mourn***, for when a man is ill, he does not desire to eat, but he begins to desire when he has just begun to be healed; and so it is in the spiritual life, for when men are in sin, they do not feel spiritual hunger, but when they abandon sin, then they feel it. And therefore he immediately adds, ***blessed are the merciful***, because justice without mercy is cruelty, while mercy without justice is the mother of laxity. And so it is necessary that both be joined together: *Let not mercy and truth leave you* (Prov. 3:3 DRB). *Mercy and truth have met each other: justice and peace have kissed* (Ps. 85:10 DRB).

430 ***Blessed are the merciful: for they will obtain mercy.*** To be merciful is to have a miserable heart at the misery of others. Moreover, we have pity on the miseries of others when we think of them as our own. Now, we sorrow for our miseries, and we are eager to drive them away; therefore you are truly merciful when you are eager to drive away the misery of others.

And the misery of one's neighbor is twofold. *First*, in temporal things, and for this we should have a miserable heart; *if anyone has the world's goods and sees his brother in need, yet closes his heart against him, how does God's love abide in him?* (1 John 3:17). *Second*, when a man is made miserable through sin; because, just as there is beatitude in the works of the virtues, so there is a particular misery in vices. *Sin is a reproach to any people* (Prov. 14:34). And therefore, when we warn those falling so that they may return, we are merciful; ***when he saw the crowds, he had compassion for them*** (Matt. 9:36). Therefore, these merciful ones are blessed.

431 And why? ***For they will obtain mercy.*** And one should know that the gifts of God always exceed our merit; *the Lord is the one who repays, and he will repay you sevenfold* (Sir. 35:11). Therefore the mercy which our Lord has on us is much greater than that which we have on our neighbor.

This mercy is begun in this life in two ways. *First*, because sins are loosed: *[The Lord] forgives all your iniquities* (Ps. 103:3). *Second*, because he removes temporal defects, such that he ***makes his sun rise*** (Matt. 5:45); yet it will be perfected in the future, when every misery, both of guilt and of punishment, will be taken away. *O Lord, your mercy is in heaven* (Ps. 36:5 DRB). And this is ***for they will obtain mercy.***

432 This beatitude is reduced to the gift of counsel; because this is a unique counsel, that we should obtain mercy amidst the dangers of this world. *Godliness is of value in every way* (1 Tim. 4:8); *O king, let my counsel be acceptable to you* (Dan. 4:27).

433 So in this way are set down the acts of the virtues by which we are withdrawn from what is evil and do what is good. Now are set down the acts by which we are disposed to what is best; hence, ***Blessed are the clean of heart.*** This beatitude consists in two things: in the vision of God and in the love of neighbor. Hence, *first*, he sets out the beatitude which pertains to the vision of God; *second*, the beatitude which pertains to the love of neighbor, at ***Blessed are the peacemakers.***

434 He says then, ***Blessed are the clean of heart: for they will see God.*** Here there is first a question of literal meaning. For we know that God cannot be seen: *No man has ever seen God* (1 John 4:12). And lest someone say that although no one sees at present, he will see in the future, the Apostle takes this possibility away: *[He] alone has immortality and dwells in unapproachable light, whom no man has ever seen, or can see* (1 Tim. 6:16).

But one should know that there are different opinions about this. For some have held that God is never seen in his essence, but in some reflection of his glory; but the *Gloss* condemns this, commenting on Exodus, *Man shall not see me and live* (33:20), with two arguments. *First*, because this opposes the authority of Sacred Scripture: *We will see him as he is* (1 John 3:2). Similarly, *Now we see in a mirror dimly, but then face to face* (1 Cor. 13:12). It is likewise opposed to reason, because the beatitude of man is the last good of man, in which his desire is set to rest. Now, it is a natural desire that a man, seeing an effect, inquires about the cause; hence also the philosophers' wonder was the origin of philosophy, because when they saw effects, they wondered and sought the cause. Therefore, that desire will not be set to rest until it arrives at the first cause, which is God, namely at the divine essence itself. Therefore, he will be seen through his essence.

Others have erred even more, holding the contrary position, for they said that we will see the essence of God not only with the eye of the mind, but with the eye of the body as well, and that Christ sees the divine essence with his bodily eye. But this does not hold together, which is clear, *first* from the Scriptural text which is mentioned here, because he would not say, ***blessed are the clean of heart***, but, 'blessed are they who have clean and pure eyes.' So he gives one to understand that he will not see except with the heart, i.e., the intellect, for heart is taken this way: *the eyes of your heart enlightened* (Eph. 1:18). *Second*, because the sense of a body can only attain to its own object; but if it be said that then it will have a greater power, one should say that then it would not be bodily vision, because the bodily eye sees only colors, and sees the essence *per accidens*, according to Augustine.[22] Just as when I see something living, we can say that I see life, insofar as I see certain indications by which its

22. Augustine, *The City of God* 22.29.

life is pointed out to me, so it will be in the divine vision, because the reflection of God in the new heaven and the new earth and the glorified bodies will be so great that by it we will be said to see God as though with the bodily eyes. Therefore, ***blessed are the clean of heart.***

He resolves the text, *No man has ever seen God* (1 John 4:12), in three ways. *First*, that it will not be by a comprehensive vision; *second*, not with bodily eyes; *third*, not in this life: because if it were given to someone to see God in this life, this would be because he is entirely estranged and lifted above the bodily senses. And this is why he said, ***blessed are the clean of heart***; because just as the eye seeing color must be free from impurities, so it is with the mind seeing God; *think of the Lord in goodness, and seek him in simplicity of heart. For he is found by those who tempt him not: and he shows himself to those who have faith in him* (Wis. 1:1 DRB), for the heart is purified by faith. *[He] cleansed their hearts by faith* (Acts 15:9). And because vision follows upon faith, therefore it is said, ***for they will see God.***

435 ***Blessed are the clean of heart***, namely those who have a general cleanness from unworthy thoughts, by which their heart is a holy temple of God, in which they see God by contemplating; for 'temple' seems to be said from 'contemplating.' But in a particular way, ***blessed are the clean of heart***, i.e., those who have cleanness of body; for nothing so impedes spiritual contemplation as uncleanness of body does. They obtain the *peace . . . and holiness, without which no one will see God* (Heb. 12:14).

And therefore, some say that the moral virtues, especially chastity, advance one toward the contemplative life. And according to this, ***blessed are the clean of heart*** can be understood as about the vision in this life; for the saints who have a heart filled by justice see more excellently than some who see through bodily effects, for to the degree that effects are closer to God, to that degree God is more known through them. Hence the saints, who have justice, charity, and other such effects, which are most like God, know more than others. *O taste and see that the Lord is good* (Ps. 34:8).

436 ***Blessed are the peacemakers: for they will be called children of God.*** Here the *seventh* beatitude is set down; and, as was said, the virtues which dispose one to what is best dispose one to two things, namely to the vision of God and to love. And just as cleanness of heart disposes one to the vision of God, so peace disposes one to the love of God, by which we are called and are sons of God; and thus it disposes one to the love of neighbor, because, *he who does not love his brother whom he has seen cannot love God whom he has not seen* (1 John 4:20).

437 And one should note that two rewards of beatitude are set down here, namely ***blessed are the peacemakers*** and ***blessed are they who suffer persecution for justice's sake.*** And all the preceding beatitudes are reduced to these two,

and these are the effects of all the preceding. For what is caused by poverty of spirit, by mourning, by meekness, except that one has a clean heart? What by justice and mercy, except that we have peace? *And the work of justice will be peace, and the service of justice quietness, and security forever* (Isa. 32:17 DRB).

438 ***Blessed*** therefore ***are the peacemakers***. But one should see what peace is, and how we can arrive at it. Peace is the tranquility of order. Now, order is the arrangement allotting the proper place to equals and unequals. Therefore peace resides in this, that all hold their own places. Hence the mind of man ought first to be subject to God. *Second*, the motions and inferior powers which are common to us and the brutes should be subject to man, for man has dominion over the animals by reason: *Let us make man in our image, after our likeness; and let them have dominion over the fish of the sea, and over the birds of the air, and over the cattle, and over all the earth, and over every creeping thing that creeps upon the earth* (Gen. 1:26). *Third*, that a man have peace toward others, because thus he will be entirely ordered.

However, this ordering can only exist in holy men; *much peace have they who love your law* (Ps. 119:165); "*there is no peace," says the Lord, "for the wicked"* (Isa. 48:22), for they cannot have interior peace. *They live in great strife due to ignorance, and they call such great evils peace* (Wis. 14:22). Such peace the world cannot give; *not as the world gives, do I give unto you* (John 14:27). Similarly, all this is not enough, but they ought to make peace among those who quarrel; *joy follows them that take counsels of peace* (Prov. 12:20 DRB).

Nevertheless, one should know that this peace is begun here, but not perfected, because no one can have the animal movements entirely subject to reason; *but I see another law in my members, fighting against the law of my mind, and captivating me in the law of sin, that is in my members* (Rom. 7:23). Hence true peace will be in eternal life; *in peace I will both lie down and sleep* (Ps. 4:8); *the peace of God . . . surpasses all understanding* (Phil. 4:7).

439 ***For they will be called children of God***, for three reasons. The *first* is because they have the duty of a son of God, for the Son is said to have come into the world for this purpose, that he might gather together the scattered; *for he is our peace* (Eph. 2:14); *making peace through the blood of his cross* (Col. 1:20). *Second*, because through peace with charity one arrives at the eternal kingdom, in which all will be called sons of God; *how they are numbered among the children of God, and their lot is among the saints* (Wis. 5:5 DRB). *Careful to keep the unity of the Spirit in the bond of peace* (Eph. 4:3). *Third*, because a man is made like God by this, because where there is peace, there is no resistance; but no one can resist God. *Who has hardened himself against him, and succeeded?* (Job 9:4).

440 And one should note that these beatitudes add onto one another. For it is greater to obtain mercy than to have one's fill, because to have one's fill is to complete what is proportioned to oneself, but mercy goes beyond oneself. Similarly, not all who receive mercy are admitted by the king to see the king.
441 Similarly, it is more to be a son of the king than to see the king. And yet one should know that by all these beatitudes one reward is designated. But why did the Lord will to signify it through many things this way?

One should say that all things which are divided in lower things are brought together in higher things. And since in human affairs those things are found scattered about, and we are led by the hand through sensible things, for this reason the Lord signified the eternal reward through many things.

442 Now, this seventh beatitude is adapted to the gift of wisdom, for wisdom makes men to be sons of God. One should note likewise that peace is placed in the seventh beatitude, just as rest in the seventh day (Gen. 2:2).

443 Next is set down the eighth beatitude, which indicates the perfection of all the preceding beatitudes; for a man is perfect in all these things when he does not give up at all because of afflictions. *The furnace tries the potter's vessels, and the trial of affliction just men* (Sir. 27:5 DRB). ***Blessed*** therefore ***are they who suffer persecution.***

But perhaps someone hearing ***Blessed are the peacemakers*** would say that these men are not blessed on account of persecution, because persecution disturbs peace, or takes it away entirely. But certainly not interior peace, but exterior peace; *great peace have those who love your law* (Ps. 119:165).

Now, the persecution itself does not make one blessed, but the cause of the persecution; hence he says, ***for justice's sake***: *If also you suffer anything for justice's sake, blessed are you* (1 Pet. 3:14 DRB). Chrysostom: *He does not say,* 'from the pagans and for the faith,' but ***for justice's sake.***[23]

23. Thomas Aquinas, *Catena Aurea on Matthew* 5.10 ascribes this quote to a Pseudo-Chrysostom, *Phil.* 3.2.3.

Galatians 5:22–23

The Fruits of the Spirit

On Galatians 5.6 (327–335)

5:22 ***But the fruit of the Spirit is charity, joy, peace, patience, benignity, goodness, longanimity,***

5:23 ***mildness, faith, modesty, continency, chastity. Against such there is no law.***

327 Having listed the works of the flesh, the Apostle then manifests the works of the Spirit.[24] *First*, he manifests them; *second*, he shows how the law is related to the works of the Spirit and to the works of the flesh, at ***against such*** (Gal. 5:23).

328 As to the *first*, he enumerates the spiritual goods which he calls ***fruits***. But here a question arises, because fruit is something we enjoy; but we should enjoy not our acts, but God alone. Therefore, acts of this kind, which the Apostle lists here, ought not be called ***fruits***.

Furthermore, a gloss says that these works of the Spirit are to be sought for themselves; but that which is sought for itself is not referred to something else. Therefore virtues and their works are not to be referred to happiness.

I answer that ***fruit*** is said in two ways: namely, as something acquired, for example, from labor or study—*The fruit of good labors is renowned* (Wis. 3:15)—and as something produced, as fruit is produced from a tree: *A sound tree cannot bear evil fruit* (Matt. 7:18). Now the works of the Spirit are called fruits, not as something earned or acquired, but as produced. Furthermore, fruit which is acquired has the character of an ultimate end; not, however, fruit which is produced. Nevertheless, fruit so understood implies two things: namely, that it is the last thing of the producer, as the last thing produced by a tree is its fruit, and that it is sweet or delightful: *His fruit was sweet to my taste* (Song of Sol. 2:3). So, then, the works of the virtues and of the Spirit are something last in us. For the Holy Spirit is in us through grace, through which we acquire the habit of the virtues; these in turn make us capable of working according to virtue.

Furthermore, they are delightful and even fruitful: *You have your fruit unto sanctification* (Rom. 6:22 DRB), i.e., in holy works. And that is why they are called ***fruits***. But they are also called flowers, namely, in relation to future happiness; because just as from flowers hope of fruit is taken, so from works of

24. See Gal. 5:18–21 and Thomas Aquinas *On Galatians* 5.5 (not included in this collection).

the virtues is obtained hope of eternal life and happiness. And as in the flower there is a beginning of the fruit, so in the works of the virtues is a beginning of happiness, which will exist when knowledge and charity are made perfect.

From this the answer to the *second* objection is plain. For something can be said to be worthy of being sought for itself in two ways, according as 'for' designates formal cause or final cause. Works of the virtues are to be sought for themselves formally but not finally, because they are a delight in themselves. For a sweet medicine is formally sought for itself, because it has something within itself that makes it pleasant, namely, sweetness, which however is sought for an end, namely, for the sake of health. But a bitter medicine is not sought formally for itself, because it does not please by reason of its form; yet it is sought for something else finally, namely, for health, which is its end.

This explains why the Apostle calls the effects of the flesh ***works***, but the fruits of the Spirit he calls ***fruits***. For it has been pointed out that a fruit is something last and sweet, produced from a thing. On the other hand, that which is produced from something but not according to nature does not have the character of fruit but is, as it were, an alien growth. Now the works of the flesh and sins are alien to the nature of those things which God has planted in our nature. For God planted in human nature certain seeds, namely, a natural desire of good and knowledge, and he added gifts of grace: and therefore, because the works of the virtues are produced naturally from these, they are called ***fruits***, but the works of the flesh are not. And for this reason, the Apostle says: *what fruit . . . had you then in those things of which you are now ashamed?* (Rom. 6:21 DRB).

It is plain, therefore, from what has been said, that the works of the virtues are called ***fruits of the Spirit***, both because they have a sweetness and delight in themselves and because they are the last and congruous products of the gifts.
329 The difference from one another of the gifts, beatitudes, virtues, and fruits is taken in the following way.

In a virtue can be considered the habit and the act. Now the habit of a virtue qualifies a person to act well. If it enables him to act well in a human mode, it is called a virtue. But if it qualifies one for acting well, above the human mode, it is called a gift. Hence the Philosopher, above the common virtues, puts certain heroic virtues:[25] thus, to know the invisible things of God darkly is in keeping with the human mode, and such knowledge pertains to the virtue of faith; but to know the same things more penetratingly and above the human mode pertains to the gift of understanding. But as to the act of a virtue, it is either perfective, and in this way is a beatitude; or it is a source of

25. Aristotle, *Nicomachean Ethics* 7.1.

delight, and in this way it is a fruit. Of these fruits it is said in Revelation: *On either side of the river [was] the tree of life with its twelve kinds of fruit* (22:2).

330 He says, therefore, ***the fruit of the Spirit***, which arises in the soul from the sowing of spiritual grace, is ***charity, joy, peace, patience, longanimity***, which indeed are thus distinguished because fruits perfect one either inwardly or outwardly. *First*, he mentions those that perfect inwardly; *second*, those that perfect outwardly. Now a man is perfected and directed inwardly both as to good things and as to evil: *with the weapons of righteousness for the right hand and for the left* (2 Cor. 6:7).

With respect to good things a person is perfected, first of all, in his heart through love. For just as in natural movements there is first an inclination of a nature's appetite to its end, so the first of the inward movements is the inclination to good, i.e., love; accordingly, the first fruit is ***charity***: *The charity of God is poured forth in our hearts by the Holy Spirit who is given to us* (Rom. 5:5 DRB). And through charity the others are perfected; wherefore, the Apostle says in Colossians: *Above all these put on love which binds everything together in perfect harmony* (3:14). But the ultimate end that perfects man inwardly is ***joy***, which proceeds from the presence of the thing loved. And he that has charity already has what he loves: *He that abides in charity abides in God and God in him* (1 John 4:16 DRB). And from this springs joy: *Rejoice in the Lord always; again I say, rejoice* (Phil. 4:4).

But this joy should be perfect, and for this two things are required: *first*, that the object loved be enough to perfect the lover. And as to this he says, ***peace***. For it is then that the lover has peace, when he adequately possesses the object loved: *I am become in his presence as one finding peace* (Song of Sol. 8:10 DRB). *Second*, that there be perfect enjoyment of the thing loved, which is likewise obtained by peace, because whatever else happens, if someone perfectly enjoys the object loved, say God, he cannot be hindered from enjoying it: *Great peace have those who love your law; nothing can make them stumble* (Ps. 119:165). In this way, therefore, joy connotes the fruition of charity, but peace the perfection of charity. And by these is man inwardly made perfect as to good things.

331 Also with respect to evils, the Holy Spirit perfects and adjusts a person: *first*, against the evil that disturbs peace, which is disturbed by adverse objects. Touching this the Holy Spirit perfects one by patience, which makes for patient endurance of adversities; hence he says, ***patience***: *In your patience you shall possess your souls* (Luke 21:19 DRB); and *patience has a perfect work* (James 1:4 DRB). *Second*, against the evil which hinders joy, namely, the deferment of the object loved, the Spirit opposes long-suffering, which is not broken by delay. As to this he says, ***longanimity***: *If it seem slow, wait for it; it will surely come, it will*

not delay (Hab. 2:3): in *forbearance* (2 Cor. 6:6). Hence the Lord says, *He who endures to the end will be saved* (Matt. 10:22).

332 Then when he says, ***goodness, benignity***, he mentions the fruits of the Spirit that perfect a man with respect to external things. Now external to man are things next to him, above him, and beneath him. Next to him is the neighbor; above him is God; beneath him is his sensitive nature and body.

In regard to his neighbor he perfects men, first of all, from the heart with a right and good will. Concerning this he says, ***goodness***, i.e., rectitude and gentleness of spirit. For even if all a person's other powers should be good, he cannot be said to be good unless he has a good will, according to which he uses all the others well. The reason for this is that the good denotes something perfect. But perfection is twofold: the first concerns the being of a thing; the second, its operation; and the latter is greater than the former. For that is called perfect in the absolute sense which has attained its perfect operation, which is its second perfection. Therefore, since it is by his will that man exercises the act of any power, right will makes for the good use of all the powers, and, consequently, makes the man himself good. Of this fruit it is said in Ephesians: The fruit of the light is found in all that is good and right and true (5:9).

Second, he perfects a man in his deeds, so that he will share with his neighbor. Concerning this he says, ***benignity***, i.e., giving: *God loves a cheerful giver* (2 Cor. 9:7). For benignity is said to be, as it were, a good fire, which makes a man melt to relieve the needs of others: *Wisdom is a kindly spirit* (Wis. 1:6); *put one then, as God's chosen ones, holy and beloved compassion, kindness, meekness, and patience* (Col. 3:12). Again, they perfect one with respect to evils inflicted by others, so that one meekly bears and endures harassment from another. Touching this he says, ***mildness***: *Learn from me, for I am gentle and lowly in heart* (Matt. 11:29); *to the humble he shows favor* (Prov. 3:34).

333 With respect to what is above us, namely, God, the Spirit establishes right order through faith; hence he says, ***faith***, which is a knowledge of invisible things with certainty: *[Abram] believed the Lord and; and he reckoned it to him as righteousness* (Gen. 15:6); *whoever would draw near to God must believe that he exists* (Heb. 11:6). On this account it is said in Sirach: *That which is agreeable to the Lord is faith and meekness* (1:34–35 DRB).

334 Touching what is beneath us, namely, the body, the Spirit directs us *first* as to the outward acts of the body by modesty, which moderates its deeds or utterances; concerning this he says, ***modesty*** (Gal. 5:23): *Let your modesty be known to all men* (Phil. 4:5 DRB).

Second, as to the interior appetite, and concerning this he says ***continency***, which abstains even from things that are lawful; and ***chastity***, which correctly uses what is lawful, as a gloss says.

Or, another way: continence refers to the fact that although a man be assailed by base desires, yet by the vigor of his reason he holds fast lest he be carried away. According to this the word 'continence' is taken from a person's holding fast under attack. But chastity is taken from the fact that one is neither attacked nor carried away and is derived from 'chastening.' For we call him well-chastened who is rightly tempered in all things.

335 Concerning the aforesaid, two problems arise. The *first* is that since the fruits of the Spirit are opposed to the works of the flesh, it seems that the Apostle should have mentioned as many fruits of the spirit as he mentioned works of the flesh—which he did not do. I answer that he did not do so, because there are more vices than virtues. The *second* problem is that the fruits of the Spirit mentioned do not correspond to the works of the flesh.

I answer that since it is not the Apostle's intention here to teach the art of the virtues and vices, he does not set one against the other; but he mentions as many of the one and as many of the other as are suited to his present objective.

Yet a more diligent consideration discloses that they are in some fashion set in opposition. For in opposition to ***fornication***, which is illicit love, is set ***charity***; in opposition to ***uncleanness***, ***immodesty***, and ***lust***, which are allurements of the flesh that arise from fornication, is set ***joy***, which is the spiritual delight produced by charity, as has been said. In opposition to what are called ***witchcrafts, enmities, contentions, dissensions***, are set ***patience, longanimity***, and ***goodness***. To what are called ***sects***, ***faith*** is set in opposition. To what is called ***murder***, ***benignity***. To what are called ***drunkenness, revelings***, and the like, are opposed ***modesty, continency***, and ***chastity***.[26]

26. The "allurements of the flesh" enumerated here are from Gal. 5:18–21. See also Thomas Aquinas *On Galatians* 5.5 (not included in this collection).

Chapter 15
THE THEOLOGICAL VIRTUES

Hebrews 11:1
Faith: The Beginning of Eternal Life
On Hebrews 11.1 (551–560)

11:1 ***Now, faith is the substance of things to be hoped for, the evidence of things that appear not.***

551 Above, the Apostle showed Christ's superiority in many ways by preferring him to the angels, to Moses, and to Aaron, and advised the faithful to be united to Christ.[1] Since this union consists principally in faith and begins with faith *that Christ may dwell by faith in your hearts* (Eph. 3:17), the Apostle proceeds to recommend this faith.

And he does three things: *first*, he describes faith; *second*, he gives various examples of it, at ***for by this*** (Heb. 11:2); *third*, he exhorts them to the things which pertain to faith at ***and therefore we also*** (Heb. 12:1).

552 He gives a definition of faith which is complete but obscure. Hence, it should be noted that in attempting to define any virtue perfectly, one must mention its proper matter with which it deals and its end, because habits are recognized by their acts, and acts by their objects. Therefore, it is necessary to mention the act and its order to its object and end. Thus, the definition of courage must mention its proper matter with which it deals, namely, fears and aggressions, and its end, which is the good of the republic.

Now, since faith is a theological virtue, its object and end are the same, namely, God. *First*, he mentions its order to the end; *second*, its proper matter,
553 at ***the evidence of things that appear not***. But it should be noted that the act of faith is to believe, because it is an act of the intellect narrowed to one thing by the command of the will. Hence, to believe is to think with assent, as Augustine says.[2] Therefore, the object of faith and of the will must coincide.

But the object of faith is the first truth, in which the end of the will consists, namely, happiness. But it is present one way on earth and another way in heaven, because on earth the first truth is not possessed and consequently not seen: for in regard to things that are above the soul, to possess and to see are the

1. See Thomas Aquinas, *On Hebrews* 5.1 and 10.2 (neither lecture included in this collection).

2. Augustine, *The Predestination of the Saints* 2.5.

same, as Augustine says.[3] Hence, they are only hoped for, *but hope that is seen is not hope. For who hopes for what he sees?* (Rom. 8:24). Therefore, the first truth, not seen but hoped for, is the end of the will on earth and, consequently, is the object of faith, because its end and object are the same. But the ultimate end of faith in heaven, which we tend toward by faith, is happiness, which consists in the clear vision of God: *This is eternal life, that they know you the only true God, and Jesus Christ whom you have sent* (John 17:3). And: *Blessed are they that have not seen and have believed* (John 20:29). But such is the hope of believers: *We have been born anew to a living hope* (1 Pet. 1:3). The end, therefore, of faith on earth is the attainment of the thing hoped for, namely, of eternal happiness; hence, he says, ***of things to be hoped for***.

554 But a question arises: since faith is prior to hope, why is it defined in terms of hope? For it is customary to define the later by the previous, and not vice versa. I answer that the answer should be obvious from what has been said, namely, that the object and end of faith are the same. Therefore, since the attainment of the things hoped for is its end, it must also be its object.

For it has been stated above that a habit must be defined by the order of its act to its object. But the true and the good, even though when considered in themselves are convertible as far as their supposits are concerned, differ in conception. Hence, they are diversely related to each other, because the true is a good and a good is true. In like manner, the intellect and will, which are distinguished on the basis of the distinction between the true and the good, have a diverse relationship to each other. For inasmuch as the intellect apprehends truth and anything contained in it, the true is a good; hence, the good is under the true; but inasmuch as the will moves, the true is under the good. Therefore, in the order of knowing, the intellect is prior; but in the order of moving, the will is prior.

Therefore, because the intellect is moved to the act of faith by the command of the will, in the order of moving, the will is prior. Therefore, the prior is not being defined in terms of the later because, as has been stated, in the definition of faith, the order of the act to its object, which is the same as the end, must be mentioned. But the end and the good are the same, as it says in the *Physics*.[4] But in the order to the good, the will, which is the subject of hope, is prior.

555 But why not say, 'of things to be loved,' rather than ***of things to be hoped for***? The reason is because charity is concerned with things that are present or absent. Therefore, because the unpossessed end is the object of faith, he says, ***of things to be hoped for***.

3. Augustine, *Eighty-Three Different Questions* 35.

4. Aristotle, *Physics* 2.

Nor does it make any difference that the thing to be hoped for is also the object of hope, because it is necessary that faith be ordained to an end which coincides with the object of those virtues by which the will is made perfect;
556 since faith pertains to the intellect as moved by the will. But since faith is one virtue, because it is called one habit (for its object is one), why not say 'of the thing to be hoped for,' instead ***of things to be hoped for***?

I answer that happiness, which is essentially one thing in itself, because it consists in the vision of God, is the principle and root from which the many good things contained under it are derived: for example, the characteristics of the body, companionship with the saints, and many other good things. Therefore, in order to show that all these pertain to faith, he speaks in the plural.

557 The word ***substance***, which appears in the definition, can be explained in a number of ways: in one way, causally, and then it has two senses: one which is substance, i.e., making the things hoped for be present in us. This it does in two ways: in one way, by meriting, as it were; for from the fact that a person makes his intellect captive and submissive to the things of faith, he deserves some day to see the things he hopes for, for vision is the reward of faith. In another way, as though by its property, bringing it about that what is believed really to lie in the future, be somehow already possessed, provided one believe in God.

In another way, we can explain the word ***substance*** essentially, as if faith is the substance, i.e., the essence of things to be hoped for. Hence, in Greek it is defined as 'the hypostasis of things to be hoped for.' For the essence of happiness is no less than the vision of God: *This is eternal life: that they know you, the only true God* (John 17:3). Hence, Augustine says: *This contemplation is promised to us; the end of all actions.*[5] Therefore, the full vision of God is the essence of happiness.

We also see this in the liberal sciences, which, if a person wishes to learn them, he must first accept their principles, which he must believe when they are delivered to him by the teacher. For a learner must believe, as it is stated in *Posterior Analytics*.[6] And in those principles the entire science is somehow contained, as conclusions are contained in their principles, and an effect in its cause. Therefore, one who has the principles of a science, say geometry, has its substance. And if geometry were the substance of happiness, a person who possessed the principles of geometry would, in a sense, have the substance of happiness.

But our faith consists in believing that the blessed will see and enjoy God. Therefore, if we will to reach that state, it is necessary that we believe the prin-

5. Augustine, *The Trinity* 1.3.8.

6. Aristotle, *Posterior Analytics* 1.

ciples of that knowledge. And these principles are the articles of faith, which contain the summary of this knowledge, because the vision of the triune God makes us happy. And this is one article; hence we believe this. Consequently, he says, ***the substance of things to be hoped for***: *Now we see in a mirror dimly, but then face to face* (1 Cor. 13:12). As if to say: 'we shall be happy when we see face to face that which we now see in a glass and in a dark manner.'

In these words is shown the relationship of the act of faith to its end because faith is ordained to things to be hoped for, being, as it were, a beginning in which the whole is, as it were, virtually contained, as conclusions
558 in principles. Then when he says, ***the evidence of things that appear not***, he touches the act of faith in regard to its proper matter. But the act proper to faith, even though it is in relation to the will, as has been said, is nevertheless in the intellect, as in a subject, because its object is the true, which properly pertains to the intellect.

But there is a difference among the acts of the intellect: for some are habits of the intellect which imply complete certitude and perfect understanding of that which is understood, as is clear in the habit of understanding, which is the habit of first principles, because one who understands that every whole is greater than its part sees this and is certain. But the habit of science also does this: thus the habits of understanding and of science will produce certitude and vision. But there are others which beget neither, namely, doubt and opinion.

But faith is midway between these: because, as has been stated, faith produces assent in the intellect, which can be caused in two ways: in one way, because the intellect is moved to assent because of the evidence of the object which is *per se* knowable, as in the habit of principles, or known through something else that is *per se* knowable, as in the science of astronomy. In another way, it assents to something not because of the evidence of the object, by which it is not sufficiently moved (hence it is not certain), but it either doubts, namely, when there is no more evidence for one side than for the other; or it opines, if it does have reason for one side, but without satisfying the intellect, so that there is fear in regard to the opposite side.

But faith does not suggest either of these absolutely because neither is it evident to itself, as with the first, nor does it doubt, as with the last two; but it fixes on one side with certainty and firm adherence by a voluntary choice. But this choice rests on God's authority, and by it the intellect is fixed, so that it clings firmly to the things of faith and assents to them with the greatest of certainty. Therefore, to believe is to think with assent. Therefore, the proper matter of the habit of faith are things that appear not. For appearance has knowledge, but not faith, as Gregory says.[7]

7. Gregory the Great, *Forty Gospel Homilies* 26.

But the act of faith is certain adherence, which the Apostle calls ***evidence,*** taking the cause for the effect, because evidence produces faith about a doubtful matter. For evidence is the reason for believing a doubted thing. Or if we follow the etymology of the word ***evidence*** [*argumentum*], as arguing-the-mind, then he is taking the effect for the cause, because the mind is compelled to assent because of the thing's certainty.[8] Hence, it is called the ***evidence of things that appear not***, i.e., a sure and certain apprehension of things it does not see.

Now, if someone were to reduce those words to their due form, he could say that faith is a habit of the mind by which eternal life is begun in us and makes the intellect assent to things that it does not see. (Where we have ***evidence***, another version has ***conviction***, because on God's authority the intellect is convinced about things it does not see.) Therefore, it is obvious that the
559 Apostle has defined faith completely, although obscurely. By that definition, faith is distinguished from all the other habits of the intellect.

By the fact that it is called ***evidence***, faith is distinguished from opinion, doubt, and suspicion, because these three do not cause the intellect to adhere to something firmly. By the words ***of things to be hoped for***, it is distinguished from ordinary faith, which is not ordained to happiness. For by proper definition a thing is made known and distinguished from all else, as in this case; hence, all the others are reduced to it.

560 But it seems incorrect to say, ***of things that appear not***, as it says in John, that Thomas saw and believed (20:26). Furthermore, we believe that there is one God, a fact which is demonstrated by philosophers. I answer that faith is taken in two senses: in the proper sense, it is concerned with things not seen and not known, as is clear from the above. And accordingly, as there cannot be greater certainty of a conclusion than of the principle from which it is drawn, because principles are always more certain than the conclusions, it follows that since the principles of faith are not evident, neither are its conclusions. Hence, the intellect does not assent to the conclusions as to things known or seen. But taken in a general sense, it excludes all knowledge that is certain; that is the sense in which it is taken by Augustine, when he says that faith is concerned with things that are seen. But the Apostle is speaking in the first

8. To appreciate St. Thomas' point here it is necessary to observe the form of the Latin *argumentum*, the perfect passive participle of *arguo*, which means both 'to argue' and, more originally, 'to illuminate' or 'to make bright' (e.g., relating to the Greek *argos*: 'bright'). St. Thomas is exploiting the fact that the suffix -mentum of *argumentum* appears very similar to the Latin word for *mind* in its objective or accusative case (i.e. *mentem*). Hence the word *argumentum* almost looks like *arguens mentem*, which means 'to argue (or 'illuminate') the mind.'

sense.[9] Furthermore, it must be said of Thomas that, as Gregory says, he saw one thing and believed something else, for he saw the humanity and believed the divinity.[10]

To the objection based on demonstration, the answer is that nothing prohibits one thing being seen by one person and believed by another, as is obvious in diverse states.[11] For what is not seen on earth is seen by the angels. Therefore, what I believe, an angel sees. Similarly, what is seen by the prophets, for example, that God is one and incorporeal, must be believed by the illiterate; just as an illiterate person believes in an eclipse, which an astronomer sees. However, in such matters faith is taken in a different sense. But there are some things which absolutely transcend the state of the present life; and in regard to these there is faith in the strict sense.

---

9. The passage cited here (Augustine, *Questions on the Gospel* 2.39.1) says precisely the opposite of what is quoted: . . . *faith, whereby one believes those things that are not seen*. There appears to be a rather crucial error (a missing negation) in the manuscript here as can be seen both on the basis of context and in light of the fact that the *not* is present in the quotation where St. Thomas quotes it elsewhere (*Summa theologiae* 2-2.4.1).

10. Gregory the Great, *Forty Gospel Homilies* 26.

11. The *objection based on demonstration* mentioned here was raised in the preceding paragraph where St. Thomas acknowledged that the existence of one God is demonstrable by philosophers. The thrust of the objection is that if these philosophers can be said to have faith in virtue of their demonstrations, then faith cannot be the kind of belief in the inevident that Thomas has here defined it to be. Thomas' answer, in short, is that although the philosopher's knowledge of the one God and the philosophical lay person's belief on the basis of testimony might seem to amount to the same thing (e.g., a belief in the existence of one God), they are not both rightly regarded as faith. The philosopher's belief constitutes knowledge, not faith. Likewise, the angels' vision or insight into the invisible amounts to something distinct from faith.

Romans 5:1–5

Hope: The Glory of the Sons of God

On Romans 5.1 (381–393)

5:1 ***Being justified therefore by faith, let us have peace with God, through our Lord Jesus Christ:***

5:2 ***By whom also we have access through faith into this grace wherein we stand: and glory in the hope of the glory of the sons of God.***

5:3 ***And not only so: but we glory also in tribulation, knowing that tribulation works patience;***

5:4 ***and patience trial; and trial hope;***

5:5 ***and hope does not confound: because the charity of God is poured forth in our hearts, by the Holy Spirit who is given to us.***

381 After showing the need for Christ's grace, because without it neither the knowledge of the truth benefited the gentiles nor circumcision and the law benefited the Jews unto salvation, the Apostle now begins to extol the power of grace.[12] Concerning this, he does two things. *First*, he shows what goods we obtain through grace; *second*, from what evils we are freed by it, at ***through one man*** (Rom. 5:12).

In regard to the *first* he does two things. *First*, he indicates the manner of reaching or the way by which we come to grace; *second*, the good things we obtain through grace, at ***and glory in the hope of the glory***.

In regard to the *first* he does two things. *First*, he exhorts to the due use of grace; *second*, he shows us the entrance to grace, at ***by whom also we have access***.

382 *First*, therefore, he says: it has been stated that faith will be reputed as justice to all who believe in Christ's resurrection, which is the cause of our justification. ***Being justified therefore by faith***, inasmuch as through faith in the resurrection we participate in its effect, ***let us have peace with God***, namely, by submitting ourselves and obeying him: *Agree with God and be at peace* (Job 22:21); *Who has hardened himself against him, and suceeded?* (Job 9:4).

And this ***through our Lord Jesus Christ***, who has led us to that peace: *He is*
383 *our peace* (Eph. 2:14). Hence he continues, ***by whom***, namely, Christ, ***we have***

12. See Romans 3:21–4:25 and Thomas Aquinas, *On Romans* 3.3–4.3 (not included in this collection).

access as through a mediator: *There is one mediator between God and men, the man Christ Jesus* (1 Tim. 2:5); *through him we both have access in one Spirit to the Father* (Eph. 2:18).

Access, I say, ***into this grace***, i.e., to the state of grace: *Grace and truth came through Jesus Christ* (John 1:17). ***Wherein***, i.e., through which grace we have not only risen from sin but ***we stand*** firm and erect in the heavens through love: *Our feet have been standing within your gates, O Jerusalem* (Ps. 122:2); *we shall rise and stand upright* (Ps. 20:8). And this ***through faith***, through which we obtain grace, not because faith precedes grace, since it is rather through grace that there is faith: *By grace you have been saved through faith* (Eph. 2:8), i.e., because the first effect of grace in us is faith.

384 Then when he says, ***and glory in the hope of the glory***, he indicates the blessings that have come to us through grace. *First*, he says that through grace we have the glory of hope; *second*, that through grace we have the glory of God, at ***and not only so***.

In regard to the *first* he does three things. *First*, he shows the greatness of the hope in which we glory; *second*, its vehemence, at ***and not only so***; *third*, its firmness, at ***and hope does not confound***.

385 The greatness of hope is considered in terms of the greatness of things hoped for. He sets this out when he says, ***and glory in the hope of the glory of the sons of God***, i.e., in the fact that we hope to obtain the glory of sons of God. For through Christ's grace ***you have received the spirit of sonship*** (Rom. 8:15); *how they have been numbered among the sons of God* (Wis. 5:5 DRB). But to sons is due the father's inheritance: ***If children, then heirs*** (Rom. 8:17). This inheritance is the glory which God has in himself: *Have you an arm like God, and can you thunder with a voice like his?* (Job 40:9). Our hope for this has been given to us by Christ: *We have been born anew to a living hope through the resurrection of Jesus Christ from the dead and to an inheritance which is imperishable* (1 Pet. 1:3–4). This glory, which will be completed in us in the future, is in the meantime begun in us through hope, ***for we are saved by hope*** (Rom. 8:24); *all they that love your name will glory in you* (Ps. 5:11 DRB).

386 Then when he says, ***and not only so***, he shows the vehemence of this hope. For anyone who vehemently hopes for something endures difficult and bitter things for it, as a sick person who strongly desires health gladly drinks a bitter medicine to be healed by it. Therefore, the sign of the vehement hope we have for Christ is that we glory not only in virtue of our hope of future glory but also in the evils we suffer for it. Hence he says, ***and not only so***, i.e., we not only glory in the hope of glory, ***but we glory also in tribulation***, through which we arrive at glory: *Through many tribulations we must enter the kingdom of God* (Acts 14:22); *count it all joy . . . when you meet various trials* (James 1:2).

387 Then he shows the cause when he says, ***knowing that***. Here he mentions four things in order: the *first* is tribulation, about which he says, ***tribulation works patience***, not in the sense that tribulation is the cause that begets it, but because suffering is the material and occasion for exercising the act of patience: ***be patient in tribulation*** (Rom. 12:12).

388 *Second*, he mentions the effect of patience when he says, ***and patience trial***: *Gold is tested in the fire and acceptable men in the furnace of humiliation* (Sir. 2:5). For it is plain that we accept the loss of something easily for the sake of another thing we love more. Hence, if a person endures patiently the loss of bodily and temporal goods for the sake of obtaining eternal benefits, this is sufficient proof that such a person loves eternal blessings more than temporal.

However, James seems to say the opposite: *The trying of your faith works patience* (1:3 DRB). The answer is that 'trial' can be understood in two ways. In one way, as it takes place in the one tested; then the trial is the very suffering through which a man is tested. Hence, it is the same to say that tribulation produces patience and that tribulation tests patience. In another way, trial is taken for the fact of having been tested. This is the way it is taken here, because if a person endures sufferings patiently, he has been tested.

389 *Third*, he mentions the third, saying, ***and trial hope***, namely, trial brings about hope, because after a person has been tested, hope can be had by himself and by others that he will be admitted to God's inheritance: *God tested them and found them worthy of himself* (Wis. 3:5). Therefore, from the first to the last it is clear that suffering paves the way to hope. Hence, if a person rejoices strongly in hope, it follows that he will glory in his sufferings.

390 Then when he says, ***and hope does not confound***, he shows the firmness of such hope. *First*, he asserts it, saying, ***hope***, namely, by which we hope for the glory of the sons of God, ***does not confound***, i.e., does not fail, unless the man fails it. For a person is said to be confounded in his hope, when he falls away from the thing he hoped for: *In you, O Lord, have I hoped; let me never be disappointed* (Ps. 31:1 DRB); *no one has hoped in the Lord and has been confounded* (Sir. 2:10 DRB).

391 *Second*, at ***because the charity of God***, he presents two arguments for the certainty of hope. The *first* is based on a gift of the Holy Spirit; the *second* on the death of Christ, at ***Christ died for the ungodly*** (Rom. 5:6).

392 *First*, therefore, he says: we can be certain that hope does not confound, ***because the charity of God is poured forth in our hearts, by the Holy Spirit who is given to us***. The love of God can be taken in two ways: in one way, for the love by which God loves us: *I have loved you with an everlasting love* (Jer. 31:3); in another way for the love by which we love God: ***I am sure that neither death, nor life . . . shall be able to separate us from the love of God*** (Rom. 8:38–39).

Both these loves of God are poured into our hearts by the Holy Spirit who has been given to us.

For the Holy Spirit, who is the love of the Father and of the Son, to be given to us is our being brought to participate in the love who is the Holy Spirit, and by this participation we are made lovers of God. The fact that we love him is a sign that he loves us: *I love those who love me* (Prov. 8:17); *not as though we had loved God but because he has first loved us* (1 John 4:10 DRB).

The love by which he loves us is said to be poured into our hearts, because it is clearly shown in our hearts by the gift of the Holy Spirit sealed in us: *By this we know that he abides in us, by the Spirit he has given us* (1 John 3:24).

But the love by which we love God is said to be poured into our hearts, because it reaches to the perfecting of all the moral habits and acts of the soul; for, as is stated in 1 Corinthians: *Love is patient and kind; love is not jealous or boastful* (13:4).

393 Both interpretations of these words lead to the conclusion that ***hope does not confound.*** For if they are taken to mean the love of God by which he loves us, it is clear that God does not deny himself to those whom he loves: *He loved his people; all those consecrated to him were in his hand* (Deut. 33:3). Similarly, if they are taken as referring to the love by which we love God, it is clear that he has prepared eternal goods for those who love him: *He who loves me will be loved by my Father and I will love him and manifest myself to him* (John 14:21).

1 Corinthians 13:4–7

Charity: The Greatest Virtue

On 1 Corinthians 13.2 (771–785)

13:4 ***Charity is patient, is kind: charity envies not, deals not perversely, is not puffed up,***

13:5 ***is not ambitious, seeks not her own, is not provoked to anger, thinks no evil:***

13:6 ***Rejoices not in iniquity, but rejoices with the truth:***

13:7 ***Bears all things, believes all things, hopes all things, endures all things.***

771 After showing that charity is so necessary that without it no spiritual gifts are sufficient for salvation,[13] the Apostle now shows that it is so useful and of such efficacious strength that through it all virtuous works are completed. *First*, he makes two quasi-general statements; *second*, he mentions in particular the virtuous works which are completed by charity, at ***charity envies not***.

772 In regard to the *first* he does two things. For every virtue consists in this, that in acting, one is well disposed for enduring evil things, or in accomplishing good things. Therefore, in regard to enduring evil, he says, ***charity is patient***, i.e., makes one endure evils patiently. For when a man loves someone on account of the beloved's love, he endures all difficulties with ease; similarly, a person who loves God patiently endures any adversity for love of him. Hence it is said: *Many waters cannot quench love, neither can floods drown it* (Song of Sol. 8:7); *patience has a perfect work* (James 1:4 DRB).

773 But as to performing good works, he adds: ***is kind***; benignity is described as 'a good fire,' so that just as fire by melting metal makes it flow, so charity inclines a person not to keep the good things he has, but makes them flow to others: *Let your fountains be conveyed abroad, and in the streets divide thy waters* (Prov. 5:16 DRB), and this is what charity does: hence, it is said: *If anyone has the world's goods and sees a brother in need, yet closes his heart against him, how does God's love abide in him?* (1 John 3:17). Hence, it is also said: *Be kind to one another, tenderhearted, forgiving one another* (Eph. 4:32); *wisdom is a kindly spirit* (Wis. 1:6).

13. See 1 Cor. 13:1–3 and Thomas Aquinas, *On 1 Corinthians* 13.1 (not included in this collection).

774 Then when he says, ***charity envies not***, he mentions in particular the virtuous works which charity produces, and because two things pertain to a virtue, namely, to refrain from evil and to do good: *Depart from evil and do good* (Ps. 34:14); *cease to do evil, learn to do good* (Isa. 1:16). *First*, he shows how charity avoids all evil; *second*, how it accomplishes the good, at ***but rejoices with the truth***.

But man cannot do evil effectively to God, but only to himself and to his neighbor: *If you have sinned, what do you accomplish against him?* (Job 35:6); *your wickedness concerns a man like yourself* (Job 35:8). *First*, therefore, he shows how charity avoids evils against one's neighbor; *second*, how evils are avoided by which someone is disarranged in himself, at ***is not puffed up***.

775 Evil against one's neighbor can exist in the will or emotions and externally. It exists in the former especially, as when a person through envy grieves over his neighbor's good. This is directly contrary to charity which inclines a person to love his neighbor as himself (Lev. 19:18). Hence it pertains to charity that just as a person rejoices in his own goods, so he should rejoice in the goods of his neighbor. It follows from this that charity excludes envy. And this is what he says: ***Charity envies not***. Hence it is said: *Be not envious of wrongdoers* (Ps. 37:1); *let not your heart envy sinners* (Prov. 23:17).

As to the outward effect he adds: ***deals not perversely***, i.e., against anyone.
776 For no one deals unjustly against one he loves: *Cease to do evil* (Isa. 1:16). Then
when he says, ***is not puffed up***, he shows that charity makes one avoid evils by
which one is disarranged in himself. *First*, as to passions; *second*, as to choice,
777 at ***thinks no evil***. Therefore, he first shows that charity drives away inordinate
passions in regard to three things.

First, indeed, as to pride, which is a disarranged desire for one's own excellence. One seeks his own excellence in a disarranged manner, when it does not satisfy him to be contained in that station which has been established for him by God. Therefore it is said: *The beginning of man's pride is to depart from the Lord* (Sir. 10:12). This happens when a man does not wish to be contained under the rule of God's arrangement. And this is opposed to charity, by which one loves God above all things: *puffed up without reason by this sensuous mind and not holding fast to the Head* (Col. 2:18).

It is right to compare pride to arrogance. For that which is puffed up does not have solidity but its appearance; so the proud seem to themselves to be great, while they really lack true greatness, which cannot exist without the divine order: *He will dash them speechless to the ground* (Wis. 4:19).

778 The chief daughter of pride is ambition, through which one seeks to be foremost, which charity also excludes, seeking rather to serve: *Through love be servants of one another* (Gal. 5:13). Therefore, he adds: ***is not ambitious***, i.e.,

makes a man avoid ambition: *Do not seek from the Lord the highest office nor the seat of honor from the king* (Sir. 7:4).

779 *Second*, he shows how charity excludes the disorder of cupidity, when he says: ***seeks not her own***. This is understood precisely, i.e., it does not neglect the good of others. For one who loves others as himself seeks the good of others just as his own. Hence the Apostle said above: ***not seeking my own advantage, but that of many*** (1 Cor. 10:33). Against which it is said of some: *They all look after their own interests, not those of Jesus Christ* (Phil. 2:21).

It is possible to understand in another way that charity ***seeks not her own***, i.e., it does not seek the return of what has been taken from it, namely, in a court case with scandal; because he loves the salvation of his neighbor more than money: *Not that I seek the gift; but I seek the fruit which increases to your credit* (Phil. 4:17).

780 *Third*, he shows how charity excludes the disorder of anger, saying: ***It is not provoked to anger***. For anger is an inordinate desire for revenge. But it pertains to charity rather to forgive offenses than to seek revenge beyond measure: *forbearing one another and, if one has a complaint against another, forgiving* (Col. 3:13); *the anger of man does not work the righteousness of God* (James 1:20).

781 Then when he says, ***thinks no evil***, he shows how by charity disordered choosing is excluded. Now choice is, as it says in the *Ethics*, *the desire for what has already been thought about and weighed.*[14] Therefore, a man sins from choice and not from passion, when by a plan of his reason his affections are bestirred to evil.

Charity, therefore, *first* of all, excludes perverse counsel. Therefore, he says: charity ***thinks no evil***, i.e., does not permit devising how to complete something evil: *Woe to those who devise wickedness and work evil upon their beds* (Mic. 2:1); *remove the evil of your doings from before my eyes* (Isa. 1:16). Or charity ***thinks no evil***, because it does not permit one to think evil about his neighbor by various suspicions and rash judgments: *Why do you think evil in your hearts?* (Matt. 9:4).

782 *Second*, charity excludes an inordinate love for evil; hence he says: ***rejoices not in iniquity***. For one who sins from passion commits sin with some remorse and sorrow, but one who sins from choice rejoices in the fact that he commits sin: *[They] rejoice in doing evil and delight in the perverseness of evil* (Prov. 2:14). But charity prevents this, inasmuch as it is the love of the supreme good, to whom all sin is obnoxious.

Or he says that charity ***rejoices not in iniquity***, namely, committed by a neighbor: in fact it laments over it, inasmuch as it is opposed to our neighbor's salvation, which it desires: *I fear that when I come again my God will humble me before you, and I may have to mourn over many of those who sinned* (2 Cor. 12:21).

---

14. Aristotle, *Nicomachean Ethics* 3.

783 Then when he says, ***but rejoices***, he shows how charity makes one do the
784 good: *first*, as to one's neighbor; *second*, as to God, at ***believes all things***. In
regard to his neighbor, man does the good in two ways: *first*, by rejoicing in his good. In regard to this he says: ***but rejoices with the truth***, namely, of the neighbor or of life or doctrine or justice, inasmuch as he loves his neighbor as himself: *I greatly rejoiced when some of the brethren arrived and testified to the truth of your life, as indeed you do follow the truth* (3 John 1:3).

Second, in the fact that a person endures the evils of his neighbor to the extent that it is fitting. In regard to this he says: ***bears all things***, i.e., without disquiet it tolerates all the shortcomings of the neighbor of any adversity whatever: *We who are strong ought to bear with the failings of the weak* (Rom. 15:1); *carry one another's burdens and so you will fulfill the law of Christ* (Gal. 6:2), namely, charity.

785 Then when he says: ***believes all things***, he shows how charity makes one do the good in relation to God. This is done especially through the theological virtues which have God for their object. In addition to charity the other two, as will be said below, are faith and hope.

Therefore, in regard to faith he says: ***believes all things***, namely, which are divinely revealed. *[Abram] believed the Lord and; and he reckoned it to him as righteousness* (Gen. 15:6). But to believe all things said by men is lightmindedness: *One who trusts others too quickly is light-minded* (Sir. 19:4).

In regard to hope he says: ***hopes all things***, namely, which are promised by God: *You who fear the Lord hope for good things* (Sir. 2:9). And in order that hope not be discouraged by the delay, he adds: ***endures all things***, i.e., patiently awaits what God has promised in spite of delay: *If it seem slow, wait for it* (Hab. 2:3); *let your heart take courage . . . wait for the Lord* (Ps. 27:14).

CONCLUSION

John 21:24–25

The Epilogue of John's Gospel

On John 21.6 (2652–2660)

21:24 ***This is the disciple who gives testimony of these things, and has written these things; and we know that his testimony is true.***

21:25 ***But there are also many other things which Jesus did; which, if every one of them were to be written, the world itself, I think, would not be able to contain the books that should be written.***

2652 Now we have the last part of this Gospel, which is like an epilogue. *First*, the Gospel is commended; and then the vastness of the subject treated: ***There are also many other things which Jesus did.*** The Gospel is commended because of two things: its author, and its truth, ***We know that his testimony is true.*** Three things are mentioned about the author.

2653 *First*, there is the authority of the author, because ***this is the disciple***, understanding what was mentioned before who was loved above the others, intimate with Christ, able to question him with confidence, and to whom it was granted to remain ***till I come.*** All these things refer to the authority of the author.

John is said to have been loved more than the others because of his unique charity: ***By this will all men know that you are my disciples, if you have love one for another*** (John 13:35). None of the other apostles speak so much of love for others as does John in his letters. We also read that as an old man he was carried to the church by his followers to teach the faithful. He taught only one thing: *Little children, love one another.* This is the perfection of the Christian life.

2654 *Second*, John's office is mentioned, which was to give testimony, for he says, ***who gives testimony of these things.*** This is the special office of apostles: *You shall be my witnesses* (Acts 1:8); *you are my witnesses!* (Isa. 44:8).

2655 *Third*, he refers to his zeal when he says, ***and has written these things.*** As an apostle he testified to the actions of Christ to those who were present; and in his zeal he recorded these actions in writing for those who were not with him and were to come after him: *Take a large tablet and write upon it in common characters* (Isa. 8:1); *the wisdom of the scribe depends on the opportunity of leisure; and he who has little business may become wise* (Sir. 38:24).

For it was granted to John to live until the time when the Church was at peace; and this is the time when he wrote all these things. John mentions such things so that we will not think that his Gospel has less authority than the other three, seeing that he wrote after the death of all the other apostles, and that the other Gospels, especially that of Matthew, had been approved by them.

2656 Now John states that his Gospel is true, and he speaks in the person of the entire Church which received it: *My mouth will utter truth* (Prov. 8:7). Note that although many have written about universal truth, there is a difference among them: those who wrote the canonical Scriptures, such as the evangelists and apostles and the like, so constantly and firmly affirm this truth that it cannot be doubted. Thus John says, ***We know that his testimony is true***: *If anyone is preaching to you a gospel contrary to that which you received, let him be accursed* (Gal. 1:9). The reason for this is that only the canonical Scriptures are the standard of faith. Others have set forth this truth but in such a way that they do not want to be believed except in those things in which they say what is true.

2657 Now John states that his Gospel is incomplete as compared with the reality, as if to downplay what he had written in order to hand over the glory to the one who loved him, because Christ not only did these things: ***There are also many other things which Jesus did.***

2658 His statement, ***if every one of them were to be written, I suppose that the world itself could not contain the books that should be written***, can be understood in two ways. *First*, the word ***contain*** can refer to the capacity of our minds to understand. So the meaning is: so much could be said about Christ that the world could not understand all that could be written: ***I have yet many things to say to you, but you cannot bear them now***, that is, understand them (John 16:12).

We could also regard this statement as a deliberate exaggeration; and it
2659 then indicates the abundance of Christ's works. How can we reconcile this?
He had just said, ***we know that his testimony is true***, and then immediately resorts to hyperbole, exceeding the truth. According to Augustine, Scripture does use figures of speech, such as *I saw the Lord sitting upon a throne, high and lifted up* (Isa. 6:1), and such statements are not false.[15] This is so when hyperbole is used. The desire of the speaker is not that we accept the literal meaning of the words, but what they were intended to mean, that is, the great number of Christ's works. Hyperbole is not used to explain what is obscure or doubtful, but to exaggerate or minimize what is obvious. For example, to emphasize how plentiful something is, one can say that there is enough for a hundred or a thousand people. And to minimize something, one could say that there is hardly enough for three. This is not speaking falsely, because it is so obvious that the words contort the reality that they show that one does not intend to lie, but to indicate that something is great or small.

15. Augustine, *Tractates on the Gospel of John* 124.8.

2660 Or, this statement could be understood to refer to the power of Christ, who performed these signs; and the emphasis is on ***every one of them***. For to write about each and every word and deed of Christ is to reveal the power of every word and deed. Now the words and deeds of Christ are also those of God. Thus, if one tried to write and tell of the nature of every one, he could not do so; indeed, the entire world could not do this. This is because even an infinite number of human words cannot equal one word of God. From the beginning of the Church, Christ has been written about; but this is still not equal to the subject. Indeed, even if the world lasted a hundred thousand years and books were written about Christ, his words and deeds could not be completely revealed: *Of making many books there is no end* (Eccles. 12:12); the works of God are *more than can be numbered* (Ps. 40:5).

Devoutly I Adore You, Hidden Deity

A PRAYER OF THOMAS AQUINAS

Devoutly I adore You, hidden Deity
under these appearances concealed.
To You my heart surrenders self
for, seeing You, all else must yield.

Sight and touch and taste here fail;
hearing only can be believed.
I trust what God's own Son has said.
Truth from truth is best received.

Divinity on the Cross was hid;
humanity here comes not to thought.
Believing and confessing both,
I seek out what the good thief sought.

I see no wounds, as Thomas did,
but I profess You God above.
Draw me deeply into faith,
into your hope, into your love.

O memorial of the Lord's sad death,
show life to man, O living bread.
Grant that my soul may live through you,
by your sweet savor ever fed.

Jesus Lord, my Pelican devout,
With your blood my sins dismiss.
One single drop could surely save
from sin this world's dark edifice.

Jesus, whom now I see enveiled,
what I desire, when will it be?
Beholding your fair face revealed,
your glory shall I be blessed to see.

Amen

BIBLIOGRAPHIES

RECOMMENDED ENGLISH TRANSLATIONS OF ANCIENT WORKS CITED IN THIS COLLECTION

Ambrose. *Commentary of Saint Ambrose on the Gospel According to Saint Luke.* Translated by Ide M. Ni Riain. Dublin: Halcyon, 2001.

———. *Exposition of the Christian Faith.* In Nicene and Post-Nicene Fathers of the Christian Church, Second Series, vol. 10: *Ambrose: Select Works and Letters,* translated by H. De Romestin, edited by Philip Schaff and Henry Wace, 199–314. Grand Rapids, MI: Eerdmans, 1955.

Ambrosiaster. *Commentary on 1 Corinthians.* In *Commentaries on Romans and 1–2 Corinthians: Ambrosiaster.* Translated and edited by Gerald L. Bray. Ancient Christian Texts. Downers Grove, IL: IVP Academic, 2009.

Anselm. *Anselm: Monologion and Proslogion.* Translated, with Introduction and Notes, by Thomas Williams. Indianapolis, IN: Hackett, 1996.

Aristotle. *Categories and De Interpretatione.* Translated with Notes and Glossary by J.L. Ackrill. Oxford: Oxford University Press, 1975.

———. *The Nicomachean Ethics.* Translated by Robert C. Bartlett and Susan D. Collins. Chicago: University of Chicago Press, 2011.

———. *Physics.* Translated by C.D.C. Reeve. Indianapolis, IN: Hackett, 2018.

———. *Politics.* 2nd ed. Translated by Carnes Lord. Chicago: Chicago University Press, 2013.

———. *Posterior Analytics.* 2nd ed. Translated by Jonathan Barnes. Oxford: Oxford University Press, 1994.

Augustine. *Agreement among the Evangelists.* Translated by Kim Paffenroth. In The Works of Saint Augustine: A Translation for the 21st Century, pt. 1, vols. 15–16: *The New Testament I and II,* edited by Boniface Ramsey, 131–333. Hyde Park, NY: New City, 2014.

———. *Answer to Maximinus the Arian.* In The Works of Saint Augustine: A Translation for the 21st Century, pt. 1, vol. 18: *Arianism and Other Heresies,* translated by Roland J. Teske, 246–336. Hyde Park, NY: New City, 1995.

Augustine. *Baptism (De baptismo)*. In The Works of Saint Augustine: A Translation for the 21st Century, pt. 1, vol. 21: *The Donatist Controversy I*, translated by Maureen Tilley and Boniface Ramsey, edited by Boniface Ramsey and David G. Hunter, 391–604. Hyde Park, NY: New City, 2019.

———. *A Book on Seeing God* [*Letter 147: Augustine to Paulina*]. In The Works of Saint Augustine: A Translation for the 21st Century, pt. 2, vol. 2: *Letters 100–155*. Translated by Roland J. Teske, edited by Boniface Ramsey, 317–349. Hyde Park, NY: New City, 2003.

———. *The City of God*. Translated by William Babcock. Edited by Boniface Ramsey. The Works of Saint Augustine: A Translation for the 21st Century, pt. 1, vols. 6–7. Hyde Park, NY: New City, 2012–2013.

———. *The Confessions*. Translated by Maria Boulding. Edited by John E. Rotelle. The Works of Saint Augustine: A Translation for the 21st Century, pt. 1, vol. 1. Hyde Park, NY: New City, 1997.

———. *Eighty-Three Different Questions*. Translated by David L. Mosher. The Fathers of the Church: A New Translation, vol. 70. Washington, DC: The Catholic University of America Press, 1982.

———. *The Enchiridion on Faith, Hope, and Charity*. Translated by Bruce Harbert. In The Works of Saint Augustine: A Translation for the 21st Century, pt. 1, vol. 8: *On Christian Belief*, edited by Boniface Ramsey, 276–344. Hyde Park, NY: New City, 2005.

———. *Instructing Beginners in Faith*. Translated by Raymond Canning. Edited by Boniface Ramsey. The Augustine Series, vol. 5. Hyde Park, NY: New City, 2006.

———. *The Literal Meaning of Genesis*. In The Works of Saint Augustine: A Translation for the 21st Century, pt. 1, vol. 13: *On Genesis*, translated by Edmund Hill, edited by John E. Rotelle, 168–506. Hyde Park, NY: New City, 2002.

———. *The Nature of the Good*. In The Works of Saint Augustine: A Translation for the 21st Century, pt. 1, vol. 19: *The Manichean Debate*, translated by Roland J. Teske, edited by Boniface Ramsey, 325–348. Hyde Park, NY: New City, 2006.

———. *On the Lord's Sermon on the Mount*. Translated by Michael Campbell. In The Works of Saint Augustine: A Translation for the 21st Century, pt. 1, vols. 15–16: *The New Testament I and II*, edited by Boniface Ramsey, 23–114. Hyde Park, NY: New City, 2014.

Augustine. *The Predestination of the Saints.* In The Works of Saint Augustine: A Translation for the 21st Century, pt. 1, vol. 26: *Answer to the Pelagians, IV: To the Monks of Hadrumetum and Provence*, translated by Roland J. Teske, edited by John E. Rotelle, 149–187. Hyde Park, NY: New City, 1999.

———. *The Presence of God: Letter 187.* In The Works of Saint Augustine: A Translation for the 21st Century, pt. 2, vol. 3: *Letters 156–210.* Translated by Roland J. Teske, edited by Boniface Ramsey, 230–250. Hyde Park, NY: New City, 2004.

———. *The Punishment and Forgiveness of Sins and the Baptism of Little Ones.* In The Works of Saint Augustine: A Translation for the 21st Century, pt. 1, vol. 23: *Answer to the Pelagians I*, translated by Roland J. Teske, edited by John E. Rotelle, 34–134. Hyde Park, NY: New City, 1997.

———. *Questions on the Gospels.* Translated by Roland J. Teske. In The Works of Saint Augustine: A Translation for the 21st Century, pt. 1, vols. 15–16: *The New Testament I and II*, edited by Boniface Ramsey, 359–415. Hyde Park, NY: New City, 2014.

———. *Revisions.* Translated and edited by Boniface Ramsey. The Works of Saint Augustine: A Translation for the 21st Century, pt. 1, vol. 2. Hyde Park, NY: New City, 2010.

———. *Sermons (94A–147A) on the New Testament.* Translated by Edmund Hill. Edited by John E. Rotelle. The Works of Saint Augustine: A Translation for the 21st Century, pt. 3, vol. 4. Brooklyn, NY: New City, 1992.

———. *Sermons (341–400) on Various Subjects.* Translated by Edmund Hill. Edited by John E. Rotelle. The Works of Saint Augustine: A Translation for the 21st Century, pt. 3, vol. 10. Hyde Park, NY: New City, 1995.

———. *Teaching Christianity: De Doctrina Christiana.* Translated by Edmund Hill. Edited by John E. Rotelle. The Works of Saint Augustine: A Translation for the 21st Century, pt. 1, vol. 11. Hyde Park, NY: New City, 2014.

———. *Tractates on the Gospel of John.* Translated by John W. Rettig. The Fathers of the Church: A New Translation. Vols. 78–79, 88, 90, 92. Washington, DC: The Catholic University of America Press, 1988–1995.

———. *The Trinity.* Translated by Edmund Hill. Edited by John E. Rotelle. The Works of Saint Augustine: A Translation for the 21st Century, pt. 1, vol. 5. Hyde Park, NY: New City, 1991.

———. *True Religion.* Translated by Edmund Hill. In The Works of Saint Augustine: A Translation for the 21st Century, pt. 1, vol. 8: *On Christian Belief*, edited by Boniface Ramsey, 29–104. Hyde Park, NY: New City, 2006.

Basil the Great. *Homily on the Beginning of the Gospel of John (Jn. 1:1–12)*. In *On Christian Doctrine and Practice*. Translated by Mark DelCogliano. St. Vladimir's Seminary, 2012.

Bernard of Clairvaux. *Sermons on the Feast of the Purification of Holy Mary*. In *Bernard of Clairvaux: Sermons for Lent and the Easter Season*, translated by Irene Edmonds, edited by Mark A. Scott, 3–13. Collegeville, MN: Liturgical, 2013.

Council of Ephesus. "Canonical Epistle of St. Cyril, *Cum Salvator Noster*." In Nicene and Post-Nicene Fathers of the Church, Second Series, vol. 14: *The Seven Ecumenical Councils*, ed. Philip Schaff and Henry Wace, 201–205. Buffalo, NY: Christian Literature, 1900.

Gregory the Great. *Forty Gospel Homilies*. Translated by Dom David Hurst. Kalamazoo, MI: Cistercian, 1990.

———. *The Homilies on the Book of the Prophet Ezekiel*. 2nd ed. Translated by Theodosia Tomkinson. Etna, CA: Center for Traditionalist Orthodox Studies, 2008.

———. *Moralia in Job or Morals on the Book of Job*. 3 vols. Translated by James Bliss and Charles Marriott. Oxford: Ex Fontibus, 2012–2020.

Hilary of Poitiers. *Commentary on Matthew*. Translated by D.H. Williams. The Fathers of the Church: A New Translation. Vol. 125. Washington, DC: The Catholic University of America Press, 2012.

———. *The Trinity*. Translated by Stephen McKenna. The Fathers of the Church: A New Translation. Vol. 25. Washington, DC: The Catholic University of America Press, 1954.

Jerome. "The Books of Samuel and Kings." In *Jerome: The Principal Works of St. Jerome*, translated by W.H. Freemantle, The Nicene and Post-Nicene Fathers of the Christian Church, Second Series, 6:489–490. Grand Rapids, MI: Eerdmans, 1892.

———. *Commentary on Daniel*. Translated by Gleason L. Archer, Jr. Grand Rapids, MI: Baker, 1958.

———. *Commentary on Isaiah: Including St. Jerome's Translation of Origen's Homilies 1–9 on Isaiah*. Translated by Thomas P. Scheck. Ancient Christian Writers, vol. 68. Mahwah, NJ: Newman, 2015.

———. *Commentary on Matthew*. Translated by Thomas P. Scheck. The Fathers of the Church: A New Translation. Vol. 117. Washington, DC: The Catholic University of America Press, 2008.

Jerome. *On the Perpetual Virginity of the Blessed Mary Against Helvidius*. In The Fathers of the Church: A New Translation, vol. 53: *Saint Jerome: Dogmatic and Polemical Works*, translated by John N. Hritzu, 3–46. Washington, DC: The Catholic University of America Press, 1965.

———. "Preface to the Commentary on Ecclesiastes." In *Jerome: The Principal Works of St. Jerome*, translated by W.H. Freemantle, The Nicene and Post-Nicene Fathers of the Christian Church, Second Series, 6:487. Grand Rapids, MI: Eerdmans, 1892.

———. "Prologue to Daniel." Translated by Kevin P. Edgecomb. Early Church Fathers: Additional Texts. 2006. https://www.tertullian.org/fathers/jerome_preface_daniel.htm.

———. "Prologue to Judith." Translated by Kevin P. Edgecomb. Early Church Fathers: Additional Texts. 2006. https://www.tertullian.org/fathers/jerome_preface_judith_e.htm.

———. "To Paulinus." In *Jerome: The Principal Works of St. Jerome*, translated by W.H. Freemantle, The Nicene and Post-Nicene Fathers of the Christian Church, Second Series, 6:96–102. Grand Rapids, MI: Eerdmans, 1892.

John Chrysostom. *Commentary on Saint John the Apostle and Evangelist*. Translated by Sister Thomas Aquinas Goggin. The Fathers of the Church: A New Translation. Vols. 33, 41. Washington, DC: The Catholic University of America Press, 1957–1959.

———. *Homilies of St. John Chrysostom on the Epistles of St. Paul to the Corinthians*. Edited by Paul A Böer Sr. Toledo, OH: Veritatis Splendor, 2012.

———. *Homilies of St. John Chrysostom on the Epistle to the Hebrews*. Translated by T. Keble and Frederic Gardiner. Edited by Philip Schaff. In, The Nicene and Post-Nicene Fathers of the Church, 14:333–522. Grand Rapids, MI: Eerdmans, 1889.

———. *Homilies on the Gospel of Saint Matthew*. The Nicene and Post-Nicene Fathers of the Church, First Series, vol. 10, translated by George Prevost, edited by Philip Schaff. Grand Rapids, MI: Eerdmans, 1888.

John of Damascus. *An Exact Exposition of the Orthodox Faith*. In *St. John of Damascus Writings*, translated by Frederic H. Chase Jr., The Fathers of the Church: A New Translation. 37:165–406. Washington, DC: The Catholic University of America Press, 1958.

John Scotus Eriugena. *The Voice of the Eagle: The Heart of Celtic Christianity: John Scotus Eriugena's Homily on the Prologue to the Gospel of John*. Translated by Christopher Bamford. Great Barrington, MA: Lindisfarne Books, 2000.

Lactantius. *The Epitome of the Divine Institutes.* Translated by E.H. Blakeney. London: SPCK, 1950.

Lombard, Peter. *The Sentences: Book 3: On the Incarnation of the Word.* Translated by Giulio Silano. Mediaeval Sources in Translation. Ontario: Pontifical Institute of Mediaeval Studies, 2008.

Origen. *The Commentary of Origen on the Gospel of St. Matthew.* 2 vols. Translated with Introduction and Brief Annotations by Ronald E. Heine. Oxford: Oxford University Press, 2018.

———. *Commentary on the Gospel According to John.* Translated by Ronald E. Heine. The Fathers of the Church: A New Translation. Vols. 80, 89. Washington, DC: The Catholic University of America Press, 1989, 1993.

———. *Origen: Homilies on Luke.* Translated by Joseph T. Lienhard. The Fathers of the Church: A New Translation, vol. 94. Washington, DC: The Catholic University of America Press, 1996.

———. *Origen: On First Principles.* 2 vols. Edited and translated by John Behr. Oxford: Oxford University Press, 2017.

Plotinus. *The Enneads.* Edited by Lloyd P. Gerson. Translated by George Boys-Stones, John M. Dillon, Lloyd P. Gerson, R.A.H. King, Andrew Smith, and James Wilberding. Cambridge: Cambridge University Press, 2018.

Pseudo-Dionysius. *The Celestial Hierarchy.* In *Pseudo-Dionysius: The Complete Works,* translated by Colm Luibheid, 143–191. Mahwah, NJ: Paulist, 1987.

———. *The Divine Names.* In *Pseudo-Dionysius: The Complete Works,* translated by Colm Luibheid, 47–131. Mahwah, NJ: Paulist, 1987.

———. *The Ecclesiastical Hierarchy.* In *Pseudo-Dionysius: The Complete Works,* translated by Colm Luibheid, 143–259. Mahwah, NJ: Paulist, 1987.

———. "Letter Seven: To Polycarp, a Hierarch." In *Pseudo-Dionysius: The Complete Works,* translated by Colm Luibheid, 266–269. Mahwah, NJ: Paulist, 1987.

Theophylact of Ochrid. *The Explanation of the Holy Gospel According to John.* Translated by Christopher Stade. House Springs, MO: Chrysostom, 2007.

UNTRANSLATED ANCIENT WORKS CITED IN THIS COLLECTION

Alcuin. *Commentaria in sancti Joannis Evangelium.* In Patrologia cursus completus, series Latina, edited by J.-P. Migne, 100:743–1008. Paris, 1863.

Athanasius. *Epistola IV ad Serapionem.* In Patrologia cursus completus, series Latina, edited by J.-P. Migne, 26:638–676. Paris, 1845.

Bede. *Expositio in Evangelium Sancti Joannis.* In Patrologia cursus completus, series Latina, edited by J.-P. Migne, 92:633–938. Paris, 1862.

Jerome. *Epistle 119: Ad Minervium et Alexandrum Monachos.* In Patrologia cursus completus, series Latina, edited by J.-P. Migne, 22:966–980. Paris, 1845.

Rabanus. *Expostio in Epistolam ad Philippenses.* In Patrologia cursus completus, series Latina, edited by J.-P. Migne, 112:477–508. Paris, 1852.

RECENTLY PUBLISHED OR REPUBLISHED TRANSLATIONS OF THE WORKS OF THOMAS AQUINAS CITED IN THIS COLLECTION

Catena Aurea: Commentary on the Four Gospels. 4 vols. Translated by John Henry Newman. London: Baronius, 2009.

Commentary on Saint Paul's Epistle to the Ephesians. Translated with an introduction by Matthew L. Lamb. Albany, NY: Magi Books, 1966.

Commentary on St. Paul's Epistles to Timothy, Titus, and Philemon. Translated by Chrysostom Baer. South Bend, IN: St. Augustine's, 2006.

Commentary on the Epistle to the Hebrews. Translated by Chrysostom Baer. South Bend, IN: St. Augustine's, 2006.

Commentary on the Gospel of John. Translated by Fabian R. Larcher. Edited by The Aquinas Institute. Latin/English Edition of the Works of St. Thomas Aquinas, vols. 35–36. Lander, WY: Aquinas Institute, 2013. This translation is published also in an English-only edition, revised by James A. Weisheipl with an introduction and notes by Daniel Keating and Matthew Levering. Washington, DC: The Catholic University of America Press, 2010.

Commentary on the Gospel of Matthew. Translated by Jeremy Holmes and Beth Mortensen. Edited by The Aquinas Institute. Latin/English Edition of the Works of St. Thomas Aquinas, vols. 33–34. Lander, WY: Aquinas Institute, 2013.

Commentary on the Letter of Saint Paul to the Romans. Translated by Fabian R. Larcher. Edited by John Mortensen and Enrique Alarcón. Latin/English Edition of the Works of St. Thomas Aquinas, vol. 37. Lander, WY: Aquinas Institute, 2012.

Commentary on the Letters of Saint Paul to the Corinthians. Translated by Fabian R. Larcher, Beth Mortensen, and Daniel Keating. Edited by John Mortensen and Enrique Alarcón. Latin/English Edition of the Works of St. Thomas Aquinas, vol. 38. Lander, WY: Aquinas Institute, 2012.

Commentary on the Letters of Saint Paul to the Galatians and Ephesians. Translated by Fabian R. Larcher. Edited by the Aquinas Institute. Latin/English Edition of the Works of St. Thomas Aquinas, vol. 39. Lander, WY: Aquinas Institute, 2012.

Commentary on the Metaphysics of Aristotle. Translated by John P. Rowan. Notre Dame, IN: Dumb Ox Books, 1995.

Literal Commentary on Job. Translated by Brian Mullady. Edited by the Aquinas Institute. Latin/English Edition of the Works of St. Thomas Aquinas, vol. 38. Lander, WY: Aquinas Institute, 2012.

The Power of God. Translated by Richard J. Regan. Oxford: Oxford University Press, 2012.

RECOMMENDED BIOGRAPHIES AND GENERAL INTRODUCTIONS

Barron, Robert. *Thomas Aquinas: Spiritual Master*. Park Ridge, IL: Word on Fire Academic, 2022.

Chenu, Marie-Dominique. *Toward Understanding Saint Thomas*. Translated by Albert M. Landry and Dominic Hughes. Chicago, Henry Regnery, 1964.

Chesterton, G.K. *St. Thomas Aquinas: "The Dumb Ox."* New York: Sheed & Ward, 1933.

Copleston, F.C. Aquinas: *An Introduction to the Life and Work of the Great Medieval Thinker*. Baltimore, MD: Penguin Books, 1955.

Dauphinais, Michael and Matthew Levering. *Knowing the Love of Christ: An Introduction to the Theology of St. Thomas Aquinas*. Notre Dame, IN: University of Notre Dame Press, 2002.

Foster, Kenelm, ed. and trans. *The Life of St. Thomas Aquinas: Biographical Documents*. Baltimore, MD: Helicon, 1959.

Hütter, Reinhard. *Dust Bound for Heaven: Explorations in the Theology of Thomas Aquinas*. Grand Rapids, MI: Eerdmans, 2012.

Murray, Paul. *Aquinas at Prayer: The Bible, Mysticism and Poetry*. London: Bloomsbury, 2013.

Nieuwenhove, Rik Van and Joseph Wawrykow, eds. *The Theology of Thomas Aquinas.* Notre Dame, IN: University of Notre Dame Press, 2005.

Sertillanges, A.G. *St. Thomas Aquinas and His Work.* Translated by Godfrey Anstruther. London: Burns, Oates, and Washbourne, 1933.

Torrell, Jean-Pierre. *Saint Thomas Aquinas*, translated by Robert Royal, vol. 1: *The Person and His Work* and vol. 2: *Spiritual Master*. Washington, DC: The Catholic University of America Press, 1996–2003.

Weisheipl, James A. *Friar Thomas D'Aquino: His Life, Though, and Works*. Garden City, NY: Doubleday, 1974.

BOOKS ON THOMAS AQUINAS' USE OF SCRIPTURE

Baglow, Christopher. *"Modus et Forma": A New Approach to the Exegesis of Saint Thomas Aquinas with an Application to the* Lectura Super Epistolam Ad Ephesios.

Boyle, John F. *The Order and Division of Divine Truth: St. Thomas Aquinas as Scholastic Master of the Sacred Page*. Steubenville, OH: Emmaus Academic, 2021.

Klimczak, Pawel. *Christus Magister: Le Christ Maître dans les Commentaires Évangéliques de Saint Thomas d'Aquin*. Fribourg, CH: Academic Press Freibourg, 2013.

Levering, Matthew. *Paul in the* Summa Theologiae. Washington, DC: The Catholic University of America Press, 2014.

Levering, Matthew and Michael Dauphinais, eds. *Reading John with St. Thomas Aquinas*. Washington, DC: The Catholic University of America Press, 2005.

———. *Reading Romans with St. Thomas Aquinas*. Washington, DC: The Catholic University of America Press, 2011.

Nutt, Roger and Michael Dauphinais, eds. *Thomas Aquinas: Biblical Theologian*. Steubenville, OH: Emmaus Academic, 2021.

Roszak, Piotr and Jörgen Vijgen, eds. *Towards A Biblical Thomism: Thomas Aquinas and the Renewal of Biblical Theology*. Pamplona, ES: Ediciones Universidad de Navarra, 2018.

———. *Reading the Church Fathers with St. Thomas Aquinas: Historical and Systematical Perspectives*. Turnhout, BE: Brepols, 2021.

Ryan, Thomas F. *Thomas Aquinas as Reader of the Psalms*. Notre Dame, IN: University of Notre Dame Press, 2000.

Sabathé, Martin. *La Trinité Rédemptrice: Dans le Commentaire de L'Évangile de Saint Jean par Thomas d'Aquin*. Paris: Vrin, 2011.

Sirilla, Michael G. *The Ideal Bishop: Aquinas's Commentaries on the Pastoral Epistles*. Washington, DC: The Catholic University of America Press, 2017.

Smith, Randall B. *Aquinas, Bonaventure, and the Scholastic Culture of Medieval Paris: Preaching, Prologues, and Biblical Commentary*. Cambridge: Cambridge University Press, 2021.

Valkenberg, Wilhelmus. *Words of the Living God: Place and Function of Holy Scripture in the Theology of St. Thomas Aquinas*. Leuven, BE: Peeters, 2000.

Weinandy, Thomas G., Daniel A. Keating, and John P. Yocum, eds. *Aquinas on Scripture: An Introduction to His Biblical Commentaries*. New York: T&T Clark, 2005.

OTHER STUDY RESOURCES

Deferrari, Roy J. *A Lexicon of Saint Thomas Aquinas*. Fitzwilliam, NH: Loreto, 2004.

Wawrykow, Joseph P. *The Westminster Handbook to Thomas Aquinas*. Lexington, KY: John Knox, 2005.

GENERAL INDEX

INDEX OF ANCIENT SOURCES

1. OLD TESTAMENT

John

Romans (*continued*)

3. PATRISTIC AND MEDIEVAL WORKS